HENRY VI
Parts I, II, and III

The RSC Shakespeare

Edited by Jonathan Bate and Eric Rasmussen

Chief Associate Editors: Jan Sewell and Will Sharpe

Associate Editors: Trey Jansen, Eleanor Lowe, Lucy Munro,
Dee Anna Phares, Héloïse Sénéchal

Henry VI Parts I, II, and III

Textual editing: Eleanor Lowe and Eric Rasmussen

Introduction and Shakespeare's Career in the Theater: Jonathan Bate

Commentary: Charlotte Scott and Héloïse Sénéchal

Plot Synopses: Will Sharpe

In Performance: Karin Brown (RSC stagings), Peter Kirwan (overview)

The Director's Cut (interviews by Will Sharpe and Kevin Wright):
Edward Hall and Michael Boyd

Designing *Henry VI*: Tom Piper

The RSC Shakespeare

William Shakespeare

HENRY VI
Parts I, II, and III

Edited by Jonathan Bate and Eric Rasmussen

Introduction by Jonathan Bate

Modern Library
New York

2012 Modern Library Paperback Edition

Published in the United States by Modern Library, an imprint of
The Random House Publishing Group, a division of
Random House, Inc., New York.

The version of *Henry VI* and the corresponding footnotes that appear
in this volume were originally published in *William Shakespeare:
Complete Works*, edited by Jonathan Bate and Eric Rasmussen,
published in 2007 by Modern Library, an imprint of The Random
House Publishing Group, a division of Random House, Inc.

ISBN 978-0-8129-6940-5
eBook ISBN 978-1-58836-887-4

Printed in the United States of America

www.modernlibrary.com

2 4 6 8 9 7 5 3

CONTENTS

INTRODUCTION TO THE THREE PARTS OF *HENRY VI*

AFTER AGINCOURT

Shakespeare's epic drama of *Henry V* ends with the Chorus speaking an epilogue in sonnet form. It offers a forward look that somewhat deflates the triumph of Agincourt. King Henry, the "star of England," will live but a small time. "The world's best garden," having been brought to order by his charismatic arts, will soon be choked with weeds. His son will be crowned King of France and England while still an infant. So many rivals then had the managing of his state "That they lost France and made his England bleed, / Which oft our stage hath shown." Shakespeare thus reminds his audience that his cycle of history plays is complete: the sequence from *Richard II* to *Henry V* at this point joins on to the earlier written tetralogy of the three parts of *Henry VI* and *Richard III*. Sometimes gathered together in modern productions under a title such as *The Wars of the Roses* or *The Plantagenets*, these plays tell the story of England's self-scarring and "dire division."

In *Henry VI Part I*, Henry V's miraculous conquest of France goes into reverse, despite the exploits of the noble Talbot; meanwhile civil war brews at home. In *Part II*, the war with France is brought to an end by the marriage of King Henry VI to Margaret of Anjou, but the weak king cannot prevent the rise of the Yorkist faction. At the beginning of *Part III*, the succession is surrendered to Richard Duke of York, but his ascendancy is halted on a Yorkshire battlefield, where Queen Margaret brings his life to an undignified end; his sons spend the rest of the play avenging him—and it is one of those sons, Richard of Gloucester, the future Richard III, who proves most unscrupulous and therefore most to be feared.

SEQUENCE AND AUTHORSHIP

The Romantic poet and Shakespearean commentator Samuel Taylor Coleridge did not think well of this bloody triple-header. He said of the opening lines of *Part I*, "if you do not feel the impossibility of this speech having been written by Shakespeare, all I dare suggest is, that you may have ears—for so has another animal—but an ear you cannot have." To his own finely tuned ear for poetry, the rhythm of the verse was crude and far inferior to that of even Shakespeare's earliest plays. Coleridge was lecturing on Shakespeare only a few years after the publication of Edmond Malone's scholarly *Dissertation on the Three Parts of King Henry VI, tending to show that these plays were not written originally by Shakespeare.* Ever since Shakespeare rose in the course of the eighteenth century to his status as supreme cultural icon, there has been a tendency to assume that any less than perfect work—*Titus Andronicus*, say, or *Pericles*—must have been the product of some lesser dramatist, or at the very least that Shakespeare was merely patching up a rickety old play for which he was not originally responsible. In the case of the *Henry VI* plays, support for the latter possibility seemed to come from the existence of early editions of versions of the second and third parts under the titles *The First Part of the Contention of the two Famous Houses of York and Lancaster with the Death of the Good Duke Humphrey* (published in 1594) and *The True Tragedy of Richard Duke of York and the Death of Good King Henry the Sixth, with the Whole Contention between the two houses Lancaster and York* (1595). Malone and his successors argued that these were the originals, written by another dramatist (probably one of the so-called "university wits," Robert Greene or George Peele), and that Shakespeare merely undertook the work of a reviser. As for *Henry VI Part I*, Malone regarded it as almost wholly un-Shakespearean. Though grounded in textual scholarship, his arguments were driven by critical distaste for the play's style of verse, the "stately march" whereby "the sense concludes or pauses uniformly at the end of every line."

More recently, scholars have suggested that *The First Part of the Contention* and *Richard Duke of York* are in fact texts of works by Shakespeare, albeit poorly transcribed ones. The titles *The First Part* and *The Whole Contention* strongly suggest that the plays that we now call *Part II* and *Part III* of *Henry VI* originally constituted a two-part work. They were probably first produced in the early 1590s, when Christopher Marlowe's mighty *Tamburlaine the Great* had established a vogue for two-part plays filled with battles, processions, and high-sounding verse.

What we now call *Henry VI Part I* would then stand slightly apart. Since it appears to have been premiered—to considerable acclaim—in 1592, it was probably written *after* the two Wars of the Roses plays that are now called the second and third parts. Perhaps it was what in modern film parlance is called a "prequel," designed to cash in on the success of a blockbuster. Its lack of unity, and its use of different source materials for different scenes, suggest that it may have been a collaborative work. Thomas Nashe, who also wrote in partnership with Marlowe, has been suggested as a prime contributor, but there may have been three or even four hands in the composition. The possibility that Shakespeare was not the principal author of the Talbot/Joan of Arc play would account for some of the inconsistencies in the sequence considered as a trilogy. Among these are the fact that in *Part II* Humphrey Duke of Gloucester is a statesmanlike figure, a Lord Protector worthy of his late brother Henry V, whereas in *Part I* he is more rough-hewn, and the plot discrepancy whereby the surrender of Anjou and Maine, a condition of the marriage between King Henry VI and Margaret of Anjou, is much resented in *Part II* yet not mentioned in the marriage negotiations in *Part I*.

There is a long tradition of attempting to establish literary authorship by stylistic tests—preference for feminine endings in verse lines, contractions (*them* versus *'em*), frequency of grammatical function words, and so forth. The availability of large-scale databases of texts and computer programs to crunch them means that such tests are becoming ever more sophisticated and reliable. When an array of different tests gives the same result, one can speak tentatively of the evidence attaining scientific standards of probability. Twenty-first-century stylometric research of this kind suggests that nearly all of *Part II* can be confidently attributed to Shakespeare, that there are some doubts about *Part III*, and that Shakespeare probably only wrote a few scenes of *Part I*. Perhaps the only thing that makes one hesitate about these results is that they seem too convenient, in that they so neatly mirror the consensus about the relative dramatic quality of the three plays: *Part II* has gloriously Shakespearean energy and variety, and nearly always works superbly in the theater; *Part III* has some immensely powerful rhetorical encounters but many longueurs; *Part I* is generally the least admired—save for the rose-plucking scene in the second act and the moving dialogue of Talbot and his son in the fourth-act battle, the very sequences which the computer tests ascribe to Shakespeare.

It cannot be determined whether the traces of non-Shakespearean language are the vestiges of older plays that Shakespeare was revising or whether they are signs of active collaboration. Nor do we know whether the plays were ever staged as a trilogy in Shakespeare's lifetime. They only came to be labeled as such in the posthumously published 1623 Folio, where all his histories were collected and ordered by the chronology of their subject matter as opposed to their composition. Since the charismatic villain Richard of Gloucester appears in *Part II* and *Part III*, it becomes very tempting to think of the whole group as a tetralogy capped by *The Tragedy of Richard the Third*. Perhaps the best approach is to try to treat each of the plays both on its own terms—they were, after all, designed to be performed one at a time—and as part of Shakespeare's unfolding panorama of English history.

STRUCTURE AND STYLE

Richard III, probably first staged between 1592 and 1594, does seem to represent a quantum leap in Shakespeare's dramatic art. While Crookback Richard has been a role that has made the names of great actors from David Garrick in the eighteenth century to Edmund Kean in the nineteenth to Antony Sher in the twentieth, the *Henry VI* plays have not fared well on the English (or any other) stage. The second and third parts were given a few outings in heavily adapted and compressed form between the Restoration and Regency periods, but almost three hundred years elapsed before there was a full-scale revival of the entire sequence, and even the twentieth century, which restored to favor such previously unpopular early Shakespearean plays as *Love's Labour's Lost* and *Titus Andronicus*, only saw some half dozen major productions: those of F. R. Benson at the beginning of the century, Sir Barry Jackson shortly after the Second World War, John Barton and Peter Hall (rewritten and compressed into two plays under the title *The Wars of the Roses*) at Stratford-upon-Avon in the early 1960s, Terry Hands and Adrian Noble in succeeding decades at Stratford (the latter reducing the tetralogy to a trilogy entitled *The Plantagenets*), and Michael Bogdanov as part of a brave attempt to stage all of the history plays in modern dress, with a strong anti-Thatcherite political agenda, for the touring English Shakespeare Company in the 1980s.

The early twenty-first century, however, witnessed a reversal of fortune: Michael Boyd directed a much-admired version with full texts under the title *This England* in the intimate space of the Swan theater in Stratford-upon-Avon, then on becoming artistic director of the Royal Shakespeare Company revived his productions on a larger stage. Edward Hall, meanwhile, followed his father Peter in reducing three to two, with an energetic version set in a slaughter-house and entitled *Rose Rage*. In a new millennium, at a time of renewed religious war and deep uncertainty about the meaning of nation and national identity, Shakespeare's exploration of the foundations of the fractured Tudor polity seemed powerfully prescient.

Sometimes even the directors who have taken it upon themselves to give the plays a chance have sounded apologetic. For Jackson, they were "ill-shaped, lacking the cohesion brought of practice, a spate of events viewed from a wide angle." The succession of battles, busy messengers, and bombastic exhortations has been ridiculed by critics ever since the playwright Robert Greene, in what is the earliest extant allusion to Shakespeare, mocked Stratford Will as "an upstart Crow, beautified with our feathers, that with his 'Tiger's heart wrapped in a Player's hide,' supposes he is as well able to bombast out a blank verse as the best of you." Greene's quotation is a parody of a line in *Part III*, where the Duke of York is in the full flood of a formal rhetorical vituperation directed at Queen Margaret, the "She-wolf of France." There is, however, a note of anxiety in Greene's mockery: he doesn't like provincial Master Shakespeare's easy adoption of the grand style which had hitherto been regarded as the hallmark of the university-educated dramatists who dominated the London stage in the early 1590s, such as Marlowe and Greene himself.

The Henry VI plays reveal Shakespeare learning his art with great rapidity. Poetic styles and stage business are snapped up from the university men, source material from the prose chronicles of English history. Edward Hall's *Union of the Two Noble and Illustrious Families of Lancaster and York* (1548) is compressed in such a way as to give a pattern to the march of history. The action is concerned less with individual characters than with the roles that individuals play in the drama of the nation's destiny. Shakespeare is quite willing to change someone's age or even their nature in order to subordinate them to his overall scheme. The demonization of Joan of Arc in *Part I* is among the most striking examples. Whereas we associate the mature Shakespeare with contemplation—King Harry or Prince Hamlet in troubled soliloquy—the driving force of these early plays is action. *Part I* deploys a set of variations on an underlying structure in which dramatic action precedes explanation, then a scene will end with epigrammatic recapitulation; each scene is presented in such a way that a different character's viewpoint is emphasized or a new aspect of an existing character developed. The scene with Talbot in the Countess of Auvergne's castle, for instance, highlights the courtesy and prudence of a man who has previously been seen as the exemplar of heroic courage. It also provides a contrast against which the later confrontation of Suffolk and Margaret can be measured: Talbot is a relic from the days of Henry V and England's conquest of France, while Suffolk is a harbinger of division and the Wars of the Roses.

In *Part II*, Shakespeare used a structural pattern to which he returned in later tragedies such as *King Lear* and *Timon of Athens:* the hero, Duke Humphrey of Gloucester, is progressively isolated as prominence is given to the legalistic conspiracies of his malicious enemies. But since the subject is the nation, not an individual hero, Humphrey is dispatched in the third act, and the remainder of the play turns to the subject of rebellion (Jack Cade's proletarian rising in Act 4) and attempted usurpation (the altogether more dangerous Duke of York's march on London). *Part III* begins in chaos, with each of the first two acts ending in a battle (at Wakefield, then Towton), then proceeds in an uneasy equilibrium which sees two kings alive simultaneously and their respective claims only resolved after a bewildering series of encounters, parleys, and changes of allegiance.

Balanced scene structure is paralleled by formal rhetorical style. The formality of the world of these plays is also apparent from the use of dramatic tableaux. The civil strife of the Wars of the Roses could have no better epitome than the paired entrances in Act 2 Scene 5 of *Part III*, where a son that has killed his father appears at one stage door and a moment later a father that has killed his son emerges through the other. Their entry rudely interrupts King Henry's meditation on how he only wants a quiet life, how he'd rather be a shepherd than a king. The aspirations of the weak but pious king are formally visualized in the stage direction for his next entry, in Act 3 Scene 1: "Enter the King, [disguised,] with a prayer-book." Only in retreat and disguise can he fulfill his desire to be a holy man. And even then his peace lasts only an instant, for two gamekeepers overhear and apprehend him, taking him to captivity in the hands of usurping King Edward. By contrast, when Richard of Gloucester becomes King Richard in the next play, a prayer-book is itself a form of disguise.

The unifying theme that makes the plays work as a trilogy, whatever the circumstances of their origin, is the pitching of two world-pictures against each other. Opposites cannot coexist in harmony, so chaos ensues. In *Part I* the opposition takes the form of French against English, Joan against Talbot, magical thinking against rationality, female against male, and implicitly Catholic against Protestant. The historical Talbot was a Catholic, but to an audience in the early 1590s, his plain-speaking Englishness and his heroic deeds on the continental mainland would inevitably have evoked the knightly warriors such as Sir Philip Sidney who fought with Robert Dudley, Earl of Leicester, in the religious wars of the 1580s in the Spanish Netherlands. Joan, meanwhile, is a figure familiar from anti-Catholic propaganda: a virgin branded whore ("pucelle" means "maiden" but "puzzel" connotes prostitute), a saint and martyr converted into a conjuror of devils, a figure linked to papist veneration of the Virgin Mary by way of the suggestion of miraculous pregnancy.

The dialectic of *Part II* pits honest old Duke Humphrey of Gloucester and pious young King Henry VI against the scheming Plantag-enets. Richard Duke of York's brain, "more busy than the labouring spider," "weaves tedious snares to trap" his enemies; his son Richard, future Duke of Gloucester and eventual Richard III, will develop both this kind of language and his father's strategizing to chilling effect. As various characters shift allegiance between the houses of York and Lancaster, so audience sympathies shift as the fast-moving action unfolds: the power-hungry York of *Part II* becomes a figure of pathos when he is forced to wear a paper crown in the final moments before he is stabbed to death in *Part III.*

THE POPULAR VOICE

Shakespeare does not reveal his own allegiances, but he knows the direction in which history is moving. A key incident in this regard is the fake miracle of Simpcox in *Part II:* King Henry is taken in, a mark of his naive faith, whereas Humphrey of Gloucester adopts the skep-tical, interrogative voice of a witchfinder—for which the contempo-rary equivalent would have been a seeker after closet Catholics. Revealingly, the source for this scene was not the pro-Tudor chroni-cle of Edward Hall but the anti-Catholic martyrology of John Foxe. Other "medieval," and thus implicitly Catholic, elements are also subverted: the Duchess of Gloucester's reliance on conjuration and the trial by combat between the armorer Horner and his man Peter both backfire.

Protestantism, with its rejection of the hierarchies of saints and cardinals, its commitment to the Bible in the language of the people, was associated with a democratization of religious faith. *Part II* is the element of the trilogy that toys with the popular voice (hence its significant proportion of prose writing, which is entirely absent from the first and third parts), but it cannot be said to endorse a modern notion of democracy. Jack Cade is a highly attractive figure onstage because he speaks in the same language as the commoners in the audience; his clowning offers welcome respite from the high rhetoric and low cunning of the aristocrats, and such lines as "the first thing we do, let's kill all the lawyers" elicit an approving laugh in every age. But Shakespeare, who made his living by the literacy that his father lacked, can hardly be said to approve of a character who orders the hanging of a village clerk for the crime of being able to read and write. And Cade's vision of England is self-contradictory to the core:

> CADE   Be brave, then, for your captain is brave, and vows reformation. There shall be in England seven halfpenny loaves sold for a penny: the three-hooped pot shall have ten hoops, and I will make it felony to drink small beer. All the realm shall be in common, and in Cheapside shall my palfrey go to grass: and when I am king, as king I will be—
>
> ALL   God save your majesty!

This is a double-edged "reformation": cheap bread, unwatered ale, and the land held in common sound Utopian, but Cade does not really want representative government. He wants to be king himself. Shakespeare plays the same trick against the "commonwealth" idealism of the courtier Gonzalo twenty years later in *The Tempest:* "No sovereignty— / Yet he would be king on't." If Shakespeare has an Eden, it is not a place anterior to class distinction on the lines of the old rhyme "When Adam delved and Eve span / Who was then the gentleman?" but rather an English gentleman's country estate, a place of peace and retreat where Cade is an intruder: the Kentish garden of Alexander Iden.

THE TRAGIC AGON

There is a primal quality to the three plays of *Henry VI.* The basis of drama is *agon,* the Greek word for "struggle" or "contest." According to Aristotle, the origin of tragedy was the moment when an actor split off from a chorus and began to enter into dialogue with them. Later came a second actor and a further opportunity for confrontation— the term for the first actor was "protagonist" and the second "deuteragonist." Conversation in the theater of historical tragedy is always a form of agon, which rapidly escalates into emotional intensity (agony) and thence to physical violence. Shakespeare, with his highly self-conscious theatrical art, is always acutely aware of the several agons that coexist in the theater: between the actor and his role (the struggle to master a part), between the players and the audience (the struggle to grab attention, to move a crowd of onlookers to woe and wonder), within each individual character (the play of conflicting desires and duties), as well as between the characters in their dialogue and stage disposition.

War is the logical culmination of an agonistic world: it is the beginning and end of the three parts of *Henry the Sixth.* The process of escalation is such that *Part III* in particular portrays the complete breakdown of society. The play has the harrowing, relentless quality of Greek tragedy, where people live and die according to a code of revenge, the sins of the fathers are visited upon the children, and the language moves between rhetorical, proto-operatic arias of anger, anguish, invective, and rapid-fire one-line exchanges in which the essential conflicts between Lancastrians and Yorkists, men and women, old and young, self-servers and seekers after justice, winners and losers, are stripped to their essentials. In this world, words are weapons, but just occasionally they are harbingers of hope, as when King Henry VI lays his hands on young Henry Richmond's head and says:

Come hither, England's hope. If secret powers
Suggest but truth to my divining thoughts,
This pretty lad will prove our country's bliss.
His looks are full of peaceful majesty,
His head by nature framed to wear a crown,
His hand to wield a sceptre, and himself
Likely in time to bless a regal throne.
Make much of him, my lords, for this is he
Must help you more than you are hurt by me.

This anointing looks forward to the establishment of the Tudor dynasty when Richmond becomes Henry VII, Queen Elizabeth's grandfather. But, as always seems to happen at moments of apparent stasis in these plays, a messenger then rushes on with the news that the rival king, Edward, has escaped. The violence continues apace. And before the final victory of Richmond at Bosworth Field, England must endure the darkness and blood of Crookback Richard's reign, to which Shakespeare will turn his attention in his next tragedy.

ABOUT THE TEXT

Shakespeare endures through history. He illuminates later times as well as his own. He helps us to understand the human condition. But he cannot do this without a good text of the plays. Without editions there would be no Shakespeare. That is why every twenty years or so throughout the last three centuries there has been a major new edition of his complete works. One aspect of editing is the process of keeping the texts up to date—modernizing the spelling, punctuation, and typography (though not, of course, the actual words), providing explanatory notes in the light of changing educational practices (a generation ago, most of Shakespeare's classical and biblical allusions could be assumed to be generally understood, but now they can't).

But because Shakespeare did not personally oversee the publication of his plays, editors also have to make decisions about the relative authority of the early printed editions. Half of the sum of his plays only appeared posthumously, in the elaborately produced First Folio text of 1623, the original "Complete Works" prepared for the press by Shakespeare's fellow actors, the people who knew the plays better than anyone else. The other half had appeared in print in his lifetime, in the more compact and cheaper form of "Quarto" editions, some of which reproduced good quality texts, others of which were to a greater or lesser degree garbled and error-strewn. In the case of a few plays there are hundreds of differences between the Quarto and Folio editions, some of them far from trivial.

If you look at printers' handbooks from the age of Shakespeare, you quickly discover that one of the first rules was that, whenever possible, compositors were recommended to set their type from existing printed books rather than manuscripts. This was the age before mechanical typesetting, where each individual letter had to be picked out by hand from the compositor's case and placed on a stick (upside down and back to front) before being laid on the press. It was an age of murky rush-light and of manuscripts written in a secretary hand that had dozens of different, hard-to-decipher forms. Printers' lives were a lot easier when they were reprinting existing books rather than struggling with handwritten copy. Easily the quickest way to have created the First Folio would have been simply to reprint those eighteen plays that had already appeared in Quarto and only work from manuscript on the other eighteen.

But that is not what happened. Whenever Quartos were used, playhouse "promptbooks" were also consulted and stage directions copied in from them. And in the case of several major plays where a reasonably well-printed Quarto was available, the Folio printers were instructed to work from an alternative, playhouse-derived manuscript. This meant that the whole process of producing the first complete Shakespeare took months, even years, longer than it might have done. But for the men overseeing the project, John Hemings and Henry Condell, friends and fellow actors who had been remembered in Shakespeare's will, the additional labor and cost were worth the effort for the sake of producing an edition that was close to the practice of the theater. They wanted all the plays in print so that people could, as they wrote in their prefatory address to the reader, "read him and again and again," but they also wanted "the great variety of readers" to work from texts that were close to the theater life for which Shakespeare originally intended them. For this reason, the *RSC Shakespeare*, in both *Complete Works* and individual volumes, uses the Folio as base text wherever possible. Significant Quarto variants are, however, noted in the Textual Notes.

All three parts of *Henry VI* were printed in the Folio, where, incidentally, they were first referred to as the *First, Second,* and *Third Parts of Henry VI*. The play we now know as *Part I* made its first appearance in the Folio, while *Part II* and *Part III* had been printed in the early 1590s under the names *The First Part of the Contention of the two Famous Houses of York and Lancaster* and *The True Tragedy of Richard Duke of York* (see Introduction). The Folio text of *Part I* is the only early version we have, and seems to have been set from authorial papers, its multiple authorship in some way attested to by the different spelling habits and inconsistent speech headings from scene to scene that would have been in some measure smoothed if a scribe had prepared the copy. Other deficiencies in performance considerations seem to attest that the copy used by the printer was never used in the theater (which is not to say that the play wasn't performed— we know it was). The quarto and octavo texts of *Contention* and *True Tragedy* respectively are much shorter and linguistically poorer than their Folio counterparts, leading many to hypothesize that they are memorial reports of versions that had been shortened for performance. The Folio texts, *Part II* and *Part III*, are substantially longer, better versions which bear similar evidence to *Part I* of being set from authorial—as opposed to scribal/theatrical—papers.

The following notes highlight various aspects of the editorial process and indicate conventions used in the text of this edition:

Lists of Parts are supplied in the First Folio for only six plays, not including *Henry VI*, so the list here is editorially supplied. Capitals indicate that part of the name which is used for speech headings in the script (thus "Duke Humphrey of GLOUCESTER, Lord Protector, the king's uncle").

Locations are provided by Folio for only two plays, which does not include the *Henry VI* plays. Eighteenth-century editors, working in an age of elaborately realistic stage sets, were the first to provide detailed locations ("Another part of the palace/battlefield," etc.). Given that Shakespeare wrote for a bare stage and often an imprecise sense of place, we have relegated locations to the explanatory notes at the foot of the page, where they are given at the beginning of each scene where the imaginary location is different from the one before.

Act and Scene Divisions were provided in Folio in a much more thoroughgoing way than in the Quartos. Sometimes, however, they were erroneous or omitted; corrections and additions supplied by editorial tradition are indicated by square brackets. Five-act division is based on a classical model, and act breaks provided the opportunity to replace the candles in the indoor Blackfriars playhouse the King's Men used after 1608, but Shakespeare did not necessarily think in terms of a five-part structure of dramatic composition. The Folio convention is that a scene ends when the stage is empty. Nowadays, partly under the influence of film, we tend to consider a scene to be a dramatic unit that ends with either a change of imaginary location or a significant passage of time within the narrative. Shakespeare's fluidity of composition accords well with this convention, so in addition to act and scene numbers we provide a ***running scene*** count in the right margin at the beginning of each new scene, in the typeface used for editorial directions. Where there is a scene break caused by a momentary bare stage, but the location does not change and extra time does not pass, we use the convention ***running scene continues***. There is inevitably a degree of editorial judgment in making such calls, but the system is very valuable in suggesting the pace of the plays.

Speakers' Names are often inconsistent in Folio. We have regularized speech headings, but retained an element of deliberate inconsistency in entry directions, in order to give the flavor of Folio. For example, in *Part I* and *Part II* GLOUCESTER is always so-called in speech headings but is sometimes "Duke Humphrey" or "Protector" in entry directions; in *Part III*, QUEEN MARGARET is always so-called in speech headings but often simply "Queen" in entry directions.

Verse is indicated by lines that do not run to the right margin and by capitalization of each line. The Folio printers sometimes set verse as prose, and vice versa (either out of misunderstanding or for reasons of space). We have silently corrected in such cases, although in some instances there is ambiguity, in which case we have leaned toward the preservation of Folio layout. Folio sometimes uses contraction ("turnd" rather than "turned") to indicate whether or not the final "-ed" of a past participle is sounded, an area where there is variation for the sake of the five-beat iambic pentameter rhythm. We use the convention of a grave accent to indicate sounding (thus "turnèd" would be two syllables), but would urge actors not to overstress. In cases where one speaker ends with a verse half line and the next begins with the other half of the pentameter, editors since the late eighteenth century have indented the second line. We have abandoned this convention, since the Folio does not use it, nor did actors' cues in the Shakespearean theater. An exception is made when the second speaker actively interrupts or completes the first speaker's sentence.

Spelling is modernized, but older forms are occasionally maintained where necessary for rhythm or aural effect.

Punctuation in Shakespeare's time was as much rhetorical as grammatical. "Colon" was originally a term for a unit of thought in an argument. The semicolon was a new unit of punctuation (some of the Quartos lack them altogether). We have modernized punctuation throughout, but have given more weight to Folio punctuation than many editors, since, though not Shakespearean, it reflects the usage of his period. In particular, we have used the colon far more than many editors: it is exceptionally useful as a way of indicating how many Shakespearean speeches unfold clause by clause in a developing argument that gives the illusion of enacting the process of thinking in the moment. We have also kept in mind the origin of punctuation in classical times as a way of assisting the actor and orator: the comma suggests the briefest of pauses for breath, the colon a middling one, and a full stop or period a longer pause. Semicolons, by contrast, belong to an era of punctuation that was only just coming in during Shakespeare's time and that is coming to an end now: we have accordingly only used them where they occur in our copy texts (and not always then). Dashes are sometimes used for parenthetical interjections where the Folio has brackets. They are also used for interruptions and changes in train of thought. Where a change of addressee occurs within a speech, we have used a dash preceded by a period (or occasionally another form of punctuation). Often the identity of the respective addressees is obvious from the context. When it is not, this has been indicated in a marginal stage direction.

Entrances and Exits are fairly thorough in Folio, which has accordingly been followed as faithfully as possible. Where characters are omitted or corrections are necessary, this is indicated by square brackets (e.g. "[*and Attendants*]"). *Exit* is sometimes silently normalized to *Exeunt* and *Manet* anglicized to "remains." We trust Folio positioning of entrances and exits to a greater degree than most editors.

Editorial Stage Directions such as stage business, asides, indications of addressee and of characters' position on the gallery stage are only used sparingly in Folio. Other editions mingle directions of this kind with original Folio and Quarto directions, sometimes marking them by means of square brackets. We have sought to distinguish what could be described as *directorial* interventions of this kind from Folio-style directions (either original or supplied) by placing them in the right margin in a different typeface. There is a degree of subjectivity about which directions are of which kind, but the procedure is intended as a reminder to the reader and the actor that Shakespearean stage directions are often dependent upon editorial inference alone and are not set in stone. We also depart from editorial tradition in sometimes admitting uncertainty and thus printing permissive stage directions, such as an **Aside?** (often a line may be equally effective as an aside or a direct address—it is for each production or reading to make its own decision) or a **may exit** or a piece of business placed between arrows to indicate that it may occur at various different moments within a scene.

Line Numbers in the left margin are editorial, for reference and to key the explanatory and textual notes.

Explanatory Notes at the foot of each page explain allusions and gloss obsolete and difficult words, confusing phraseology, occasional major textual cruxes, and so on. Particular attention is given to non-standard usage, bawdy innuendo, and technical terms (e.g. legal and military language). Where more than one sense is given, commas indicate shades of related meaning, slashes alternative or double meanings.

Textual Notes at the end of the play indicate major departures from the Folio. They take the following form: the reading of our text is given in bold and its source given after an equals sign. In relation to

Part I, "F2" signifies a correction introduced in the Second Folio of 1632, and "Ed" one from the subsequent editorial tradition. With *Part II,* "Q" means a reading from the First Quarto text of 1594, "Q2" one from the Second Quarto of 1600, "Q3" from the Third Quarto of 1619, "F2" a correction from the Second Folio of 1632, "F4" a correction from the Fourth Folio of 1685, and "Ed" a reading from the subsequent editorial tradition. For *Part III,* "O" signifies a reading from the First Octavo text of 1595, "Q3" one from the Third Quarto text of 1619, "F2" a correction from the Second Folio of 1632, "F3" a correction from the Third Folio of 1663–64, and "Ed" one from the subsequent editorial tradition. The rejected Folio reading is then given. Thus, for example, in *Part II:* "**5.1.201 household** = Q. F = housed. F2 = house's" means that we have preferred the Quarto reading "household" and rejected the First Folio's "housed" and the Second Folio's "house's" in the phrase "thy household badge." We have also included interestingly different readings even when we have accepted the reading of the First Folio.

HENRY VI
Parts I, II, and III

HENRY VI PART I:
KEY FACTS

MAJOR PARTS: (*with percentage of lines/number of speeches/scenes onstage*) Talbot (15%/59/12), Joan la Pucelle (9%/46/10), Richard Plantagenet, later Duke of York (7%/56/7), Duke of Gloucester (7%/48/7), King Henry VI (7%/29/5), Earl of Suffolk (6%/41/3), Charles, King of France (5%/41/8), Winchester (4%/27/6), Edmund Mortimer (3%/9/1), Sir William Lucy (3%/14/3), Duke of Bedford (3%/19/4), Earl of Warwick (3%/24/4), Duke of Somerset (2%/27/4), Duke of Exeter (2%/11/5), Reignier (2%/24/6), Duke of Alençon (2%/18/7), John Talbot (2%/11/2), Countess of Auvergne (2%/13/1), Duke of Burgundy (2%/17/6).

LINGUISTIC MEDIUM: 100% verse.

DATE: 1592. Generally assumed to be the "harey the vi" performed at the Rose Theatre in March 1592 (marked as "ne"—new?—by proprietor Philip Henslowe). Nashe's pamphlet *Pierce Penniless* (registered for publication August 1592) refers to the Talbot scenes inspiring "the tears of ten thousand spectators."

SOURCES: Different chronicle sources seem to have been used, perhaps by the play's different authors. So, for example, Edward Hall's *The Union of the Two Noble and Illustre Famelies of Lancastre and Yorke* (1548) is the main source for the civil contention in England, whereas the account of Joan of Arc draws on Holinshed's *Chronicles* (1587 edition). Strikingly, the scenes most likely to be Shakespeare's—the Temple garden and Talbot with his son—seem to be pure dramatic invention, with no source in the chronicles.

TEXT: 1623 Folio is the only text. There is dispute over whether it was set from (multi-?)authorial holograph or scribal copy, and the extent to which it was influenced by the playhouse bookkeeper. Some textual inconsistencies (e.g. whether Winchester is a bishop or a cardinal) may have been the result of different authors making different assumptions. The Folio editors introduced act and scene divisions that are perhaps more literary than theatrical.

TRILOGY?: Modern scholarship leans to the view that the plays which the Folio calls the second and third parts of *Henry the Sixth* were originally a two-part "Wars of the Roses" drama (*The First Part of the Contention* and *The True Tragedy of Richard Duke of York*) and that this play was a (collaborative) "prequel," written later to cash in on their success. This argument supposes that the three plays only became a "trilogy" when they were renamed and ordered by historical sequence in the 1623 Folio. Some scholars, however, adhere to the minority view that all three parts were written in sequence as a trilogy.

THE FIRST PART OF HENRY THE SIXTH

The English side

KING HENRY VI, probably a boy player

Duke of BEDFORD, Regent of France

Duke of GLOUCESTER, Lord Protector, brother of the late Henry V, uncle of the king

Duke of EXETER, uncle of the late Henry V, great-uncle of the king

Bishop of WINCHESTER, later a Cardinal, Exeter's younger brother, family name Beaufort

Duke of SOMERSET, Exeter's nephew

RICHARD PLANTAGENET, later DUKE OF YORK and Regent of France

Earl of WARWICK

Earl of SALISBURY

Earl of SUFFOLK, William de la Pole

Lord TALBOT, later Earl of Shrewsbury

JOHN Talbot, his son

Edmund MORTIMER, Earl of March

Sir Thomas GARGRAVE

Sir William GLASDALE

Sir John FALSTAFF (historically Fastolf, not the same character as in *Henry IV* and *The Merry Wives of Windsor*)

Sir William LUCY

WOODVILLE, Lieutenant of the Tower of London

MAYOR of London

OFFICER to the Mayor of London

VERNON

BASSET

A LAWYER

A Papal LEGATE

JAILERS

English CAPTAIN

FIRST SERVINGMAN

FIRST MESSENGER

SECOND MESSENGER

THIRD MESSENGER

FIRST WARDER

SECOND WARDER

The French side

CHARLES the Dauphin, later King of France

REIGNIER, Duke of Anjou, King of Naples

MARGARET, his daughter

Duke of ALENÇON

BASTARD of Orléans

Duke of BURGUNDY

French GENERAL

Joan la PUCELLE, also called Joan of Arc

SHEPHERD, father of Joan

MASTER GUNNER of Orléans

Master Gunner's BOY, his son

COUNTESS of Auvergne

Her PORTER

French SERGEANT

FIRST SENTINEL

WATCH

FIRST SOLDIER

French SCOUT

Soldiers, Attendants, Ambassadors,
the Governor of Paris, French
herald, Servingmen,
Messengers, Sentinels, Captains,
Fiends, Trumpeters

Act 1 Scene 1

running scene 1

*Dead march. Enter the funeral of King Henry the Fifth, attended on by
the Duke of Bedford, Regent of France; the Duke of Gloucester,
Protector; the Duke of Exeter, [the Earl of] Warwick, the Bishop of
Winchester, and the Duke of Somerset, [and Heralds]*

BEDFORD   Hung be the heavens with black: yield, day, to night!
Comets, importing change of times and states,
Brandish your crystal tresses in the sky,
And with them scourge the bad revolting stars
5   That have consented unto Henry's death:
King Henry the Fifth, too famous to live long:
England ne'er lost a king of so much worth.
GLOUCESTER   England ne'er had a king until his time:
Virtue he had, deserving to command:
10   His brandished sword did blind men with his beams:
His arms spread wider than a dragon's wings:
His sparkling eyes, replete with wrathful fire,
More dazzlèd and drove back his enemies
Than midday sun, fierce bent against their faces.

1.1   Location: Westminster Abbey, London   Dead march solemn piece of music
accompanying a funeral; probably played with a muffled drum   **1 Hung . . . black** some
scholars believe that the projecting roof or canopy over the Elizabethan stage (**the heavens**)
was conventionally draped with black for the performance of a tragedy   **2 Comets** these were
thought to presage **change** and were often deemed to be evil omens   **states** circumstances/
ruling bodies   **3 Brandish** flourish/shine, flash   **crystal tresses** clear, gleaming strands
(of hair—i.e. the comets' tails)   **4 scourge** punish, whip   **revolting** rebellious   **stars**
thought to influence human destiny   **5 consented unto** conspired in   **6 too . . . long** Henry
died when he was thirty-five, after a nine-year reign   **9 Virtue** merit/grace/power   **10 his** its
12 replete with full of

15   What should I say? His deeds exceed all speech:
        He ne'er lift up his hand but conquerèd.
            EXETER   We mourn in black: why mourn we not in blood?
        Henry is dead and never shall revive:
        Upon a wooden coffin we attend,
20   And death's dishonourable victory
        We with our stately presence glorify,
        Like captives bound to a triumphant car.
        What, shall we curse the planets of mishap,
        That plotted thus our glory's overthrow?
25   Or shall we think the subtle-witted French
        Conjurers and sorcerers, that, afraid of him,
        By magic verses have contrived his end?
            WINCHESTER   He was a king blessed of the King of Kings.
        Unto the French the dreadful judgement day
30   So dreadful will not be as was his sight.
        The battles of the Lord of hosts he fought:
        The church's prayers made him so prosperous.
            GLOUCESTER   The church? Where is it? Had not churchmen
                prayed,
        His thread of life had not so soon decayed.
35   None do you like but an effeminate prince,
        Whom like a schoolboy you may overawe.
            WINCHESTER   Gloucester, whate'er we like, thou art Protector
        And lookest to command the Prince and realm.

---

15 What . . . say? i.e. I have not words to express it   **16 He . . . conquerèd** he never raised his
arm (i.e. sword) without conquering the enemy   **17 in blood** i.e. by declaring war against the
French   **18 revive** live again   **19 wooden** plays on the sense of "unfeeling, lifeless"   **22 car**
chariot (to which **captives** were traditionally **bound**, to be paraded through the streets by the
victors)   **23 of mishap** of evil influence, that bring misfortune   **24 plotted** schemed/mapped
out   **25 subtle-witted** crafty, clever   **27 verses** spells, incantations   **contrived** plotted
28 King of Kings name for Christ, used especially during descriptions of **judgement day**
(Revelation 19:16)   **30 dreadful** awe-inspiring, causing dread and fear   **31 Lord of hosts**
frequent biblical name for God   **32 prosperous** successful, fortunate   **33 prayed** i.e. for
Henry's downfall; puns on "preyed"   **34 thread of life** in classical mythology, the three Fates
spun, measured out, and cut the thread of a person's life   **35 effeminate prince** weak,
unmanly ruler   **36 overawe** i.e. repress and control   **37 Protector** surrogate ruler of the
realm, while the new king was too young to reign; Henry VI was a baby when Henry V died
38 lookest expect

Thy wife is proud: she holdeth thee in awe,

40   More than God or religious churchmen may.

GLOUCESTER   Name not religion, for thou lov'st the flesh,

And ne'er throughout the year to church thou go'st

Except it be to pray against thy foes.

BEDFORD   Cease, cease these jars, and rest your minds in
peace:

45   Let's to the altar: heralds, wait on us:

[*Exeunt funeral procession*]

Instead of gold, we'll offer up our arms:

Since arms avail not now that Henry's dead:

Posterity, await for wretched years,

When, at their mothers' moistened eyes, babes shall suck,

50   Our isle be made a nourish of salt tears,

And none but women left to wail the dead.

Henry the Fifth, thy ghost I invocate:

Prosper this realm, keep it from civil broils,

Combat with adverse planets in the heavens:

55   A far more glorious star thy soul will make

Than Julius Caesar, or bright—

Enter a Messenger

FIRST MESSENGER   My honourable lords, health to you all:

Sad tidings bring I to you out of France,

Of loss, of slaughter and discomfiture:

60   Guyenne, Champaigne, Rouen, Rheims, Orléans,

Paris, Gisors, Poitiers, are all quite lost.

BEDFORD   What say'st thou, man, before dead Henry's
corpse?

Speak softly, or the loss of those great towns

Will make him burst his lead and rise from death.

---

41 **the flesh** worldly, material pleasures/sexual pursuits   44 **jars** discords, conflicts   47 **avail
not** are of no use or advantage   48 **await for** expect, anticipate   49 **at . . . suck** babies are
suckled only by their mother's tears   50 **nourish** nurse   52 **invocate** invoke, summon
53 **broils** turmoil, conflict   54 **adverse planets** planets of unfavorable influences
55 **star . . . Caesar** according to Roman tradition, the great ruler's soul was turned into a star
59 **discomfiture** overthrow, utter defeat?   60 **Champaigne** Compiègne (not Champagne)
64 **burst his lead** break out of the leaden inner lining of the wooden coffin

65 GLOUCESTER   Is Paris lost? Is Rouen yielded up?
     If Henry were recalled to life again,
     These news would cause him once more yield the ghost.
   EXETER   How were they lost? What treachery was used?
   FIRST MESSENGER   No treachery, but want of men and money.
70   Amongst the soldiers this is mutterèd:
     That here you maintain several factions,
     And whilst a field should be dispatched and fought,
     You are disputing of your generals.
     One would have lingering wars with little cost:
75   Another would fly swift, but wanteth wings:
     A third thinks, without expense at all,
     By guileful fair words peace may be obtained.
     Awake, awake, English nobility!
     Let not sloth dim your honours new-begot:
80   Cropped are the flower-de-luces in your arms:
     Of England's coat, one half is cut away.   [Exit]
   EXETER   Were our tears wanting to this funeral,
     These tidings would call forth her flowing tides.
   BEDFORD   Me they concern: Regent I am of France:
85   Give me my steelèd coat: I'll fight for France.
     Away with these disgraceful wailing robes!   He removes his
     Wounds will I lend the French instead of eyes,   mourning robes
     To weep their intermissive miseries.
   Enter to them another Messenger
   SECOND MESSENGER   Lords, view these letters, full of bad
       mischance.
90   France is revolted from the English quite,
     Except some petty towns of no import.

---

67 **yield the ghost** die   69 **want** lack   71 **several** separate, divisive   72 **field** battle
dispatched prepared, organized   73 **of** about   77 **guileful** deceitful, devious   79 **new-begot**
newly created   80 **flower-de-luces** fleur-de-lis, or lily of France; after Edward III claimed his
right to the French throne, the flower was incorporated into the English royal coat of arms
arms coat of arms   81 **coat** coat of arms   82 **wanting to** lacking for   83 **her** i.e. England's
tides picks up on **tidings**   84 **Regent** ruler in the king's absence   85 **steelèd coat** armor
88 **intermissive** coming at intervals   89 **mischance** misfortune   90 **quite** entirely   91 **petty**
small, insignificant

The dauphin Charles is crownèd king in Rheims:
The Bastard of Orléans with him is joined:
Reignier, Duke of Anjou, doth take his part:
95   The Duke of Alençon flieth to his side.   *Exit*

EXETER   The dauphin crownèd king! All fly to him?
O whither shall we fly from this reproach?

GLOUCESTER   We will not fly, but to our enemies' throats.
Bedford, if thou be slack, I'll fight it out.

100   BEDFORD   Gloucester, why doubt'st thou of my forwardness?
An army have I mustered in my thoughts,
Wherewith already France is overrun.

Enter another Messenger

THIRD MESSENGER   My gracious lords, to add to your laments,
Wherewith you now bedew King Henry's hearse,
105   I must inform you of a dismal fight
Betwixt the stout Lord Talbot and the French.

WINCHESTER   What? Wherein Talbot overcame — is't so?

THIRD MESSENGER   O no: wherein Lord Talbot was o'erthrown:
The circumstance I'll tell you more at large.
110   The tenth of August last, this dreadful lord,
Retiring from the siege of Orléans,
Having full scarce six thousand in his troop,
By three and twenty thousand of the French
Was round encompassèd and set upon:
115   No leisure had he to enrank his men.
He wanted pikes to set before his archers:
Instead whereof, sharp stakes plucked out of hedges

---

92 **dauphin** title of the French king's eldest son, heir to the throne   93 **Bastard** illegitimate
son of Charles, Duke of Orléans   97 **fly** flee (Gloucester shifts the sense to "rush upon in
attack")   **reproach** shame, disgrace   100 **forwardness** readiness, preparedness
104 **bedew** i.e. wet with tears   105 **dismal** disastrous, ominous   **fight** i.e. the battle of Patay,
which, historically, took place after the siege of Orléans that is depicted in the following two
scenes   109 **circumstance** details   110 **tenth of August** historically, 18 June (1429)
dreadful frightening, inspiring dread and awe   112 **full scarce** barely   114 **round**
encompassèd completely surrounded   115 **enrank** draw up in battle ranks   116 **wanted**
lacked   **pikes** stakes bound with iron and sharpened at either end, set in the ground to
protect archers from enemy cavalry

They pitchèd in the ground confusedly,
To keep the horsemen off from breaking in.
120 More than three hours the fight continuèd,
Where valiant Talbot above human thought
Enacted wonders with his sword and lance.
Hundreds he sent to hell, and none durst stand him:
Here, there, and everywhere, enraged he slew.
125 The French exclaimed the devil was in arms:
All the whole army stood agazed on him.
His soldiers spying his undaunted spirit
'A Talbot! A Talbot!' cried out amain
And rushed into the bowels of the battle.
130 Here had the conquest fully been sealed up,
If Sir John Falstaff had not played the coward.
He, being in the vanguard, placed behind
With purpose to relieve and follow them,
Cowardly fled, not having struck one stroke.
135 Hence grew the general wrack and massacre;
Enclosèd were they with their enemies.
A base Walloon, to win the dauphin's grace,
Thrust Talbot with a spear into the back,
Whom all France with their chief assembled strength
140 Durst not presume to look once in the face.
BEDFORD   Is Talbot slain then? I will slay myself,
For living idly here in pomp and ease,
Whilst such a worthy leader, wanting aid,
Unto his dastard foemen is betrayed.
145 THIRD MESSENGER   O no, he lives, but is took prisoner,
And Lord Scales with him, and Lord Hungerford:
Most of the rest slaughtered, or took likewise.

---

118 confusedly in a disorderly manner   **121 above human thought** beyond human belief
123 stand resist   **126 agazed on** amazed by, gaping at   **128 A** To   **amain** forcefully
129 bowels innards, intestines   **130 sealed up** finished   **131 Falstaff** historically "Fastolf";
not the character who features in *1* and *2 Henry IV* and is declared dead in *Henry V*   **133 With**
on   **135 wrack** wreck, ruin   **136 Enclosèd** surrounded   **137 Walloon** inhabitant of a
region that is now part of southern Belgium   **grace** favor   **142 pomp** luxury, splendor
144 dastard foemen cowardly enemies

BEDFORD   His ransom there is none but I shall pay.
I'll hale the dauphin headlong from his throne:
150   His crown shall be the ransom of my friend:
Four of their lords I'll change for one of ours.
Farewell, my masters: to my task will I.
Bonfires in France forthwith I am to make,
To keep our great Saint George's feast withal.
155   Ten thousand soldiers with me I will take,
Whose bloody deeds shall make all Europe quake.
THIRD MESSENGER   So you had need, for Orléans is besieged.
The English army is grown weak and faint:
The Earl of Salisbury craveth supply,
160   And hardly keeps his men from mutiny,
Since they, so few, watch such a multitude.   [*Exit*]
EXETER   Remember, lords, your oaths to Henry sworn:
Either to quell the dauphin utterly,
Or bring him in obedience to your yoke.
165   BEDFORD   I do remember it, and here take my leave,
To go about my preparation.   *Exit Bedford*
GLOUCESTER   I'll to the Tower with all the haste I can,
To view th'artillery and munition,
And then I will proclaim young Henry king.   *Exit Gloucester*
170   EXETER   To Eltham will I, where the young king is,
Being ordained his special governor,
And for his safety there I'll best devise.   *Exit*
WINCHESTER   Each hath his place and function to attend:
I am left out; for me nothing remains:
175   But long I will not be Jack-out-of-office.
The king from Eltham I intend to steal
And sit at chiefest stern of public weal.   *Exit*

---

149 **hale** haul, drag   151 **change** exchange   154 **keep** celebrate   **Saint George's feast**
23 April, feast day of the patron saint of England   **withal** with   159 **supply** reinforcements,
relief   160 **hardly** with difficulty   163 **quell** crush, overcome   167 **Tower** Tower of London,
which housed the royal armory   170 **Eltham** royal palace nine miles southeast of London, on
the road to Canterbury   171 **Being** as I am   **special governor** guardian   175 **Jack-out-of-
office** a knave who has been dismissed from his post   177 **sit . . . stern** control the ship of
state, i.e. assume the government   **public weal** the commonwealth, the state

[Act 1 Scene 2]   *running scene 2*

Sound a flourish. Enter Charles [the Dauphin, the Duke of] Alençon
and Reignier [Duke of Anjou], marching with Drum and Soldiers

CHARLES   Mars his true moving, even as in the heavens
             So in the earth, to this day is not known.
             Late did he shine upon the English side:
             Now we are victors: upon us he smiles.
5   What towns of any moment but we have?
             At pleasure here we lie near Orléans;
             Otherwhiles the famished English, like pale ghosts,
             Faintly besiege us one hour in a month.

ALENÇON   They want their porridge and their fat bull-beeves:
10   Either they must be dieted like mules,
             And have their provender tied to their mouths,
             Or piteous they will look, like drownèd mice.

REIGNIER   Let's raise the siege: why live we idly here?
             Talbot is taken, whom we wont to fear:
15   Remaineth none but mad-brained Salisbury,
             And he may well in fretting spend his gall,
             Nor men nor money hath he to make war.

CHARLES   Sound, sound alarum! We will rush on them.
             Now for the honour of the forlorn French:
20   Him I forgive my death that killeth me
             When he sees me go back one foot or fly.   *Exeunt*

Here alarum: they are beaten back by the English with great loss
Enter Charles, Alençon and Reignier

CHARLES   Who ever saw the like? What men have I?
             Dogs, cowards, dastards! I would ne'er have fled,
             But that they left me 'midst my enemies.

1.2   *Location: the French camp, near Orléans, a town on the River Loire, south of*
Paris   *flourish* trumpet fanfare accompanying a person in authority   *Drum* drummers
1 Mars . . . moving the exact orbit of the planet Mars (a source of uncertainty to Elizabethan
astronomers); Mars was also the Roman god of war   **3 Late** recently   **5 moment** importance
7 Otherwhiles at times   **9 want** lack   **porridge** vegetable stew   **bull-beeves** bull-beef, joints
of beef   **10 dieted** fed   **11 provender** animal feed, fodder   **13 raise** put an end to   **14 wont**
used, were accustomed   **16 fretting** impatience, bad temper   **spend his gall** wear out his
bitterness   **18 alarum** call to arms   **19 forlorn** in imminent danger of death   **23 dastards**
cowards

25 REIGNIER   Salisbury is a desperate homicide;
            He fighteth as one weary of his life:
            The other lords, like lions wanting food,
            Do rush upon us as their hungry prey.

    ALENÇON   Froissart, a countryman of ours, records
30   England all Olivers and Rowlands bred,
            During the time Edward the Third did reign:
            More truly now may this be verified;
            For none but Samsons and Goliases
            It sendeth forth to skirmish: one to ten!
35   Lean raw-boned rascals, who would e'er suppose
            They had such courage and audacity?

    CHARLES   Let's leave this town, for they are hare-brained slaves,
            And hunger will enforce them to be more eager:
            Of old I know them; rather with their teeth
40   The walls they'll tear down than forsake the siege.

    REIGNIER   I think by some odd gimmers or device
            Their arms are set, like clocks, still to strike on;
            Else ne'er could they hold out so as they do:
            By my consent, we'll even let them alone.

45 ALENÇON   Be it so.

    Enter the Bastard of Orléans

    BASTARD   Where's the Prince Dauphin? I have news for him.

    CHARLES   Bastard of Orléans, thrice welcome to us.

    BASTARD   Methinks your looks are sad, your cheer appalled.
            Hath the late overthrow wrought this offence?

---

25 homicide murderer   **28 hungry** a transferred epithet; the **lions** are hungry for the prey
29 Froissart Jean Froissart, fourteenth-century French author who chronicled contemporary
conflicts between France and England   **30 all . . . Rowlands** like the two knights in the
twelfth-century poem *La Chanson de Roland (The Song of Roland)*, who embody Christian virtue,
heroism, and true friendship   **33 Samsons and Goliases** biblical characters famed for great
strength; Samson appears in Judges 14, and Goliath (Golias), the giant killed by David, in
1 Samuel 17   **34 skirmish** do battle, fight   **one . . . ten** one (English) man for every ten
(French)   **35 raw-boned** skeleton-like, excessively lean or gaunt   **rascals** lean, inferior deer
in a herd   **37 hare-brained slaves** reckless villains   **38 eager** fierce, hungry for violence
40 forsake give up, leave   **41 gimmers** gimmals, mechanical connecting links, used especially
for transmitting motion   **device** mechanism   **42 still** continually   **44 consent** agreement
(to your suggestion to **leave this town**)   **even** completely   **48 cheer appalled** face pale
49 wrought worked, brought about   **offence** harm

50   Be not dismayed, for succour is at hand:
      A holy maid hither with me I bring,
      Which by a vision sent to her from heaven,
      Ordainèd is to raise this tedious siege
      And drive the English forth the bounds of France:
55   The spirit of deep prophecy she hath,
      Exceeding the nine sibyls of old Rome:
      What's past and what's to come she can descry.
      Speak, shall I call her in? Believe my words,
      For they are certain and unfallible.
60 **CHARLES**   Go, call her in.   [*Exit Bastard of Orléans*]
                 But first, to try her skill,
      Reignier, stand thou as dauphin in my place:
      Question her proudly: let thy looks be stern:
      By this means shall we sound what skill she hath.
      Enter [the Bastard of Orléans, with] Joan [la] Pucelle [armed]
      REIGNIER   Fair maid, is't thou wilt do these wondrous
          feats?   *As Charles*
65 **PUCELLE**   Reignier, is't thou that thinkest to beguile me?
      Where is the dauphin?— Come, come from behind: *To Charles*
      I know thee well, though never seen before.
      Be not amazed, there's nothing hid from me;
      In private will I talk with thee apart:
70   Stand back, you lords, and give us leave awhile.   *Reignier, Alençon,*
      REIGNIER   She takes upon her bravely at first dash.   *and Bastard*
      PUCELLE   Dauphin, I am by birth a shepherd's   *stand apart*
          daughter,
      My wit untrained in any kind of art:
      Heaven and our Lady gracious hath it pleased

---

53 Ordainèd destined, appointed by God   **raise** put an end to   **tedious** harrowing, lengthy
54 forth out of   **bounds** territory   **56 nine sibyls** female prophets from classical times,
not exclusively from **Rome** and usually said to be ten in number   **57 descry** discern, see
60 try test   **62 proudly** haughtily, with authority   **63 sound** probe, measure   ***Joan [la]***
Pucelle i.e. Joan of Arc; *pucelle* is French for "maid, virgin," with play on "puzzel," i.e. "whore"
65 beguile deceive   **69 *apart*** aside   **71 takes upon her** takes the initiative boldly/plays
her part splendidly   **at first dash** from the outset, at the first encounter (with sexual
connotations)   **73 wit** intellect   **art** scholarship, learning   **74 our Lady gracious** the Virgin
Mary, **God's** (Christ's) **mother**

75 To shine on my contemptible estate.
    Lo, whilst I waited on my tender lambs,
    And to sun's parching heat displayed my cheeks,
    God's mother deignèd to appear to me,
    And in a vision full of majesty,
80 Willed me to leave my base vocation
    And free my country from calamity:
    Her aid she promised, and assured success.
    In complete glory she revealed herself:
    And whereas I was black and swart before,
85 With those clear rays which she infused on me
    That beauty am I blessed with, which you may see.
    Ask me what question thou canst possible,
    And I will answer unpremeditated:
    My courage try by combat, if thou dar'st,
90 And thou shalt find that I exceed my sex.
    Resolve on this, thou shalt be fortunate,
    If thou receive me for thy warlike mate.
CHARLES   Thou hast astonished me with thy high terms:
    Only this proof I'll of thy valour make,
95 In single combat thou shalt buckle with me,
    And if thou vanquishest, thy words are true:
    Otherwise I renounce all confidence.
PUCELLE   I am prepared: here is my keen-edged sword,
    Decked with five flower-de-luces on each side,
100 The which at Touraine, in Saint Katherine's churchyard,
    Out of a great deal of old iron I chose forth.
CHARLES   Then come, a God's name: I fear no woman.

---

75 **contemptible estate** lowly, humble condition   **76 Lo** look (a general speech marker; may pun on "low")   **tender** young   **83 complete** perfect   **84 black and swart** dark, unattractive, and swarthy   **85 infused on** shed on, poured into   **88 unpremeditated** spontaneous   **91 Resolve on** be assured of   **92 mate** companion, brother-in-arms (with play on the sense of "sexual partner"; **warlike** may pun on "whore-like")   **93 high terms** lofty/eloquent words   **94 proof** test   **95 buckle** fight at close quarters, grapple (plays on sense of "have sex")   **96 vanquishest** overcome me   **97 confidence** trust, belief/intimacy   **98 keen-edged** sharp   **99 Decked** adorned   **flower-de-luces** fleurs-de-lis, the lily on French coat of arms   **100 Touraine** region in central France   **Saint Katherine** fourth-century saint and virgin martyr who was beheaded for her Christian faith; Joan of Arc claimed to have seen her in a vision   **102 a** in

PUCELLE   And while I live, I'll ne'er fly from a man.

Here they fight, and Joan la Pucelle overcomes

CHARLES   Stay, stay thy hands! Thou art an Amazon

105   And fightest with the sword of Deborah.

PUCELLE   Christ's mother helps me, else I were too weak.

CHARLES   Whoe'er helps thee, 'tis thou that must help me:
     Impatiently I burn with thy desire:
     My heart and hands thou hast at once subdued.

110   Excellent Pucelle, if thy name be so,
     Let me thy servant and not sovereign be:
     'Tis the French dauphin sueth to thee thus.

PUCELLE   I must not yield to any rites of love,
     For my profession's sacred from above:

115   When I have chased all thy foes from hence,
     Then will I think upon a recompense.

CHARLES   Meantime, look gracious on thy prostrate thrall.

REIGNIER   My lord, methinks, is very long in   *To the others, apart*
     talk.

ALENÇON   Doubtless he shrives this woman to her smock,

120   Else ne'er could he so long protract his speech.

REIGNIER   Shall we disturb him, since he keeps no mean?

ALENÇON   He may mean more than we poor men do know.
     These women are shrewd tempters with their tongues.

REIGNIER   My lord, where are you? What devise you on?

125   Shall we give o'er Orléans, or no?

---

103 **I'll . . . man** unwitting sexual innuendo   104 **Amazon** mythical race of female warriors
105 **Deborah** Old Testament prophetess who led the Israelites in revolt against their Canaanite
oppressors (Judges 4 and 5)   106 **else** otherwise   108 **thy desire** the same urge to fight that
you feel/sexual desire for you   111 **servant** plays on the notion of sexual service   112 **sueth
to** begs, woos   114 **profession** religious calling, profession of faith   116 **recompense** return,
repayment   117 **gracious** with divine grace/with favor   **prostrate** either figurative
("adoring, submissive"), or Charles may literally still be on the floor after the fight   **thrall** slave
119 **shrives** hears confession and grants absolution/undresses/has sex with   **smock**
undergarment   120 **protract** extend (plays on notion of penile erection)   121 **mean** limit,
measure   122 **know** perhaps with sexual connotations (to know: to have sex with)
123 **shrewd** cunning, artful   **tongues** speech/tongues used sexually   124 **where are you**
what are your intentions   **devise you on** do you decide upon, are you planning   125 **give
o'er** abandon, leave

PUCELLE   Why, no, I say: distrustful recreants,
          Fight till the last gasp: I'll be your guard.

CHARLES   What she says, I'll confirm: we'll fight it out.

PUCELLE   Assigned am I to be the English scourge.
130   This night the siege assuredly I'll raise:
          Expect Saint Martin's summer, halcyon's days,
          Since I have entered into these wars.
          Glory is like a circle in the water,
          Which never ceaseth to enlarge itself
135   Till by broad spreading, it disperse to naught.
          With Henry's death, the English circle ends:
          Dispersèd are the glories it included:
          Now am I like that proud insulting ship
          Which Caesar and his fortune bare at once.

140 CHARLES   Was Mahomet inspirèd with a dove?
          Thou with an eagle art inspirèd then.
          Helen, the mother of great Constantine,
          Nor yet Saint Philip's daughters were like thee.
          Bright star of Venus, fall'n down on the earth,
145   How may I reverently worship thee enough?

ALENÇON   Leave off delays, and let us raise the siege.

REIGNIER   Woman, do what thou canst to save our honours;
          Drive them from Orléans, and be immortalized.

CHARLES   Presently we'll try: come, let's away about it:
150   No prophet will I trust, if she prove false.   *Exeunt*

---

126 recreants cowards, deserters, those who abandon the true cause   **129 scourge** one sent
by God to punish   **131 Saint Martin's summer** a late spell of fine weather; Saint Martin's day
is 11 November   **halcyon's days** a period of calm (from the legend that the kingfisher laid its
eggs in a nest on the surface of the water; while they incubated the waters remained
untroubled)   **138 insulting** exultant, mocking   **139 Caesar . . . once** in a story related by the
ancient writer Plutarch, Caesar tells a sea captain not to fear the rough weather as his ship
contains both Caesar and Caesar's good **fortune**   **140 Mahomet . . . dove** Mohammed, the
prophet and founder of Islam who received divine revelations from a dove that whispered in his
ear; skeptics said that he had merely trained the bird to nibble corn lodged there   **141 with** by
eagle a Christian symbol   **142 Helen** mother of the emperor **Constantine**; after being led by a
vision to the discovery of the true cross, she converted her son to Christianity, which he made
the official religion in the Roman Empire   **143 Saint Philip's daughters** four virgins said to
have prophetic powers (Acts 21:9)   **144 Venus** Roman goddess of love; the planet Venus is
known as the Morning **Star**   **148 immortalized** gain immortal fame   **149 Presently**
immediately

[Act 1 Scene 3]   *running scene 3*

Enter Gloucester, with his Servingmen [in blue coats]

GLOUCESTER   I am come to survey the Tower this day:
Since Henry's death, I fear, there is conveyance:
Where be these warders, that they wait not here?   *Servingmen*
Open the gates; 'tis Gloucester that calls.   *knock on gates*

5   FIRST WARDER   Who's there that knocks so imperiously?   *Within*
FIRST SERVINGMAN   It is the noble Duke of Gloucester.
SECOND WARDER   Whoe'er he be, you may not be let in.   *Within*
FIRST SERVINGMAN   Villains, answer you so the Lord Protector?
FIRST WARDER   The Lord protect him, so we answer him: *Within*
10   We do no otherwise than we are willed.
GLOUCESTER   Who willèd you? Or whose will stands but mine?
There's none protector of the realm but I.
Break up the gates, I'll be your warrantize: *To Servingmen*
Shall I be flouted thus by dunghill grooms?
*Gloucester's men rush at the Tower Gates, and Woodville the
Lieutenant speaks within*

15   WOODVILLE   What noise is this? What traitors have we here?
GLOUCESTER   Lieutenant, is it you whose voice I hear?
Open the gates: here's Gloucester that would enter.
WOODVILLE   Have patience, noble duke: I may not open:
The Cardinal of Winchester forbids:
20   From him I have express commandment
That thou nor none of thine shall be let in.
GLOUCESTER   Faint-hearted Woodville, prizest him 'fore me?
Arrogant Winchester, that haughty prelate,
Whom Henry, our late sovereign, ne'er could brook?
25   Thou art no friend to God or to the king:
Open the gates, or I'll shut thee out shortly.

1.3   *Location: the Tower of London   blue coats* Gloucester's livery and the typical color
of Elizabethan servants' uniforms   **2 conveyance** trickery, theft   **3 warders** guards
8 Villains scoundrels/base servants   **10 willed** ordered   **12 none** no other   **13 Break up**
open   **warrantize** guarantee, surety   **14 flouted** mocked, taunted   **19 Cardinal** an error; he
has only just been made a cardinal in Act 5 Scene 1   **22 prizest him 'fore** do you esteem him
more than   **24 brook** endure   **26 shut . . . shortly** have you dismissed immediately

SERVINGMEN   Open the gates unto the Lord Protector,
Or we'll burst them open, if that you come not quickly.
Enter to the [Lord] Protector at the Tower Gates, [the Bishop of]
Winchester and his men in tawny coats

WINCHESTER   How now, ambitious umpire! What means this?

30   GLOUCESTER   Peeled priest, dost thou command me to be shut
out?

WINCHESTER   I do, thou most usurping proditor,
And not 'Protector', of the king or realm.

GLOUCESTER   Stand back, thou manifest conspirator,
Thou that contrived'st to murder our dead lord:

35   Thou that giv'st whores indulgences to sin:
I'll canvass thee in thy broad cardinal's hat,
If thou proceed in this thy insolence.

WINCHESTER   Nay, stand thou back, I will not budge a foot:
This be Damascus, be thou cursèd Cain,

40   To slay thy brother Abel, if thou wilt.

GLOUCESTER   I will not slay thee, but I'll drive thee back:
Thy scarlet robes as a child's bearing-cloth
I'll use to carry thee out of this place.

WINCHESTER   Do what thou dar'st, I beard thee to thy face.

45   GLOUCESTER   What? Am I dared and bearded to my face?
Draw, men, for all this privilegèd place;   *All draw their swords*
Blue coats to tawny coats. Priest, beware your beard,
I mean to tug it and to cuff you soundly.

---

28 tawny yellowish brown, the color of the uniform worn by summoners or officers of an
ecclesiastical court   **29 umpire** one who sets himself up as arbitrator (Second Folio's
emendation of Folio's "Vmpheir"; some editors emend to "Humphrey," but there is no reason
for the bishop to use his adversary's Christian name)   **30 Peeled** bald, tonsured   **31 proditor**
traitor   **34 contrived'st** plotted   **dead lord** i.e. Henry V   **35 whores . . . sin** the see of the
Bishop of Winchester owned and leased land in Southwark, an area south of the Thames
notorious for brothels; prostitutes were known as "Winchester geese"   **indulgences** official
documents, purchasable from the Church, that granted absolution from sin   **36 canvass**
entangle in a net/sift, examine, as through a canvas sieve/punish (literally toss in a canvas
sheet)   **cardinal's hat** also the name of a long-standing Southwark brothel; the Bishop of
Winchester does not actually become a cardinal until later in the play   **39 Damascus . . .**
Cain the city of Damascus, in Syria, was thought to have been built at the place where Adam
and Eve's son Cain murdered his **brother Abel**   **42 bearing-cloth** christening robe   **44 beard**
defy (literally, pull insultingly by the beard)   **45 dared** challenged   **46 for all this** despite this
being   **privilegèd place** i.e. royal residence, where it was illegal to draw swords

Under my feet I stamp thy cardinal's hat:

50 In spite of Pope or dignities of Church,

Here by the cheeks I'll drag thee up and down.

WINCHESTER   Gloucester, thou wilt answer this before the Pope.

GLOUCESTER   Winchester goose, I cry, 'A rope, a rope!'—

Now beat them hence: why do you let them

stay?—   *To Servingmen*

55 Thee I'll chase hence, thou wolf in sheep's array.— *To Winchester*

Out, tawny coats!— Out, scarlet hypocrite!

Here Gloucester's men beat out the [Bishop of Winchester's] men, and
enter in the hurly-burly the Mayor of London and his Officers

MAYOR   Fie, lords, that you, being supreme magistrates,

Thus contumeliously should break the peace!

GLOUCESTER   Peace, mayor, thou know'st little of my wrongs:

60 Here's Beaufort, that regards nor God nor king,

Hath here distrained the Tower to his use.

WINCHESTER   Here's Gloucester — a foe to citizens,

One that still motions war and never peace,

O'ercharging your free purses with large fines—

65 That seeks to overthrow religion,

Because he is Protector of the realm,

And would have armour here out of the Tower,

To crown himself king and suppress the prince.

GLOUCESTER   I will not answer thee with words, but blows.

Here they skirmish again

70 MAYOR   Naught rests for me, in this tumultuous strife,

But to make open proclamation.

Come, officer, as loud as e'er thou canst, cry.   *Handing a paper to*

OFFICER   All manner of men assembled here in   *the Officer, who*

arms this day against God's peace and the king's,   *reads*

75 we charge and command you, in his highness' name, to repair

---

50 **dignities** dignitaries   53 **Winchester goose** syphilitic swelling in the groin/client of
prostitutes   **A rope** i.e. for flogging (dominant sense); also "hangman's noose/penis/
parrot's cry (abusive)"   56 *hurly-burly* tumult, uproar   57 **Fie** expression of impatience
58 **contumeliously** disgracefully, insolently   61 **distrained** seized   63 **still** constantly, always
motions promotes, urges   64 **O'ercharging . . . fines** i.e. overburdening with heavy taxation
(levied to fund war)   **free** generous   68 **prince** ruler, king   70 **rests** remains   75 **repair**
return

to your several dwelling-places, and not to wear, handle, or
use any sword, weapon, or dagger, henceforward, upon pain
of death.   *The skirmish ends*

GLOUCESTER   Cardinal, I'll be no breaker of the law:
80   But we shall meet, and break our minds at large.

WINCHESTER   Gloucester, we'll meet to thy cost, be sure:
Thy heart-blood I will have for this day's work.

MAYOR   I'll call for clubs, if you will not away:
This cardinal's more haughty than the devil.

85   GLOUCESTER   Mayor, farewell: thou dost but what thou mayst.

WINCHESTER   Abominable Gloucester, guard thy head,
For I intend to have it ere long.

*Exeunt [separately, Gloucester and Bishop of Winchester with their
Servingmen]*

MAYOR   See the coast cleared, and then we will depart.
Good God, these nobles should such stomachs bear!
90   I myself fight not once in forty year.   *Exeunt*

[Act 1 Scene 4]   *running scene 4*

Enter the Master Gunner of Orléans and his Boy

MASTER GUNNER   Sirrah, thou know'st how Orléans is besieged,
And how the English have the suburbs won.

BOY   Father, I know, and oft have shot at them,
Howe'er, unfortunate, I missed my aim.

5   MASTER GUNNER   But now thou shalt not. Be thou ruled by me:
Chief Master Gunner am I of this town,
Something I must do to procure me grace:
The prince's espials have informèd me
How the English, in the suburbs close entrenched,
10   Wont, through a secret grate of iron bars

---

76 **several** various   80 **break** reveal, broach   **at large** in full   83 **call for clubs** give the
rallying cry for apprentices armed with clubs (used to suppress a riot)   86 **Abominable**
loathsome (often popularly "inhuman, unnatural")   87 **ere** before   89 **stomachs** tempers,
anger   **1.4   *Location: Orléans, France***   1 **Sirrah** sir (used to inferiors)   2 **suburbs**
outskirts, areas outside the city walls   7 **grace** honor/favor   8 **espials** spies   9 **close
entrenched** securely dug-in/fortified nearby   10 **Wont** are accustomed

In yonder tower, to overpeer the city,
And thence discover how with most advantage
They may vex us with shot or with assault.
To intercept this inconvenience,
15 A piece of ordnance gainst it I have placed,
And even these three days have I watched,
If I could see them. Now do thou watch
For I can stay no longer.
If thou spy'st any, run and bring me word,
20 And thou shalt find me at the governor's.
BOY   Father, I warrant you, take you no care:

                                        Exit [Master Gunner]

I'll never trouble you, if I may spy them.   *Exit*
Enter Salisbury and Talbot on the turrets, with others [including Sir
Thomas Gargrave and Sir William Glasdale]
SALISBURY   Talbot, my life, my joy, again returned?
How wert thou handled, being prisoner?
25 Or by what means got'st thou to be released?
Discourse, I prithee, on this turret's top.
TALBOT   The Earl of Bedford had a prisoner,
Called the brave Lord Ponton de Santrailles:
For him was I exchanged and ransomèd.
30 But with a baser man of arms by far
Once in contempt they would have bartered me:
Which I, disdaining, scorned, and cravèd death,
Rather than I would be so pilled esteemed:
In fine, redeemed I was as I desired.
35 But O, the treacherous Falstaff wounds my heart,
Whom with my bare fists I would execute,
If I now had him brought into my power.
SALISBURY   Yet tell'st thou not how thou wert entertained.

---

14 inconvenience harm, injury   **15 ordnance** cannon, artillery   **gainst** aimed at
21 take . . . care do not worry   **30 baser** of lower birth or rank   **man of arms** soldier
32 cravèd entreated   **33 pilled** peeled, i.e. reduced, worthless, deprived of honor   **34 In fine**
in short, to sum up   **redeemed** ransomed   **38 entertained** treated

TALBOT   With scoffs and scorns and contumelious taunts:
40   In open market-place produced they me,
        To be a public spectacle to all:
        'Here', said they, 'is the terror of the French,
        The scarecrow that affrights our children so.'
        Then broke I from the officers that led me,
45   And with my nails digged stones out of the ground,
        To hurl at the beholders of my shame.
        My grisly countenance made others fly:
        None durst come near for fear of sudden death.
        In iron walls they deemed me not secure:
50   So great fear of my name 'mongst them was spread,
        That they supposed I could rend bars of steel,
        And spurn in pieces posts of adamant.
        Wherefore a guard of chosen shot I had,
        That walked about me every minute while:
55   And if I did but stir out of my bed,
        Ready they were to shoot me to the heart.

Enter the Boy [who passes over the stage and exits] with a linstock
[lit and burning]

SALISBURY   I grieve to hear what torments you endured,
        But we will be revenged sufficiently.
        Now it is supper-time in Orléans:
60   Here, through this grate, I count each one
        And view the Frenchmen how they fortify:
        Let us look in: the sight will much delight thee:
        Sir Thomas Gargrave, and Sir William Glasdale,
        Let me have your express opinions
65   Where is best place to make our batt'ry next.   *They look through*

GARGRAVE   I think, at the north gate, for there stands   *the grate*
        lords.

GLASDALE   And I, here, at the bulwark of the bridge.

---

39 contumelious contemptuous, insolent   **47 grisly** grim, terrifying   **48 sudden** immediate
52 spurn kick   **adamant** a legendary substance of unsurpassed hardness   **53 Wherefore**
for which reason   **chosen shot** specially selected marksman   **54 every minute while** at
one-minute intervals   **56 *linstock*** forked stick for holding the gunner's lighted match
64 express precise, considered   **65 batt'ry** assault, bombardment   **67 bulwark** manned
fortification

TALBOT   For aught I see, this city must be famished,
Or with light skirmishes enfeeblèd.

Here they shoot [within] and Salisbury [and Gargrave] fall down

70 SALISBURY   O Lord have mercy on us, wretched sinners!

GARGRAVE   O Lord have mercy on me, woeful man!

TALBOT   What chance is this that suddenly hath crossed us?
Speak, Salisbury; at least, if thou canst, speak:
How far'st thou, mirror of all martial men?
75 One of thy eyes and thy cheek's side struck off?
Accursèd tower! Accursèd fatal hand
That hath contrived this woeful tragedy.
In thirteen battles Salisbury o'ercame:
Henry the Fifth he first trained to the wars:
80 Whilst any trump did sound, or drum struck up,
His sword did ne'er leave striking in the field.
Yet liv'st thou, Salisbury? Though thy speech doth fail,
One eye thou hast to look to heaven for grace.
The sun with one eye vieweth all the world.
85 Heaven, be thou gracious to none alive,
If Salisbury wants mercy at thy hands.
Sir Thomas Gargrave, hast thou any life?
Speak unto Talbot: nay, look up to him.
Bear hence his body: I will help to bury it.

[Exit one with Gargrave's body]

90 Salisbury, cheer thy spirit with this comfort:
Thou shalt not die whiles—
He beckons with his hand and smiles on me:
As who should say 'When I am dead and gone,
Remember to avenge me on the French.'
95 Plantagenet, I will; and like thee, Nero,
Play on the lute, beholding the towns burn:
Wretched shall France be only in my name.

---

68 **aught** anything, what   69 **enfeeblèd** weakened   72 **chance** unfortunate event
crossed thwarted   74 **mirror** i.e. model, image   76 **fatal** deadly/that deals fate   80 **trump**
trumpet   86 **wants** lacks   93 **As** as one   95 **Plantagenet** Salisbury (Thomas Montacute)
was a descendant of Edward III   **Nero . . . burn** Roman emperor, Nero supposedly played
music (popularly "fiddled") while Rome burned   97 **only in** at the mere sound of

Here an alarum, and it thunders and lightens

What stir is this? What tumult's in the heavens?
Whence cometh this alarum and the noise?

Enter a Messenger

100 MESSENGER   My lord, my lord, the French have gathered head.
The dauphin, with one Joan la Pucelle joined,
A holy prophetess new risen up,
Is come with a great power to raise the siege.

Here Salisbury lifteth himself up and groans

TALBOT   Hear, hear, how dying Salisbury doth groan!
105 It irks his heart he cannot be revenged.
Frenchmen, I'll be a Salisbury to you.
Puzzel or pucelle, dolphin or dogfish,
Your hearts I'll stamp out with my horse's heels,
And make a quagmire of your mingled brains.
110 Convey me Salisbury into his tent,
And then we'll try what these dastard Frenchmen dare.

Alarum.   Exeunt

[Act 1 Scene 5]   *running scene 4 continues*

Here an alarum again, and Talbot pursueth the Dauphin, and driveth
him: then enter Joan la Pucelle, driving Englishmen before her, [and
exeunt]. Then enter Talbot

TALBOT   Where is my strength, my valour, and my force?
Our English troops retire, I cannot stay them:
A woman clad in armour chaseth them.

Enter [Joan la] Pucelle

Here, here she comes. I'll have a bout with thee:
5 Devil or devil's dam, I'll conjure thee:

---

lightens lightning flashes   **100 gathered head** raised an army, drawn their forces together
103 power army   **105 irks** distresses   **107 Puzzel or pucelle** though it means the opposite,
the word had in England taken on a slang sense of "whore"   **dolphin** i.e. Dauphin
(pronounced in the same way)   **109 mingled** mixed together/mangled   **110 Convey me**
convey (**me** is emphatic)   **1.5   2 stay** prevent   **4 bout** of fighting/of sex   **5 dam** mother
conjure control with incantations, exorcise (perhaps "have sex with")

Blood will I draw on thee — thou art a witch —
And straightway give thy soul to him thou serv'st.

PUCELLE   Come, come, 'tis only I that must disgrace thee.

Here they fight

TALBOT   Heavens, can you suffer hell so to prevail?
10   My breast I'll burst with straining of my courage
And from my shoulders crack my arms asunder.
But I will chastise this high-minded strumpet.

They fight again

PUCELLE   Talbot, farewell: thy hour is not yet come:
I must go victual Orléans forthwith.

A short alarum: then [the French] enter the town with soldiers

15   O'ertake me if thou canst: I scorn thy strength.
Go, go, cheer up thy hungry-starvèd men:
Help Salisbury to make his testament:
This day is ours, as many more shall be.   *Exit*

TALBOT   My thoughts are whirlèd like a potter's wheel:
20   I know not where I am, nor what I do:
A witch by fear, not force, like Hannibal,
Drives back our troops and conquers as she lists:
So bees with smoke and doves with noisome stench
Are from their hives and houses driven away.
25   They called us, for our fierceness, English dogs:
Now, like to whelps, we crying run away.   *A short alarum*
Hark, countrymen: either renew the fight,
Or tear the lions out of England's coat:
Renounce your soil, give sheep in lions' stead:
30   Sheep run not half so treacherous from the wolf,
Or horse or oxen from the leopard,
As you fly from your oft-subduèd slaves.

---

6 Blood . . . witch superstition held anyone who drew blood from a witch was then protected from her spells   **7 him** the devil/the dauphin   **10 courage** vigor, spirit   **12 high-minded** arrogant   **14 victual** supply with provisions   **17 testament** will   **21 Hannibal** famous third-century Carthaginian general who once outwitted his Roman enemies by tying firebrands to the horns of a vast herd of oxen so that they thought they were outnumbered   **22 lists** pleases   **23 noisome** noxious   **26 whelps** puppies   **28 England's coat** coat of arms, in which three **lions** featured, quartered with the French fleur-de-lis   **29 give** display   **stead** place   **30 treacherous** cowardly   **32 subduèd** overcome, subjugated

Alarum. Here another skirmish

It will not be: retire into your trenches:

You all consented unto Salisbury's death,

35   For none would strike a stroke in his revenge.

Pucelle is entered into Orléans,

In spite of us or aught that we could do.

O would I were to die with Salisbury!

The shame hereof will make me hide my head.   *Exit Talbot*

Alarum: retreat: flourish

[Act 1 Scene 6]   *running scene 4 continues*

Enter on the walls, [Joan la] Pucelle, Charles [the Dauphin], Reignier,
Alençon and Soldiers [with colours]

PUCELLE   Advance our waving colours on the walls:

Rescued is Orléans from the English.

Thus Joan la Pucelle hath performed her word.

CHARLES   Divinest creature, Astraea's daughter,

5   How shall I honour thee for this success?

Thy promises are like Adonis' garden

That one day bloomed and fruitful were the next.

France, triumph in thy glorious prophetess!

Recovered is the town of Orléans:

10   More blessèd hap did ne'er befall our state.

REIGNIER   Why ring not out the bells aloud throughout the
town?

Dauphin, command the citizens make bonfires

And feast and banquet in the open streets,

To celebrate the joy that God hath given us.

15   ALENÇON   All France will be replete with mirth and joy,

When they shall hear how we have played the men.

---

33 It . . . be i.e. it is useless   34 consented unto conspired to bring about   35 his revenge
revenge of him   38 would if only, I wish   1.6 *walls* city walls   1 Advance raise aloft
colours military banners or flags   4 Astraea Greek goddess of justice   6 Adonis' garden
mythical garden of extraordinary fertility   10 hap chance, fortune   16 played the men
performed our role of soldier, displayed manliness

CHARLES   'Tis Joan, not we, by whom the day is won:
              For which I will divide my crown with her,
              And all the priests and friars in my realm
20   Shall in procession sing her endless praise.
              A statelier pyramid to her I'll rear
              Than Rhodope's of Memphis' ever was.
              In memory of her, when she is dead,
              Her ashes, in an urn more precious
25   Than the rich-jewelled coffer of Darius,
              Transported shall be at high festivals
              Before the kings and queens of France.
              No longer on Saint Denis will we cry,
              But Joan la Pucelle shall be France's saint.
30   Come in, and let us banquet royally,
              After this golden day of victory.   *Flourish. Exeunt*

Act 2 Scene 1   *running scene 5*

Enter [above] a [French] Sergeant of a band with two Sentinels

SERGEANT   Sirs, take your places and be vigilant:
              If any noise or soldier you perceive
              Near to the walls, by some apparent sign
              Let us have knowledge at the court of guard.
5   FIRST SENTINEL   Sergeant, you shall.   *[Exit Sergeant]*
                                Thus are poor servitors,
              When others sleep upon their quiet beds,
              Constrained to watch in darkness, rain and cold.
Enter Talbot, Bedford, Burgundy, [and soldiers], with scaling-ladders,
their drums beating a dead march

---

21 pyramid . . . Memphis Rhodope was a Greek courtesan, who married a king of Memphis
and supposedly built the third Egyptian pyramid   **25 rich-jewelled . . . Darius** King of Persia,
conquered by Alexander the Great; the **coffer** is either Darius' jeweled treasure chest (in
which Alexander stored the works of Homer), or his coffin   **26 high** elaborate, important
28 Saint Denis patron saint of France   **2.1**   *band* company of soldiers guarding the town
3 apparent clear, manifest   **4 court of guard** guardhouse   **5 servitors** soldiers, those who
perform military service   **7 Constrained** obliged   *scaling-ladders* used by soldiers to climb
defensive fortifications   *dead march* funeral march or simply march played on muffled
drums

TALBOT   Lord Regent, and redoubted Burgundy,
               By whose approach the regions of Artois,
10   Wallon, and Picardy are friends to us:
               This happy night the Frenchmen are secure,
               Having all day caroused and banqueted:
               Embrace we then this opportunity,
               As fitting best to quittance their deceit,
15   Contrived by art and baleful sorcery.

BEDFORD   Coward of France! How much he wrongs his fame,
               Despairing of his own arm's fortitude,
               To join with witches and the help of hell.

BURGUNDY   Traitors have never other company.
20   But what's that Pucelle whom they term so pure?

TALBOT   A maid, they say.

BEDFORD   A maid? And be so martial?

BURGUNDY   Pray God she prove not masculine ere long,
               If underneath the standard of the French
25   She carry armour as she hath begun.

TALBOT   Well, let them practise and converse with spirits.
               God is our fortress, in whose conquering name
               Let us resolve to scale their flinty bulwarks.

BEDFORD   Ascend, brave Talbot, we will follow thee.

30 TALBOT   Not all together: better far, I guess,
               That we do make our entrance several ways:
               That, if it chance the one of us do fail,
               The other yet may rise against their force.

BEDFORD   Agreed: I'll to yond corner.

35 BURGUNDY   And I to this.

---

8 **redoubted** revered/feared   9 **approach** arrival   10 **Wallon** region that is now part of
southern Belgium   11 **happy** fortunate   **secure** carefree/overconfident   14 **quittance**
requite, repay   15 **art** magic   **baleful** malignant, deadly   16 **Coward of France!** i.e. the
dauphin   **fame** reputation   17 **fortitude** strength   23 **prove not masculine** does not turn
out to be a man/turns out to be a woman (by getting pregnant)   24 **standard** military
banner/soldier who carries the banner/erect penis   25 **carry armour** wear armor/bear the
weight of a man in armor (during sex)   26 **practise and converse** scheme and talk,
associate/have sex   28 **flinty** hard, stony   31 **several** separate, various   34 **yond** yonder,
that (over there)

TALBOT   And here will Talbot mount, or make his grave.
              Now, Salisbury, for thee, and for the right
              Of English Henry, shall this night appear
              How much in duty I am bound to both.

40 SENTINELS   Arm! Arm! The enemy doth make assault!
[English soldiers, having scaled the walls] cry: 'Saint George,'
'A Talbot.'
The French leap o'er the walls in their shirts. Enter several ways [the]
Bastard [of Orléans], Alençon [and] Reignier, half ready, and half
unready

ALENÇON   How now, my lords? What, all unready so?

BASTARD   Unready? Ay, and glad we scaped so well.

REIGNIER   'Twas time, I trow, to wake and leave our beds,
              Hearing alarums at our chamber doors.

45 ALENÇON   Of all exploits since first I followed arms,
              Ne'er heard I of a warlike enterprise
              More venturous or desperate than this.

BASTARD   I think this Talbot be a fiend of hell.

REIGNIER   If not of hell, the heavens sure favour him.

50 ALENÇON   Here cometh Charles: I marvel how he sped.
Enter Charles and Joan [la Pucelle]

BASTARD   Tut, holy Joan was his defensive guard.

CHARLES   Is this thy cunning, thou deceitful dame?
              Didst thou at first, to flatter us withal,
              Make us partakers of a little gain,

55   That now our loss might be ten times so much?

PUCELLE   Wherefore is Charles impatient with his friend?
              At all times will you have my power alike?
              Sleeping or waking must I still prevail,
              Or will you blame and lay the fault on me?

---

ready dressed   **43 I trow** I am sure   **47 venturous** risky   **desperate** reckless, hazardous
50 marvel . . . sped wonder how he fared   **51 holy** may pun on "holey" (i.e. "with a vagina,"
imaging Joan in her sexual capacity)   **52 cunning** magic/skill/craftiness   **53 flatter** falsely
encourage   **withal** with it   **56 impatient** angry   **57 alike** in the same way   **58 prevail** be
victorious

60   Improvident soldiers, had your watch been good,
       This sudden mischief never could have fall'n.

     CHARLES   Duke of Alençon, this was your default,
       That, being captain of the watch tonight,
       Did look no better to that weighty charge.

65   ALENÇON   Had all your quarters been as safely kept
       As that whereof I had the government,
       We had not been thus shamefully surprised.

     BASTARD   Mine was secure.

     REIGNIER   And so was mine, my lord.

70   CHARLES   And for myself, most part of all this night,
       Within her quarter and mine own precinct
       I was employed in passing to and fro,
       About relieving of the sentinels.
       Then how or which way should they first break in?

75   PUCELLE   Question, my lords, no further of the case,
       How or which way: 'tis sure they found some place
       But weakly guarded, where the breach was made:
       And now there rests no other shift but this:
       To gather our soldiers, scattered and dispersed,

80   And lay new platforms to endamage them.

     Alarum. Enter an [English] Soldier, crying 'A Talbot! A Talbot!' [The
     French] fly, leaving their clothes behind

     SOLDIER   I'll be so bold to take what they have left:
       The cry of 'Talbot' serves me for a sword,
       For I have loaden me with many spoils,
       Using no other weapon but his name.   *Exit*

---

60 Improvident careless, short-sighted   **61 mischief** calamity, harm   **fall'n** befallen,
happened   **62 default** failure, negligence   **64 weighty charge** important responsibility
65 quarters part of an army camp/rooms, apartments   **kept** guarded, secured
66 government control, management   **67 surprised** ambushed, assaulted   **71 her quarter**
Joan's rooms (possibly plays sexually on sense of "hindquarters")   **precinct** sector, area of
control   **72 passing** moving   **73 About** concerned with   **relieving . . . sentinels** possibly
plays on the sense of "sexually relieving my erection"   **77 But** only   **78 rests** remains
shift strategy   **80 platforms** plans   **endamage them** harm the enemy   **83 spoils** plunder,
booty

[Act 2 Scene 2]

Enter Talbot, Bedford, Burgundy, [a Captain, and others]

BEDFORD   The day begins to break, and night is fled,
Whose pitchy mantle over-veiled the earth.
Here sound retreat, and cease our hot pursuit.

Retreat [sounded]

TALBOT   Bring forth the body of old Salisbury,
5   And here advance it in the market-place,
The middle centre of this cursèd town.
Now have I paid my vow unto his soul:
For every drop of blood was drawn from him,
There hath at least five Frenchmen died tonight.
10   And that hereafter ages may behold
What ruin happened in revenge of him,
Within their chiefest temple I'll erect
A tomb, wherein his corpse shall be interred:
Upon the which, that everyone may read,
15   Shall be engraved the sack of Orléans,
The treacherous manner of his mournful death,
And what a terror he had been to France.
But, lords, in all our bloody massacre,
I muse we met not with the dauphin's grace,
20   His new-come champion, virtuous Joan of Arc,
Nor any of his false confederates.

BEDFORD   'Tis thought, Lord Talbot, when the fight began,
Roused on the sudden from their drowsy beds,
They did amongst the troops of armèd men
25   Leap o'er the walls for refuge in the field.

BURGUNDY   Myself, as far as I could well discern
For smoke and dusky vapours of the night,
Am sure I scared the dauphin and his trull,

2.2   **2 pitchy** black (as pitch, a tarlike substance)   ***Retreat*** trumpet signal recalling the pursuing force   **5 advance** display/raise   **7 vow** i.e. of vengeance   **11 ruin** death, destruction   **16 mournful** sorrowful, causing grief   **19 muse** wonder   **20 champion** one who fights for another, defendant   **virtuous** said with irony   **28 trull** whore

When arm in arm they both came swiftly running,
30 Like to a pair of loving turtle-doves
That could not live asunder day or night.
After that things are set in order here,
We'll follow them with all the power we have.

Enter a Messenger

MESSENGER   All hail, my lords! Which of this princely train
35 Call ye the warlike Talbot, for his acts
So much applauded through the realm of France?

TALBOT   Here is the Talbot: who would speak with him?

MESSENGER   The virtuous lady, Countess of Auvergne,
With modesty admiring thy renown,
40 By me entreats, great lord, thou wouldst vouchsafe
To visit her poor castle where she lies,
That she may boast she hath beheld the man
Whose glory fills the world with loud report.

BURGUNDY   Is it even so? Nay, then I see our wars
45 Will turn unto a peaceful comic sport,
When ladies crave to be encountered with.
You may not, my lord, despise her gentle suit.

TALBOT   Ne'er trust me then: for when a world of men
Could not prevail with all their oratory,
50 Yet hath a woman's kindness overruled:
And therefore tell her I return great thanks,
And in submission will attend on her.
Will not your honours bear me company?

BEDFORD   No, truly, 'tis more than manners will:
55 And I have heard it said, unbidden guests
Are often welcomest when they are gone.

TALBOT   Well then, alone, since there's no remedy,
I mean to prove this lady's courtesy.

---

30 turtle-doves emblematic of faithful love, they supposedly formed couples for life   **33 power** military force   **40 vouchsafe** grant, deign   **41 poor** humble   **lies** lives   **43 report** plays on the sense of "explosion of a gun or cannon"   **45 comic sport** amusing entertainment (**sport** plays on the sense of "sexual activity")   **46 encountered with** met/fought with/had sex with   **47 despise** scorn   **gentle** kind/courteous/honorable   **48 world** i.e. great number   **49 oratory** eloquence, rhetorical skill   **50 overruled** prevailed   **52 attend on** visit, wait on   **55 unbidden** uninvited   **57 remedy** alternative   **58 prove** try/test sexually

Come hither, captain.

60   You perceive my mind?   *Whispers*

CAPTAIN   I do, my lord, and mean accordingly.   *Exeunt*

[Act 2 Scene 3]

Enter [the] Countess [of Auvergne and her Porter]

COUNTESS   Porter, remember what I gave in charge,
And when you have done so, bring the keys to me.

PORTER   Madam, I will.   *Exit*

COUNTESS   The plot is laid: if all things fall out right,

5   I shall as famous be by this exploit
As Scythian Tomyris by Cyrus' death.
Great is the rumour of this dreadful knight,
And his achievements of no less account:
Fain would mine eyes be witness with mine ears,

10   To give their censure of these rare reports.

Enter Messenger and Talbot

MESSENGER   Madam, according as your ladyship desired,
By message craved, so is Lord Talbot come.

COUNTESS   And he is welcome. What, is this the man?

MESSENGER   Madam, it is.

15   COUNTESS   Is this the scourge of France?
Is this the Talbot, so much feared abroad
That with his name the mothers still their babes?
I see report is fabulous and false:
I thought I should have seen some Hercules,

20   A second Hector, for his grim aspect,
And large proportion of his strong-knit limbs.

---

60 mind intention   61 mean mean to act   **2.3 *Location: the castle of the Countess of Auvergne, near Orléans, France*   1 gave in charge** ordered   **6 Tomyris . . . death** in revenge for her son's death, Queen Tomyris killed his murderer, the Persian King Cyrus, and put his head in a wineskin full of blood   **9 Fain** willingly   **10 censure** opinion (not necessarily negative)   **rare** exceptional/splendid   **16 abroad** everywhere, out in the world   **17 still** silence   **18 fabulous** fantastical, fictitious   **19 Hercules** famous Greek hero and demigod, possessed of exceptional strength   **20 Hector** famed Trojan warrior   **for** in terms of   **grim aspect** stern expression   **21 proportion** size, bulk   **strong-knit** powerfully built, well constructed

Alas, this is a child, a silly dwarf:
It cannot be this weak and writhled shrimp
Should strike such terror to his enemies.

25 TALBOT   Madam, I have been bold to trouble you:
But since your ladyship is not at leisure,
I'll sort some other time to visit you.

COUNTESS   What means he now? Go ask him whither he goes.

MESSENGER   Stay, my lord Talbot, for my lady craves
30 To know the cause of your abrupt departure.

TALBOT   Marry, for that she's in a wrong belief,
I go to certify her Talbot's here.

Enter Porter with keys

COUNTESS   If thou be he, then art thou prisoner.

TALBOT   Prisoner? To whom?

35 COUNTESS   To me, bloodthirsty lord;
And for that cause I trained thee to my house.
Long time thy shadow hath been thrall to me,
For in my gallery thy picture hangs:
But now the substance shall endure the like,
40 And I will chain these legs and arms of thine,
That hast by tyranny these many years
Wasted our country, slain our citizens,
And sent our sons and husbands captive.

TALBOT   Ha, ha, ha!

45 COUNTESS   Laughest thou, wretch? Thy mirth shall turn to
moan.

TALBOT   I laugh to see your ladyship so fond
To think that you have aught but Talbot's shadow
Whereon to practise your severity.

COUNTESS   Why, art not thou the man?

50 TALBOT   I am indeed.

---

22 silly feeble, weak   **23 writhled** wrinkled   **27 sort** arrange, choose   **31 Marry** by the
Virgin Mary   **for that** because   **in . . . belief** under a misapprehension   **32 I . . . here** i.e. by
leaving I demonstrate that I am the real Talbot, independent-minded and not inclined to listen
to insults/I go as a means of demonstrating my presence   **36 trained** lured   **37 shadow**
portrait/(illusory) image built on reputation/insubstantial thing   **thrall** slave   **41 tyranny**
cruelty, oppressive violence   **42 Wasted** ravaged/exhausted   **43 captive** into captivity
46 fond foolish   **47 aught** nothing

COUNTESS   Then have I substance too.

TALBOT   No, no, I am but shadow of myself:
You are deceived, my substance is not here;
For what you see is but the smallest part
55   And least proportion of humanity:
I tell you, madam, were the whole frame here,
It is of such a spacious lofty pitch,
Your roof were not sufficient to contain't.

COUNTESS   This is a riddling merchant for the nonce:
60   He will be here, and yet he is not here:
How can these contrarieties agree?

TALBOT   That will I show you presently.

Winds his horn, drums strike up, a peal of ordnance. Enter Soldiers
How say you, madam? Are you now persuaded
That Talbot is but shadow of himself?
65   These are his substance, sinews, arms and strength,
With which he yoketh your rebellious necks,
Razeth your cities and subverts your towns
And in a moment makes them desolate.

COUNTESS   Victorious Talbot, pardon my abuse:
70   I find thou art no less than fame hath bruited,
And more than may be gathered by thy shape.
Let my presumption not provoke thy wrath,
For I am sorry that with reverence
I did not entertain thee as thou art.

75   TALBOT   Be not dismayed, fair lady, nor misconster
The mind of Talbot, as you did mistake
The outward composition of his body.
What you have done hath not offended me:
Nor other satisfaction do I crave,
80   But only, with your patience, that we may

---

55 least . . . humanity smallest part of humankind (here referring to the army)   56 frame
structure, i.e. the body/the army   57 pitch height   59 merchant fellow/trader (in **riddles**)
for the nonce as the occasion requires   61 contrarieties paradoxes, contradictions
62 presently immediately   *Winds* blows   *ordnance* artillery   66 yoketh subjects,
imprisons, yokes like an animal   67 Razeth wipes out, obliterates   subverts overthrows
69 abuse insulting, aggressive behavior/delusion, misconception   70 bruited reported,
proclaimed   74 entertain receive   75 misconster misconstrue   80 patience permission

Taste of your wine and see what cates you have,
For soldiers' stomachs always serve them well.

COUNTESS   With all my heart, and think me honourèd
To feast so great a warrior in my house.   *Exeunt*

[Act 2 Scene 4]   *running scene 7*

Enter Richard Plantagenet, Warwick, Somerset, Suffolk,   A rose brier
[*Vernon, and a Lawyer*]   revealed

RICHARD PLANTAGENET   Great lords and gentlemen, what means
this silence?
Dare no man answer in a case of truth?

SUFFOLK   Within the Temple hall we were too loud:
The garden here is more convenient.

5   RICHARD PLANTAGENET   Then say at once if I maintained the
truth:
Or else was wrangling Somerset in th'error?

SUFFOLK   Faith, I have been a truant in the law,
And never yet could frame my will to it,
And therefore frame the law unto my will.

10   SOMERSET   Judge you, my lord of Warwick, then between us.

WARWICK   Between two hawks, which flies the higher pitch,
Between two dogs, which hath the deeper mouth,
Between two blades, which bears the better temper,
Between two horses, which doth bear him best,

15   Between two girls, which hath the merriest eye,
I have perhaps some shallow spirit of judgement:

---

81 **cates** delicacies   82 **stomachs** appetites   **2.4   Location:** *London, a garden at the Temple (area west of the City that housed the Inns of Court, where young men studied law)*   2 **case of truth** legal term for a case that is to be resolved by considering the facts rather than any ethical implications; given the ensuing dialogue, the dispute may have been one concerning Plantagenet's claim to the throne   3 **were** would have been   6 **Or else** perhaps "or alternatively, to put it another way," but probably Plantagenet simply inquires, "Was I right or was Somerset wrong?" to which he can only receive a favorable answer   **wrangling** quarreling/disputing (formally on an academic issue)   7 **a truant** negligent   8 **frame** adapt   11 **pitch** height (falconry term: highest point in the flight of a bird of prey)   12 **mouth** bark   13 **blades** swords' blades   **temper** quality, hardness   14 **bear him** carry himself   16 **shallow** naive

But in these nice sharp quillets of the law,
Good faith, I am no wiser than a daw.

RICHARD PLANTAGENET   Tut, tut, here is a mannerly forbearance:
20   The truth appears so naked on my side
That any purblind eye may find it out.

SOMERSET   And on my side it is so well apparelled,
So clear, so shining, and so evident
That it will glimmer through a blind man's eye.

25   RICHARD PLANTAGENET   Since you are tongue-tied and so loath to
speak,
In dumb significants proclaim your thoughts:
Let him that is a true-born gentleman
And stands upon the honour of his birth,
If he suppose that I have pleaded truth,
30   From off this brier pluck a white rose with me.   *He plucks a*

SOMERSET   Let him that is no coward nor no flatterer,   *white rose*
But dare maintain the party of the truth,
Pluck a red rose from off this thorn with me.   *He plucks a red rose*

WARWICK   I love no colours, and without all colour
35   Of base insinuating flattery
I pluck this white rose with Plantagenet.

SUFFOLK   I pluck this red rose with young Somerset
And say withal I think he held the right.

VERNON   Stay, lords and gentlemen, and pluck no more
40   Till you conclude that he upon whose side
The fewest roses are cropped from the tree
Shall yield the other in the right opinion.

SOMERSET   Good Master Vernon, it is well objected:
If I have fewest, I subscribe in silence.

---

17 nice precise, fastidious   **sharp** subtle, discerning   **quillets** fine distinctions   **18 daw**
jackdaw, a proverbially stupid bird   **19 mannerly forbearance** courteous reluctance (to be
involved)   **20 naked** evident, palpable   **21 purblind** partially blind   **22 apparelled** dressed
(as opposed to being **naked**)   **24 blind** i.e. totally blind as opposed to merely **purblind**
26 significants signs   **28 stands** insists   **29 pleaded** stated (legal sense)   **30 white rose**
badge of the Mortimers (from whom Richard is descended) and then the House of York
32 party side   **33 red rose** badge of the House of Lancaster   **34 colours** literally, hues/
corroborative evidence (legal sense)/military banners   **colour** outward appearance
38 withal with it   **42 yield** concede in law   **43 objected** urged, brought forward as an
argument   **44 subscribe** submit, agree (literally, sign a document)

45   RICHARD PLANTAGENET   And I.

VERNON   Then for the truth and plainness of the case.
I pluck this pale and maiden blossom here,
Giving my verdict on the white rose side.

SOMERSET   Prick not your finger as you pluck it off,

50   Lest bleeding you do paint the white rose red
And fall on my side so against your will.

VERNON   If I, my lord, for my opinion bleed,
Opinion shall be surgeon to my hurt
And keep me on the side where still I am.

55   SOMERSET   Well, well, come on, who else?

LAWYER   Unless my study and my books be false,
The argument you held was wrong in law: *To Somerset*
In sign whereof I pluck a white rose too.

RICHARD PLANTAGENET   Now, Somerset, where is your argument?

60   SOMERSET   Here in my scabbard, meditating that
Shall dye your white rose in a bloody red.

RICHARD PLANTAGENET   Meantime your cheeks do counterfeit our
roses:
For pale they look with fear, as witnessing
The truth on our side.

65   SOMERSET   No, Plantagenet,
'Tis not for fear, but anger, that thy cheeks
Blush for pure shame to counterfeit our roses,
And yet thy tongue will not confess thy error.

RICHARD PLANTAGENET   Hath not thy rose a canker, Somerset?

70   SOMERSET   Hath not thy rose a thorn, Plantagenet?

RICHARD PLANTAGENET   Ay, sharp and piercing, to maintain his
truth,
Whiles thy consuming canker eats his falsehood.

SOMERSET   Well, I'll find friends to wear my bleeding roses,
That shall maintain what I have said is true,

75   Where false Plantagenet dare not be seen.

---

47 maiden unblemished, pure   **53 Opinion** public opinion, reputation (a shift from the usual sense in the previous line)   **54 still** always   **60 scabbard** sheath for a sword   **meditating that** thinking on that which   **62 counterfeit** imitate   **69 canker** parasitic grub that destroys plants   **71 his** its   **75 false** dishonest (also continues Somerset's accusation that Richard is **counterfeit**)

RICHARD PLANTAGENET   Now, by this maiden blossom in my hand,
I scorn thee and thy fashion, peevish boy.

SUFFOLK   Turn not thy scorns this way, Plantagenet.

RICHARD PLANTAGENET   Proud Pole, I will, and scorn both him
and thee.

80   SUFFOLK   I'll turn my part thereof into thy throat.

SOMERSET   Away, away, good William de la Pole:
We grace the yeoman by conversing with him.

WARWICK   Now, by God's will, thou wrong'st him, Somerset:
His grandfather was Lionel Duke of Clarence,

85   Third son to the third Edward King of England:
Spring crestless yeomen from so deep a root?

RICHARD PLANTAGENET   He bears him on the place's privilege,
Or durst not for his craven heart say thus.

SOMERSET   By him that made me, I'll maintain my words

90   On any plot of ground in Christendom.
Was not thy father, Richard Earl of Cambridge,
For treason executed in our late king's days?
And by his treason, stand'st not thou attainted,
Corrupted, and exempt from ancient gentry?

95   His trespass yet lives guilty in thy blood,
And till thou be restored, thou art a yeoman.

RICHARD PLANTAGENET   My father was attachèd, not attainted,
Condemned to die for treason, but no traitor;
And that I'll prove on better men than Somerset,

100   Were growing time once ripened to my will.

---

77 fashion sort/fashion of wearing a red rose   **peevish** foolish/stubborn   **79 Pole** Suffolk's family name   **80 turn . . . throat** throw the slanders back down your throat   **82 grace** favor, ennoble   **yeoman** man who owns property but is not a gentleman   **84 grandfather** ancestor (actually his great-great-grandfather)   **86 crestless** without heraldic crest/without a top to his family tree (an image picked up on in **root**)/with lowered (cock's) crest, i.e. cowardly   **87 bears . . . privilege** relies on the fact that this is a privileged place (where it was forbidden to draw swords)   **88 craven** cowardly   **89 maintain** stand by, defend   **93 attainted** tainted, corrupt/subject to attainder (legal term), i.e. unable to inherit property or title from a relative who received the death penalty   **96 be restored** have title and property returned, be reinstated   **97 attachèd, not attainted** arrested, but not made legally subject to attainder (perhaps having been executed on the king's orders, without being formally indicted by bill of attainder)   **100 Were . . . will** i.e. given the opportunity

For your partaker Pole and you yourself,
I'll note you in my book of memory,
To scourge you for this apprehension:
Look to it well, and say you are well warned.

105 SOMERSET   Ah, thou shalt find us ready for thee still,
And know us by these colours for thy foes,
For these my friends in spite of thee shall wear.

RICHARD PLANTAGENET   And by my soul, this pale and angry rose,
As cognizance of my blood-drinking hate,
110 Will I for ever and my faction wear,
Until it wither with me to my grave,
Or flourish to the height of my degree.

SUFFOLK   Go forward and be choked with thy ambition:
And so farewell until I meet thee next.   *Exit*

115 SOMERSET   Have with thee, Pole.— Farewell, ambitious
Richard.   *Exit*

RICHARD PLANTAGENET   How I am braved and must perforce
endure it!

WARWICK   This blot that they object against your house
Shall be wiped out in the next parliament,
Called for the truce of Winchester and Gloucester:
120 And if thou be not then created York,
I will not live to be accounted Warwick.
Meantime, in signal of my love to thee,
Against proud Somerset and William Pole,
Will I upon thy party wear this rose.
125 And here I prophesy: this brawl today,
Grown to this faction in the Temple garden,
Shall send, between the red rose and the white,
A thousand souls to death and deadly night.

---

101 **partaker** part-taker, supporter   102 **note** record/brand   103 **apprehension** opinion
104 **Look to it** beware it, expect it   107 **spite** contempt   109 **cognizance** badge,
distinguishing mark   112 **degree** rank   115 **Have with thee** I will go with you   116 **braved**
defied, insulted   **perforce** of necessity   117 **object** bring forward as a charge, an accusation
119 **for . . . of** to make peace between   122 **in signal** as a sign   124 **party** side   126 **faction**
dissent, forming of factions

RICHARD PLANTAGENET   Good Master Vernon, I am bound to you,

130   That you on my behalf would pluck a flower.

VERNON   In your behalf still will I wear the same.

LAWYER   And so will I.

RICHARD PLANTAGENET   Thanks, gentles.

Come, let us four to dinner: I dare say

135   This quarrel will drink blood another day.   *Exeunt*

[Act 2 Scene 5]   *running scene 8*

Enter Mortimer, brought in a chair, and Jailers

MORTIMER   Kind keepers of my weak decaying age,

Let dying Mortimer here rest himself.

Even like a man new haled from the rack,

So fare my limbs with long imprisonment:

5   And these grey locks, the pursuivants of death,

Nestor-like agèd in an age of care,

Argue the end of Edmund Mortimer.

These eyes, like lamps whose wasting oil is spent,

Wax dim, as drawing to their exigent:

10   Weak shoulders, overborne with burdening grief,

And pithless arms, like to a withered vine,

That droops his sapless branches to the ground.

Yet are these feet, whose strengthless stay is numb,

Unable to support this lump of clay,

15   Swift-wingèd with desire to get a grave,

As witting I no other comfort have.

But tell me, keeper, will my nephew come?

---

131 still always   133 gentles gentlemen   **2.5**   *Location: the Tower of London*
1 keepers carers, nurses/jailers   3 haled hauled, dragged   rack torture instrument that
stretched the limbs   5 pursuivants messengers (one of whose tasks was to announce the
imminent arrival of their master)   6 Nestor oldest of the Greek leaders who fought at Troy;
famed for his wisdom   care anxiety, sorrow   9 Wax grow   exigent end   10 overborne
overburdened   11 pithless feeble, lacking "pith" or vital essence   13 stay is numb support is
paralyzed   16 witting knowing

FIRST JAILER   Richard Plantagenet, my lord, will come:
We sent unto the Temple, unto his chamber,
20   And answer was returned that he will come.
MORTIMER   Enough: my soul shall then be satisfied.
Poor gentleman, his wrong doth equal mine.
Since Henry Monmouth first began to reign,
Before whose glory I was great in arms,
25   This loathsome sequestration have I had:
And even since then hath Richard been obscured,
Deprived of honour and inheritance.
But now, the arbitrator of despairs,
Just death, kind umpire of men's miseries,
30   With sweet enlargement doth dismiss me hence:
I would his troubles likewise were expired,
That so he might recover what was lost.
Enter Richard [Plantagenet]
FIRST JAILER   My lord, your loving nephew now is come.
MORTIMER   Richard Plantagenet, my friend, is he come?
35   RICHARD PLANTAGENET   Ay, noble uncle, thus ignobly used,
Your nephew, late despisèd Richard, comes.
MORTIMER   Direct mine arms I may embrace his neck,
And in his bosom spend my latter gasp.
O tell me when my lips do touch his cheeks,
40   That I may kindly give one fainting kiss.   *He embraces Richard*
And now declare, sweet stem from York's great stock,
Why didst thou say of late thou wert despised?
RICHARD PLANTAGENET   First, lean thine agèd back against mine
        arm,
And in that ease I'll tell thee my disease.
45   This day in argument upon a case,
Some words there grew 'twixt Somerset and me:

---

22 his wrong the wrong done to him   **23 Henry Monmouth** Henry V, so nicknamed because
he was born at Monmouth, a town in southern Wales near the English border
25 sequestration imprisonment/loss of income   **26 even** exactly   **28 arbitrator** one who
decides and settles a matter between opposed parties   **29 umpire** one brought in to decide a
matter when arbitrators cannot agree   **30 enlargement** release   **31 his** i.e. Richard's
35 used treated   **36 late** lately, recently   **38 latter** last   **40 kindly** in kinship   **41 stock**
main body of a tree or plant   **44 disease** pronounced "dis-ease"

Among which terms he used his lavish tongue
And did upbraid me with my father's death:
Which obloquy set bars before my tongue,
50   Else with the like I had requited him.
Therefore, good uncle, for my father's sake,
In honour of a true Plantagenet,
And for alliance' sake, declare the cause
My father, Earl of Cambridge, lost his head.
55 MORTIMER   That cause, fair nephew, that imprisoned me
And hath detained me all my flowering youth
Within a loathsome dungeon, there to pine,
Was cursèd instrument of his decease.
RICHARD PLANTAGENET   Discover more at large what cause that
was,
60   For I am ignorant and cannot guess.
MORTIMER   I will, if that my fading breath permit
And death approach not ere my tale be done.
Henry the Fourth, grandfather to this king,
Deposed his nephew Richard, Edward's son,
65   The first begotten and the lawful heir
Of Edward king, the third of that descent,
During whose reign the Percies of the north,
Finding his usurpation most unjust,
Endeavoured my advancement to the throne.
70   The reason moved these warlike lords to this
Was for that — young King Richard thus removed,
Leaving no heir begotten of his body —
I was the next by birth and parentage:
For by my mother I derivèd am

---

47 lavish unrestrained, excessive   **49 obloquy** disgrace, slander   **set . . . tongue** made me
speechless/made me grit my teeth (in rage)   **50 requited** repaid, answered   **53 alliance'**
kinship's, family's   **declare** explain   **59 Discover** reveal   **at large** fully   **64 nephew**
relative (here, cousin)   **Richard, Edward's son** Richard II, son to Edward III; the deposition is
dramatized in *Richard II*   **67 whose** i.e. Henry IV's   **Percies** Henry Percy, Earl of
Northumberland, and his son (nicknamed "Hotspur"); these events are dramatized in *1* and
2 Henry IV   **70 moved** that moved   **74 mother** actually his grandmother, daughter to the
Duke of Clarence; probably this Edmund Mortimer is being confused with his uncle of the
same name, although "mother" can mean "female ancestor"   **derivèd** descended

75 From Lionel Duke of Clarence, the third son
To King Edward the Third; whereas the king
From John of Gaunt doth bring his pedigree,
Being but fourth of that heroic line.
But mark: as in this haughty great attempt
80 They laboured to plant the rightful heir,
I lost my liberty and they their lives.
Long after this, when Henry the Fifth,
Succeeding his father Bullingbrook, did reign,
Thy father, Earl of Cambridge then, derived
85 From famous Edmund Langley, Duke of York,
Marrying my sister that thy mother was,
Again, in pity of my hard distress,
Levied an army, weening to redeem
And have installed me in the diadem:
90 But, as the rest, so fell that noble earl,
And was beheaded. Thus the Mortimers,
In whom the title rested, were suppressed.

RICHARD PLANTAGENET   Of which, my lord, your honour is the
last.

MORTIMER   True, and thou see'st that I no issue have,
95 And that my fainting words do warrant death:
Thou art my heir; the rest I wish thee gather:
But yet be wary in thy studious care.

RICHARD PLANTAGENET   Thy grave admonishments prevail
with me:
But yet methinks my father's execution
100 Was nothing less than bloody tyranny.

MORTIMER   With silence, nephew, be thou politic:
Strong-fixèd is the house of Lancaster,
And like a mountain, not to be removed.

---

77 **John of Gaunt** Edward III's **fourth** son   79 **mark** pay attention   **haughty** proud, aspiring
80 **They** i.e. the Mortimers and the Percies   83 **Bullingbrook** i.e. Henry IV, known by this name
before he was king   87 **hard** severe   88 **weening** aiming, thinking   89 **diadem** crown
94 **issue** children   95 **warrant** guarantee   96 **gather** infer/regain (the inheritance)
97 **studious** diligent   98 **admonishments** warnings   101 **politic** prudent

But now thy uncle is removing hence,

105 As princes do their courts, when they are cloyed

With long continuance in a settled place.

RICHARD PLANTAGENET   O uncle, would some part of my young years

Might but redeem the passage of your age.

MORTIMER   Thou dost then wrong me, as that slaughterer doth

110 Which giveth many wounds when one will kill.

Mourn not, except thou sorrow for my good,

Only give order for my funeral.

And so farewell, and fair be all thy hopes,

And prosperous be thy life in peace and war.   *Dies*

115 RICHARD PLANTAGENET   And peace, no war, befall thy parting soul.

In prison hast thou spent a pilgrimage,

And like a hermit overpassed thy days.

Well, I will lock his counsel in my breast,

And what I do imagine, let that rest.

120 Keepers, convey him hence, and I myself

Will see his burial better than his life.

                    Exeunt [Jailers with Mortimer's body]

Here dies the dusky torch of Mortimer,

Choked with ambition of the meaner sort.

And for those wrongs, those bitter injuries,

125 Which Somerset hath offered to my house,

I doubt not but with honour to redress.

And therefore haste I to the parliament,

Either to be restorèd to my blood,

Or make mine ill the advantage of my good.   *Exit*

---

104 removing departing (i.e. dying)   **105 cloyed** sickened, satiated   **108 passage** passing
111 except unless   **sorrow . . . good** mourn for the good in me/can use your grief for
my (posthumous) advantage, i.e. revenge   **112 give order** make arrangements
117 overpassed lived out, spent   **119 let that rest** leave that alone   **122 dusky** dim,
flickering (perhaps referring to his failing eyesight)   **123 of . . . sort** belonging to less noble
people (i.e. Bullingbrook and his supporters)   **124 for** as for   **125 house** family   **128 blood**
i.e. inheritance rights   **129 make . . . good** turn the wrongs done to me to my advantage, let
my injuries fuel my ambition

Act 3 Scene 1

Flourish. Enter King [Henry VI], Exeter, Gloucester, [Bishop of]
Winchester, Warwick, Somerset, Suffolk, Richard Plantagenet.
Gloucester offers to put up a bill: Winchester snatches it, tears it

WINCHESTER   Com'st thou with deep premeditated lines?
    With written pamphlets studiously devised?
    Humphrey of Gloucester, if thou canst accuse,
    Or aught intend'st to lay unto my charge,
5   Do it without invention, suddenly,
    As I with sudden and extemporal speech
    Purpose to answer what thou canst object.
GLOUCESTER   Presumptuous priest, this place commands my
      patience,
    Or thou shouldst find thou hast dishonoured me.
10   Think not, although in writing I preferred
    The manner of thy vile outrageous crimes,
    That therefore I have forged, or am not able
    Verbatim to rehearse the method of my pen.
    No, prelate, such is thy audacious wickedness,
15   Thy lewd, pestiferous and dissentious pranks,
    As very infants prattle of thy pride.
    Thou art a most pernicious usurer,
    Froward by nature, enemy to peace,
    Lascivious, wanton, more than well beseems
20   A man of thy profession and degree.
    And for thy treachery, what's more manifest?

3.1   *Location: London, parliament   offers . . . bill attempts to present a list of accusations
1 deep premeditated lines carefully planned statements   **5 invention** stratagem/fabrication/
written exposition   **suddenly** spontaneously   **6 extemporal** unplanned   **7 object** bring
forward in accusation   **8 commands my patience** obliges me to endure this   **10 preferred**
put forward   **11 vile** contemptible, shameful   **12 forged** fabricated, invented   **13 Verbatim**
word for word/orally   **rehearse** relate, repeat   **method . . . pen** order and arrangement of
what I have written   **15 lewd** low, wicked   **pestiferous** poisonous, deadly   **dissentious**
quarrelsome, provoking disorder   **pranks** wicked deeds, malicious acts   **16 As very** that
even   **17 pernicious** destructive   **usurer** moneylender who charges (often very high)
interest; another reference to the leasing of land in Southwark and sanctioning of brothels
there   **18 Froward** demanding, stubborn   **19 wanton** dissolute   **beseems** befits, is
appropriate to   **20 degree** position, status   **21 for** as for

In that thou laid'st a trap to take my life,
As well at London Bridge as at the Tower.
Beside, I fear me, if thy thoughts were sifted,
25   The king, thy sovereign, is not quite exempt
From envious malice of thy swelling heart.

WINCHESTER Gloucester, I do defy thee. Lords, vouchsafe
To give me hearing what I shall reply.
If I were covetous, ambitious or perverse,
30   As he will have me, how am I so poor?
Or how haps it I seek not to advance
Or raise myself, but keep my wonted calling?
And for dissension, who preferreth peace
More than I do? — Except I be provoked.
35   No, my good lords, it is not that offends:
It is not that that hath incensed the Duke:
It is because no one should sway but he,
No one but he should be about the king:
And that engenders thunder in his breast
40   And makes him roar these accusations forth.
But he shall know I am as good—

GLOUCESTER As good?
Thou bastard of my grandfather.

WINCHESTER Ay, lordly sir: for what are you, I pray,
45   But one imperious in another's throne?

GLOUCESTER Am I not Protector, saucy priest?

WINCHESTER And am not I a prelate of the Church?

GLOUCESTER Yes, as an outlaw in a castle keeps
And useth it to patronage his theft.

50   **WINCHESTER** Unreverent Gloucester.

GLOUCESTER Thou art reverent
Touching thy spiritual function, not thy life.

---

24 sifted closely examined   **26 envious** malicious   **swelling** arrogant   **31 haps** happens, chances   **32 wonted** customary, usual   **34 except** unless   **35 that** that which   **37 sway** rule, have influence   **38 about** concerned with   **43 bastard** Winchester was the illegitimate son of John of Gaunt by Catherine Swynford (whom Gaunt later married)   **45 imperious** acting like a king   **46 saucy** insolent   **48 keeps** resides for defense   **49 patronage** protect   **51 reverent** worthy of respect   **52 Touching** concerning   **function** role, occupation

WINCHESTER   Rome shall remedy this.

WARWICK   Roam thither then.

55   My lord, it were your duty to forbear.   *To Gloucester*

SOMERSET   Ay, see the bishop be not overborne.

Methinks my lord should be religious   *To Winchester*

And know the office that belongs to such.

WARWICK   Methinks his lordship should be humbler:

60   It fitteth not a prelate so to plead.

SOMERSET   Yes, when his holy state is touched so near.

WARWICK   State holy or unhallowed, what of that?

Is not his grace Protector to the king?

RICHARD PLANTAGENET   Plantagenet, I see, must hold his

tongue,   *Aside*

65   Lest it be said 'Speak, sirrah, when you should:

Must your bold verdict enter talk with lords?'

Else would I have a fling at Winchester.

KING HENRY VI   Uncles of Gloucester and of Winchester,

The special watchmen of our English weal,

70   I would prevail, if prayers might prevail,

To join your hearts in love and amity.

O what a scandal is it to our crown,

That two such noble peers as ye should jar!

Believe me, lords, my tender years can tell

75   Civil dissension is a viperous worm

That gnaws the bowels of the commonwealth.

A noise within: 'Down with the tawny-coats!'

What tumult's this?

WARWICK   An uproar, I dare warrant,

Begun through malice of the Bishop's men.

A noise again: 'Stones, stones!' *Enter Mayor [of London]*

---

53 **Rome** i.e. the Pope   55 **forbear** desist   56 **overborne** overruled, subdued   58 **office** duty,
behavior   **such** i.e. **religious** persons   59 **his lordship** i.e. Winchester   61 **holy state**
ecclesiastical status   **touched . . . near** so closely concerned   65 **sirrah** term of address for
social inferiors   67 **fling** verbal attack   69 **weal** commonwealth, state   73 **jar** clash, quarrel
74 **tender years** historically, Henry, a baby when his father died, was five at the time of this
dispute   75 **viperous worm** malevolent, poisonous snake   76 **bowels** insides, intestines
tawny-coats i.e. ecclesiastical officials, supporters of Winchester

80   **MAYOR**   O my good lords, and virtuous Henry,
        Pity the city of London, pity us!
        The Bishop and the Duke of Gloucester's men,
        Forbidden late to carry any weapon,
        Have filled their pockets full of pebble stones
85   And, banding themselves in contrary parts,
        Do pelt so fast at one another's pate
        That many have their giddy brains knocked out:
        Our windows are broke down in every street,
        And we, for fear, compelled to shut our shops.

Enter [Servingmen] in skirmish with bloody pates

90   **KING HENRY VI**   We charge you, on allegiance to ourself,
        To hold your slaught'ring hands and keep the peace.
        Pray, uncle Gloucester, mitigate this strife.

  FIRST SERVINGMAN   Nay, if we be forbidden stones, we'll fall to it
        with our teeth.

  SECOND SERVINGMAN   Do what ye dare, we are as resolute.

Skirmish again

95   **GLOUCESTER**   You of my household, leave this peevish broil
        And set this unaccustomed fight aside.

  THIRD SERVINGMAN   My lord, we know your grace to be a man
        Just and upright and, for your royal birth,
        Inferior to none but to his majesty:
100   And ere that we will suffer such a prince,
        So kind a father of the commonweal,
        To be disgracèd by an inkhorn mate,
        We and our wives and children all will fight
        And have our bodies slaughtered by thy foes.

105   **FIRST SERVINGMAN**   Ay, and the very parings of our nails
        Shall pitch a field when we are dead.

Begin again

---

83 **late** lately   85 **banding themselves** forming groups   **contrary parts** opposing parties
86 **pate** head(s)   87 **giddy** consumed by disorder, mad with fury   92 **mitigate** calm, lessen
94 **as** just as   95 **peevish** foolish/stubborn   100 **suffer** allow   102 **disgracèd** insulted;
treated without reverent respect   **inkhorn mate** mere scribe (i.e. low status)   105 **parings**
trimmings   106 **pitch a field** prepare for battle   **pitch** prepare defensive stakes

GLOUCESTER   Stay, stay, I say!
And if you love me, as you say you do,
Let me persuade you to forbear awhile.

110   KING HENRY VI   O how this discord doth afflict my soul!
Can you, my lord of Winchester, behold
My sighs and tears and will not once relent?
Who should be pitiful, if you be not?
Or who should study to prefer a peace,
115   If holy churchmen take delight in broils?

WARWICK   Yield, my Lord Protector, yield, Winchester:
Except you mean with obstinate repulse
To slay your sovereign and destroy the realm.
You see what mischief and what murder too
120   Hath been enacted through your enmity:
Then be at peace, except ye thirst for blood.

WINCHESTER   He shall submit, or I will never yield.

GLOUCESTER   Compassion on the king commands me stoop,
Or I would see his heart out, ere the priest
125   Should ever get that privilege of me.

WARWICK   Behold, my lord of Winchester, the duke
Hath banished moody discontented fury,
As by his smoothèd brows it doth appear:
Why look you still so stern and tragical?

130   GLOUCESTER   Here, Winchester, I offer thee my hand.   *Winchester*

KING HENRY VI   Fie, uncle Beaufort! I have heard you   *turns away*
preach   *To Winchester*
That malice was a great and grievous sin:
And will not you maintain the thing you teach,
But prove a chief offender in the same?

135   WARWICK   Sweet king: the bishop hath a kindly gird.
For shame, my lord of Winchester, relent:
What, shall a child instruct you what to do?

---

114 **study** endeavor, labor   **prefer** put forward, favor   117 **repulse** refusal, rejection
119 **mischief** harm, calamity   124 **his** i.e. Winchester's   125 **privilege of** advantage over
127 **moody** angry, disordered   129 **tragical** foreboding/sorrowful   135 **hath . . . gird** has
been given a suitable rebuke

WINCHESTER   Well, Duke of Gloucester, I will yield to thee
Love for thy love and hand for hand I give.

140   GLOUCESTER   Ay, but I fear me with a hollow heart.—   *Aside*
See here, my friends and loving countrymen,   *To the others*
This token serveth for a flag of truce
Betwixt ourselves and all our followers:
So help me God, as I dissemble not.

145   WINCHESTER   So help me God,— as I intend it not.   *Aside*

KING HENRY VI   O loving uncle, kind Duke of Gloucester,
How joyful am I made by this contract.—
Away, my masters, trouble us no more,
But join in friendship, as your lords have done.

150   FIRST SERVINGMAN   Content: I'll to the surgeon's.

SECOND SERVINGMAN   And so will I.

THIRD SERVINGMAN   And I will see what physic the tavern affords.
Exeunt [the Mayor and Servingmen]

WARWICK   Accept this scroll, most gracious sovereign,
Which in the right of Richard Plantagenet

155   We do exhibit to your majesty.

GLOUCESTER   Well urged, my lord of Warwick — for sweet
prince,
And if your grace mark every circumstance,
You have great reason to do Richard right,
Especially for those occasions

160   At Eltham Place I told your majesty.

KING HENRY VI   And those occasions, uncle, were of force:
Therefore, my loving lords, our pleasure is
That Richard be restorèd to his blood.

WARWICK   Let Richard be restorèd to his blood;

165   So shall his father's wrongs be recompensed.

---

140 **hollow** empty, insincere, deceptive   142 **token** i.e. the handshake   144 **dissemble**
deceive, pretend   147 **contract** accord, agreement   148 **masters** i.e. the servants (a
condescending though not offensive form of address)   150 **surgeon** more particularly,
physician   152 **physic** medicine   155 **exhibit** show, submit for consideration   157 **mark**
note, pay attention to   **circumstance** detail, particular   159 **occasions** reasons,
circumstances   161 **of force** convincing, forceful   163 **blood** hereditary rights (to property
and titles)   165 **wrongs** i.e. wrongs suffered by him

WINCHESTER   As will the rest, so willeth Winchester.

KING HENRY VI   If Richard will be true, not that alone
But all the whole inheritance I give
That doth belong unto the House of York,
170   From whence you spring by lineal descent.

RICHARD PLANTAGENET   Thy humble servant vows obedience
And humble service till the point of death.

KING HENRY VI   Stoop then and set your knee against my
    foot,   *Richard kneels*
And, in reguerdon of that duty done,
175   I gird thee with the valiant sword of York:
Rise Richard, like a true Plantagenet,
And rise created princely Duke of York.

RICHARD DUKE OF YORK   And so thrive Richard as thy foes may
    fall: *Plantagenet is henceforth*
And as my duty springs, so perish they   *known as Richard*
180   That grudge one thought against your majesty.   *Duke of York*

ALL   Welcome, high prince, the mighty Duke of York!

SOMERSET   Perish, base prince, ignoble Duke of York!   *Aside*

GLOUCESTER   Now will it best avail your majesty
To cross the seas and to be crowned in France:
185   The presence of a king engenders love
Amongst his subjects and his loyal friends,
As it disanimates his enemies.

KING HENRY VI   When Gloucester says the word, King Henry
    goes,
For friendly counsel cuts off many foes.

190   GLOUCESTER   Your ships already are in readiness.

Sennet. Flourish   *Exeunt all but Exeter*

EXETER   Ay, we may march in England or in France,
Not seeing what is likely to ensue:
This late dissension grown betwixt the peers
Burns under feignèd ashes of forged love,

---

174 reguerdon recompense, reward   **175 gird** invest (with a title; picks up on the sound of **reguerdon**)   **177 princely** of the royal blood   **180 grudge one thought** have one resentful thought   **187 disanimates** discourages, disheartens   **Sennet** trumpet call signaling a procession   **194 forged** false (may play on the sense of "molded in fire")

195 And will at last break out into a flame:
As festered members rot but by degree,
Till bones and flesh and sinews fall away,
So will this base and envious discord breed.
And now I fear that fatal prophecy
200 Which, in the time of Henry named the Fifth,
Was in the mouth of every sucking babe:
That Henry born at Monmouth should win all
And Henry born at Windsor lose all:
Which is so plain that Exeter doth wish
205 His days may finish ere that hapless time.   *Exit*

Act 3 Scene 2   *running scene 10*

Enter [Joan la] Pucelle disguised, with four [French] Soldiers with
sacks upon their backs

PUCELLE   These are the city gates, the gates of Rouen,
Through which our policy must make a breach.
Take heed, be wary how you place your words:
Talk like the vulgar sort of market men
5 That come to gather money for their corn.
If we have entrance, as I hope we shall,
And that we find the slothful watch but weak,
I'll by a sign give notice to our friends,
That Charles the Dauphin may encounter them.
10 FIRST SOLDIER   Our sacks shall be a mean to sack the city,
And we be lords and rulers over Rouen:
Therefore we'll knock.   *[They] knock*
WATCH   *Qui là?*   *Within*
PUCELLE   *Paysans, la pauvre gens de France*:
15 Poor market folks that come to sell their corn.

196 **festered** rotten, decomposing   **members** limbs   **by degree** gradually, in stages
198 **envious** malicious   202 **Henry . . . Monmouth** i.e. Henry V   203 **Henry . . . Windsor** i.e.
Henry VI   205 **hapless** unlucky   **3.2   Location: Rouen, a French town on the River**
Seine, between Le Havre and Paris   2 **policy** strategy, cunning   4 **vulgar** common,
ordinary   7 **that** if   9 **encounter** assail, confront   10 **mean** means   11 **be** shall be
13 **Qui là?** "Who goes there?" (French)   14 **Paysans . . . France** "Peasants, the poor folk of
France"

WATCH   Enter, go in: the market bell is rung.   *Opening the gates*

PUCELLE   Now, Rouen, I'll shake thy bulwarks to the ground.

          Exeunt

Enter Charles, [the] Bastard [of Orléans], Alençon, [Reignier, and forces]

CHARLES   Saint Denis bless this happy stratagem,

And once again we'll sleep secure in Rouen.

20   BASTARD   Here entered Pucelle and her practisants:

Now she is there, how will she specify

Here is the best and safest passage in?

REIGNIER   By thrusting out a torch from yonder tower,

Which, once discerned, shows that her meaning is,

25   No way to that, for weakness, which she entered.

Enter [Joan la] Pucelle on the top, thrusting out a torch burning

PUCELLE   Behold, this is the happy wedding torch

That joineth Rouen unto her countrymen,

But burning fatal to the Talbonites!

BASTARD   See, noble Charles, the beacon of our friend:

30   The burning torch in yonder turret stands.

CHARLES   Now shine it like a comet of revenge,

A prophet to the fall of all our foes!

REIGNIER   Defer no time, delays have dangerous ends:

Enter and cry, 'The dauphin!', presently,

35   And then do execution on the watch.   *Alarum*   [*Exeunt*]

An alarum. [Enter] Talbot in an excursion

TALBOT   France, thou shalt rue this treason with thy tears,

If Talbot but survive thy treachery.

Pucelle, that witch, that damnèd sorceress,

Hath wrought this hellish mischief unawares,

40   That hardly we escaped the pride of France.   *Exit*

---

18 happy fortunate   **20 practisants** conspirators, plotters   **25 No . . . entered** no entrance is as weakly guarded as the one she entered   *top* i.e. gallery, upper staging level   **26 wedding torch** Hymen, the Greek and Roman god of marriage, was traditionally depicted carrying a burning torch   **31 shine it** may it shine   **32 prophet to** portent of (comets were thought to be bad omens)   **34 presently** immediately   **35 do . . . watch** kill the guards   *excursion* a bout of fighting across the stage   **39 unawares** unexpectedly   **40 hardly** with difficulty **pride** power and arrogance/the dauphin (and his fellow nobles)

*An alarum: excursions. Bedford brought in sick in a chair. Enter Talbot
and Burgundy without: within, [Joan la] Pucelle, Charles, Bastard of
Orléans, [Alençon] and Reignier on the walls*

PUCELLE   Good morrow, gallants: want ye corn for bread?
I think the Duke of Burgundy will fast
Before he'll buy again at such a rate.
'Twas full of darnel: do you like the taste?

45   BURGUNDY   Scoff on, vile fiend and shameless courtesan:
I trust ere long to choke thee with thine own
And make thee curse the harvest of that corn.

CHARLES   Your grace may starve, perhaps, before that time.

BEDFORD   O, let no words, but deeds, revenge this treason.

50   PUCELLE   What will you do, good grey-beard? Break a lance
And run a-tilt at death within a chair?

TALBOT   Foul fiend of France, and hag of all despite,
Encompassed with thy lustful paramours,
Becomes it thee to taunt his valiant age

55   And twit with cowardice a man half dead?
Damsel, I'll have a bout with you again,
Or else let Talbot perish with this shame.

PUCELLE   Are ye so hot, sir? Yet, Pucelle, hold thy peace:
If Talbot do but thunder, rain will follow.

[The English] whisper together in counsel

60   God speed the parliament: who shall be the speaker?

TALBOT   Dare ye come forth and meet us in the field?

PUCELLE   Belike your lordship takes us then for fools,
To try if that our own be ours or no.

TALBOT   I speak not to that railing Hecate,

65   But unto thee, Alençon, and the rest.
Will ye, like soldiers, come and fight it out?

---

without on the main stage   **within** probably, but not necessarily, on the upper staging level,
conventionally used to represent city walls   **41 gallants** fine young gentlemen (sarcastic)
43 rate cost   **44 darnel** weeds   **51 run a-tilt at** joust with, charge at   **within** while seated in
52 hag witch   **of all despite** full of spite or malice   **53 Encompassed with** surrounded by
55 twit taunt   **56 bout** of fighting/of sex   **58 hot** hot-tempered/lustful   **60 speed** aid/
hurry up   **speaker** spokesperson/chairman (of the parliament)   **61 in the field** for battle
62 Belike presumably   **64 Hecate** in classical mythology, the goddess of night and the
underworld and the patroness of witches

ALENÇON   Seigneur, no.

TALBOT   Seigneur, hang! Base muleteers of France,
Like peasant footboys do they keep the walls,
70   And dare not take up arms like gentlemen.

PUCELLE   Away, captains, let's get us from the walls,
For Talbot means no goodness by his looks.
Goodbye, my lord: we came but to tell you
That we are here.   *Exeunt from the walls*

75   TALBOT   And there will we be too, ere it be long,
Or else reproach be Talbot's greatest fame.
Vow, Burgundy, by honour of thy house,
Pricked on by public wrongs sustained in France,
Either to get the town again or die.
80   And I, as sure as English Henry lives,
And as his father here was conqueror,
As sure as in this late betrayèd town
Great Coeur-de-lion's heart was buried,
So sure I swear to get the town or die.

85   BURGUNDY   My vows are equal partners with thy vows.

TALBOT   But ere we go, regard this dying prince,
The valiant Duke of Bedford.— Come, my lord,   *To Bedford*
We will bestow you in some better place,
Fitter for sickness and for crazy age.

90   BEDFORD   Lord Talbot, do not so dishonour me:
Here will I sit before the walls of Rouen
And will be partner of your weal or woe.

BURGUNDY   Courageous Bedford, let us now persuade you.

BEDFORD   Not to be gone from hence: for once I read
95   That stout Pendragon, in his litter sick,
Came to the field and vanquishèd his foes.

---

67 **Seigneur** lord   68 **base muleteers** lowly mule-drivers   69 **footboys** boy servants, often
assistants to footmen   **keep** stay near   78 **Pricked** spurred   81 **his . . . conqueror** Henry V
besieged and captured Rouen in 1419   83 **Coeur-de-lion** Richard I of England, nicknamed
"the Lionheart" after he fought a lion and tore its heart out; he asked that his heart be buried
in Rouen   86 **regard** observe/tend to   89 **crazy** infirm, fragile   92 **weal** happiness
95 **stout** brave   **Pendragon** Uther Pendragon, father of King Arthur; the story referred to
here is related in Geoffrey of Monmouth's *Historia Regnum Britanniae*   **litter** transportable bed
for the sick

Methinks I should revive the soldiers' hearts,
Because I ever found them as myself.

TALBOT   Undaunted spirit in a dying breast!
100   Then be it so: heavens keep old Bedford safe.
And now no more ado, brave Burgundy,
But gather we our forces out of hand,
And set upon our boasting enemy.

Exit [with Burgundy and forces]

An alarum: excursions. Enter Sir John Falstaff and a Captain

CAPTAIN   Whither away, Sir John Falstaff, in such haste?
105   FALSTAFF   Whither away? To save myself by flight:
We are like to have the overthrow again.

CAPTAIN   What? Will you fly, and leave Lord Talbot?

FALSTAFF   Ay, all the Talbots in the world, to save my life.   *Exit*

CAPTAIN   Cowardly knight, ill fortune follow thee!   *Exit*

Retreat: excursions. [Joan la] Pucelle, Alençon and Charles fly

110   BEDFORD   Now, quiet soul, depart when heaven please,
For I have seen our enemies' overthrow.
What is the trust or strength of foolish man?
They that of late were daring with their scoffs
Are glad and fain by flight to save themselves.

Bedford dies, and is carried in by two in his chair.
An alarum. Enter Talbot, Burgundy and the rest [of the
English soldiers]

115   TALBOT   Lost, and recovered in a day again!
This is a double honour, Burgundy:
Yet heavens have glory for this victory.

BURGUNDY   Warlike and martial Talbot, Burgundy
Enshrines thee in his heart, and there erects
120   Thy noble deeds as valour's monuments.

TALBOT   Thanks, gentle duke. But where is Pucelle now?
I think her old familiar is asleep.
Now where's the Bastard's braves, and Charles his gleeks?

---

98 ever always   **101 ado** business, fuss   **102 out of hand** at once, immediately   **106 have
the overthrow** be defeated   **113 daring** challenging, defiant   **114 glad** here, relieved   **fain**
willing   **121 gentle** noble/kind   **122 familiar** witch's attendant spirit, demon   **123 braves**
boasts   **Charles his gleeks** Charles' scoffs, jests

What, all amort? Rouen hangs her head for grief
125   That such a valiant company are fled.
Now will we take some order in the town,
Placing therein some expert officers,
And then depart to Paris, to the king,
For there young Henry with his nobles lie.
130 BURGUNDY   What wills Lord Talbot pleaseth Burgundy.
TALBOT   But yet, before we go, let's not forget
The noble Duke of Bedford late deceased,
But see his exequies fulfilled in Rouen.
A braver soldier never couchèd lance,
135   A gentler heart did never sway in court.
But kings and mightiest potentates must die,
For that's the end of human misery.   *Exeunt*

Act 3 Scene 3   *running scene 11*

*Enter Charles, [the] Bastard [of Orléans], Alençon, [Joan la] Pucelle
[and French soldiers]*

PUCELLE   Dismay not, princes, at this accident,
Nor grieve that Rouen is so recoverèd:
Care is no cure, but rather corrosive,
For things that are not to be remedied.
5   Let frantic Talbot triumph for a while
And like a peacock sweep along his tail:
We'll pull his plumes and take away his train,
If Dauphin and the rest will be but ruled.
CHARLES   We have been guided by thee hitherto,
10   And of thy cunning had no diffidence:
One sudden foil shall never breed distrust.

---

124 **amort** downcast, dispirited   126 **take some order** establish order, make arrangements
127 **expert** experienced   129 **lie** dwells   133 **exequies** funeral rites   134 **couchèd lance**
leveled his lance in attack   135 **sway** exert influence   136 **potentates** powerful rulers
137 **end** sum, final destination/purpose/ending, death   **3.3** *Location: near Rouen*
1 **accident** unforeseen event   2 **recoverèd** regained by the English   3 **Care . . . cure** sorrow,
anxiety   7 **train** peacock's tail/army   8 **be but ruled** merely follow advice   10 **cunning** skill/
magical powers   **diffidence** distrust   11 **foil** defeat

BASTARD   Search out thy wit for secret policies,
And we will make thee famous through the world.
ALENÇON   We'll set thy statue in some holy place,
15   And have thee reverenced like a blessèd saint.
Employ thee then, sweet virgin, for our good.
PUCELLE   Then thus it must be: this doth Joan devise:
By fair persuasions, mixed with sugared words,
We will entice the Duke of Burgundy
20   To leave the Talbot and to follow us.
CHARLES   Ay, marry, sweeting, if we could do that,
France were no place for Henry's warriors,
Nor should that nation boast it so with us,
But be extirpèd from our provinces.
25   ALENÇON   For ever should they be expulsed from France
And not have title of an earldom here.
PUCELLE   Your honours shall perceive how I will work
To bring this matter to the wishèd end.

Drum sounds afar off

Hark! By the sound of drum you may perceive
30   Their powers are marching unto Paris-ward.

Here sound an English march

There goes the Talbot, with his colours spread,
And all the troops of English after him.

[Here sound a] French march

Now in the rearward comes the duke and his:
Fortune in favour makes him lag behind.
35   Summon a parley: we will talk with him.

Trumpets sound a parley

CHARLES   A parley with the Duke of Burgundy.

[Enter Burgundy with soldiers]

BURGUNDY   Who craves a parley with the Burgundy?
PUCELLE   The princely Charles of France, thy countryman.

---

12 wit intelligence   **secret policies** surprise stratagems   **18 fair** plausible, flattering
21 sweeting sweetheart, darling   **24 extirpèd** uprooted   **25 expulsed** expelled   **30 unto**
Paris-ward toward Paris   **31 colours spread** flags unfurled   **34 in** in our   **35 parley**
negotiation between opposing sides (summoned with a particular trumpet call)

BURGUNDY   What say'st thou, Charles? For I am marching
      hence.

40 CHARLES   Speak, Pucelle, and enchant him with thy words.

PUCELLE   Brave Burgundy, undoubted hope of France,
      Stay, let thy humble handmaid speak to thee.

BURGUNDY   Speak on, but be not over-tedious.

PUCELLE   Look on thy country, look on fertile France,
45   And see the cities and the towns defaced
      By wasting ruin of the cruel foe,
      As looks the mother on her lowly babe
      When death doth close his tender-dying eyes.
      See, see the pining malady of France:
50   Behold the wounds, the most unnatural wounds,
      Which thou thyself hast given her woeful breast.
      O turn thy edgèd sword another way:
      Strike those that hurt, and hurt not those that help:
      One drop of blood drawn from thy country's bosom
55   Should grieve thee more than streams of foreign gore.
      Return thee therefore with a flood of tears,
      And wash away thy country's stainèd spots.

BURGUNDY   Either she hath bewitched me with her words,
      Or nature makes me suddenly relent.

60 PUCELLE   Besides, all French and France exclaims on thee,
      Doubting thy birth and lawful progeny.
      Who join'st thou with, but with a lordly nation
      That will not trust thee but for profit's sake?
      When Talbot hath set footing once in France
65   And fashioned thee that instrument of ill,
      Who then but English Henry will be lord
      And thou be thrust out like a fugitive?
      Call we to mind, and mark but this for proof:
      Was not the Duke of Orléans thy foe?

---

40 **enchant** bewitch   43 **tedious** laborious, lengthy   46 **wasting** destructive, ravaging
47 **lowly** laid low, prostrate/tiny   48 **tender-dying** youthful dying   49 **pining** wasting
malady of France plays on the sense of "syphilis" ("the French disease")   50 **unnatural**
against the natural order/against one's own country   52 **edgèd** sharp   57 **stainèd** i.e.
staining   59 **nature** natural, inherent feeling/a sense of kinship   60 **exclaims on** accuses,
condemns loudly   61 **lawful progeny** legitimate lineage   68 **mark but** only note

70   And was he not in England prisoner?
      But when they heard he was thine enemy,
      They set him free without his ransom paid,
      In spite of Burgundy and all his friends.
      See, then, thou fight'st against thy countrymen,
75   And join'st with them will be thy slaughtermen.
      Come, come, return; return, thou wandering lord:
      Charles and the rest will take thee in their arms.

BURGUNDY   I am vanquished: these haughty words of   *Aside*
            hers
      Have battered me like roaring cannon-shot,
80   And made me almost yield upon my knees.
      Forgive me, country, and sweet countrymen:
      And, lords, accept this hearty kind embrace.
      My forces and my power of men are yours.
      So farewell, Talbot: I'll no longer trust thee.

85   PUCELLE   Done like a Frenchman: turn and turn again.   *Aside*
      CHARLES   Welcome, brave duke: thy friendship makes us
                 fresh.
      BASTARD   And doth beget new courage in our breasts.
      ALENÇON   Pucelle hath bravely played her part in this,
                 And doth deserve a coronet of gold.
90   CHARLES   Now let us on, my lords, and join our powers,
                 And seek how we may prejudice the foe.   *Exeunt*

Act 3 Scene 4   *running scene 12*

*Enter King [Henry VI], Gloucester, [Bishop of] Winchester, [Richard
Plantagenet, now Duke of] York, Suffolk, Somerset, Warwick, Exeter,
[Vernon, Basset and others]. To them, with his Soldiers, Talbot*

TALBOT   My gracious prince, and honourable peers,
          Hearing of your arrival in this realm,

---

75 them those who   **76 wandering** straying, erring   **78 haughty** high, lofty   **82 hearty**
sincere, heartfelt   **83 power** force, army   **86 makes us fresh** invigorates, renews us, makes
us eager   **87 beget** breed, create   **88 bravely** courageously/splendidly   **89 coronet** small
crown worn by members of the nobility   **91 prejudice** injure, damage   **3.4 *Location:
Paris, France***

I have awhile given truce unto my wars,
To do my duty to my sovereign:
5   In sign whereof, this arm, that hath reclaimed
To your obedience fifty fortresses,
Twelve cities and seven walled towns of strength,
Beside five hundred prisoners of esteem,
Lets fall his sword before your highness' feet,
10   And with submissive loyalty of heart
Ascribes the glory of his conquest got
First to my God and next unto your grace.   *He kneels*

KING HENRY VI   Is this the lord Talbot, uncle Gloucester,
That hath so long been resident in France?

15   GLOUCESTER   Yes, if it please your majesty, my liege.

KING HENRY VI   Welcome, brave captain and victorious   *To Talbot*
lord.
When I was young, as yet I am not old,
I do remember how my father said
A stouter champion never handled sword.
20   Long since we were resolvèd of your truth,
Your faithful service and your toil in war,
Yet never have you tasted our reward,
Or been reguerdoned with so much as thanks,
Because till now we never saw your face.
25   Therefore stand up, and for these good deserts   *Talbot rises*
We here create you Earl of Shrewsbury,
And in our coronation take your place.

Sennet. Flourish   *Exeunt all but Vernon and Basset*

VERNON   Now sir, to you that were so hot at sea,
Disgracing of these colours that I wear
30   In honour of my noble lord of York,
Dar'st thou maintain the former words thou spak'st?

---

4 do my duty pay homage   **5 reclaimed** won back   **8 esteem** high rank   **19 stouter** bolder,
more hardy   **champion** one who fights on behalf of another   **20 resolvèd** convinced   **truth**
loyalty   **23 reguerdoned** rewarded   **25 deserts** deservings, merits   **28 hot** hot-tempered,
angry   **29 Disgracing . . . colours** insulting the badge (that identifies his loyalty)

BASSET   Yes, sir, as well as you dare patronage

The envious barking of your saucy tongue

Against my lord the Duke of Somerset.

35   VERNON   Sirrah, thy lord I honour as he is.

BASSET   Why, what is he? As good a man as York.

VERNON   Hark ye, not so: in witness, take ye that.

Strikes him

BASSET   Villain, thou know'st the law of arms is such

That whoso draws a sword 'tis present death,

40   Or else this blow should broach thy dearest blood.

But I'll unto his majesty, and crave

I may have liberty to venge this wrong,

When thou shalt see I'll meet thee to thy cost.

VERNON   Well, miscreant, I'll be there as soon as you,

45   And after meet you sooner than you would.   *Exeunt*

Act 4 Scene 1   *running scene 13*

Enter King [Henry VI], Gloucester, [Bishop of] Winchester, York,
Suffolk, Somerset, Warwick, Talbot, and [the] Governor [of Paris and]
Exeter

GLOUCESTER   Lord Bishop, set the crown upon his head.

WINCHESTER   God save King Henry, of that name the

sixth!   *Crowns King Henry*

GLOUCESTER   Now, Governor of Paris, take your oath,

That you elect no other king but him;

5   Esteem none friends but such as are his friends,

And none your foes but such as shall pretend

Malicious practices against his state:

This shall ye do, so help you righteous God.

Enter Falstaff

---

32 patronage defend, uphold   **33 envious** malicious   **saucy** insolent   **35 Sirrah** sir (used to
an inferior; here, contemptuous)   **as he is** i.e. for what he's worth (implying not much)
38 law of arms law that forbade fighting near a royal residence   **39 present** immediate
40 broach set flowing   **41 crave** request earnestly   **42 liberty** permission   **44 miscreant**
villain, wretch   **45 after** i.e. after the king's permission to fight has been obtained
4.1   **4 elect** acknowledge, accept   **5 Esteem** consider   **6 pretend** intend, plan

FALSTAFF   My gracious sovereign, as I rode from Calais
10   To haste unto your coronation,
      A letter was delivered to my hands,   *He shows the letter*
      Writ to your grace from th'Duke of Burgundy.
TALBOT   Shame to the Duke of Burgundy and thee!
      I vowed, base knight, when I did meet thee next,
15   To tear the Garter from thy craven's leg,   *Plucks it off*
      Which I have done, because unworthily
      Thou wast installèd in that high degree.
      Pardon me, princely Henry, and the rest:
      This dastard, at the battle of Patay,
20   When but in all I was six thousand strong
      And that the French were almost ten to one,
      Before we met or that a stroke was given,
      Like to a trusty squire did run away:
      In which assault we lost twelve hundred men.
25   Myself and divers gentlemen beside
      Were there surprised and taken prisoners.
      Then judge, great lords, if I have done amiss:
      Or whether that such cowards ought to wear
      This ornament of knighthood: yea or no?
30 GLOUCESTER   To say the truth, this fact was infamous
      And ill beseeming any common man,
      Much more a knight, a captain and a leader.
TALBOT   When first this order was ordained, my lords,
      Knights of the Garter were of noble birth,
35   Valiant and virtuous, full of haughty courage,
      Such as were grown to credit by the wars:
      Not fearing death, nor shrinking for distress,
      But always resolute in most extremes.
      He then that is not furnished in this sort

---

15 Garter sign of membership of the Order of the Garter, the highest order of English
knighthood, consisting of a blue and gold ribbon tied below the left knee   **craven's** coward's
19 dastard despicable coward   **25 divers** several, various   **30 fact** deed, crime
31 common ordinary, without rank   **32 captain** commander of a regiment   **35 haughty
courage** high spirit, exalted bravery   **36 grown to credit** risen to honor   **37 for** from
distress hardship, adversity   **39 furnished . . . sort** so equipped

40   Doth but usurp the sacred name of knight,
      Profaning this most honourable order,
      And should, if I were worthy to be judge,
      Be quite degraded, like a hedge-born swain
      That doth presume to boast of gentle blood.

45   KING HENRY VI   Stain to thy countrymen, thou hear'st thy doom:
      Be packing, therefore, thou that wast a knight:
      Henceforth we banish thee on pain of death.   [*Exit Falstaff*]
      And now, my Lord Protector, view the letter
      Sent from our uncle Duke of Burgundy.

50   GLOUCESTER   What means his grace, that he hath changed his
            style?
      No more but plain and bluntly 'To the king'?
      Hath he forgot he is his sovereign?
      Or doth this churlish superscription
      Pretend some alteration in good will?

55   What's here? — 'I have upon especial cause,   *Reads*
      Moved with compassion of my country's wrack,
      Together with the pitiful complaints
      Of such as your oppression feeds upon,
      Forsaken your pernicious faction

60   And joined with Charles, the rightful King of France.'
      O monstrous treachery! Can this be so?
      That in alliance, amity and oaths,
      There should be found such false dissembling guile?

      KING HENRY VI   What? Doth my uncle Burgundy revolt?

65   GLOUCESTER   He doth, my lord, and is become your foe.

      KING HENRY VI   Is that the worst this letter doth contain?

      GLOUCESTER   It is the worst, and all, my lord, he writes.

      KING HENRY VI   Why then Lord Talbot there shall talk with him
      And give him chastisement for this abuse.

70   How say you, my lord? Are you not content?

---

43 degraded lowered in rank   **hedge-born swain** person of very low birth, peasant born out
of doors   **44 gentle** noble   **45 doom** sentence, judgment   **46 Be packing** be off, get
packing   **50 style** form of address   **51 but** than   **53 churlish** ungracious, blunt
superscription form of address appearing at the head of the letter   **54 Pretend** imply, intend
56 wrack ruin   **59 pernicious** destructive   **64 revolt** rebel; literally, perform a complete
turnaround   **69 chastisement** punishment, retribution

TALBOT   Content, my liege? Yes: but that I am prevented,
I should have begged I might have been employed.

KING HENRY VI   Then gather strength and march unto him
straight:
Let him perceive how ill we brook his treason
75   And what offence it is to flout his friends.

TALBOT   I go, my lord, in heart desiring still
You may behold confusion of your foes.   [*Exit*]

Enter Vernon and Basset

VERNON   Grant me the combat, gracious sovereign.

BASSET   And me, my lord, grant me the combat too.

80   RICHARD DUKE OF YORK   This is my servant: hear him, noble
prince.   *Pointing to Vernon*

SOMERSET   And this is mine, sweet Henry, favour him.   *Pointing to*

KING HENRY VI   Be patient, lords, and give them leave to   *Basset*
speak.
Say, gentlemen, what makes you thus exclaim,
And wherefore crave you combat, or with whom?

85   VERNON   With him, my lord, for he hath done me wrong.

BASSET   And I with him, for he hath done me wrong.

KING HENRY VI   What is that wrong whereof you both complain?
First let me know, and then I'll answer you.

BASSET   Crossing the sea from England into France,
90   This fellow here with envious carping tongue,
Upbraided me about the rose I wear,
Saying the sanguine colour of the leaves
Did represent my master's blushing cheeks,
When stubbornly he did repugn the truth
95   About a certain question in the law
Argued betwixt the Duke of York and him:
With other vile and ignominious terms:

---

71 **but . . . prevented** were it not for the fact that I have been anticipated (by you)
73 **strength** troops   **straight** straightaway   74 **brook** tolerate   75 **flout** mock, abuse
76 **still** (that) always   77 **confusion** destruction, overthrow   78 **the combat** permission to
fight a duel   80 **servant** follower   83 **exclaim** outcry, protest   90 **envious** malicious
92 **sanguine** bloodred   **leaves** petals   94 **repugn** reject, oppose   95 **question . . . law** i.e.
the question of succession, and the attainder of York's father (see Act 2 Scene 4)

In confutation of which rude reproach
And in defence of my lord's worthiness,
100   I crave the benefit of law of arms.

VERNON   And that is my petition, noble lord:
For though he seem with forgèd quaint conceit
To set a gloss upon his bold intent,
Yet know, my lord, I was provoked by him,
105   And he first took exceptions at this badge,
Pronouncing that the paleness of this flower
Bewrayed the faintness of my master's heart.

RICHARD DUKE OF YORK   Will not this malice, Somerset, be left?

SOMERSET   Your private grudge, my lord of York, will out,
110   Though ne'er so cunningly you smother it.

KING HENRY VI   Good Lord, what madness rules in brainsick men,
When for so slight and frivolous a cause
Such factious emulations shall arise?
Good cousins both of York and Somerset,
115   Quiet yourselves, I pray, and be at peace.

RICHARD DUKE OF YORK   Let this dissension first be tried by fight,
And then your highness shall command a peace.

SOMERSET   The quarrel toucheth none but us alone:
Betwixt ourselves let us decide it then.

120   RICHARD DUKE OF YORK   There is my pledge: accept it, Somerset.

VERNON   Nay, let it rest where it began at first.

BASSET   Confirm it so, mine honourable lord.

GLOUCESTER   Confirm it so? Confounded be your strife,
And perish ye with your audacious prate:
125   Presumptuous vassals, are you not ashamed
With this immodest clamorous outrage

---

98 confutation refutation (legal term)   **rude** ignorant   **100 benefit** (legal) privilege
101 petition formal request   **102 forgèd** false, crafted   **quaint conceit** cunning invention/
ingenious rhetoric   **103 set . . . upon** give a plausible, attractive appearance to   **105 took
exceptions at** objected to   **107 Bewrayed** betrayed, revealed   **faintness** cowardice, timidity
111 brainsick foolish, demented   **113 factious emulations** divisive rivalries   **114 cousins**
kinsmen; also a term used to fellow nobles   **118 toucheth** concerns   **120 pledge** gage, i.e.
item (often a glove or gauntlet) that signified the giver's commitment to a duel   **121 rest**
remain   **123 Confounded** destroyed, overcome   **124 prate** prattle, chatter   **125 vassals**
servants   **126 immodest** arrogant, outspoken

To trouble and disturb the king and us?
And you, my lords, methinks you do not well
To bear with their perverse objections:
130   Much less to take occasion from their mouths
To raise a mutiny betwixt yourselves.
Let me persuade you take a better course.

EXETER   It grieves his highness: good my lords, be friends.

KING HENRY VI   Come hither, you that would be combatants:
135   Henceforth I charge you, as you love our favour,
Quite to forget this quarrel and the cause.
And you, my lords, remember where we are:
In France, amongst a fickle wavering nation:
If they perceive dissension in our looks
140   And that within ourselves we disagree,
How will their grudging stomachs be provoked
To wilful disobedience, and rebel!
Beside, what infamy will there arise,
When foreign princes shall be certified,
145   That for a toy, a thing of no regard,
King Henry's peers and chief nobility
Destroyed themselves, and lost the realm of France!
O, think upon the conquest of my father,
My tender years, and let us not forgo
150   That for a trifle that was bought with blood.
Let me be umpire in this doubtful strife:
I see no reason, if I wear this rose,   *Putting on a red rose*
That any one should therefore be suspicious
I more incline to Somerset than York:
155   Both are my kinsmen, and I love them both.
As well they may upbraid me with my crown,
Because, forsooth, the King of Scots is crowned.

---

129 objections accusations, allegations   **130 occasion** grounds, opportunity   **131 mutiny** strife, riot   **140 within ourselves** among ourselves (plays on the sense of "within our own bodies")   **141 grudging stomachs** resentful tempers/stomachs exhibiting signs of disease   **142 rebel** rebellion   **144 certified** informed, shown   **145 toy** trifle   **regard** value, consequence   **149 forgo** forfeit, lose   **150 That . . . that** for a trifle that which was   **151 doubtful** precarious, generating fear   **153 suspicious** anxious   **154 incline to** favor   **156 As . . . may** they might as well   **157 forsooth** in truth

But your discretions better can persuade
Than I am able to instruct or teach:
160   And therefore, as we hither came in peace,
So let us still continue peace and love.
Cousin of York, we institute your grace
To be our regent in these parts of France:
And good my lord of Somerset, unite
165   Your troops of horsemen with his bands of foot,
And like true subjects, sons of your progenitors,
Go cheerfully together and digest
Your angry choler on your enemies.
Ourself, my Lord Protector and the rest,
170   After some respite, will return to Calais;
From thence to England, where I hope ere long
To be presented, by your victories,
With Charles, Alençon and that traitorous rout.

Exeunt all but York, Warwick, Exeter [and] Vernon. Flourish

WARWICK   My lord of York, I promise you, the king
175   Prettily, methought, did play the orator.

RICHARD DUKE OF YORK   And so he did: but yet I like it not,
In that he wears the badge of Somerset.

WARWICK   Tush, that was but his fancy, blame him not:
I dare presume, sweet prince, he thought no harm.

180   RICHARD DUKE OF YORK   An if I wist he did— but let it rest:
Other affairs must now be managèd.   *Exeunt [all but] Exeter*

EXETER   Well didst thou, Richard, to suppress thy voice:
For had the passions of thy heart burst out,
I fear we should have seen deciphered there
185   More rancorous spite, more furious raging broils,
Than yet can be imagined or supposed:
But howsoe'er, no simple man that sees

---

158 **discretions** judgments   162 **institute** appoint   163 **parts** regions   165 **bands of foot** regiments of infantry, foot soldiers   166 **progenitors** forefathers   167 **digest** i.e. break down, assimilate, get rid of   168 **angry choler** anger   170 **respite** interval, delay   173 **rout** rabble
175 **Prettily** charmingly/ingeniously   178 **fancy** whim   180 **An . . . wist** if I knew
183 **passions** powerful feelings   184 **deciphered** revealed, detected   187 **simple** common, ordinary

This jarring discord of nobility,
This shouldering of each other in the court,
190   This factious bandying of their favourites,
But that it doth presage some ill event.
'Tis much when sceptres are in children's hands:
But more, when envy breeds unkind division,
There comes the ruin, there begins confusion.   *Exit*

[Act 4 Scene 2]   *running scene 14*

Enter Talbot, with Trump and Drum before Bordeaux

TALBOT   Go to the gates of Bordeaux, trumpeter:
Summon their general unto the wall.
[Trumpet] sounds. Enter General aloft
English John Talbot, captains, calls you forth,
Servant in arms to Harry King of England,
5   And thus he would: open your city gates,
Be humble to us, call my sovereign yours,
And do him homage as obedient subjects,
And I'll withdraw me and my bloody power.
But if you frown upon this proffered peace,
10   You tempt the fury of my three attendants,
Lean famine, quartering steel, and climbing fire,
Who in a moment even with the earth
Shall lay your stately and air-braving towers,
If you forsake the offer of their love.
15   GENERAL   Thou ominous and fearful owl of death,
Our nation's terror and their bloody scourge,
The period of thy tyranny approacheth.
On us thou canst not enter but by death:

---

189 **shouldering** jostling   190 **bandying** verbal contests   **favourites** supporters   **191 that**
sees that   **event** outcome   192 **much** a weighty business   193 **envy** malice, enmity
unkind unnatural   194 **confusion** chaos, destruction   **4.2**   *Location: outside the gates
of Bordeaux (a major port on the River Garonne in southwest France)   Trump and
Drum* trumpeter and drummer   *aloft* gallery, upper staging level, conventionally used to
represent city walls   5 **would** wishes   8 **bloody** bloodthirsty, warlike   11 **quartering**
dismembering   12 **even** level   13 **air-braving** defying the heavens, lofty   14 **forsake** reject
15 **ominous . . . death** the owl's cry was thought to portend evil or death   17 **period** end

For I protest we are well fortified
20 And strong enough to issue out and fight.
If thou retire, the dauphin well appointed
Stands with the snares of war to tangle thee.
On either hand thee there are squadrons pitched,
To wall thee from the liberty of flight;
25 And no way canst thou turn thee for redress,
But death doth front thee with apparent spoil,
And pale destruction meets thee in the face:
Ten thousand French have ta'en the sacrament
To rive their dangerous artillery
30 Upon no Christian soul but English Talbot:
Lo, there thou stand'st, a breathing valiant man
Of an invincible unconquered spirit:
This is the latest glory of thy praise
That I thy enemy due thee withal:
35 For ere the glass that now begins to run
Finish the process of his sandy hour,
These eyes that see thee now well colourèd
Shall see thee withered, bloody, pale and dead.

Drum afar off

Hark, hark, the dauphin's drum, a warning bell,
40 Sings heavy music to thy timorous soul,
And mine shall ring thy dire departure out.   *Exit*

TALBOT   He fables not: I hear the enemy:
Out, some light horsemen, and peruse their wings.
O negligent and heedless discipline,
45 How are we parked and bounded in a pale?

---

20 issue out come forth   **21 appointed** equipped   **23 hand thee** side of you   **pitched** drawn up in battle formation   **24 wall** block, shut off   **25 redress** relief, aid   **26 front** confront, face   **apparent spoil** obvious destruction   **27 pale** i.e. deathly   **28 ta'en the sacrament** taken Communion as a means of confirming their oaths   **29 rive** split open (with explosions)   **33 latest** last   **34 due** endow   **35 glass** hourglass   **37 well colourèd** in good health   **39 warning bell** bell rung to warn of fire or invasion   **40 heavy** solemn, sad, burdensome   **41 dire** dreadful   **departure** i.e. death   **42 fables** lies, fabricates   **43 peruse** investigate, survey   **wings** flanks, forces at the sides of a main body of troops   **44 heedless** careless, slack   **discipline** military strategy   **45 parked . . . pale** fenced in and confined within an enclosure

A little herd of England's timorous deer,
Mazed with a yelping kennel of French curs.
If we be English deer, be then in blood,
Not rascal-like to fall down with a pinch,
50   But rather, moody-mad: and desperate stags
Turn on the bloody hounds with heads of steel
And make the cowards stand aloof at bay:
Sell every man his life as dear as mine,
And they shall find dear deer of us, my friends.
55   God and Saint George, Talbot and England's right,
Prosper our colours in this dangerous fight!   [*Exeunt*]

[Act 4 Scene 3]   *running scene 15*

*Enter a Messenger that meets York. Enter York with Trumpet and
many Soldiers*

RICHARD DUKE OF YORK   Are not the speedy scouts returned
again,
That dogged the mighty army of the dauphin?
MESSENGER   They are returned, my lord, and give it out
That he is marched to Bordeaux with his power
5   To fight with Talbot: as he marched along,
By your espials were discoverèd
Two mightier troops than that the dauphin led,
Which joined with him and made their march for
Bordeaux.
RICHARD DUKE OF YORK   A plague upon that villain Somerset,
10   That thus delays my promisèd supply
Of horsemen, that were levied for this siege.
Renownèd Talbot doth expect my aid,

---

47 **Mazed** bewildered, confused   **kennel** pack   **curs** hounds   **48 in blood** full of life, in fine
condition (hunting term)   49 **rascal-like** like young, inferior deer   **pinch** bite, nip
50 **moody-mad** wild with rage   51 **heads of steel** antlers like swords   52 **stand . . . bay**
back off as we, like the maddened, cornered deer, turn to face our pursuers   54 **dear** costly
(with obvious pun)   **4.3** *Location: France; six hours' journey from Bordeaux, exact
location unspecified*   2 **dogged** tracked, followed   3 **give it out** assert   6 **espials** spies

And I am louted by a traitor villain,
And cannot help the noble chevalier:
15 God comfort him in this necessity:
If he miscarry, farewell wars in France.

Enter another messenger [Sir William Lucy]

LUCY   Thou princely leader of our English strength,
Never so needful on the earth of France,
Spur to the rescue of the noble Talbot,
20 Who now is girdled with a waist of iron
And hemmed about with grim destruction:
To Bordeaux, warlike duke, to Bordeaux, York,
Else farewell Talbot, France, and England's honour.

RICHARD DUKE OF YORK   O God, that Somerset, who in proud
heart
25 Doth stop my cornets, were in Talbot's place,
So should we save a valiant gentleman
By forfeiting a traitor and a coward:
Mad ire and wrathful fury makes me weep,
That thus we die, while remiss traitors sleep.

30 LUCY   O, send some succour to the distressed lord.

RICHARD DUKE OF YORK   He dies, we lose: I break my warlike word:
We mourn, France smiles: we lose, they daily get,
All 'long of this vile traitor Somerset.

LUCY   Then God take mercy on brave Talbot's soul,
35 And on his son young John, who two hours since
I met in travel toward his warlike father:
This seven years did not Talbot see his son,
And now they meet where both their lives are done.

RICHARD DUKE OF YORK   Alas, what joy shall noble Talbot have
40 To bid his young son welcome to his grave?
Away, vexation almost stops my breath,
That sundered friends greet in the hour of death.

---

13 louted made a fool of, mocked; or possibly "delayed"   **15 necessity** unavoidable event
16 miscarry come to harm   **18 needful** necessary   **20 girdled** belted, surrounded   **waist**
belt (puns on "waste," i.e. vast expanse)   **25 stop** detain, delay   **cornets** cavalry, troops of
horsemen   **29 remiss** careless   **30 distressed** undergoing adversity   **33 'long of** because of
41 vexation terrible anguish, affliction   **42 sundered** separated   **friends** relatives

Lucy, farewell: no more my fortune can,
But curse the cause I cannot aid the man.
45 Maine, Blois, Poitiers, and Tours are won away,
'Long all of Somerset and his delay.   *Exeunt [all but Lucy]*
LUCY   Thus, while the vulture of sedition
Feeds in the bosom of such great commanders,
Sleeping neglection doth betray to loss
50 The conquest of our scarce-cold conqueror,
That ever-living man of memory,
Henry the Fifth: whiles they each other cross,
Lives, honours, lauds, and all hurry to loss.   *[Exit]*

[Act 4 Scene 4]   *running scene 16*

Enter Somerset with his army, [a Captain of Talbot's with him]

SOMERSET   It is too late, I cannot send them now:
This expedition was by York and Talbot
Too rashly plotted. All our general force
Might with a sally of the very town
5   Be buckled with: the over-daring Talbot
Hath sullied all his gloss of former honour
By this unheedful, desperate, wild adventure:
York set him on to fight and die in shame,
That, Talbot dead, great York might bear the name.
10 CAPTAIN   Here is Sir William Lucy, who with me
Set from our o'ermatched forces forth for aid.
[Enter Sir William Lucy]
SOMERSET   How now, Sir William, whither were you sent?

---

43 can can do   44 cause i.e. Somerset   46 'Long all all because   47 sedition disputes
between factions/mutiny, revolt   49 Sleeping neglection careless, lazy neglect   50 scarce-
cold recently dead (historically, however, the events of this scene took place thirty-one years
after the death of Henry V)   51 ever-living . . . memory man who will live forever in memory
52 cross thwart, obstruct   53 lauds praises   *Exit* some editors have Lucy remaining onstage; he speaks again shortly after the beginning of the following scene   4.4   2 expedition
speedy action, military enterprise   4 sally sudden attack, sortie   very town merely the
town's garrison, unsupported by further troops   5 buckled with encountered, tackled
6 gloss luster   7 unheedful careless, negligent   11 o'ermatched outnumbered

LUCY   Whither, my lord? From bought and sold Lord
              Talbot,
              Who, ringed about with bold adversity,
15   Cries out for noble York and Somerset,
              To beat assailing death from his weak legions:
              And whiles the honourable captain there
              Drops bloody sweat from his war-wearied limbs,
              And, in advantage ling'ring, looks for rescue,
20   You, his false hopes, the trust of England's honour,
              Keep off aloof with worthless emulation:
              Let not your private discord keep away
              The levied succours that should lend him aid,
              While he, renownèd noble gentleman,
25   Yields up his life unto a world of odds.
              Orléans the Bastard, Charles, Burgundy,
              Alençon, Reignier. compass him about,
              And Talbot perisheth by your default.
SOMERSET   York set him on: York should have sent him aid.
30 LUCY   And York as fast upon your grace exclaims,
              Swearing that you withhold his levied host,
              Collected for this expedition.
SOMERSET   York lies: he might have sent and had the horse:
              I owe him little duty, and less love,
35   And take foul scorn to fawn on him by sending.
LUCY   The fraud of England, not the force of France,
              Hath now entrapped the noble-minded Talbot:
              Never to England shall he bear his life,
              But dies betrayed to fortune by your strife.
40 SOMERSET   Come, go: I will dispatch the horsemen straight:
              Within six hours they will be at his aid.

---

13 bought and sold betrayed   **16 legions** troops   **19 in advantage ling'ring** trying to draw
out any kind of benefit through delaying tactics/desperately protracting his superior military
position for as long as possible   **20 trust** trustee, guardian   **21 Keep off aloof** stand aside
worthless emulation ignoble ambition, rivalry   **22 private discord** personal disagreement
23 levied succours mustered military assistance   **25 world of** immense, overwhelming
27 compass him about surround him   **28 default** negligence, failure to act   **29 set him on**
incited him   **31 host** army, specifically cavalry   **33 sent** sent for   **35 take foul scorn** think
scornfully, find it disgraceful

LUCY   Too late comes rescue: he is ta'en or slain.
              For fly he could not, if he would have fled,
              And fly would Talbot never, though he might.
45   SOMERSET   If he be dead, brave Talbot, then adieu.
      LUCY   His fame lives in the world, his shame in you.

                                                      Exeunt

[Act 4 Scene 5]   *running scene 17*

Enter Talbot and his son [John]

TALBOT   O young John Talbot, I did send for thee
              To tutor thee in stratagems of war,
              That Talbot's name might be in thee revived
              When sapless age and weak unable limbs
5   Should bring thy father to his drooping chair.
              But — O malignant and ill-boding stars —
              Now thou art come unto a feast of death,
              A terrible and unavoided danger:
              Therefore, dear boy, mount on my swiftest horse,
10   And I'll direct thee how thou shalt escape
              By sudden flight. Come, dally not, be gone.
      JOHN   Is my name Talbot? And am I your son?
              And shall I fly? O, if you love my mother,
              Dishonour not her honourable name,
15   To make a bastard and a slave of me:
              The world will say, he is not Talbot's blood,
              That basely fled when noble Talbot stood.
      TALBOT   Fly to revenge my death if I be slain.
      JOHN   He that flies so will ne'er return again.
20   TALBOT   If we both stay, we both are sure to die.
      JOHN   Then let me stay and, father, do you fly:
              Your loss is great, so your regard should be;

---

44 though even if   **4.5   *Location: a battlefield near Bordeaux, France*   5 drooping**
transferred epithet: decaying, failing   **6 malignant** of evil influence   **ill-boding** inauspicious
8 unavoided unavoidable   **11 sudden** rapid/immediate   **22 Your . . . great** the loss of you
would have a devastating impact   **regard** self-regard, care of yourself

My worth unknown, no loss is known in me.

Upon my death the French can little boast;

25   In yours they will, in you all hopes are lost.

Flight cannot stain the honour you have won,

But mine it will, that no exploit have done.

You fled for vantage, everyone will swear:

But if I bow, they'll say it was for fear.

30   There is no hope that ever I will stay,

If the first hour I shrink and run away:

Here on my knee I beg mortality,

Rather than life preserved with infamy.

TALBOT   Shall all thy mother's hopes lie in one tomb?

35   JOHN   Ay, rather than I'll shame my mother's womb.

TALBOT   Upon my blessing I command thee go.

JOHN   To fight I will, but not to fly the foe.

TALBOT   Part of thy father may be saved in thee.

JOHN   No part of him but will be shame in me.

40   TALBOT   Thou never hadst renown, nor canst not lose it.

JOHN   Yes, your renownèd name: shall flight abuse it?

TALBOT   Thy father's charge shall clear thee from that stain.

JOHN   You cannot witness for me, being slain.

If death be so apparent, then both fly.

45   TALBOT   And leave my followers here to fight and die?

My age was never tainted with such shame.

JOHN   And shall my youth be guilty of such blame?

No more can I be severed from your side,

Than can yourself yourself in twain divide:

50   Stay, go, do what you will, the like do I;

For live I will not, if my father die.

TALBOT   Then here I take my leave of thee, fair son,

Born to eclipse thy life this afternoon:

Come, side by side, together live and die,

55   And soul with soul from France to heaven fly.   *Exeunt*

---

27 mine i.e. my **honour**   **exploit** warlike deeds   28 **vantage** military advantage   **29 bow**
retreat   32 **mortality** death   41 **abuse** dishonor   42 **charge** order, command
44 **apparent** certain, evident   46 **age** whole life   53 **eclipse** extinguish

[Act 4 Scene 6]   *running scene 17 continues*

Alarum: excursions, wherein Talbot's son [John] is hemmed about
[by French soldiers], and Talbot rescues him

TALBOT   Saint George and victory! Fight, soldiers, fight:
      The Regent hath with Talbot broke his word
      And left us to the rage of France his sword.
      Where is John Talbot? Pause, and take thy breath:
5   I gave thee life and rescued thee from death.

JOHN   O, twice my father, twice am I thy son:
      The life thou gav'st me first was lost and done,
      Till with thy warlike sword, despite of fate,
      To my determined time thou gav'st new date.

10 TALBOT   When from the dauphin's crest thy sword struck
            fire,
      It warmed thy father's heart with proud desire
      Of bold-faced victory. Then leaden age,
      Quickened with youthful spleen and warlike rage,
      Beat down Alençon, Orléans, Burgundy,
15   And from the pride of Gallia rescued thee.
      The ireful bastard Orléans, that drew blood
      From thee, my boy, and had the maidenhood
      Of thy first fight, I soon encountered,
      And interchanging blows I quickly shed
20   Some of his bastard blood, and in disgrace
      Bespoke him thus: 'Contaminated, base
      And misbegotten blood I spill of thine,
      Mean and right poor, for that pure blood of mine
      Which thou didst force from Talbot, my brave boy.'
25   Here, purposing the Bastard to destroy,
      Came in strong rescue. Speak, thy father's care:

4.6   2 Regent i.e. York, who was appointed regent in Act 4 Scene 1   **3 France his** France's
9 determined limited, with an appointed ending   **date** limit, term   **10 crest** helmet
13 Quickened was reanimated, lived   **spleen** fiery temper, impetuosity   **15 pride** arrogance/
foremost nobility   **Gallia** France   **16 ireful** enraged   **17 maidenhood** virginity   **20 in
disgrace** with contempt, insultingly   **22 misbegotten** illegitimate, wrongly created
23 Mean base   **25 purposing** as I was intending

Art thou not weary, John? How dost thou fare?
Wilt thou yet leave the battle, boy, and fly,
Now thou art sealed the son of chivalry?
30   Fly, to revenge my death when I am dead:
The help of one stands me in little stead.
O, too much folly is it, well I wot,
To hazard all our lives in one small boat.
If I today die not with Frenchmen's rage,
35   Tomorrow I shall die with mickle age.
By me they nothing gain, and if I stay
'Tis but the short'ning of my life one day.
In thee thy mother dies, our household's name,
My death's revenge, thy youth, and England's fame:
40   All these and more we hazard by thy stay;
All these are saved if thou wilt fly away.

JOHN   The sword of Orléans hath not made me smart:
These words of yours draw life-blood from my heart.
On that advantage, bought with such a shame,
45   To save a paltry life and slay bright fame,
Before young Talbot from old Talbot fly,
The coward horse that bears me fall and die:
And like me to the peasant boys of France,
To be shame's scorn and subject of mischance.
50   Surely, by all the glory you have won,
An if I fly, I am not Talbot's son.
Then talk no more of flight, it is no boot:
If son to Talbot, die at Talbot's foot.

TALBOT   Then follow thou thy desp'rate sire of Crete,
55   Thou Icarus: thy life to me is sweet:
If thou wilt fight, fight by thy father's side,
And commendable proved, let's die in pride.   *Exeunt*

---

29 sealed confirmed   **32 wot** know   **35 mickle** great   **42 smart** suffer, feel pain   **44 On that advantage** for the sake of that advantage (i.e. safety)   **47 The** may the   **48 like** liken
49 scorn object of scorn   **subject of mischance** victim of misfortune   **52 boot** use
54 follow . . . Icarus Icarus and his father, Daedalus, tried to escape imprisonment in Crete using wings made out of feathers and wax; Icarus flew too close to the sun and the wax melted so that he fell to his death   **57 pride** honor, glory

[Act 4 Scene 7]   *running scene 17 continues*

Alarum. Excursions. Enter old Talbot led [by a Servant]

TALBOT   Where is my other life? Mine own is gone.
O, where's young Talbot? Where is valiant John?
Triumphant death, smeared with captivity,
Young Talbot's valour makes me smile at thee.
5   When he perceived me shrink and on my knee,
His bloody sword he brandished over me,
And like a hungry lion did commence
Rough deeds of rage and stern impatience:
But when my angry guardant stood alone,
10   Tend'ring my ruin and assailed of none,
Dizzy-eyed fury and great rage of heart
Suddenly made him from my side to start
Into the clust'ring battle of the French:
And in that sea of blood my boy did drench
15   His over-mounting spirit, and there died,
My Icarus, my blossom, in his pride.

SERVANT   O my dear lord, lo where your son is borne.

Enter [Soldiers] with [the body of] John Talbot borne

TALBOT   Thou antic death, which laugh'st us here to scorn,
Anon, from thy insulting tyranny,
20   Couplèd in bonds of perpetuity,
Two Talbots, wingèd through the lither sky,
In thy despite shall scape mortality.
O thou whose wounds become hard-favoured death,   *To John*
Speak to thy father ere thou yield thy breath.
25   Brave death by speaking, whether he will or no:
Imagine him a Frenchman and thy foe.

4.7   3 Triumphant victorious, celebrating victory   **captivity** the blood of injured captives
8 stern impatience cruel fury   **9 guardant** protector, guard   **10 Tend'ring my ruin** tending to
my injuries, caring for me in my fall   **of** by   **11 Dizzy-eyed** with dazzled, glazed eyes
13 clust'ring crowded, swarming   **14 drench** drown   **15 over-mounting** over-ambitious
17 lo look   **18 antic** grinning, grotesque   **19 Anon** soon   **21 lither** yielding, supple   **22 In
thy despite** in contempt, in spite of you   **scape mortality** escape death (through the
immortality of the soul)   **23 become hard-favoured** suit ugly, hideous   **25 Brave** defy,
challenge

Poor boy, he smiles, methinks, as who should say,
'Had death been French, then death had died today.'
Come, come, and lay him in his father's arms:

30   My spirit can no longer bear these harms.
Soldiers, adieu: I have what I would have,
Now my old arms are young John Talbot's grave.   *Dies*

Enter Charles, Alençon, Burgundy, Bastard [of Orléans] and [Joan la]
Pucelle

CHARLES   Had York and Somerset brought rescue in,
We should have found a bloody day of this.

35   BASTARD   How the young whelp of Talbot's, raging wood,
Did flesh his puny sword in Frenchmen's blood.

PUCELLE   Once I encountered him, and thus I said:
'Thou maiden youth, be vanquished by a maid.'
But with a proud majestical high scorn,

40   He answered thus: 'Young Talbot was not born
To be the pillage of a giglot wench':
So rushing in the bowels of the French,
He left me proudly, as unworthy fight.

BURGUNDY   Doubtless he would have made a noble knight:

45   See where he lies inhearsèd in the arms
Of the most bloody nurser of his harms.

BASTARD   Hew them to pieces, hack their bones asunder
Whose life was England's glory, Gallia's wonder.

CHARLES   O no, forbear: for that which we have fled

50   During the life, let us not wrong it dead.

Enter Lucy [with a French herald]

LUCY   Herald, conduct me to the dauphin's tent,
To know who hath obtained the glory of the day.

CHARLES   On what submissive message art thou sent?

---

27 who one who   **35 whelp** puppy (plays on the fact that a "talbot" is a type of hunting dog)
wood mad   **36 flesh** initiate (from the practice of feeding hunting dogs raw meat to excite
them)   **puny** inexperienced, novice   **38 maiden** virginal, inexperienced   **41 pillage** plunder
giglot strumpet, whorish   **42 bowels** depths, core   **45 inhearsèd** laid as in a coffin
46 bloody bloodthirsty/covered in blood   **nurser . . . harms** person who taught him to harm
his enemies/person who has caused his injuries (by allowing him into battle)/person bent or
slumped over him and seemingly tending his wounds   **48 wonder** source of amazement and
awe   **49 that . . . fled** i.e. Talbot   **53 submissive message** message of submission, surrender

LUCY   Submission, dauphin? 'Tis a mere French word:
55   We English warriors wot not what it means.
         I come to know what prisoners thou hast ta'en
         And to survey the bodies of the dead.
CHARLES   For prisoners ask'st thou? Hell our prison is.
         But tell me whom thou seek'st?
60 LUCY   But where's the great Alcides of the field,
         Valiant Lord Talbot, Earl of Shrewsbury,
         Created for his rare success in arms
         Great Earl of Washford, Waterford, and Valence,
         Lord Talbot of Goodrich and Urchinfield,
65   Lord Strange of Blackmere, Lord Verdun of Alton,
         Lord Cromwell of Wingfield, Lord Furnival of Sheffield,
         The thrice victorious lord of Falconbridge,
         Knight of the noble order of Saint George,
         Worthy Saint Michael and the Golden Fleece,
70   Great Marshal to Henry the Sixth
         Of all his wars within the realm of France?
PUCELLE   Here is a silly stately style indeed:
         The Turk, that two-and-fifty kingdoms hath,
         Writes not so tedious a style as this.
75   Him that thou magnifi'st with all these titles,
         Stinking and fly-blown lies here at our feet.
LUCY   Is Talbot slain, the Frenchmen's only scourge,
         Your kingdom's terror and black Nemesis?
         O were mine eyeballs into bullets turned,
80   That I in rage might shoot them at your faces!
         O, that I could but call these dead to life!
         It were enough to fright the realm of France.
         Were but his picture left amongst you here,

---

54 a mere an exclusively   **55 wot** know   **57 survey** examine, take note of   **60 But . . .
France** this epic list of Talbot's many titles may have been derived from an epitaph on his
original tomb in France   **Alcides** Hercules, the mythical hero famed for feats of strength
62 rare extraordinary/splendid   **69 Worthy** equal to/worthy of   **Saint Michael** the Order of
Saint Michael, a French chivalric order in fact not established until 1469, after the events of
the play occurred   **Golden Fleece** another French order of knights, set up in 1429   **72 style**
list of titles, mode of expression   **73 The Turk** conventional title for the Turkish sultan
76 fly-blown putrefied, rotting (literally, with fly's eggs laid in his decomposing flesh)
78 Nemesis Greek goddess of justice and retribution, who punished pride and arrogance

It would amaze the proudest of you all.
85 Give me their bodies, that I may bear them hence
And give them burial as beseems their worth.

PUCELLE   I think this upstart is old Talbot's ghost,
He speaks with such a proud commanding spirit:
For God's sake let him have them: to keep them here,
90 They would but stink, and putrefy the air.

CHARLES   Go take their bodies hence.

LUCY   I'll bear them hence: but from their ashes shall be reared
A phoenix that shall make all France afeard.

CHARLES   So we be rid of them, do with them what thou wilt.
95 And now to Paris in this conquering vein:
All will be ours, now bloody Talbot's slain.   *Exeunt*

Act 5 Scene 1   *running scene 18*

Sennet. Enter King [Henry VI], Gloucester, and Exeter [attended]

KING HENRY VI   Have you perused the letters from the Pope,
The Emperor, and the Earl of Armagnac?

GLOUCESTER   I have, my lord, and their intent is this:
They humbly sue unto your excellence
5 To have a godly peace concluded of
Between the realms of England and of France.

KING HENRY VI   How doth your grace affect their motion?

GLOUCESTER   Well, my good lord, and as the only means
To stop effusion of our Christian blood
10 And stablish quietness on every side.

KING HENRY VI   Ay, marry, uncle, for I always thought
It was both impious and unnatural
That such immanity and bloody strife
Should reign among professors of one faith.

---

84 **amaze** terrify, alarm   86 **beseems** befits, is appropriate to   92 **ashes . . . phoenix** the phoenix, a mythical bird, was said to live for five hundred years, consume itself in fire, and then rise again from its own ashes   94 **So** provided   **5.1**   *Location: the royal court, London*
4 **sue unto** entreat   5 **concluded of** resolved, settled   7 **affect their motion** incline to their proposal   10 **stablish** establish   13 **immanity** barbarity, atrocities

15 GLOUCESTER   Beside, my lord, the sooner to effect
And surer bind this knot of amity,
The Earl of Armagnac, near knit to Charles,
A man of great authority in France,
Proffers his only daughter to your grace
20 In marriage, with a large and sumptuous dowry.
KING HENRY VI   Marriage, uncle? Alas, my years are young:
And fitter is my study and my books
Than wanton dalliance with a paramour.
Yet call th'ambassadors, and as you please,
25 So let them have their answers every one: *Exit Attendant*
I shall be well content with any choice
Tends to God's glory and my country's weal.
Enter Winchester [in Cardinal's habit], and three Ambassadors
[one a Papal legate]
EXETER   What, is my lord of Winchester installed,   *Aside*
And called unto a cardinal's degree?
30 Then I perceive that will be verified
Henry the Fifth did sometime prophesy:
'If once he come to be a cardinal,
He'll make his cap co-equal with the crown.'
KING HENRY VI   My lords ambassadors, your several suits
35 Have been considered and debated on:
Your purpose is both good and reasonable:
And therefore are we certainly resolved
To draw conditions of a friendly peace,
Which by my lord of Winchester we mean
40 Shall be transported presently to France.
GLOUCESTER   And for the proffer of my lord your
master,   *To Armagnac*
I have informed his highness so at large   *ambassador*
As liking of the lady's virtuous gifts,

---

17 **near knit** closely related   21 **young** historically Henry was actually twenty-one
23 **wanton** lascivious   27 **Tends** that tends   **weal** welfare   *legate* representative
29 **degree** rank   30 **verified** come true   31 **sometime** at one time, formerly   33 **cap** i.e.
Cardinal's red hat   34 **several** separate, respective   38 **draw** draw up   40 **presently**
immediately   42 **at large** in full   43 **As** that

Her beauty and the value of her dower,

45   He doth intend she shall be England's queen.

KING HENRY VI   In argument and proof of which contract,

Bear her this jewel, pledge of my affection.

And so, my Lord Protector, see them guarded

And safely brought to Dover, wherein shipped

50   Commit them to the fortune of the sea.

Exeunt [all but Winchester and Legate]

WINCHESTER   Stay, my lord legate, you shall first receive

The sum of money which I promisèd

Should be delivered to his holiness

For clothing me in these grave ornaments.

55   LEGATE   I will attend upon your lordship's leisure.   *[Exit]*

WINCHESTER   Now Winchester will not submit, I trow,

Or be inferior to the proudest peer:

Humphrey of Gloucester, thou shalt well perceive

That neither in birth or for authority,

60   The bishop will be overborne by thee:

I'll either make thee stoop and bend thy knee,

Or sack this country with a mutiny.   *Exit*

Act 5 Scene 2   *running scene 19*

Enter Charles, Burgundy, Alençon, Bastard [of Orléans], Reignier and Joan [la Pucelle]

CHARLES   These news, my lords, may cheer our drooping

spirits:

'Tis said the stout Parisians do revolt

And turn again unto the warlike French.

ALENÇON   Then march to Paris, royal Charles of France,

5   And keep not back your powers in dalliance.

PUCELLE   Peace be amongst them, if they turn to us,

Else ruin combat with their palaces.

---

46 **In argument** as evidence   49 **wherein shipped** where once embarked   54 **grave ornaments** dignified robes of office   56 **trow** am sure   62 **a mutiny** an open revolt, rebellion   **5.2   *Location: France, exact location unspecified***   2 **stout** brave, resolute   5 **powers** troops   **dalliance** idleness, time wasting   7 **combat with** fight, bring down

Enter Scout

SCOUT   Success unto our valiant general,
             And happiness to his accomplices.
10 CHARLES   What tidings send our scouts? I prithee speak.
    SCOUT   The English army that divided was
             Into two parties, is now conjoined in one,
             And means to give you battle presently.
    CHARLES   Somewhat too sudden, sirs, the warning is,
15   But we will presently provide for them.
    BURGUNDY   I trust the ghost of Talbot is not there:
             Now he is gone, my lord, you need not fear.
    PUCELLE   Of all base passions, fear is most accursed.
             Command the conquest, Charles, it shall be thine:
20   Let Henry fret and all the world repine.
    CHARLES   Then on, my lords, and France be fortunate!

                                                   Exeunt

[Act 5 Scene 3]   *running scene 19 continues*

Alarum. Excursions. Enter Joan la Pucelle

PUCELLE   The regent conquers, and the Frenchmen fly.
             Now help, ye charming spells and periapts,
             And ye choice spirits that admonish me,
             And give me signs of future accidents.   *Thunder*
5   You speedy helpers, that are substitutes
             Under the lordly monarch of the north,
             Appear, and aid me in this enterprise.
Enter Fiends
             This speedy and quick appearance argues proof
             Of your accustomed diligence to me.
10   Now, ye familiar spirits that are culled

---

9 **accomplices** allies   15 **provide** prepare ourselves   20 **repine** complain
5.3   2 **charming** magic   **periapts** amulets, charms (worn on the body)   3 **choice** excellent,
worthy   **admonish** forewarn   4 **accidents** events, chance happenings   5 **substitutes**
servants, agents   6 **lordly . . . north** i.e. the devil   8 **quick** lively, in living form/alert, vigorous
10 **familiar spirits** attendant spirits that served a witch, often inhabiting the bodies of animals
culled selected

Out of the powerful regions under earth,
Help me this once, that France may get the field.

They walk, and speak not

O hold me not with silence over-long:
Where I was wont to feed you with my blood,
15   I'll lop a member off and give it you
In earnest of a further benefit,
So you do condescend to help me now.

They hang their heads

No hope to have redress? My body shall
Pay recompense, if you will grant my suit.

They shake their heads

20   Cannot my body nor blood-sacrifice
Entreat you to your wonted furtherance?
Then take my soul — my body, soul and all —
Before that England give the French the foil.   *They depart*
See, they forsake me! Now the time is come
25   That France must vail her lofty-plumèd crest
And let her head fall into England's lap.
My ancient incantations are too weak,
And hell too strong for me to buckle with:
Now, France, thy glory droopeth to the dust.   *Exit*

Excursions. Burgundy and York fight hand to hand. [The] French fly
[leaving Joan la Pucelle in York's power]

30   **RICHARD DUKE OF YORK**   Damsel of France, I think I have you fast:
Unchain your spirits now with spelling charms
And try if they can gain your liberty.
A goodly prize, fit for the devil's grace!
See how the ugly witch doth bend her brows,
35   As if with Circe she would change my shape!

---

12 get the field win the battle   **14 Where** whereas   **wont** accustomed   **15 member** limb
16 earnest advance payment   **18 redress** assistance, relief   **body . . . recompense** with
sexual connotations (to **pay**: to have sex)   **21 wonted furtherance** usual assistance   **23 the
foil** defeat   **25 vail** lower (in submission)   **lofty-plumèd crest** helmet adorned with tall
feathers   **27 ancient** former/very old   **28 buckle** fight (plays on the sense of "have sex")
Excursions sortie, bouts of fighting (during which Joan reenters)   **30 fast** secure
31 spelling conjuring   **33 devil's grace** favor; also touches on the paradoxical notion of the
devil possessing divine grace   **34 bend her brows** scowl   **35 with** like   **Circe** in Greek
mythology, an island-dwelling sorceress who turned men into pigs with a magic potion

PUCELLE   Changed to a worser shape thou canst not be.

RICHARD DUKE OF YORK   O, Charles the Dauphin is a proper man:
No shape but his can please your dainty eye.

PUCELLE   A plaguing mischief light on Charles and thee,

40   And may ye both be suddenly surprised
By bloody hands, in sleeping on your beds!

RICHARD DUKE OF YORK   Fell banning hag, enchantress, hold thy
tongue.

PUCELLE   I prithee, give me leave to curse awhile.

RICHARD DUKE OF YORK   Curse, miscreant, when thou com'st to
the stake.   *Exeunt*

Alarum. Enter Suffolk with Margaret in his hand

45   SUFFOLK   Be what thou wilt, thou art my prisoner.

Gazes on her

O fairest beauty, do not fear nor fly:
For I will touch thee but with reverent hands:
I kiss these fingers for eternal peace,
And lay them gently on thy tender side.

50   Who art thou? Say, that I may honour thee.

MARGARET   Margaret my name, and daughter to a king,
The King of Naples, whosoe'er thou art.

SUFFOLK   An earl I am, and Suffolk am I called.
Be not offended, nature's miracle,

55   Thou art allotted to be ta'en by me:
So doth the swan her downy cygnets save,
Keeping them prisoner underneath her wings:
Yet if this servile usage once offend,
Go, and be free again, as Suffolk's friend.   *She is going*

60   O stay!— I have no power to let her pass;   *Aside*
My hand would free her, but my heart says no.
As plays the sun upon the glassy streams,
Twinkling another counterfeited beam,

---

37 proper handsome, perfect   **38 dainty** fastidious, scrupulous   **39 plaguing mischief**
tormenting calamity   **41 in** while   **42 Fell banning hag** fierce cursing witch   **44 miscreant**
heretic   ***in his hand*** led by the hand   **48 for** to signify   **49 lay . . . side** i.e. release her hand
so that it hangs by her side   **55 allotted** destined   **56 save** protect   **58 usage** treatment
62 glassy mirror-like   **63 Twinkling** causing to twinkle   **counterfeited** mirrored, reflected

So seems this gorgeous beauty to mine eyes.

65   Fain would I woo her, yet I dare not speak:

I'll call for pen and ink, and write my mind:

Fie, de la Pole, disable not thyself!

Hast not a tongue? Is she not here?

Wilt thou be daunted at a woman's sight?

70   Ay, beauty's princely majesty is such

Confounds the tongue and makes the senses rough.

MARGARET   Say, Earl of Suffolk — if thy name be so —

What ransom must I pay before I pass?

For I perceive I am thy prisoner.

75   SUFFOLK   How canst thou tell she will deny thy suit,   *Aside*

Before thou make a trial of her love?

MARGARET   Why speak'st thou not? What ransom must I pay?

SUFFOLK   She's beautiful, and therefore to be wooed: *Aside*

She is a woman, therefore to be won.

80   MARGARET   Wilt thou accept of ransom, yea or no?

SUFFOLK   Fond man, remember that thou hast a wife: *Aside*

Then how can Margaret be thy paramour?

MARGARET   I were best to leave him, for he will not hear.   *Aside*

SUFFOLK   There all is marred: there lies a cooling card.   *Aside*

85   MARGARET   He talks at random: sure, the man is mad.   *Aside*

SUFFOLK   And yet a dispensation may be had.   *Aside*

MARGARET   And yet I would that you would answer me.

SUFFOLK   I'll win this Lady Margaret. For whom?   *Aside*

Why, for my king: tush, that's a wooden thing.

90   MARGARET   He talks of wood: it is some carpenter.   *Aside*

SUFFOLK*   Yet so my fancy may be satisfied,   *Aside*

And peace establishèd between these realms.

But there remains a scruple in that too:

---

67 de la Pole Suffolk's family name   **disable** devalue, disparage   **69 a woman's sight** the sight of a woman/the gaze of a woman   **71 Confounds** that it destroys the power of   **rough** dulls/agitated   **81 Fond** foolish   **84 cooling card** opponent's card that, when played, ruins one's hopes of winning (plays on the idea of "cooling" down hot desire)   **86 dispensation** special permission from the Pope to dissolve a marriage   **89 wooden thing** stupid idea/man (the king) not moved by passion/(Suffolk's) erect penis   **91 fancy** infatuation/love
93 scruple difficulty

For though her father be the King of Naples,

95   Duke of Anjou and Maine, yet is he poor,

And our nobility will scorn the match.

MARGARET   Hear ye, captain? Are you not at leisure?

SUFFOLK   It shall be so, disdain they ne'er so much.   *Aside*

Henry is youthful and will quickly yield.—

100   Madam, I have a secret to reveal.   *To Margaret*

MARGARET   What though I be enthralled, he seems a   *Aside*
      knight,

And will not any way dishonour me.

SUFFOLK   Lady, vouchsafe to listen what I say.

MARGARET   Perhaps I shall be rescued by the French,   *Aside*

105   And then I need not crave his courtesy.

SUFFOLK   Sweet madam, give me a hearing in a cause.

MARGARET   Tush, women have been captivate ere now.   *Aside*

SUFFOLK   Lady, wherefore talk you so?

MARGARET   I cry you mercy, 'tis but *quid* for *quo*.

110   SUFFOLK   Say, gentle princess, would you not suppose

Your bondage happy to be made a queen?

MARGARET   To be a queen in bondage is more vile

Than is a slave in base servility,

For princes should be free.

115   SUFFOLK   And so shall you,

If happy England's royal king be free.

MARGARET   Why, what concerns his freedom unto me?

SUFFOLK   I'll undertake to make thee Henry's queen,

To put a golden sceptre in thy hand

120   And set a precious crown upon thy head,

If thou wilt condescend to be my—

MARGARET   What?

SUFFOLK   His love.

MARGARET   I am unworthy to be Henry's wife.

---

98 disdain . . . much however disdainful they are   **101 enthralled** taken captive
107 captivate taken prisoner, both literally and metaphorically (either in love or servitude)
109 cry you mercy beg your pardon   ***quid* for *quo*** *quid pro quo* (Latin), i.e. tit for tat
111 bondage happy imprisonment fortunate were you   **112 vile** degraded, low (punned on
in **servility**)   **113 servility** slavery

125 SUFFOLK   No, gentle madam, I unworthy am
　　　　　　To woo so fair a dame to be his wife,
　　　　　　And have no portion in the choice myself.
　　　　　　How say you, madam, are ye so content?

MARGARET   An if my father please, I am content.

130 SUFFOLK   Then call our captains and our colours forth,
　　　　　　And, madam, at your father's castle walls
　　　　　　We'll crave a parley, to confer with him.

[Enter Captains, Colours and Trumpeters]
Sound [a parley]. Enter Reignier on the walls
　　　　　　See, Reignier, see, thy daughter prisoner.

REIGNIER   To whom?

135 SUFFOLK   To me.

REIGNIER   Suffolk, what remedy?
　　　　　　I am a soldier, and unapt to weep,
　　　　　　Or to exclaim on fortune's fickleness.

SUFFOLK   Yes, there is remedy enough, my lord:

140 　　　　Consent, and for thy honour give consent,
　　　　　　Thy daughter shall be wedded to my king,
　　　　　　Whom I with pain have wooed and won thereto:
　　　　　　And this her easy-held imprisonment
　　　　　　Hath gained thy daughter princely liberty.

145 REIGNIER   Speaks Suffolk as he thinks?

SUFFOLK   Fair Margaret knows
　　　　　　That Suffolk doth not flatter, face, or feign.

REIGNIER   Upon thy princely warrant, I descend
　　　　　　To give thee answer of thy just demand.

　　　　　　　　　　　　　　　　[Exit from the walls]

150 SUFFOLK   And here I will expect thy coming.

Trumpets sound. Enter Reignier [below]

REIGNIER   Welcome, brave earl, into our territories:
　　　　　　Command in Anjou what your honour pleases.

---

127 portion share, part (plays on the sense of "marriage portion, dowry")   **choice** an act of
choice/object chosen   **129 An if** if   **130 colours** ensigns, bearers of military flags
132 parley military negotiation between opposing sides   **136 what remedy** i.e. there's no help
138 exclaim on accuse   **142 Whom** refers to Margaret   **143 easy-held** easily endured
147 face deceive, show a false face   **148 warrant** guarantee   **149 just** honorable, worthy
150 expect await   *below* i.e. the main stage

SUFFOLK   Thanks, Reignier, happy for so sweet a child,
Fit to be made companion with a king:
155   What answer makes your grace unto my suit?
REIGNIER   Since thou dost deign to woo her little worth
To be the princely bride of such a lord,
Upon condition I may quietly
Enjoy mine own, the country Maine and Anjou,
160   Free from oppression or the stroke of war,
My daughter shall be Henry's, if he please.
SUFFOLK   That is her ransom: I deliver her,
And those two counties I will undertake
Your grace shall well and quietly enjoy.
165   REIGNIER   And I again in Henry's royal name,
As deputy unto that gracious king,
Give thee her hand for sign of plighted faith.
SUFFOLK   Reignier of France, I give thee kingly thanks,
Because this is in traffic of a king.—
170   And yet, methinks, I could be well content   *Aside*
To be mine own attorney in this case.—
I'll over then to England with this news,   *To Reignier*
And make this marriage to be solemnized:
So farewell, Reignier: set this diamond safe
175   In golden palaces, as it becomes.
REIGNIER   I do embrace thee, as I would embrace
The Christian prince King Henry, were he here.
MARGARET   Farewell, my lord: good wishes, praise and prayers
Shall Suffolk ever have of Margaret.   *She is going*
180   SUFFOLK   Farewell, sweet madam: but hark you, Margaret:
No princely commendations to my king?
MARGARET   Such commendations as becomes a maid,
A virgin and his servant, say to him.

---

153 happy for fortunate in having   **156 her little worth** her relative poverty, playing on the
notion of moral value   **158 quietly** peacefully   **163 counties** i.e. regions, domains
165 again in return   **166 deputy** i.e. Suffolk   **167 plighted** pledged, promised   **169 traffic**
business, trade   **171 attorney** (legal) representative, advocate   **173 solemnized** celebrated,
formalized   **175 it becomes** befits it   **181 princely commendations** royal greetings,
compliments

SUFFOLK   Words sweetly placed and modestly directed.

185   But madam, I must trouble you again;

No loving token to his majesty?

MARGARET   Yes, my good lord, a pure unspotted heart,

Never yet taint with love, I send the king.

SUFFOLK   And this withal.   *Kisses her*

190   MARGARET   That for thyself: I will not so presume

To send such peevish tokens to a king.

[*Exeunt Reignier and Margaret*]

SUFFOLK   O, wert thou for myself! But, Suffolk, stay:

Thou mayst not wander in that labyrinth:

There Minotaurs and ugly treasons lurk.

195   Solicit Henry with her wondrous praise.

Bethink thee on her virtues that surmount,

Mad natural graces that extinguish art,

Repeat their semblance often on the seas,

That when thou com'st to kneel at Henry's feet,

200   Thou mayst bereave him of his wits with wonder.   *Exit*

[Act 5 Scene 4]   *running scene 20*

Enter York, Warwick, [a] Shepherd [and Joan la] Pucelle [guarded]

RICHARD DUKE OF YORK   Bring forth that sorceress condemned to
burn.

SHEPHERD   Ah, Joan, this kills thy father's heart outright.

Have I sought every country far and near,

And now it is my chance to find thee out,

5   Must I behold thy timeless cruel death?

Ah, Joan, sweet daughter Joan, I'll die with thee.

---

184 **placed** arranged   188 **taint** touched, tainted, stained   189 **withal** in addition
191 **peevish** foolish   192 **stay** stop   193 **labyrinth . . . Minotaurs** in Greek mythology, the
Minotaur was a legendary monster with the head of a bull and the body of a man, living in the
labyrinth of King Minos, in Crete   195 **Solicit** urge, move   **her wondrous praise** praise of
her wondrous qualities   196 **Bethink thee** reflect, remember   **surmount** excel
197 **extinguish art** outdo artifice   198 **Repeat their semblance** recall, dwell on the image of
them   200 **bereave** deprive, rob   **5.4**   *Location: France, exact location unspecified*
3 **sought every country** searched every region   4 **chance** fortune   5 **timeless** untimely,
premature

PUCELLE   Decrepit miser, base ignoble wretch,

I am descended of a gentler blood.

Thou art no father, nor no friend of mine.

10   SHEPHERD   Out, out!— My lords, an't please you, 'tis not so:

I did beget her, all the parish knows:

Her mother liveth yet, can testify

She was the first fruit of my bach'lorship.

WARWICK   Graceless, wilt thou deny thy parentage?

15   RICHARD DUKE OF YORK   This argues what her kind of life hath

been:

Wicked and vile, and so her death concludes.

SHEPHERD   Fie, Joan, that thou wilt be so obstacle:

God knows thou art a collop of my flesh,

And for thy sake have I shed many a tear:

20   Deny me not, I prithee, gentle Joan.

PUCELLE   Peasant, avaunt!— You have suborned this

man,   *To the English*

Of purpose to obscure my noble birth.

SHEPHERD   'Tis true, I gave a noble to the priest

The morn that I was wedded to her mother.

25   Kneel down and take my blessing, good my girl.

Wilt thou not stoop? Now cursèd be the time

Of thy nativity: I would the milk

Thy mother gave thee when thou sucked'st her breast,

Had been a little ratsbane for thy sake.

30   Or else, when thou didst keep my lambs afield,

I wish some ravenous wolf had eaten thee.

Dost thou deny thy father, cursèd drab?—

O burn her, burn her: hanging is too good.   *Exit*

---

7 **miser** miserable creature   8 **gentler** nobler   9 **friend** relative   10 **Out, out!** expression of
dismay and denial   **an't** if it   11 **beget** conceive, father   13 **bach'lorship** suggesting, either
intentionally or unwittingly for comic purposes, that Joan was illegitimate; the Shepherd may
intend "youth," and the word can also mean "period as a novice or apprentice"   15 **argues**
demonstrates   16 **concludes** proves/is a fitting end   17 **obstacle** i.e. "obstinate," an error
that apparently demonstrates the Shepherd's humble origins   18 **collop** piece, part
21 **avaunt** be gone   **suborned** bribed, corrupted   22 **Of** on   23 **noble** gold coin
27 **nativity** birth, with a particular emphasis on astronomy   29 **ratsbane** rat poison
30 **keep** look after   **afield** in the field   32 **drab** whore

RICHARD DUKE OF YORK   Take her away; for she hath lived too
    long,
35   To fill the world with vicious qualities.
PUCELLE   First let me tell you whom you have condemned:
    Not one begotten of a shepherd swain,
    But issued from the progeny of kings:
    Virtuous and holy, chosen from above,
40   By inspiration of celestial grace,
    To work exceeding miracles on earth.
    I never had to do with wicked spirits:
    But you that are polluted with your lusts,
    Stained with the guiltless blood of innocents,
45   Corrupt and tainted with a thousand vices:
    Because you want the grace that others have,
    You judge it straight a thing impossible
    To compass wonders but by help of devils.
    No misconceivèd, Joan of Arc hath been
50   A virgin from her tender infancy,
    Chaste and immaculate in very thought,
    Whose maiden blood thus rigorously effused
    Will cry for vengeance at the gates of heaven.
RICHARD DUKE OF YORK   Ay, ay.— Away with her to
    execution.   *To Guards*
55 **WARWICK**   And hark ye, sirs: because she is a maid,
    Spare for no faggots: let there be enough:
    Place barrels of pitch upon the fatal stake,
    That so her torture may be shortenèd.
PUCELLE   Will nothing turn your unrelenting hearts?
60   Then, Joan, discover thine infirmity,

---

37 swain rustic   **38 progeny** lineage   **41 exceeding** exceptional   **42 to do** plays on the
sense of "sexual intercourse"   **46 want** lack   **47 straight** instantly   **48 compass** bring
about   **49 No misconceivèd** not wickedly created/illegitimate; some editors emend
punctuation, e.g. to "No, misconceivèd!" meaning "No, you have misunderstood"   **50 tender**
young/mild, gentle   **52 rigorously effused** savagely spilled   **56 Spare . . . faggots** do not be
miserly with the bundles of kindling (a bigger blaze made it more likely for a victim to lose
consciousness from smoke inhalation before their flesh burned)   **57 pitch** black tarlike
substance (burning it would increase the amount of asphyxiating smoke produced)
60 discover reveal   **infirmity** weakness, vulnerability

That warranteth by law to be thy privilege.
I am with child, ye bloody homicides:
Murder not then the fruit within my womb,
Although ye hale me to a violent death.

65 RICHARD DUKE OF YORK   Now heaven forfend, the holy maid with
child?

WARWICK   The greatest miracle that e'er ye wrought.
Is all your strict preciseness come to this?

RICHARD DUKE OF YORK   She and the dauphin have been juggling.
I did imagine what would be her refuge.

70 WARWICK   Well, go to: we'll have no bastards live,
Especially since Charles must father it.

PUCELLE   You are deceived: my child is none of his:
It was Alençon that enjoyed my love.

RICHARD DUKE OF YORK   Alençon, that notorious machiavel?

75 It dies, an if it had a thousand lives.

PUCELLE   O give me leave, I have deluded you:
'Twas neither Charles nor yet the duke I named,
But Reignier, King of Naples, that prevailed.

WARWICK   A married man: that's most intolerable!

80 RICHARD DUKE OF YORK   Why, here's a girl! I think she knows not
well,
There were so many, whom she may accuse.

WARWICK   It's sign she hath been liberal and free.

RICHARD DUKE OF YORK   And yet, forsooth, she is a virgin pure.—
Strumpet, thy words condemn thy brat and thee.

85 Use no entreaty, for it is in vain.

PUCELLE   Then lead me hence, with whom I leave my curse:
May never glorious sun reflex his beams
Upon the country where you make abode:
But darkness and the gloomy shade of death

---

61 **warranteth . . . privilege** legally guarantees my exemption (as putting a pregnant woman to
death would entail killing the innocent child)   64 **hale** drag, haul   65 **forfend** forbid
67 **preciseness** morality, propriety   68 **juggling** having sex   69 **refuge** last resource, final
defense   74 **machiavel** i.e. intriguer/unscrupulous schemer (from Niccolò Machiavelli's *The
Prince*, a sixteenth-century treatise perceived as advocating ruthless political cunning)   75 **an**
if even if   78 **prevailed** seduced me   82 **liberal and free** licentious and promiscuous (perhaps
with mocking play on the senses of "generous and innocent")   87 **reflex** reflect, shine

90   Environ you, till mischief and despair
        Drive you to break your necks or hang yourselves!

                                        Exit [guarded]

RICHARD DUKE OF YORK   Break thou in pieces and consume to
        ashes,
        Thou foul accursèd minister of hell!

Enter [Bishop of Winchester, now] Cardinal [attended]

WINCHESTER   Lord Regent, I do greet your excellence
95   With letters of commission from the king.
        For know, my lords, the states of Christendom,
        Moved with remorse of these outrageous broils,
        Have earnestly implored a general peace
        Betwixt our nation and the aspiring French,
100   And here at hand the dauphin and his train
        Approacheth to confer about some matter.

RICHARD DUKE OF YORK   Is all our travail turned to this effect?
        After the slaughter of so many peers,
        So many captains, gentlemen and soldiers,
105   That in this quarrel have been overthrown
        And sold their bodies for their country's benefit,
        Shall we at last conclude effeminate peace?
        Have we not lost most part of all the towns,
        By treason, falsehood and by treachery,
110   Our great progenitors had conquerèd?
        O Warwick, Warwick, I foresee with grief
        The utter loss of all the realm of France.

WARWICK   Be patient, York: if we conclude a peace,
        It shall be with such strict and severe covenants
115   As little shall the Frenchmen gain thereby.

Enter Charles, Alençon, Bastard [of Orléans] and Reignier

CHARLES   Since, lords of England, it is thus agreed
        That peaceful truce shall be proclaimed in France,
        We come to be informèd by yourselves
        What the conditions of that league must be.

---

92 consume be burned   **93 minister** servant, agent   **95 commission** warrant, authority to
act   **97 remorse** pity   **outrageous broils** excessively violent turmoil   **99 aspiring** ambitious
102 travail labor, effort   **113 conclude** resolve, settle   **114 covenants** terms of agreement

120   RICHARD DUKE OF YORK   Speak, Winchester, for boiling choler
                chokes
          The hollow passage of my poisoned voice,
          By sight of these our baleful enemies.
      WINCHESTER   Charles and the rest, it is enacted thus:
          That, in regard King Henry gives consent,
125   Of mere compassion and of lenity,
          To ease your country of distressful war,
          And suffer you to breathe in fruitful peace,
          You shall become true liegemen to his crown.
          And, Charles, upon condition thou wilt swear
130   To pay him tribute, and submit thyself,
          Thou shalt be placed as viceroy under him,
          And still enjoy thy regal dignity.
      ALENÇON   Must he be then as shadow of himself?
          Adorn his temples with a coronet,
135   And yet in substance and authority
          Retain but privilege of a private man?
          This proffer is absurd and reasonless.
      CHARLES   'Tis known already that I am possessed
          With more than half the Gallian territories,
140   And therein reverenced for their lawful king.
          Shall I, for lucre of the rest unvanquished,
          Detract so much from that prerogative,
          As to be called but viceroy of the whole?
          No, lord ambassador, I'll rather keep
145   That which I have than, coveting for more,
          Be cast from possibility of all.
      RICHARD DUKE OF YORK   Insulting Charles, hast thou by secret
                means

---

122 **baleful** deadly, poisonous   123 **enacted** decreed   124 **in regard** insofar as   125 **mere**
pure, entire   **lenity** mildness, mercifulness   126 **distressful** devastating, ruinous
127 **suffer** permit   128 **liegemen** loyal followers   130 **tribute** (usually annual) payment
made as an act of homage   134 **coronet** small crown worn by members of the nobility
136 **but** only   137 **proffer** proposal, offer   139 **Gallian** French   140 **reverenced for** held in
respect as   141 **lucre** acquisition, gain   **the rest** remaining territories (that are)   146 **cast**
excluded, driven

Used intercession to obtain a league,
And, now the matter grows to compromise,
150   Stand'st thou aloof upon comparison?
Either accept the title thou usurp'st,
Of benefit proceeding from our king
And not of any challenge of desert,
Or we will plague thee with incessant wars.

155   REIGNIER   My lord, you do not well in obstinacy   *Aside to Charles*
To cavil in the course of this contract:
If once it be neglected, ten to one
We shall not find like opportunity.

ALENÇON   To say the truth, it is your policy   *Aside to Charles*
160   To save your subjects from such massacre
And ruthless slaughters as are daily seen
By our proceeding in hostility:
And therefore take this compact of a truce,
Although you break it when your pleasure serves.

165   WARWICK   How say'st thou, Charles? Shall our condition
    stand?

CHARLES   It shall:
Only reserved you claim no interest
In any of our towns of garrison.

RICHARD DUKE OF YORK   Then swear allegiance to his majesty,
170   As thou art knight, never to disobey
Nor be rebellious to the crown of England,
Thou, nor thy nobles, to the crown of England.
So, now dismiss your army when ye please:
Hang up your ensigns, let your drums be still,
175   For here we entertain a solemn peace.   *Exeunt*

---

149 compromise resolution   **150 upon comparison** by insisting on comparing your current
state with the one you are being offered/on comparing our position to yours   **152 Of benefit**
out of generosity/as a benefaction   **153 challenge of desert** claim based on merit
156 cavil dispute, raise quibbling objections   **157 neglected** disregarded, underestimated
163 compact agreement, contract   **165 condition** terms of agreement   **167 reserved** with
the sole reservation that   **168 towns of garrison** fortified towns   **174 ensigns** military
banners   **175 entertain** accept, receive

Act 5 [Scene 5]   *running scene 21*

Enter Suffolk in conference with King [Henry VI], Gloucester and
Exeter

KING HENRY VI   Your wondrous rare description, noble earl,
 Of beauteous Margaret hath astonished me:
 Her virtues gracèd with external gifts
 Do breed love's settled passions in my heart,
5 And like as rigour of tempestuous gusts
 Provokes the mightiest hulk against the tide,
 So am I driven by breath of her renown
 Either to suffer shipwreck or arrive
 Where I may have fruition of her love.
10   SUFFOLK   Tush, my good lord, this superficial tale
 Is but a preface of her worthy praise:
 The chief perfections of that lovely dame,
 Had I sufficient skill to utter them,
 Would make a volume of enticing lines,
15 Able to ravish any dull conceit:
 And, which is more, she is not so divine,
 So full replete with choice of all delights,
 But with as humble lowliness of mind
 She is content to be at your command:
20 Command, I mean, of virtuous chaste intents,
 To love and honour Henry as her lord.
 KING HENRY VI   And otherwise will Henry ne'er presume:
 Therefore, my Lord Protector, give consent
 That Margaret may be England's royal queen.
25   GLOUCESTER   So should I give consent to flatter sin.
 You know, my lord, your highness is betrothed
 Unto another lady of esteem:

5.5 *Location: the royal court, London*   **4 settled** rooted, firmly entrenched   **5 rigour**
the harshness   **6 Provokes** impels   **hulk** large vessel   **11 her worthy praise** praise of her
true worth   **15 conceit** imagination   **17 full** fully   **18 lowliness** meekness   **25 flatter**
gloss over, mitigate   **27 lady of esteem** i.e. the daughter of the Earl of Armagnac (see Act 5
Scene 1)

How shall we then dispense with that contract,
And not deface your honour with reproach?

30   SUFFOLK   As doth a ruler with unlawful oaths,
Or one that, at a triumph having vowed
To try his strength, forsaketh yet the lists
By reason of his adversary's odds.
A poor earl's daughter is unequal odds,
35   And therefore may be broke without offence.

GLOUCESTER   Why, what, I pray, is Margaret more than that?
Her father is no better than an earl,
Although in glorious titles he excel.

SUFFOLK   Yes, my lord, her father is a king,
40   The King of Naples and Jerusalem,
And of such great authority in France
As his alliance will confirm our peace
And keep the Frenchmen in allegiance.

GLOUCESTER   And so the Earl of Armagnac may do,
45   Because he is near kinsman unto Charles.

EXETER   Beside, his wealth doth warrant a liberal dower,
Where Reignier sooner will receive than give.

SUFFOLK   A dower, my lords? Disgrace not so your king,
That he should be so abject, base and poor,
50   To choose for wealth and not for perfect love.
Henry is able to enrich his queen,
And not to seek a queen to make him rich:
So worthless peasants bargain for their wives,
As market men for oxen, sheep, or horse.
55   Marriage is a matter of more worth
Than to be dealt in by attorneyship:
Not whom we will, but whom his grace affects,
Must be companion of his nuptial bed.
And therefore, lords, since he affects her most,

---

28 **contract** betrothal   29 **reproach** disgrace, shame   31 **triumph** jousting tournament
32 **lists** designated combat arena   35 **be broke** broken off with   42 **confirm** strengthen,
entrench   46 **warrant** guarantee   47 **Where** whereas   56 **attorneyship** legal practices,
negotiations between lawyers   57 **will** want   **affects** loves, prefers

60   Most of all these reasons bindeth us,
    In our opinions she should be preferred.
    For what is wedlock forcèd but a hell,
    An age of discord and continual strife?
    Whereas the contrary bringeth bliss,
65   And is a pattern of celestial peace.
    Whom should we match with Henry, being a king,
    But Margaret, that is daughter to a king?
    Her peerless feature, joinèd with her birth,
    Approves her fit for none but for a king:
70   Her valiant courage and undaunted spirit,
    More than in women commonly is seen,
    Will answer our hope in issue of a king.
    For Henry, son unto a conqueror,
    Is likely to beget more conquerors,
75   If with a lady of so high resolve,
    As is fair Margaret, he be linked in love.
    Then yield, my lords, and here conclude with me
    That Margaret shall be queen, and none but she.
    KING HENRY VI   Whether it be through force of your report,
80   My noble lord of Suffolk, or for that
    My tender youth was never yet attaint
    With any passion of inflaming love,
    I cannot tell: but this I am assured,
    I feel such sharp dissension in my breast,
85   Such fierce alarums both of hope and fear,
    As I am sick with working of my thoughts.
    Take therefore shipping: post, my lord, to France:
    Agree to any covenants, and procure
    That Lady Margaret do vouchsafe to come
90   To cross the seas to England, and be crowned
    King Henry's faithful and anointed queen.

---

61 **preferred** put forward, recommended, promoted   65 **pattern** model   68 **feature** physical appearance   69 **Approves** proves   72 **issue . . . king** giving a child to the king/giving birth to the future king   75 **resolve** constancy, courage, resolution   80 **for that** because
81 **attaint** touched, affected   84 **dissension** conflict   87 **post** hurry   88 **procure** ensure, contrive   91 **anointed** marked with holy oil, the sign of monarchy

For your expenses and sufficient charge,
Among the people gather up a tenth.
Be gone, I say, for, till you do return,
95 I rest perplexèd with a thousand cares.
And you, good uncle, banish all offence:
If you do censure me by what you were,
Not what you are, I know it will excuse
This sudden execution of my will.
100 And so conduct me where from company
I may revolve and ruminate my grief.   *Exit*

GLOUCESTER   Ay, grief, I fear me, both at first and last.

Exit [with Exeter]

SUFFOLK   Thus Suffolk hath prevailed, and thus he goes
As did the youthful Paris once to Greece,
105 With hope to find the like event in love,
But prosper better than the Trojan did:
Margaret shall now be queen, and rule the king:
But I will rule both her, the king, and realm.   *Exit*

---

92 charge money to spend   **93 tenth** a tax of ten percent on income or property   **96 offence** hostility, opposition   **97 censure** judge (not necessarily negatively)   **what you were** i.e. your own youthful impulsiveness   **100 from company** alone   **101 revolve and ruminate** consider, meditate on   **grief** anxieties/love melancholy (Gloucester then intensifies the sense) **104 Paris . . . Greece** in Greek legend, Paris' abduction of the beautiful Helen, wife of the king of Troy, provoked the devastating Trojan war with the Greeks   **105 like event** same outcome

TEXTUAL NOTES

F = First Folio text of 1623, the only authority for the play
F2 = a correction introduced in the Second Folio text of 1632
Ed = a correction introduced by a later editor
SD = stage direction
SH = speech heading (i.e. speaker's name)

List of parts = Ed

1.1.60 Champaigne = F. Ed = Compiègne **Rouen** = Ed. *Not in F, but implicit in the text* **92 dauphin** = Ed. F = Dolphin **94 Reignier** = Ed. F = *Reynold* **131 Falstaff** = F. Ed = Fastolf **176 steal** = Ed. F = send
1.2.21 fly = F. Ed = flee **30 bred** = Ed. F = breed **47 SH CHARLES** = Ed. F = *Dolph.* **65 SH PUCELLE** = Ed. F = *Puzel* **99 five** = Ed. F = fine
1.3.6 SH FIRST SERVINGMAN = Ed. F = *Glost. I. Man.* **19 The Cardinal** = F. Ed = My lord **29 umpire** = F2. F = Vmpheir **30 Peeled** *spelled* Piel'd *in F* **42 scarlet** = F. Ed = purple **49 cardinal's hat** = F. Ed = bishop's mitre **56 scarlet** = F. Ed = cloakèd **56 SD [*Bishop of Winchester's*]** = Ed. F = *Cardinalls* **73 SH OFFICER** = Ed. *Not in F* **79 Cardinal** = F. Ed = Bishop **84 cardinal's** = F. Ed = bishop is
1.4.10 Wont = Ed. F = Went **27 Earl** = F. Ed = Duke **66 lords** = F. Ed = Lou **69 SD** *shoot* = Ed. F = *shot* **SD *fall*** = Ed. F = *falls* **89 Bear . . . it** *moved from its position in F two lines before, since the body referred to cannot be that of Salisbury, and must be that of Gargrave* **95 Nero** = Ed
1.6.21 pyramid = Ed. F = pyramis **22 of** = Ed. F = or
2.1.5 SH FIRST SENTINEL = Ed. F = *Sent.* **80 SD [*The French*] fly** = Ed. F = *they flye* (F has additional "Exeunt" cue for the French one line above)
2.2.20 Arc = Ed. F = *Acre*
2.4.0 SD *Suffolk* = Ed. F = *Poole* **1 SH RICHARD PLANTAGENET** = Ed. F = *Yorke* **41 are . . . tree** = F. Ed = from the tree are cropped **57 law** = Ed. F = you **118 wiped** = F2 (wip't). F = whipt **133 gentles** = Ed. F = gentle. Ed = gentle sirs/gentlemen
2.5.33 SH FIRST JAILER = Ed. F = *Keeper* **71 King** = Ed. F2 = K. *Not in F* **75 the** = F2. *Not in F* **76 the king** = Ed. F = hee **129 mine ill** = Ed. F = my will
3.1.56 see = F. Ed = so **167 that** = Ed. F = that all
4.1.19 Patay = Ed. F = Poictiers. *Probably an authorial error, since the battle of Poitiers took place much earlier* **48 my** = Ed. *Not in F* **173 SD *Flourish*** = Ed. F *places in stage direction eight lines later* **180 wist** = Ed. F = wish

4.2.15 SH GENERAL = Ed. F = *Cap.*   **29 rive** = F. Ed = fire

4.3.17 SH LUCY = Ed. F = *2. Mes.*   **53 lauds** = F. Ed = lands

4.4.16 legions = Ed. F = Regions. *Suggested compositorial confusion between Shakespeare's lowercase "l" and "r," which similarly occurs in other plays*   **19 in advantage** = F. Ed = unadvantaged   **31 host** = F. Ed = horse

4.7.17 SD *Enter . . . borne* = Ed. F *places one line earlier*   **63 Washford** = F. Ed = Wexford   **89 them** = Ed. F = him   **94 them** = Ed. F = him

Act 5 Scene 1 = Ed. F = *Scena secunda*

Act 5 Scene 2 = Ed. F = *Scoena Tertia*

5.3.57 her = Ed. F = his   **159 country** = F. Ed = countries   **184 modestly** = F2. F = modestie

5.4.10 an't = Ed. F = and   **37 one** = Ed. F = me   **49 Arc** = Ed. F = *Aire*   **93 SD *Enter . . . Cardinal*** = Ed. F *places two lines earlier*

5.5.60 Most = F. Ed. = It most *or* That most

HENRY VI PART II: KEY FACTS

MAJOR PARTS: (*with percentage of lines/number of speeches/scenes on-stage*) Richard Plantagenet, Duke of York (12%/58/9), King Henry VI (10%/82/11), Duke of Gloucester (10%/69/7), Duke of Suffolk (10%/67/7), Queen Margaret (10%/61/9), Jack Cade (8%/61/6), Earl of Warwick (4%/32/8), Cardinal Beaufort (4%/31/6), Eleanor (4%/21/5), Earl of Salisbury (3%/17/8), Duke of Buckingham (2%/24/9), Lord Clifford (2%/17/4), Captain (2%/11/1), Lord Say (2%/13/2), Alexander Iden (2%/9/2), Young Clifford (2%/4/2), Dick (1%/24/4).

LINGUISTIC MEDIUM: 85% verse, 15% prose.

DATE: 1591? Unquestionably precedes the play now known as *The Third Part*, a line of which was parodied in a pamphlet entered for publication in September 1592. Almost certainly played as a two-parter with the following play by Pembroke's Men, who were active in 1592. The possibility of an earlier pre-Shakespearean version and a later Shakespearean revision cannot be ruled out.

SOURCES: The main historical source seems to have been either Edward Hall's *The Union of the Two Noble and Illustre Famelies of Lancastre and Yorke* (1548) or Richard Grafton's abridged and very slightly altered version thereof (1569); Holinshed's *Chronicles* also seems to have been used, but there are fewer signs of its influence than in any of the other English histories. The false miracle of Simpcox was added by Grafton to Hall, but Shakespeare almost certainly read it in John Foxe's hugely influential protestant martyrology *Actes and Monuments* (perhaps read in the enlarged edition of 1583).

TEXT: A short version was published in Quarto form in 1594, entitled *The First Part of the Contention betwixt the two famous Houses of*

Yorke and Lancaster, with the death of the good Duke Humphrey: And the banishment and death of the Duke of Suffolke, and the Tragicall end of the proud Cardinall of Winchester, with the notable Rebellion of Iacke Cade: And the Duke of Yorkes first claime vnto the Crowne, reprinted 1600 and, with attribution to Shakespeare and title combined with that of the following play, 1619 (*The Whole Contention betweene the two Famous Houses, Lancaster and Yorke*). The Quarto text is a reconstruction of a playing version, but there is much dispute over whether it is a short and often poorly remembered version of the play that is preserved in full in the Folio or the text of an early version (not by Shakespeare? partly by Shakespeare?) that Shakespeare then revised into the play that was printed in the Folio. It is equally unclear whether the possible linguistic signs of a non-Shakespearean hand (or hands) in the Folio text are vestiges of an older version or the result of active collaboration/coauthorship. We use the Folio text, which has the authority of Hemings and Condell; it is usually thought to represent a fairly close approximation of Shakespeare's manuscript, though the Third Quarto sometimes seems to have been consulted. The Quarto remains valuable for certain details of staging and the more significant of its variations are recorded in the textual notes.

THE SECOND PART OF HENRY THE SIXTH, WITH THE DEATH OF THE GOOD DUKE HUMPHREY

Lancastrians

KING HENRY VI

QUEEN MARGARET

Duke Humphrey of GLOUCESTER, Lord Protector, the king's uncle

ELEANOR, Duchess of Gloucester

CARDINAL Beaufort, Bishop of Winchester, the king's great-uncle

Duke of SOMERSET, the Cardinal's nephew

Duke of BUCKINGHAM, Humphrey Stafford

Marquis, later Duke, of SUFFOLK, William de la Pole

Old Lord CLIFFORD

YOUNG CLIFFORD, his son

Yorkists

Richard Plantagenet, Duke of YORK

EDWARD, Earl of March, his son

RICHARD (who will eventually become King Richard III), another son

Earl of SALISBURY, Richard Neville

Earl of WARWICK, his son

The conjuration

John HUME, a priest

John SOUTHWELL, a priest

MARGARET JORDAN, a witch

Roger BULLINGBROOK, a conjurer

ASNATH, a spirit

The petitions and combat

Thomas HORNER, an armourer

PETER Thump, the Armourer's man

FIRST PETITIONER

SECOND PETITIONER

FIRST NEIGHBOUR

SECOND NEIGHBOUR

THIRD NEIGHBOUR

FIRST PRENTICE

SECOND PRENTICE

The false miracle

Saunder SIMPCOX

Simpcox's WIFE

MAYOR of St Albans

TOWNSMAN

BEADLE

Eleanor's penance

Gloucester's SERVANT

Sir John STANLEY

A SHERIFF of London

A HERALD

The murder of Gloucester

FIRST MURDERER

SECOND MURDERER

The murder of Suffolk

LIEUTENANT, commander of a ship

MASTER of the same ship

The Master's MATE

Walter WHITMORE

Cade's rebellion

George BEVIS (probably the
    original actor's name, the
    character being an
    anonymous commoner)

John HOLLAND (probably the
    original actor's name, the
    character being an
    anonymous commoner)

Jack CADE, also known as John

DICK the butcher

SMITH the weaver

Emmanuel, a CLERK of
    Chartham

Sir Humphrey STAFFORD

William, STAFFORD'S BROTHER

MICHAEL

Lord SAYE

MESSENGER

SECOND MESSENGER

Lord SCALES

FIRST CITIZEN

SOLDIER

Alexander IDEN, an esquire of Kent

VAUX, a messenger

Petitioners, Servant, Servingman,
    Brethren of St Albans,
    Townspeople of St Albans,
    Gloucester's Men, Sheriff's
    Officers, Attendants, Commons,
    a Sawyer, Matthew Gough,
    Iden's Men, Soldiers

Act 1 Scene 1   *running scene 1*

*Flourish of trumpets, then hautboys. Enter King [Henry VI], Duke
Humphrey [of Gloucester], Salisbury, Warwick and [Cardinal]
Beaufort on the one side. The Queen [Margaret], Suffolk, York,
Somerset and Buckingham on the other*

SUFFOLK   As by your high imperial majesty
    I had in charge at my depart for France,
    As procurator to your excellence,
    To marry Princess Margaret for your grace,

**1.1   *Location: the royal court, London   Flourish* trumpet fanfare accompanying a person
in authority   *hautboys* oboelike instruments   2 had in charge** was commanded   **depart**
departure   **3 procurator to** deputy, representative for   **4 marry** i.e. by proxy, on the king's
behalf   **for** on behalf of

5   So, in the famous ancient city, Tours,
       In presence of the Kings of France and Sicil,
       The Dukes of Orléans, Calaber, Bretagne and Alençon,
       Seven earls, twelve barons and twenty reverend bishops,
       I have performed my task and was espoused,
10   And humbly now upon my bended knee,
       In sight of England and her lordly peers,
       Deliver up my title in the queen
       To your most gracious hands, that are the substance
       Of that great shadow I did represent:
15   The happiest gift that ever marquis gave,
       The fairest queen that ever king received.

KING HENRY VI   Suffolk, arise. Welcome, Queen Margaret:
       I can express no kinder sign of love
       Than this kind kiss: O Lord, that lends me life,
20   Lend me a heart replete with thankfulness:
       For thou hast given me in this beauteous face
       A world of earthly blessings to my soul,
       If sympathy of love unite our thoughts.

QUEEN MARGARET   Great King of England and my gracious lord,
25   The mutual conference that my mind hath had,
       By day, by night, waking and in my dreams,
       In courtly company or at my beads,
       With you, mine alderliefest sovereign,
       Makes me the bolder to salute my king
30   With ruder terms, such as my wit affords
       And overjoy of heart doth minister.

KING HENRY VI   Her sight did ravish, but her grace in speech,
       Her words yclad with wisdom's majesty,

---

5 **Tours** a city southwest of Orléans, located at the junction of the Rivers Cher and Loire
6 **Sicil** Sicily   7 **Calaber** Calabria, a region of southern Italy   **Bretagne** Brittany
9 **espoused** married   14 **shadow** image, reflection   15 **happiest** most fortunate   **marquis**
i.e. Suffolk   18 **kinder** more natural, affectionate   23 **sympathy** harmony, mutual feeling
25 **mutual conference** intimate conversation   27 **beads** i.e. prayers, said over a Catholic
rosary (beads used as prompts in the reciting of prayers)   28 **alderliefest** most beloved
29 **salute** address/greet   30 **ruder** unaccomplished, unpolished   **wit** skill, intellect
31 **minister** supply, provide   32 **Her sight** the sight of her   33 **yclad** decked out, clothed

Makes me from wond'ring fall to weeping joys,
35   Such is the fullness of my heart's content.
Lords, with one cheerful voice, welcome my love.

ALL   Long live Queen Margaret, England's happiness!

Kneel

QUEEN MARGARET   We thank you all.   *Flourish*   *They rise*

SUFFOLK   My Lord Protector, so it please your
grace,   *To Gloucester*
40   Here are the articles of contracted peace
Between our sovereign and the French King Charles,
For eighteen months concluded by consent.

GLOUCESTER   *Reads.* 'Imprimis, it is agreed between the French
King Charles, and William de la Pole, Marquess of Suffolk,
45   ambassador for Henry King of England, that the said Henry
shall espouse the Lady Margaret, daughter unto Reignier
King of Naples, Sicilia and Jerusalem, and crown her Queen
of England ere the thirtieth of May next ensuing.
Item: that the duchy of Anjou and the county of Maine shall
50   be released and delivered to the king her father'—   *Lets the*

KING HENRY VI   Uncle, how now?   *paper fall*

GLOUCESTER   Pardon me, gracious lord,
Some sudden qualm hath struck me at the heart
And dimmed mine eyes, that I can read no further.

55   KING HENRY VI   Uncle of Winchester, I pray, read on.

CARDINAL   'Item: it is further agreed between them,   *Reads*
that the duchies of Anjou and Maine shall be released and
delivered over to the king her father, and she sent over of the
King of England's own proper cost and charges, without
60   having any dowry.'

KING HENRY VI   They please us well.— Lord marquis, kneel
down: *To Suffolk*

---

34 wond'ring marveling, admiring   **39 Protector** surrogate ruler of the realm, while the
new king was too young to reign (Henry VI had inherited the throne as a baby)   **so** if
40 articles terms, conditions   **contracted** formally agreed   **42 concluded** resolved, settled
43 *Imprimis* "in the first place" (Latin)   **48 ere** before   **49** *Item* "likewise" (Latin)   **53 qualm**
sudden feeling of nausea/fit of misgiving   **54 that** so that   **55 Uncle** technically, Henry's
great-uncle   **58 of** at   **59 proper** personal

We here create thee the first Duke of Suffolk,   *Suffolk kneels*

And gird thee with the sword.—   *Suffolk rises*

Cousin of York,

65   We here discharge your grace from being regent

I'th'parts of France, till term of eighteen months

Be full expired. Thanks, uncle Winchester,

Gloucester, York, Buckingham, Somerset,

Salisbury and Warwick.

70   We thank you all for this great favour done,

In entertainment to my princely queen.

Come, let us in, and with all speed provide

To see her coronation be performed.

> *Exeunt King [Henry VI], Queen [Margaret] and Suffolk. The*
> *rest remain*

GLOUCESTER   Brave peers of England, pillars of the state,

75   To you Duke Humphrey must unload his grief:

Your grief, the common grief of all the land.

What? Did my brother Henry spend his youth,

His valour, coin and people, in the wars?

Did he so often lodge in open field,

80   In winter's cold and summer's parching heat,

To conquer France, his true inheritance?

And did my brother Bedford toil his wits,

To keep by policy what Henry got?

Have you yourselves, Somerset, Buckingham,

85   Brave York, Salisbury and victorious Warwick,

Received deep scars in France and Normandy:

Or hath mine uncle Beaufort and myself,

With all the learnèd Council of the realm,

Studied so long, sat in the Council house

90   Early and late, debating to and fro

How France and Frenchmen might be kept in awe,

---

63 gird invest (with the title)   **64 Cousin** a common form of address used among nobles
65 regent one who rules in the king's absence   **67 full** fully   **71 entertainment** hospitality
princely royal   **72 provide** prepare   **74 Brave** noble, splendid/valiant   **77 Henry** i.e.
Henry V   **79 lodge** dwell, sleep   **83 policy** skillful political strategy   **88 Council** i.e. the
Privy Council of the king's ministers and advisers   **91 awe** subjection, dread

And had his highness in his infancy
Crownèd in Paris in despite of foes?
And shall these labours and these honours die?
95   Shall Henry's conquest, Bedford's vigilance,
Your deeds of war and all our counsel die?
O peers of England, shameful is this league,
Fatal this marriage, cancelling your fame,
Blotting your names from books of memory,
100   Razing the characters of your renown,
Defacing monuments of conquered France,
Undoing all, as all had never been!
CARDINAL   Nephew, what means this passionate discourse?
This peroration with such circumstance:
105   For France, 'tis ours; and we will keep it still.
GLOUCESTER   Ay, uncle, we will keep it, if we can:
But now it is impossible we should.
Suffolk, the new-made duke that rules the roost,
Hath given the duchy of Anjou and Maine
110   Unto the poor King Reignier, whose large style
Agrees not with the leanness of his purse.
SALISBURY   Now by the death of him that died for all,
These counties were the keys of Normandy.—
But wherefore weeps Warwick, my valiant son?
115   WARWICK   For grief that they are past recovery.
For were there hope to conquer them again,
My sword should shed hot blood, mine eyes no tears.
Anjou and Maine? Myself did win them both:
Those provinces these arms of mine did conquer.
120   And are the cities that I got with wounds
Delivered up again with peaceful words?
Mort Dieu!

---

96 **counsel** advice, plans   97 **league** union, alliance   98 **fame** honor, reputations
100 **Razing** erasing   **characters** written records   101 **monuments** records, memorials
102 **as** as though   104 **peroration** rhetorical speech   **circumstance** elaborate details
110 **large style** grand title   112 **him . . . all** i.e. Christ   114 **wherefore** why   122 *Mort Dieu!*
"God's death!" (a French oath)

YORK   For Suffolk's duke, may he be suffocate,
That dims the honour of this warlike isle:
125 France should have torn and rent my very heart
Before I would have yielded to this league.
I never read but England's kings have had
Large sums of gold and dowries with their wives:
And our King Henry gives away his own,
130 To match with her that brings no vantages.

GLOUCESTER   A proper jest, and never heard before,
That Suffolk should demand a whole fifteenth
For costs and charges in transporting her:
She should have stayed in France and starved in France,
135 Before—

CARDINAL   My lord of Gloucester, now ye grow too hot:
It was the pleasure of my lord the king.

GLOUCESTER   My lord of Winchester, I know your mind.
'Tis not my speeches that you do mislike,
140 But 'tis my presence that doth trouble ye.
Rancour will out: proud prelate, in thy face
I see thy fury: if I longer stay,
We shall begin our ancient bickerings.—
Lordings, farewell, and say when I am gone,
145 I prophesied France will be lost ere long.

Exit Humphrey [*Gloucester*]

CARDINAL   So, there goes our Protector in a rage:
'Tis known to you he is mine enemy:
Nay more, an enemy unto you all,
And no great friend, I fear me, to the king:
150 Consider, lords, he is the next of blood
And heir apparent to the English crown:
Had Henry got an empire by his marriage,

---

123 For as for   **suffocate** suffocated (puns on **Suffolk**)   **125 rent** ripped up   **130 match**
marry   **vantages** advantages, assets   **131 proper** fine, resounding   **132 fifteenth** tax of
one-fifteenth of the value of income or property   **136 hot** angry, worked up   **137 pleasure**
will, desire   **143 ancient** former, long-standing   **144 Lordings** my lords   **150 next of blood**
next in line (to the throne; Henry VI does not, at this point, have children, and Gloucester is his
father's brother)

And all the wealthy kingdoms of the west,
There's reason he should be displeased at it.
155 Look to it, lords: let not his smoothing words
Bewitch your hearts: be wise and circumspect.
What though the common people favour him,
Calling him 'Humphrey, the good Duke of Gloucester',
Clapping their hands, and crying with loud voice,
160 'Jesu maintain your royal excellence!'
With 'God preserve the good Duke Humphrey!'
I fear me, lords, for all this flattering gloss,
He will be found a dangerous Protector.

BUCKINGHAM   Why should he then protect our sovereign,
165 He being of age to govern of himself?
Cousin of Somerset, join you with me,
And all together, with the Duke of Suffolk,
We'll quickly hoist Duke Humphrey from his seat.

CARDINAL   This weighty business will not brook delay:
170 I'll to the Duke of Suffolk presently.   *Exit Cardinal*

SOMERSET   Cousin of Buckingham, though Humphrey's pride
And greatness of his place be grief to us,
Yet let us watch the haughty cardinal:
His insolence is more intolerable
175 Than all the princes in the land beside:
If Gloucester be displaced, he'll be Protector.

BUCKINGHAM   Or thou or I, Somerset, will be Protector,
Despite Duke Humphrey or the cardinal.

Exeunt Buckingham and Somerset

SALISBURY   Pride went before, ambition follows him.
180 While these do labour for their own preferment,
Behoves it us to labour for the realm.
I never saw but Humphrey Duke of Gloucester

---

153 **wealthy . . . west** i.e. Spanish possessions in the Americas (an anachronism)
155 **smoothing** flattering, ingratiating, plausible   162 **flattering gloss** deceptively attractive
appearance   165 **He** i.e. Henry VI   169 **brook** tolerate   170 **presently** immediately
173 **haughty** proud, aspiring   175 **Than** than that of   177 **Or** either   179 **Pride** i.e. the
cardinal   **ambition** i.e. Buckingham and Somerset   180 **preferment** advancement
181 **Behoves it** it is appropriate for   182 **I . . . but** I have always seen that

Did bear him like a noble gentleman:
Oft have I seen the haughty cardinal,
185 More like a soldier than a man o'th'Church,
As stout and proud as he were lord of all,
Swear like a ruffian and demean himself
Unlike the ruler of a commonweal.
Warwick, my son, the comfort of my age,
190 Thy deeds, thy plainness and thy housekeeping
Hath won the greatest favour of the commons,
Excepting none but good Duke Humphrey.
And, brother York, thy acts in Ireland
In bringing them to civil discipline,
195 Thy late exploits done in the heart of France,
When thou wert regent for our sovereign,
Have made thee feared and honoured of the people:
Join we together for the public good,
In what we can, to bridle and suppress
200 The pride of Suffolk and the cardinal,
With Somerset's and Buckingham's ambition:
And, as we may, cherish Duke Humphrey's deeds,
While they do tend the profit of the land.

WARWICK   So God help Warwick, as he loves the land,
205 And common profit of his country.

YORK   And so says York,— for he hath greatest cause.   *Aside*

SALISBURY   Then let's make haste away, and look unto the
main.

WARWICK   Unto the main? O, father, Maine is lost,
That Maine which by main force Warwick did win,
210 And would have kept so long as breath did last:

---

183 him himself   **186 stout** arrogant, haughty   **as** as if   **187 demean** behave, conduct
190 plainness openness, frankness   **housekeeping** hospitality   **192 Excepting none but**
with the exception only of that shown to   **193 brother** brother-in-law (York was married to
Salisbury's sister, Cecily Neville)   **195 late** recent   **199 bridle** control, restrain   **202 cherish**
encourage, nurture   **203 tend** promote, encourage, tend to   **205 common** communal,
general   **206 cause** i.e. as one with a claim to the throne   **207 look . . . main** see to the most
important business at hand (from the dice game of hazard where the "main" was the
successful throw)   **208 Maine** French province lost as part of the recent treaty   **209 main**
sheer

Main chance, father, you meant, but I meant Maine,
Which I will win from France, or else be slain.

Exeunt Warwick and Salisbury, leaving York

YORK   Anjou and Maine are given to the French,
Paris is lost, the state of Normandy
215   Stands on a tickle point now they are gone:
Suffolk concluded on the articles,
The peers agreed, and Henry was well pleased
To change two dukedoms for a duke's fair daughter.
I cannot blame them all: what is't to them?
220   'Tis thine they give away, and not their own.
Pirates may make cheap pennyworths of their pillage
And purchase friends and give to courtesans,
Still revelling like lords till all be gone,
While as the silly owner of the goods
225   Weeps over them, and wrings his hapless hands,
And shakes his head, and trembling stands aloof,
While all is shared and all is borne away,
Ready to starve and dare not touch his own.
So York must sit and fret and bite his tongue,
230   While his own lands are bargained for and sold:
Methinks the realms of England, France and Ireland
Bear that proportion to my flesh and blood,
As did the fatal brand Althaea burnt
Unto the prince's heart of Calydon.
235   Anjou and Maine both given unto the French!
Cold news for me: for I had hope of France,
Even as I have of fertile England's soil.
A day will come when York shall claim his own,

---

215 **tickle** precarious   216 **concluded** settled, decided   218 **change** exchange   220 **thine**
your inheritance (York addresses himself)   221 **make . . . pillage** barter their booty for
virtually nothing   222 **purchase friends** i.e. through such generosity   **courtesans**
prostitutes; plays on the original meaning "one attached to the court of a prince"   223 **Still**
continually   224 **While as** while   **silly** helpless   225 **hapless** unfortunate   226 **trembling**
frightened   **aloof** to one side (unable to intervene)   228 **Ready** about   232 **proportion**
relation   233 **Althaea . . . Calydon** in Greek mythology, it was prophesied that Meleager,
Prince of Calydon, would only live for as long as a log burned in the fire; his mother, Althaea,
snatched the brand out, but cast it back into the flames when, years later, Meleager killed her
brothers

And therefore I will take the Nevilles' parts
240   And make a show of love to proud Duke Humphrey,
And, when I spy advantage, claim the crown,
For that's the golden mark I seek to hit:
Nor shall proud Lancaster usurp my right,
Nor hold the sceptre in his childish fist,
245   Nor wear the diadem upon his head,
Whose church-like humours fits not for a crown.
Then, York, be still awhile, till time do serve:
Watch thou, and wake when others be asleep,
To pry into the secrets of the state,
250   Till Henry, surfeiting in joys of love,
With his new bride and England's dear-bought queen,
And Humphrey with the peers be fall'n at jars:
Then will I raise aloft the milk-white rose,
With whose sweet smell the air shall be perfumed,
255   And in my standard bear the arms of York,
To grapple with the House of Lancaster:
And force perforce I'll make him yield the crown,
Whose bookish rule hath pulled fair England down.

Exit York

[Act 1 Scene 2]   *running scene 2*

Enter Duke Humphrey [of Gloucester] and his wife Eleanor

ELEANOR   Why droops my lord like over-ripened corn,
Hanging the head at Ceres' plenteous load?
Why doth the great Duke Humphrey knit his brows,

---

239 **Nevilles'** i.e. Salisbury and Warwick's   242 **mark** target   243 **Lancaster** i.e. Henry VI
244 **childish** Henry was only nine months old when he was crowned   245 **diadem** crown
246 **church-like humours** pious disposition   247 **still** quiet, patient   **time do serve** an
opportunity arises   248 **Watch** remain awake/be on guard   250 **surfeiting** overindulging
251 **dear-bought** expensive, obtained at too high a price   252 **at jars** into conflict, discord
253 **milk-white rose** emblem of the House of York   255 **standard** military banner, battle flag
256 **grapple** struggle, wrestle   257 **force perforce** through violence, by compulsion
258 **bookish** studious (perhaps with particular reference to religious texts)   **1.2** *Location:
the residence of the Duke of Gloucester*   2 **Ceres** Roman goddess of agriculture and the
harvest

As frowning at the favours of the world?

5   Why are thine eyes fixed to the sullen earth,
Gazing on that which seems to dim thy sight?
What see'st thou there? King Henry's diadem,
Enchased with all the honours of the world?
If so, gaze on, and grovel on thy face,
10   Until thy head be circlèd with the same.
Put forth thy hand, reach at the glorious gold.
What, is't too short? I'll lengthen it with mine,
And having both together heaved it up,
We'll both together lift our heads to heaven,
15   And never more abase our sight so low
As to vouchsafe one glance unto the ground.

GLOUCESTER   O Nell, sweet Nell, if thou dost love thy lord,
Banish the canker of ambitious thoughts:
And may that thought, when I imagine ill
20   Against my king and nephew, virtuous Henry,
Be my last breathing in this mortal world.
My troublous dreams this night doth make me sad.

ELEANOR   What dreamed my lord? Tell me, and I'll requite it
With sweet rehearsal of my morning's dream.

25   GLOUCESTER   Methought this staff, mine office-badge in court,
Was broke in twain: by whom I have forgot,
But, as I think, it was by th'cardinal:
And on the pieces of the broken wand
Were placed the heads of Edmund Duke of Somerset,
30   And William de la Pole, first Duke of Suffolk.
This was my dream: what it doth bode, God knows.

ELEANOR   Tut, this was nothing but an argument
That he that breaks a stick of Gloucester's grove

---

4 **As** as though   5 **sullen** drab, somber, dull in color   8 **Enchased** adorned, decorated as
with jewels   9 **grovel** lie facedown, prostrate   12 **is't** is your arm   16 **vouchsafe** allow
18 **canker** infection, ulcer   19 **imagine ill** formulate evil plans   21 **breathing** breath
22 **this night** last night   23 **requite** repay, recompense   24 **rehearsal** recounting
morning's dream according to popular belief, morning dreams were supposed to tell the truth
25 **staff** formal rod of office   **office-badge** badge of office   26 **twain** two   32 **an argument**
proof, evidence   33 **breaks . . . grove** i.e. damages Gloucester in the slightest

Shall lose his head for his presumption.
35 But list to me, my Humphrey, my sweet duke:
Methought I sat in seat of majesty
In the cathedral church of Westminster,
And in that chair where kings and queens are crowned,
Where Henry and Dame Margaret kneeled to me
40 And on my head did set the diadem.

GLOUCESTER   Nay, Eleanor, then must I chide outright:
Presumptuous dame, ill-nurtured Eleanor,
Art thou not second woman in the realm,
And the Protector's wife, beloved of him?
45 Hast thou not worldly pleasure at command,
Above the reach or compass of thy thought?
And wilt thou still be hammering treachery,
To tumble down thy husband and thyself
From top of honour to disgrace's feet?
50 Away from me, and let me hear no more!

ELEANOR   What, what, my lord? Are you so choleric
With Eleanor for telling but her dream?
Next time I'll keep my dreams unto myself,
And not be checked.

55 GLOUCESTER   Nay, be not angry: I am pleased again.

Enter [a] Messenger

MESSENGER   My Lord Protector, 'tis his highness' pleasure
You do prepare to ride unto St Albans,
Where as the king and queen do mean to hawk.

GLOUCESTER   I go. Come, Nell, thou wilt ride with us?

60 ELEANOR   Yes, my good lord, I'll follow presently.

Exit Humphrey [Duke of Gloucester with Messenger]

Follow I must: I cannot go before,
While Gloucester bears this base and humble mind.

---

35 **list** listen   38 **chair** throne   41 **chide** rebuke   42 **ill-nurtured** ill-mannered, poorly bred
44 **of** by   46 **compass** scope, limit   47 **hammering** thinking insistently on/devising
51 **choleric** angry (choler was one of the four bodily humors thought to govern temperament)
52 **but** only   54 **checked** scolded   57 **St Albans** town about twenty-five miles north of
London   58 **Where as** where   **hawk** hunt with trained hawks   60 **presently** immediately/
shortly   62 **base** unambitious, lowly

Were I a man, a duke, and next of blood,
I would remove these tedious stumbling blocks
65   And smooth my way upon their headless necks.
And, being a woman, I will not be slack
To play my part in Fortune's pageant.—
Where are you there? Sir John! Nay, fear not, man,   *Calling*
We are alone: here's none but thee and I.

Enter Hume

70   HUME   Jesus preserve your royal majesty.
     ELEANOR   What say'st thou? 'Majesty': I am but grace.
     HUME   But by the grace of God, and Hume's advice,
               Your grace's title shall be multiplied.
     ELEANOR   What say'st thou, man? Hast thou as yet conferred
75   With Margery Jordan, the cunning witch,
               With Roger Bullingbrook, the conjurer?
               And will they undertake to do me good?
     HUME   This they have promised to show your highness:
               A spirit raised from depth of underground,
80   That shall make answer to such questions
               As by your grace shall be propounded him.
     ELEANOR   It is enough: I'll think upon the questions:
               When from St Albans we do make return,
               We'll see these things effected to the full.
85   Here, Hume, take this reward: make merry, man,   *Giving him*
               With thy confederates in this weighty cause.   *money*

                                              Exit Eleanor

     HUME   Hume must make merry with the duchess' gold:
               Marry, and shall: but how now, Sir John Hume?
               Seal up your lips, and give no words but mum:
90   The business asketh silent secrecy.
               Dame Eleanor gives gold to bring the witch:
               Gold cannot come amiss, were she a devil.

---

67 **pageant** spectacle, entertainment   68 **Sir** conventional form of address for clergymen
71 **grace** the correct term of address for a duchess   73 **multiplied** amplified, increased
75 **cunning** skilled in magic   76 **conjurer** magician, one who conjures spirits
81 **propounded** asked of, put to   88 **Marry** by the Virgin Mary   89 **mum** silence

Yet have I gold flies from another coast:
I dare not say from the rich cardinal
95 And from the great and new-made Duke of Suffolk,
Yet I do find it so: for to be plain,
They, knowing Dame Eleanor's aspiring humour,
Have hired me to undermine the duchess
And buzz these conjurations in her brain.
100 They say 'A crafty knave does need no broker',
Yet am I Suffolk and the cardinal's broker.
Hume, if you take not heed, you shall go near
To call them both a pair of crafty knaves.
Well, so it stands: and thus, I fear, at last
105 Hume's knavery will be the duchess' wrack,
And her attainture will be Humphrey's fall:
Sort how it will, I shall have gold for all.   *Exit*

[Act 1 Scene 3]   *running scene 3*

Enter three or four Petitioners, [Peter] the armourer's man being one

FIRST PETITIONER   My masters, let's stand close: my Lord Protector
will come this way by and by, and then we may deliver our
supplications in the quill.

SECOND PETITIONER   Marry, the Lord protect him, for he's a good
5   man, Jesu bless him.

Enter Suffolk and Queen [Margaret]

FIRST PETITIONER   Here a comes, methinks, and the queen with
him. I'll be the first, sure.   *He goes to meet Suffolk*

SECOND PETITIONER   Come back, fool: this is the   *and the Queen*
Duke of Suffolk, and not my Lord Protector.

10 SUFFOLK   How now, fellow: wouldst anything with me?

93 flies that flies, comes   coast quarter, source   97 aspiring humour ambitious frame of
mind   99 buzz whisper   conjurations incantations   100 broker agent, go-between
102 go near come close   105 wrack wreck, ruin   106 attainture conviction for treason
107 Sort . . . will however it falls out   1.3 *Location: the royal court, London*
Petitioners those with formal requests to make to those in authority   armourer's man
servant or apprentice to a maker of armor   1 My masters gentlemen   close near one
another as a group   3 in the quill as a group; possibly "in their written forms"   4 protect
plays on the title of Lord Protector   6 a he   10 wouldst do you want

FIRST PETITIONER   I pray, my lord, pardon me: I took ye for my
    Lord Protector.

QUEEN MARGARET   'To my Lord Protector!'— Are your   *Reading*
    supplications to his lordship? Let me see them: what is thine?

15   FIRST PETITIONER   Mine is, an't please your grace, against John
    Goodman, my lord cardinal's man, for keeping my house
    and lands and wife and all from me.

SUFFOLK   Thy wife too? That's some wrong indeed.—   *To Second*
    What's yours?   *Petitioner*

20   What's here?— 'Against the Duke of Suffolk, for   *Reading*
    enclosing the commons of Melford.'— How now,   *supplication*
    Sir Knave?   *To Second*

SECOND PETITIONER   Alas, sir, I am but a poor petitioner   *Petitioner*
    of our whole township.

25   PETER   Against my master, Thomas Horner, for   *Offering his*
    saying that the Duke of York was rightful heir to the   *petition*
    crown.

QUEEN MARGARET   What say'st thou? Did the Duke of York say he
    was rightful heir to the crown?

30   PETER   That my master was? No, forsooth: my master said
    that he was, and that the king was an usurper.

SUFFOLK   Who is there?

Enter Servant

Take this fellow in, and send for his master with a pursuivant
presently.— We'll hear more of your matter before the king.

                 Exit [Servant with Peter]

35   QUEEN MARGARET   And as for you that love to be protected
    Under the wings of our Protector's grace,
    Begin your suits anew, and sue to him.   *Tears the supplication*
    Away, base cullions!— Suffolk, let them go.

ALL [PETITIONERS]   Come, let's be gone.   *Exeunt [Petitioners]*

40   QUEEN MARGARET   My lord of Suffolk, say, is this the guise?
    Is this the fashions in the court of England?

---

15 an't if it   **16 man** servant, agent   **21 enclosing the commons** fencing in common land available to all and converting it to private use   **30 forsooth** in truth   **33 pursuivant** state messenger with the power to execute warrants   **37 sue to** entreat   **38 cullions** rogues, wretches   **40 guise** manner, style   **41 fashions** customs, practices

Is this the government of Britain's isle?
And this the royalty of Albion's king?
What, shall King Henry be a pupil still
45   Under the surly Gloucester's governance?
Am I a queen in title and in style,
And must be made a subject to a duke?
I tell thee, Pole, when in the city Tours
Thou ran'st a-tilt in honour of my love
50   And stol'st away the ladies' hearts of France,
I thought King Henry had resemblèd thee
In courage, courtship and proportion:
But all his mind is bent to holiness,
To number Ave-Maries on his beads:
55   His champions are the prophets and apostles,
His weapons holy saws of sacred writ,
His study is his tilt-yard, and his loves
Are brazen images of canonizèd saints.
I would the college of the cardinals
60   Would choose him Pope, and carry him to Rome,
And set the triple crown upon his head:
That were a state fit for his holiness.

SUFFOLK   Madam, be patient: as I was cause
Your highness came to England, so will I
65   In England work your grace's full content.

QUEEN MARGARET   Beside the haughty Protector, have we
    Beaufort
The imperious churchman, Somerset, Buckingham,
And grumbling York: and not the least of these
But can do more in England than the king.

---

43 Albion ancient name for England   **46 style** mode of address, formal title   **48 Pole** de la
Pole, Suffolk's family name   **49 ran'st a-tilt** took part in a jousting tournament
52 proportion physical form   **53 bent** directed   **54 number** count   **Ave-Maries** Hail Marys,
prayers frequently recited over a rosary   **beads** rosary   **55 champions** most admired
combatants/defenders, those who fight on behalf of another   **56 saws** sayings, maxims
57 tilt-yard tournament ground   **58 brazen images** bronze statues   **59 college . . .
cardinals** highest council of the Catholic Church, responsible for electing new Popes
61 triple crown i.e. the crown worn by the Pope   **62 state** status   **his holiness** plays on the
Pope's official title   **65 work** enable, effect   **68 not . . . But** even the least of them

70   SUFFOLK   And he of these that can do most of all
               Cannot do more in England than the Nevilles:
               Salisbury and Warwick are no simple peers.
      QUEEN MARGARET   Not all these lords do vex me half so much
               As that proud dame, the Lord Protector's wife:
75   She sweeps it through the court with troops of ladies,
               More like an empress than Duke Humphrey's wife:
               Strangers in court do take her for the queen:
               She bears a duke's revenues on her back,
               And in her heart she scorns our poverty:
80   Shall I not live to be avenged on her?
               Contemptuous base-born callet as she is,
               She vaunted 'mongst her minions t'other day,
               The very train of her worst wearing gown
               Was better worth than all my father's lands,
85   Till Suffolk gave two dukedoms for his daughter.
      SUFFOLK   Madam, myself have limed a bush for her,
               And placed a choir of such enticing birds,
               That she will light to listen to the lays,
               And never mount to trouble you again.
90   So let her rest: and, madam, list to me,
               For I am bold to counsel you in this:
               Although we fancy not the cardinal,
               Yet must we join with him and with the lords,
               Till we have brought Duke Humphrey in disgrace.
95   As for the Duke of York, this late complaint
               Will make but little for his benefit:
               So one by one we'll weed them all at last,
               And you yourself shall steer the happy helm.

---

72 simple ordinary, humble   **75 sweeps it** parades, struts   **77 Strangers** foreigners
78 bears . . . back i.e. dresses in a magnificent style   **revenues** wealth, income
81 Contemptuous contemptible/scornful   **callet** whore   **82 vaunted** boasted   **minions**
favorites   **83 worst wearing** most unfashionable   **84 better worth** worth more   **85 Till . . .
daughter** before Suffolk handed over two dukedoms (Anjou and Maine) as part of the dowry
from Henry VI   **86 limed a bush** created a trap (from the process of smearing twigs with
birdlime, a sticky substance used to catch birds)   **87 enticing birds** i.e. decoys   **88 light** alight
lays songs   **92 fancy** favor, incline to   **95 late complaint** i.e. Peter's allegation that his
master said York was the rightful heir to the throne   **96 make . . . benefit** do him little service
97 weed uproot, weed out

Sound a sennet. Enter the King [Henry VI with Somerset and] York [whispering on either side of him], Duke Humphrey [of Gloucester], Cardinal, Buckingham, Salisbury, Warwick and the Duchess [Eleanor]

KING HENRY VI   For my part, noble lords, I care not which:
100   Or Somerset or York, all's one to me.

YORK   If York have ill demeaned himself in France,
Then let him be denied the regentship.

SOMERSET   If Somerset be unworthy of the place,
Let York be regent: I will yield to him.

105   WARWICK   Whether your grace be worthy, yea or no,
Dispute not that: York is the worthier.

CARDINAL   Ambitious Warwick, let thy betters speak.

WARWICK   The cardinal's not my better in the field.

BUCKINGHAM   All in this presence are thy betters, Warwick.

110   WARWICK   Warwick may live to be the best of all.

SALISBURY   Peace, son, and show some reason, Buckingham,
Why Somerset should be preferred in this.

QUEEN MARGARET   Because the king, forsooth, will have it so.

GLOUCESTER   Madam, the king is old enough himself
115   To give his censure: these are no women's matters.

QUEEN MARGARET   If he be old enough, what needs your grace
To be Protector of his excellence?

GLOUCESTER   Madam, I am Protector of the realm,
And at his pleasure will resign my place.

120   SUFFOLK   Resign it then and leave thine insolence.
Since thou wert king — as who is king but thou? —
The commonwealth hath daily run to wrack,
The dauphin hath prevailed beyond the seas,
And all the peers and nobles of the realm
125   Have been as bondmen to thy sovereignty.

---

sennet trumpet call signaling a procession   **100 Or** either   **101 ill demeaned** badly conducted   **102 regentship** position of ruling in France on the king's behalf   **108 field** battlefield   **109 presence** royal reception chamber, presence of the king   **115 censure** judgment, opinion   **120 leave** stop, give up   **123 dauphin** title of the French king's eldest son, heir to the throne (here used to refer to Charles VII as the English considered Henry VI the rightful king of France)   **prevailed** gained in strength and influence   **125 bondmen** slaves

CARDINAL   The commons hast thou racked: the clergy's bags
     Are lank and lean with thy extortions.

SOMERSET   Thy sumptuous buildings and thy wife's attire
     Have cost a mass of public treasury.

130 BUCKINGHAM   Thy cruelty in execution
     Upon offenders hath exceeded law,
     And left thee to the mercy of the law.

QUEEN MARGARET   Thy sale of offices and towns in France,
     If they were known, as the suspect is great,
135   Would make thee quickly hop without thy head.

Exit Gloucester

Queen Margaret drops her fan

     Give me my fan: what, minion, can ye not?   *To Eleanor*
She gives the Duchess [Eleanor] a box on the ear
     I cry you mercy, madam: was it you?

ELEANOR   Was't I? Yea, I it was, proud Frenchwoman:
     Could I come near your beauty with my nails,
140   I'd set my ten commandments in your face.

KING HENRY VI   Sweet aunt, be quiet: 'twas against her will.

ELEANOR   Against her will, good king? Look to't in time,
     She'll hamper thee and dandle thee like a baby:
     Though in this place most master wear no breeches,
145   She shall not strike Dame Eleanor unrevenged.

Exit Eleanor

BUCKINGHAM   Lord Cardinal, I will follow Eleanor,
     And listen after Humphrey, how he proceeds:
     She's tickled now, her fury needs no spurs,
     She'll gallop far enough to her destruction.

Exit Buckingham

Enter Humphrey [Duke of Gloucester]

---

126 **racked** ruined, exhausted (through taxation)   **bags** moneybags   127 **lank** shrunken
129 **treasury** money   133 **offices** official functions, positions   134 **suspect** suspicion
135 **hop . . . head** be beheaded, executed   136 **minion** hussy, servant   137 **cry you mercy**
beg your pardon (sarcastic)   140 **set . . . commandments** i.e. scratch with my fingernails
141 **against her will** unintentional, a mistake   142 **Look to't** beware   143 **hamper** obstruct,
fetter   **dandle** pamper, pet   144 **most master** the greatest master (i.e. the queen)
147 **listen after** watch out for   148 **tickled** vexed, provoked

150   GLOUCESTER   Now, lords, my choler being overblown
With walking once about the quadrangle,
I come to talk of commonwealth affairs.
As for your spiteful false objections,
Prove them, and I lie open to the law:
155   But God in mercy so deal with my soul,
As I in duty love my king and country.
But to the matter that we have in hand:—
I say, my sovereign, York is meetest man
To be your regent in the realm of France.

160   SUFFOLK   Before we make election, give me leave
To show some reason, of no little force,
That York is most unmeet of any man.

YORK   I'll tell thee, Suffolk, why I am unmeet:
First, for I cannot flatter thee in pride:
165   Next, if I be appointed for the place,
My Lord of Somerset will keep me here,
Without discharge, money, or furniture,
Till France be won into the dauphin's hands:
Last time I danced attendance on his will
170   Till Paris was besieged, famished, and lost.

WARWICK   That can I witness, and a fouler fact
Did never traitor in the land commit.

SUFFOLK   Peace, headstrong Warwick.

WARWICK   Image of pride, why should I hold my peace?

Enter [guarded, Horner the] armourer and his man [Peter]

175   SUFFOLK   Because here is a man accused of treason:
Pray God the Duke of York excuse himself!

YORK   Doth anyone accuse York for a traitor?

KING HENRY VI   What mean'st thou, Suffolk? Tell me, what are
these?

SUFFOLK   Please it your majesty, this is the man   *Indicating Peter*
180   That doth accuse his master of high treason:

---

153 objections accusations   **158 meetest** the most suitable   **160 election** choice   **give me leave** permit me   **164 for . . . pride** because my self-respect will not allow me to flatter you/because I cannot flatter your pride   **167 discharge** payment   **furniture** military equipment   **171 fouler fact** more wicked deed, crime   **174 Image** embodiment   **177 for** of being   **178 what** who

His words were these: that Richard, Duke of York,
Was rightful heir unto the English crown
And that your majesty was an usurper.

KING HENRY VI   Say, man, were these thy words?

185 HORNER   An't shall please your majesty, I never said nor
thought any such matter: God is my witness, I am falsely
accused by the villain.

PETER   By these ten bones, my lords, he did   *Raising his*
speak them to me in the garret one night, as we   *hands*
190 were scouring my Lord of York's armour.

YORK   Base dunghill villain and mechanical,
I'll have thy head for this thy traitor's speech.—
I do beseech your royal majesty,
Let him have all the rigour of the law.

195 HORNER   Alas, my lord, hang me if ever I spake the words: my
accuser is my prentice, and when I did correct him for his
fault the other day, he did vow upon his knees he would be
even with me — I have good witness of this — therefore I
beseech your majesty, do not cast away an honest man for a
200 villain's accusation.

KING HENRY VI   Uncle, what shall we say to this in law?   *To Gloucester*

GLOUCESTER   This doom, my lord, if I may judge:
Let Somerset be regent o'er the French,
Because in York this breeds suspicion:

205 And let these have a day appointed them   *Indicating Horner and*
For single combat in convenient place,   *Peter*
For he hath witness of his servant's malice: *Indicating Horner*
This is the law, and this Duke Humphrey's doom.

SOMERSET   I humbly thank your royal majesty.

210 HORNER   And I accept the combat willingly.

PETER   Alas, my lord, I cannot fight: for God's sake, pity my
case: the spite of man prevaileth against me. O Lord, have

---

185 An't if it   **188 ten bones** i.e. fingers   **189 garret** turret, watchtower   **190 scouring**
cleaning   **191 mechanical** manual worker, laborer   **196 prentice** apprentice   **correct**
punish   **202 doom** judgment, sentence   **204 this** i.e. the business involving Peter and
Horner   **206 convenient** appropriate, suitable

mercy upon me! I shall never be able to fight a blow. O Lord, my heart!

215   GLOUCESTER   Sirrah, or you must fight, or else be hanged.

   KING HENRY VI   Away with them to prison, and the day
Of combat shall be the last of the next month.
Come, Somerset, we'll see thee sent away.   *Flourish. Exeunt*

[Act 1 Scene 4]

Enter the Witch [Margaret Jordan], the two priests [Hume and Southwell] and Bullingbrook

   HUME   Come, my masters, the duchess, I tell you, expects performance of your promises.

   BULLINGBROOK   Master Hume, we are therefore provided: will her ladyship behold and hear our exorcisms?

5   HUME   Ay, what else? Fear you not her courage.

   BULLINGBROOK   I have heard her reported to be a woman of an invincible spirit: but it shall be convenient, Master Hume, that you be by her aloft, while we be busy below: and so, I pray you, go in God's name and leave us.   *Exit Hume*

10   Mother Jordan, be you prostrate and grovel on   *She lies down*
the earth. John Southwell, read you, and let us   *upon her face*
to our work.

Enter Eleanor aloft [Hume following]

   ELEANOR   Well said, my masters, and welcome all. To this gear the sooner the better.

15   BULLINGBROOK   Patience, good lady: wizards know their times:
Deep night, dark night, the silent of the night,
The time of night when Troy was set on fire,
The time when screech-owls cry and bandogs howl,

---

215 **Sirrah** sir (used to an inferior) **or** either **1.4** *Location: the residence of the Duke of Gloucester* 3 **therefore provided** equipped to that end 4 **exorcisms** conjuring up of spirits *aloft* i.e. on the upper staging level or gallery 13 **said** done **gear** business, matter 17 **Troy . . . fire** under cover of darkness the city of Troy was set on fire and destroyed by the Greeks, who had entered the city concealed in the Trojan horse 18 **screech-owls** barn owls, so-named from their discordant cry and considered birds of ill omen **bandogs** fierce tied-up watchdogs

And spirits walk, and ghosts break up their graves:

20   That time best fits the work we have in hand.

Madam, sit you and fear not: whom we raise,

We will make fast within a hallowed verge.

Here [they] do the ceremonies belonging, and make the circle:
Bullingbrook or Southwell reads, 'Conjuro te', etc. It thunders and
lightens terribly: then the Spirit [Asnath] riseth

ASNATH   Adsum.

MARGARET JORDAN   Asnath,

25   By the eternal God, whose name and power

Thou tremblest at, answer that I shall ask:

For till thou speak, thou shalt not pass from hence.

ASNATH   Ask what thou wilt: that I had said and done.

BULLINGBROOK   'First of the king: what shall of him   *Reads*
      become?'

30   ASNATH   The duke yet lives that Henry shall depose:

But him outlive, and die a violent death.   *As the Spirit speaks,*

BULLINGBROOK   'What fates await the Duke of   *Reads*   *Southwell*
      Suffolk?'   *writes the answer*

ASNATH   By water shall he die, and take his end.

BULLINGBROOK   'What shall befall the Duke of Somerset?'   *Reads*

35   ASNATH   Let him shun castles;

Safer shall he be upon the sandy plains

Than where castles mounted stand.

Have done, for more I hardly can endure.

BULLINGBROOK   Descend to darkness and the burning lake!

40   False fiend, avoid!   *Thunder and lightning.   Exit Spirit*
Enter the Duke of York and the Duke of Buckingham with their guard
[Sir Humphrey Stafford as Captain] and break in

YORK   Lay hands upon these traitors and their trash:

Beldam, I think we watched you at an inch.   *To Jordan*

---

19 up open, out of   **22 make fast** secure, restrain   **hallowed verge** magic circle   *belonging*
necessary, appropriate   *'Conjuro te'* "I conjure you" (Latin; the beginning of an invocation)
Asnath an anagram of "Sathan," i.e. Satan   *riseth* presumably through a trapdoor
23 *Adsum* "I am here" (Latin)   **26 that** that which   **28 that** i.e. would that (I wish that)
37 mounted situated on a mount   **40 False** treacherous   **avoid** be gone   **41 trash** rubbish,
paraphernalia   **42 Beldam** hag, witch   **at an inch** very closely

What, madam, are you there? The king and commonweal
Are deeply indebted for this piece of pains:
45   My Lord Protector will, I doubt it not,
See you well guerdoned for these good deserts.

ELEANOR   Not half so bad as thine to England's king,
Injurious duke, that threatest where's no cause.

BUCKINGHAM   True, madam, none at all: what call you
    this?   *Pointing to the papers*
50   Away with them: let them be clapped up close
And kept asunder.— You, madam, shall with us.   *To Eleanor*
Stafford, take her to thee.

                  [*Exeunt above Eleanor and Hume, guarded*]
We'll see your trinkets here all forthcoming.
All, away!

             Exeunt [*below guard with Margaret Jordan, Southwell and*
                                      Bullingbrook]

55   YORK   Lord Buckingham, methinks you watched her well:
A pretty plot, well chosen to build upon.
Now pray, my lord, let's see the devil's writ.   *Buckingham gives*
What have we here?   *him the papers*
'The duke yet lives, that Henry shall depose: *Reads*
60   But him outlive, and die a violent death.'
Why, this is just
'Aio Aeacidam, Romanos vincere posse.'
Well, to the rest:
'Tell me what fate awaits the Duke of Suffolk?'
65   'By water shall he die, and take his end.'
'What shall betide the Duke of Somerset?'
'Let him shun castles:

---

44 piece of pains trouble you have taken   **46 guerdoned** rewarded   **deserts** deserving
deeds   **48 Injurious** insulting   **threatest** threatens   **50 clapped up close** securely locked up
51 asunder apart   **52 to** with   **53 trinkets** trifles, rubbish (used for conjuring)   **all
forthcoming** safe and ready to be produced as evidence in court   **56 pretty** artful, cunning
plot scheme/plot of land   **57 devil's writ** as opposed to "holy writ," i.e. Scripture   **61 just**
exactly   **62 'Aio . . . posse'** words spoken by the oracle at Delphi to Pyrrhus when he asked
whether he would conquer Rome; they may be interpreted to mean either "I proclaim that you,
the descendant of Aeacus, can conquer the Romans" or "I proclaim that the Romans can
conquer you, the descendant of Aeacus"

Safer shall he be upon the sandy plains
Than where castles mounted stand.'
70   Come, come, my lords,
These oracles are hardly attained,
And hardly understood.
The king is now in progress towards St Albans,
With him the husband of this lovely lady:
75   Thither goes these news as fast as horse can carry them:
A sorry breakfast for my Lord Protector.

BUCKINGHAM   Your grace shall give me leave, my lord of York,
To be the post in hope of his reward.

YORK   At your pleasure, my good lord. Who's within
there, ho!   *Calling within*

Enter a Servingman

80   Invite my lords of Salisbury and Warwick
To sup with me tomorrow night. Away.   *Exeunt [severally]*

[Act 2 Scene 1]   *running scene 5*

Enter the King [Henry VI], Queen [Margaret], Protector [Gloucester],
Cardinal and Suffolk, with Falconers hallooing

QUEEN MARGARET   Believe me, lords, for flying at the brook,
I saw not better sport these seven years' day:
Yet, by your leave, the wind was very high,
And, ten to one, old Joan had not gone out.
5   KING HENRY VI   But what a point, my lord, your falcon
made,   *To Gloucester*
And what a pitch she flew above the rest:

---

71 **hardly attained** obtained with difficulty   72 **hardly** barely   73 **in progress** on a state
journey or procession   78 **post** messenger   81 **sup** take supper   *severally* separately
2.1   *Location: St. Albans (a town about twenty-five miles north of London)*   *hallooing*
calling out to the dogs   1 **flying . . . brook** hunting waterfowl by using dogs to drive the birds
from the bankside bushes so that trained hawks might swoop upon them   2 **these . . . day** for
the last seven years, i.e. for a long time (proverbial)   4 **And . . . out** i.e. the odds were against
the hawk Joan being able to fly (letting birds out in a high wind risked losing them)   5 **point**
advantageous position from which to swoop on the fowl   6 **pitch** height (literally, the highest
point in a falcon's flight)

To see how God in all his creatures works!
Yea, man and birds are fain of climbing high.

SUFFOLK   No marvel, an it like your majesty,
10   My Lord Protector's hawks do tower so well:
They know their master loves to be aloft,
And bears his thoughts above his falcon's pitch.

GLOUCESTER   My lord, 'tis but a base ignoble mind
That mounts no higher than a bird can soar.

15   CARDINAL   I thought as much: he would be above the clouds.

GLOUCESTER   Ay, my lord cardinal, how think you by that?
Were it not good your grace could fly to heaven?

KING HENRY VI   The treasury of everlasting joy.

CARDINAL   Thy heaven is on earth: thine eyes and thoughts
20   Beat on a crown, the treasure of thy heart,
Pernicious Protector, dangerous peer,
That smooth'st it so with king and commonweal!

GLOUCESTER   What, cardinal?
Is your priesthood grown peremptory?
25   *Tantaene animis coelestibus irae?*
Churchmen so hot? Good uncle, hide such malice:
With such holiness, can you do it?

SUFFOLK   No malice, sir, no more than well becomes
So good a quarrel and so bad a peer.

30   GLOUCESTER   As who, my lord?

SUFFOLK   Why, as you, my lord,
An't like your lordly Lord's Protectorship.

GLOUCESTER   Why, Suffolk, England knows thine insolence.

QUEEN MARGARET   And thy ambition, Gloucester.

35   KING HENRY VI   I prithee, peace, good queen,
And whet not on these furious peers,
For blessèd are the peacemakers on earth.

---

8 **fain of** inclined to, fond of   9 **an it like** if it please   10 **tower** soar in circling movements to
the highest point   11 **aloft** up high, dominant   16 **how . . . that** what do you mean by that
21 **Pernicious** destructive, wicked   22 **smooth'st it** flatters, speaks plausibly   24 **peremptory**
unchallengeable, overbearing   25 *Tantaene . . . irae*? "Is there so much anger in heavenly
minds?" (Latin; from Virgil's *Aeneid*, 1.11)   26 **hot** hot-tempered, angry   36 **whet not on** do
not encourage   37 **blessèd . . . earth** biblical; the king cites Matthew 5:9

CARDINAL Let me be blessèd for the peace I make
Against this proud Protector, with my sword.

40 GLOUCESTER Faith, holy uncle, would't were come to
that.   *Gloucester and*

CARDINAL Marry, when thou dar'st.   *Cardinal speak aside*

GLOUCESTER Make up no factious numbers for the matter,
In thine own person answer thy abuse.

CARDINAL Ay, where thou dar'st not peep: an if thou dar'st,

45 This evening, on the east side of the grove.

KING HENRY VI How now, my lords?

CARDINAL Believe me, cousin Gloucester,
Had not your man put up the fowl so suddenly,
We had had more sport.— Come with thy two-hand sword.

50 GLOUCESTER True, uncle.—
Are ye advised? The east side of the grove?

CARDINAL I am with you.

KING HENRY VI Why, how now, uncle Gloucester?

GLOUCESTER Talking of hawking; nothing else, my lord.—

55 Now, by God's mother, priest, I'll shave your crown for this,
Or all my fence shall fail.

CARDINAL *Medice, teipsum*—
Protector, see to't well, protect yourself.

KING HENRY VI The winds grow high: so do your stomachs,
lords:

60 How irksome is this music to my heart!
When such strings jar, what hope of harmony?
I pray, my lords, let me compound this strife.

Enter one [Townsman] crying 'A miracle!'

GLOUCESTER What means this noise?
Fellow, what miracle dost thou proclaim?

---

41 Marry by the Virgin Mary   **42 Make . . . matter** do not bring any of your supporters into
the business   **43 abuse** wrongdoing, insult (to me)   **44 peep** appear, show your face   **an if**
if   **48 your man** i.e. the falconer   **put up** raised, provoked from cover into flight   **49 had
had** would have had   **two-hand sword** long, heavy sword   **51 Are ye advised?** Do you
understand?   **55 God's mother** i.e. the Virgin Mary   **crown** the tonsure, the shaved crown of
a priest's head   **56 fence** fencing skills, swordsmanship   **57 *Medice, teipsum*** "Physician,
heal thyself" (Latin; from the Bible, Luke 4:23)   **59 stomachs** tempers, angry appetites
61 jar sound discordant   **62 compound** settle

65   TOWNSMAN   A miracle, a miracle!

SUFFOLK   Come to the king and tell him what miracle.

TOWNSMAN   Forsooth, a blind man at Saint Alban's shrine
Within this half-hour hath received his sight:
A man that ne'er saw in his life before.

70   KING HENRY VI   Now, God be praised, that to believing souls
Gives light in darkness, comfort in despair.

Enter the Mayor of St Albans, and his brethren, bearing the man
[Simpcox] between two in a chair, [Simpcox's Wife and Townspeople
following]

CARDINAL   Here comes the townsmen on procession,
To present your highness with the man.

KING HENRY VI   Great is his comfort in this earthly vale,
75   Although by his sight his sin be multiplied.

GLOUCESTER   Stand by, my masters, bring him near the king:
His highness' pleasure is to talk with him.

KING HENRY VI   Good fellow, tell us here the circumstance,
That we for thee may glorify the Lord.

80   What, hast thou been long blind and now restored?

SIMPCOX   Born blind, an't please your grace.

WIFE   Ay, indeed, was he.

SUFFOLK   What woman is this?

WIFE   His wife, an't like your worship.

85   GLOUCESTER   Hadst thou been his mother, thou couldst have
better told.

KING HENRY VI   Where wert thou born?   *To Simpcox*

SIMPCOX   At Berwick in the north, an't like your grace.

KING HENRY VI   Poor soul, God's goodness hath been great to
thee:

---

67 Forsooth in truth   **Saint Alban's shrine** allegedly the first Christian martyr in England,
Saint Alban was executed in the early fourth century for sheltering Christian converts
brethren members of the town corporation   **74 earthly vale** i.e. the earth, the mortal world
75 by ... multiplied i.e. as he will be subject to more temptations   **78 circumstance** details
85 thou ... told you would have been in a better position to say so (i.e. that he had been blind
from birth)   **87 Berwick** Berwick-upon-Tweed, town on the border between Scotland and
England

Let never day nor night unhallowed pass,

90   But still remember what the Lord hath done.

QUEEN MARGARET   Tell me, good fellow, cam'st thou   *To Simpcox*
here by chance,
Or of devotion, to this holy shrine?

SIMPCOX   God knows, of pure devotion, being called
A hundred times and oft'ner in my sleep,

95   By good Saint Alban, who said, 'Simon, come:
Come offer at my shrine, and I will help thee.'

WIFE   Most true, forsooth: and many time and oft
Myself have heard a voice to call him so.

CARDINAL   What, art thou lame?

100   SIMPCOX   Ay, God Almighty help me.

SUFFOLK   How cam'st thou so?

SIMPCOX   A fall off of a tree.

WIFE   A plum tree, master.

GLOUCESTER   How long hast thou been blind?

105   SIMPCOX   O, born so, master.

GLOUCESTER   What, and wouldst climb a tree?

SIMPCOX   But that in all my life, when I was a youth.

WIFE   Too true, and bought his climbing very dear.

GLOUCESTER   Mass, thou lov'dst plums well, that wouldst
venture so.

110   SIMPCOX   Alas, good master, my wife desired some damsons,
And made me climb, with danger of my life.

GLOUCESTER   A subtle knave, but yet it shall not serve:
Let me see thine eyes: wink now: now open them:
In my opinion, yet thou see'st not well.

115   SIMPCOX   Yes, master, clear as day, I thank God and Saint
Alban.

GLOUCESTER   Say'st thou me so: what colour is this cloak of?

SIMPCOX   Red, master, red as blood.

---

89 **unhallowed pass** i.e. pass without saying your prayers   **unhallowed** unholy   90 **still**
continually   92 **of** out of, from   96 **offer** make an offering   102 **fall . . . tree** "climbing a
plum tree" could be euphemistic for copulation   107 **But that** only that time, once
109 **Mass** by the (religious) Mass   110 **damsons** plays on sense of "testicles"   111 **climb**
plays on sense of "mount sexually"   112 **subtle** crafty   **shall not serve** will not hold, suffice
113 **wink** close your eyes   114 **yet** still   116 **Say'st . . . so** do you say so

GLOUCESTER   Why, that's well said: what colour is my gown of?

SIMPCOX   Black, forsooth, coal-black as jet.

120 KING HENRY VI   Why, then, thou know'st what colour jet is of?

SUFFOLK   And yet, I think, jet did he never see.

GLOUCESTER   But cloaks and gowns, before this day, a many.

WIFE   Never, before this day, in all his life.

GLOUCESTER   Tell me, sirrah, what's my name?

125 SIMPCOX   Alas, master, I know not.

GLOUCESTER   What's his name?

SIMPCOX   I know not.

GLOUCESTER   Nor his?

SIMPCOX   No, indeed, master.

130 GLOUCESTER   What's thine own name?

SIMPCOX   Saunder Simpcox, an if it please you, master.

GLOUCESTER   Then, Saunder, sit there, the lying'st knave in Christendom. If thou hadst been born blind, thou might'st as well have known all our names as thus to name the
135 several colours we do wear. Sight may distinguish of colours, but suddenly to nominate them all, it is impossible.— My lords, Saint Alban here hath done a miracle: and would ye not think his cunning to be great, that could restore this cripple to his legs again?

140 SIMPCOX   O master, that you could!

GLOUCESTER   My masters of St Albans, have you not beadles in your town, and things called whips?

MAYOR   Yes, my lord, if it please your grace.

GLOUCESTER   Then send for one presently.

145 MAYOR   Sirrah, go fetch the beadle hither straight.

Exit [a Townsperson]

GLOUCESTER   Now fetch me a stool hither by and by.— Now, sirrah, if you mean to save yourself from whipping, leap me over this stool and run away.

SIMPCOX   Alas, master, I am not able to stand alone: You go
150 about to torture me in vain.

---

122 **many** multitude   135 **several** various   **of** between   136 **nominate** name
138 **cunning** skill   141 **beadles** parish constables   144 **presently** immediately
145 **straight** straightaway   146 **by and by** immediately   149 **alone** unsupported

Enter a Beadle with whips

GLOUCESTER   Well, sir, we must have you find your legs.—
Sirrah beadle, whip him till he leap over that same stool.

BEADLE   I will, my lord.— Come on, sirrah, off with your
doublet quickly.

155 SIMPCOX   Alas, master, what shall I do? I am not able to stand.

*After the Beadle hath hit him once, he leaps over the stool and runs
away: and they follow and cry, 'A miracle!'*

KING HENRY VI   O God, see'st thou this, and bearest so long?

QUEEN MARGARET   It made me laugh to see the villain run.

GLOUCESTER   Follow the knave, and take this drab away.

WIFE   Alas, sir, we did it for pure need.

160 GLOUCESTER   Let them be whipped through every market town
Till they come to Berwick, from whence they came.

Exeunt [Wife, Beadle, Mayor and Townspeople]

CARDINAL   Duke Humphrey has done a miracle today.

SUFFOLK   True: made the lame to leap and fly away.

GLOUCESTER   But you have done more miracles than I:

165 You made in a day, my lord, whole towns to fly.

Enter Buckingham

KING HENRY VI   What tidings with our cousin Buckingham?

BUCKINGHAM   Such as my heart doth tremble to unfold:
A sort of naughty persons, lewdly bent,
Under the countenance and confederacy

170 Of Lady Eleanor, the Protector's wife,
The ringleader and head of all this rout,
Have practised dangerously against your state,
Dealing with witches and with conjurers,
Whom we have apprehended in the fact,

175 Raising up wicked spirits from under ground,
Demanding of King Henry's life and death,

---

154 **doublet** close-fitting jacket   156 **bearest** (do you) endure it   158 **drab** whore
165 **towns** i.e. the French towns given away as part of Margaret's dowry   168 **sort** gang
naughty wicked, villainous   **lewdly bent** bent on evil   169 **Under . . . confederacy**
supported by and in collusion with   171 **rout** gang, crowd   172 **practised** plotted
174 **apprehended . . . fact** caught in the act, arrested as they committed the crime
176 **Demanding of** asking about

And other of your highness' Privy Council,

As more at large your grace shall understand.

CARDINAL   And so, my Lord Protector, by this means

180   Your lady is forthcoming yet at London.

This news, I think, hath turned your weapon's edge:

'Tis like, my lord, you will not keep your hour.

GLOUCESTER   Ambitious churchman, leave to afflict my heart:

Sorrow and grief have vanquished all my powers:

185   And, vanquished as I am, I yield to thee,

Or to the meanest groom.

KING HENRY VI   O God, what mischiefs work the wicked ones,

Heaping confusion on their own heads thereby!

QUEEN MARGARET   Gloucester, see here the tainture of thy nest,

190   And look thyself be faultless, thou wert best.

GLOUCESTER   Madam, for myself, to heaven I do appeal,

How I have loved my king and commonweal:

And for my wife, I know not how it stands:

Sorry I am to hear what I have heard.

195   Noble she is: but if she have forgot

Honour and virtue and conversed with such

As, like to pitch, defile nobility,

I banish her my bed and company

And give her as a prey to law and shame,

200   That hath dishonoured Gloucester's honest name.

KING HENRY VI   Well, for this night we will repose us here:

Tomorrow toward London back again,

To look into this business thoroughly

And call these foul offenders to their answers,

205   And poise the cause in justice' equal scales,

Whose beam stands sure, whose rightful cause prevails.

Flourish. Exeunt

178 **at large** at length   180 **forthcoming yet** in custody, awaiting trial   181 **turned** blunted
182 **like** likely   **hour** appointed time   183 **leave to afflict** stop tormenting   186 **meanest
groom** humblest servingman   188 **confusion** destruction, devastation   189 **tainture**
defilement   190 **look** make sure, take care   193 **how it stands** the full circumstances
196 **conversed** kept company, associated   197 **like to pitch** resembling pitch (a black, tarlike
substance)   205 **poise** weigh, balance   **cause** court case   206 **beam stands sure** scales
are evenly balanced

[Act 2 Scene 2]   *running scene 6*

Enter York, Salisbury and Warwick

YORK   Now, my good lords of Salisbury and Warwick,
              Our simple supper ended, give me leave
              In this close walk to satisfy myself
              In craving your opinion of my title,
5   Which is infallible, to England's crown.
SALISBURY   My lord, I long to hear it at full.
WARWICK   Sweet York, begin: and if thy claim be good,
              The Nevilles are thy subjects to command.
YORK   Then thus:
10   Edward the Third, my lords, had seven sons:
              The first, Edward the Black Prince, Prince of Wales;
              The second, William of Hatfield: and the third,
              Lionel Duke of Clarence: next to whom
              Was John of Gaunt, the Duke of Lancaster;
15   The fifth was Edmund Langley, Duke of York;
              The sixth was Thomas of Woodstock, Duke of Gloucester;
              William of Windsor was the seventh and last.
              Edward the Black Prince died before his father,
              And left behind him Richard, his only son,
20   Who, after Edward the Third's death, reigned as king,
              Till Henry Bullingbrook, Duke of Lancaster,
              The eldest son and heir of John of Gaunt,
              Crowned by the name of Henry the Fourth,
              Seized on the realm, deposed the rightful king,
25   Sent his poor queen to France, from whence she came,
              And him to Pomfret: where, as all you know,
              Harmless Richard was murdered traitorously.
WARWICK   Father, the duke hath told the truth:
              Thus got the house of Lancaster the crown.
30   YORK   Which now they hold by force and not by right:
              For Richard, the first son's heir, being dead,
              The issue of the next son should have reigned.

2.2   *Location: York's private garden*   3 close secluded, private   **19 Richard** i.e.
Richard II   **26 Pomfret** Pontefract, near York   **32 issue** offspring

SALISBURY   But William of Hatfield died without an heir.

YORK   The third son, Duke of Clarence, from whose line

35   I claim the crown, had issue Philippa, a daughter,
Who married Edmund Mortimer, Earl of March.
Edmund had issue, Roger Earl of March;
Roger had issue, Edmund, Anne and Eleanor.

SALISBURY   This Edmund, in the reign of Bullingbrook,

40   As I have read, laid claim unto the crown,
And but for Owen Glendower, had been king,
Who kept him in captivity till he died.
But to the rest.

YORK   His eldest sister, Anne,

45   My mother, being heir unto the crown,
Married Richard Earl of Cambridge, who was son
To Edmund Langley, Edward the Third's fifth son.
By her I claim the kingdom: she was heir
To Roger Earl of March, who was the son

50   Of Edmund Mortimer, who married Philippe,
Sole daughter unto Lionel Duke of Clarence.
So, if the issue of the elder son
Succeed before the younger, I am king.

WARWICK   What plain proceedings is more plain than this?

55   Henry doth claim the crown from John of Gaunt,
The fourth son: York claims it from the third:
Till Lionel's issue fails, his should not reign.
It fails not yet, but flourishes in thee
And in thy sons, fair slips of such a stock.

60   Then, father Salisbury, kneel we together,
And in this private plot be we the first
That shall salute our rightful sovereign
With honour of his birthright to the crown.

---

38 Edmund i.e. Edmund Mortimer, fifth Earl of March, declared heir presumptive by Richard II
39 This Edmund following an error in the historical sources he used, Shakespeare now
confuses Edmund Mortimer with his uncle of the same name, the man who was captured by
Welsh rebel leader **Owen Glendower** but went on to marry Glendower's daughter and fight on
the rebel side   **42 Who** i.e. Glendower   **captivity . . . died** another error   **54 proceedings**
line of descent   **57 issue** descendants, line of descent   **fails** dies out, comes to an end
59 slips cuttings   **stock** tree   **61 plot** ground

BOTH	Long live our sovereign Richard, England's king!

65   YORK   We thank you, lords: but I am not your king
     Till I be crowned and that my sword be stained
     With heart-blood of the house of Lancaster:
     And that's not suddenly to be performed,
     But with advice and silent secrecy.
70   Do you as I do in these dangerous days:
     Wink at the Duke of Suffolk's insolence,
     At Beaufort's pride, at Somerset's ambition,
     At Buckingham, and all the crew of them,
     Till they have snared the shepherd of the flock,
75   That virtuous prince, the good Duke Humphrey:
     'Tis that they seek, and they, in seeking that,
     Shall find their deaths, if York can prophesy.

SALISBURY   My lord, break we off: we know your mind at full.

WARWICK   My heart assures me that the Earl of Warwick
80   Shall one day make the Duke of York a king.

YORK   And, Neville, this I do assure myself:
     Richard shall live to make the Earl of Warwick
     The greatest man in England but the king.   *Exeunt*

[Act 2 Scene 3]   *running scene 7*

---

*Sound trumpets. Enter the King [Henry VI] and state [Queen
Margaret, Gloucester, Suffolk, Buckingham and Cardinal], with Guard,
to banish the Duchess [Eleanor, with Margaret Jordan, Southwell,
Hume and Bullingbrook, all guarded. Enter to them York, Salisbury
and Warwick]*

KING HENRY VI   Stand forth, Dame Eleanor Cobham,
     Gloucester's wife:
     In sight of God, and us, your guilt is great:
     Receive the sentence of the law for sins

---

65 **We** York uses the royal pronoun   66 **that** until the time that   68 **suddenly** immediately/
impetuously   69 **with advice** advisedly, prudently   71 **Wink at** shut your eyes to, ignore
81 **Neville** Warwick's family name   83 **but** except for   **2.3**   *Location: London, a place of
judgment (exact location unspecified)*

Such as by God's book are adjudged to death.—

5　You four, from hence to prison back again:

From thence unto the place of execution:

The witch in Smithfield shall be burned to ashes,

And you three shall be strangled on the gallows.

You, madam, for you are more nobly born,

10　Despoilèd of your honour in your life,

Shall, after three days' open penance done,

Live in your country here in banishment,

With Sir John Stanley, in the Isle of Man.

ELEANOR　Welcome is banishment, welcome were my death.

15　GLOUCESTER　Eleanor, the law, thou see'st, hath judged thee:

I cannot justify whom the law condemns.—

[Exeunt Eleanor and other prisoners, guarded]

Mine eyes are full of tears, my heart of grief.

Ah, Humphrey, this dishonour in thine age

Will bring thy head with sorrow to the ground.

20　I beseech your majesty, give me leave to go:

Sorrow would solace and mine age would ease.

KING HENRY VI　Stay, Humphrey Duke of Gloucester: ere thou go,

Give up thy staff: Henry will to himself

Protector be, and God shall be my hope,

25　My stay, my guide, and lantern to my feet:

And go in peace, Humphrey, no less beloved

Than when thou wert Protector to thy king.

QUEEN MARGARET　I see no reason why a king of years

Should be to be protected like a child:

30　God and King Henry govern England's realm:

Give up your staff, sir, and the king his realm.

---

4 God's book i.e. the Bible　**adjudged to** judged in advance to be worthy of　**7 Smithfield** area in the City of London; the customary place for the execution of heretics　**8 strangled** i.e. hanged　**9 for** because　**10 Despoilèd** stripped, deprived　**in** i.e. for the rest of　**11 open** public　**13 With** i.e. in the custody of　**Isle of Man** small island off the northwest coast of England　**14 were** would be　**16 justify** excuse　**21 would** desires, would have　**22 Stay** wait　**23 staff** the official symbol of the Protector's role　**24 God . . . feet** Henry draws on the words of several Psalms　**25 stay** support　**28 of years** of maturity　**29 be to be** need to be　**31 king his** king's

GLOUCESTER   My staff? Here, noble Henry, is my staff:

As willingly do I the same resign

As e'er thy father Henry made it mine:

35   And even as willingly at thy feet I leave it

As others would ambitiously receive it.   *He lays the staff at*

Farewell, good king: when I am dead and gone,   *Henry's feet*

May honourable peace attend thy throne!   *Exit Gloucester*

QUEEN MARGARET   Why, now is Henry king, and Margaret
queen,

40   And Humphrey Duke of Gloucester scarce himself,

That bears so shrewd a maim: two pulls at once:

His lady banished, and a limb lopped off.   *She picks up the staff*

This staff of honour raught, there let it stand

Where it best fits to be, in Henry's hand.   *She gives the staff to Henry*

45   SUFFOLK   Thus droops this lofty pine and hangs his sprays:

Thus Eleanor's pride dies in her youngest days.

YORK   Lords, let him go.— Please it your majesty,

This is the day appointed for the combat,

And ready are the appellant and defendant,

50   The armourer and his man, to enter the lists,

So please your highness to behold the fight.

QUEEN MARGARET   Ay, good my lord: for purposely therefore

Left I the court, to see this quarrel tried.

KING HENRY VI   A God's name, see the lists and all things fit:

55   Here let them end it, and God defend the right.

YORK   I never saw a fellow worse bestead,

Or more afraid to fight, than is the appellant,

The servant of this armourer, my lords.

Enter at one door [Horner] the armourer and his [three] Neighbours,
drinking to him so much that he is drunk: and he enters with a Drum
before him and his staff with a sandbag fastened to it: and at the other

---

41 bears . . . maim suffers such a serious injury   **pulls** wrenches   **43 raught** seized
45 pine possibly alludes to the emblem adopted by Henry IV, Gloucester's father   **sprays**
branches (offspring)   **46 her youngest days** its prime   **47 let him go** i.e. forget him
49 appellant challenger, accuser   **50 lists** designated combat area   **52 purposely therefore**
specifically for that reason   **54 A** in   **fit** prepared   **56 bestead** prepared   *Drum* drummer
staff . . . it a basic but potentially vicious type of weapon

door [Peter] his man, with a drum and sandbag, and Prentices drinking to him

FIRST NEIGHBOUR   Here, neighbour Horner, I drink to you in a cup of sack: and fear not, neighbour, you shall do well enough.

SECOND NEIGHBOUR   And here, neighbour, here's a cup of charneco.

THIRD NEIGHBOUR   And here's a pot of good double beer, neighbour: drink, and fear not your man.

HORNER   Let it come, i'faith, and I'll pledge you all, and a fig for Peter!   *Horner drinks with them*

FIRST PRENTICE   Here, Peter, I drink to thee, and be not afraid.

SECOND PRENTICE   Be merry, Peter, and fear not thy master: fight for credit of the prentices.   *Peter rejects their*

PETER   I thank you all: drink, and pray for me,   *offers of drinks*
I pray you, for I think I have taken my last draught in this world. Here, Robin, an if I die, I give thee my apron: and, Will, thou shalt have my hammer: and here, Tom, take all the money that I have. O Lord bless me, I pray God, for I am never able to deal with my master: he hath learnt so much fence already.

SALISBURY   Come, leave your drinking, and fall to blows. Sirrah, what's thy name?

PETER   Peter, forsooth.

SALISBURY   Peter! What more?

PETER   Thump.

SALISBURY   Thump? Then see thou thump thy master well.

HORNER   Masters, I am come hither, as it were, upon my man's instigation, to prove him a knave and myself an honest man: and touching the Duke of York, I will take my death I never meant him any ill, nor the king, nor the queen: and therefore, Peter, have at thee with a downright blow.

---

60 sack type of Spanish sweet white wine   **63 charneco** sweet Portuguese wine, a kind of port   **64 double** very strong   **66 pledge** toast   **fig** from old Spanish *figo*; exclamation of contempt, often accompanied by an obscene gesture that consisted of thrusting the thumb between the index and middle fingers   **76 deal** fight   **fence** fencing   **86 touching** concerning   **take my death** stake my life on it   **88 have at thee** i.e. here I come (standard utterance at the opening of a fight)   **downright** forthright, literally "vertically downwards"

YORK   Dispatch: this knave's tongue begins to double.

90   Sound, trumpets, alarum to the combatants!

[*Alarum.*] *They fight, and Peter strikes him* [*Horner*] *down*

HORNER   Hold, Peter, hold! I confess, I confess treason.   *Dies*

YORK   Take away his weapon.— Fellow, thank God, and
the good wine in thy master's way.

PETER   O God, have I overcome mine enemies in this

95   presence? O Peter, thou hast prevailed in right.

KING HENRY VI   Go, take hence that traitor from our sight,
For by his death we do perceive his guilt,
And God in justice hath revealed to us
The truth and innocence of this poor fellow,

100   Which he had thought to have murdered wrongfully.
Come, fellow, follow us for thy reward.

Sound a flourish.   Exeunt

[Act 2 Scene 4]   *running scene 8*

Enter Duke Humphrey [*Gloucester*] *and his Men in mourning cloaks*

GLOUCESTER   Thus sometimes hath the brightest day a cloud:
And after summer evermore succeeds
Barren winter, with his wrathful nipping cold:
So cares and joys abound, as seasons fleet.

5   Sirs, what's o'clock?

SERVANT   Ten, my lord.

GLOUCESTER   Ten is the hour that was appointed me
To watch the coming of my punished duchess:
Uneath may she endure the flinty streets,

10   To tread them with her tender-feeling feet.
Sweet Nell, ill can thy noble mind abrook
The abject people gazing on thy face,
With envious looks laughing at thy shame,

---

89 **Dispatch** get on with it   **double** slur (perhaps plays on the sense of "deceive")   **90 alarum**
trumpet call to arms   **93 in . . . way** in between you and your master/hindering your master
95 presence i.e. of the king   **100 he** i.e. Horner   **2.4   *Location: a London street***
2 **evermore succeeds** always follows   **4 fleet** pass swiftly away   **9 Uneath** not easily   **flinty**
hard, stony   **11 abrook** endure   **12 abject** base, lowly   **13 envious** malicious

That erst did follow thy proud chariot-wheels
15 When thou didst ride in triumph through the streets.
But soft, I think she comes: and I'll prepare
My tear-stained eyes to see her miseries.

Enter the Duchess [Eleanor barefoot] in a white sheet, [with verses pinned on her back] and a taper burning in her hand, with [Sir John Stanley,] the Sheriff and Officers

SERVANT   So please your grace, we'll take her from the sheriff.

GLOUCESTER   No, stir not for your lives, let her pass by.

20 ELEANOR   Come you, my lord, to see my open shame?
Now thou dost penance too. Look how they gaze,
See how the giddy multitude do point,
And nod their heads, and throw their eyes on thee.
Ah, Gloucester, hide thee from their hateful looks,
25 And, in thy closet pent up, rue my shame,
And ban thine enemies, both mine and thine.

GLOUCESTER   Be patient, gentle Nell: forget this grief.

ELEANOR   Ah, Gloucester, teach me to forget myself,
For whilst I think I am thy married wife
30 And thou a prince, Protector of this land,
Methinks I should not thus be led along,
Mailed up in shame, with papers on my back,
And followed with a rabble that rejoice
To see my tears and hear my deep-fet groans.
35 The ruthless flint doth cut my tender feet,
And when I start, the envious people laugh
And bid me be advisèd how I tread.
Ah, Humphrey, can I bear this shameful yoke?
Trowest thou that e'er I'll look upon the world,
40 Or count them happy that enjoys the sun?

---

14 erst formerly   **proud** splendid, luxurious   **chariot-wheels . . . triumph** the image is of a glorious military victor returning home in ceremony   **verses . . . back** wrongdoers undertaking public penance were required to wear papers listing their crimes   **taper** candle
22 giddy fickle, unstable, heady, excited   **23 throw** turn, cast   **24 hateful** hate-filled
25 closet private chamber   **rue** pity, grieve for   **26 ban** curse   **32 Mailed up** enveloped, wrapped up (falconry term referring to the covering of the hawk to quiet it)   **34 deep-fet** fetched up from deep within, profound   **36 start** flinch (in pain)   **37 advisèd** careful
39 Trowest thou do you think

No: dark shall be my light, and night my day.
To think upon my pomp shall be my hell.
Sometime I'll say, I am Duke Humphrey's wife,
And he a prince and ruler of the land:

45   Yet so he ruled and such a prince he was,
As he stood by, whilst I, his forlorn duchess,
Was made a wonder and a pointing-stock
To every idle rascal follower.
But be thou mild and blush not at my shame,

50   Nor stir at nothing till the axe of death
Hang over thee, as sure it shortly will.
For Suffolk, he that can do all in all
With her that hateth thee and hates us all,
And York and impious Beaufort, that false priest,

55   Have all limed bushes to betray thy wings,
And fly thou how thou canst, they'll tangle thee.
But fear not thou, until thy foot be snared,
Nor never seek prevention of thy foes.

GLOUCESTER   Ah, Nell, forbear: thou aimest all awry.

60   I must offend before I be attainted:
And had I twenty times so many foes,
And each of them had twenty times their power,
All these could not procure me any scathe,
So long as I am loyal, true and crimeless.

65   Wouldst have me rescue thee from this reproach?
Why yet thy scandal were not wiped away
But I in danger for the breach of law.
Thy greatest help is quiet, gentle Nell:
I pray thee sort thy heart to patience,

70   These few days' wonder will be quickly worn.

---

42 pomp (former) splendor   **46 As that**   **47 wonder** spectacle   **pointing-stock** object of
ridicule   **48 idle** useless/foolish/trifling   **rascal** lowborn   **49 mild** placid, calm   **53 her** i.e.
Queen Margaret   **55 limed** smeared with birdlime (sticky substance used to catch birds)
56 how thou canst as best you may   **59 forbear** desist   **aimest** guess, conjecture   **awry**
mistakenly   **60 attainted** convicted of treason   **63 procure . . . scathe** bring about any
damage   **66 scandal were not** disgrace would not be   **68 quiet** acceptance, calm   **69 sort**
fashion, adapt   **70 few days' wonder** passing spectacle (proverbial: "a wonder lasts but nine
days")   **worn** worn away, forgotten

Enter a Herald

HERALD   I summon your grace to his majesty's parliament,
Holden at Bury the first of this next month.

GLOUCESTER   And my consent ne'er asked herein before?
This is close dealing. Well, I will be there.—   [*Exit Herald*]

75   My Nell, I take my leave: and, Master Sheriff,
Let not her penance exceed the king's commission.

SHERIFF   An't please your grace, here my commission stays,
And Sir John Stanley is appointed now
To take her with him to the Isle of Man.

80   GLOUCESTER   Must you, Sir John, protect my lady here?

STANLEY   So am I given in charge, may't please your grace.

GLOUCESTER   Entreat her not the worse in that I pray
You use her well: the world may laugh again,
And I may live to do you kindness if

85   You do it her. And so, Sir John, farewell.   *He begins to leave*

ELEANOR   What, gone, my lord, and bid me not farewell?

GLOUCESTER   Witness my tears, I cannot stay to speak.

Exeunt Gloucester [and his Men]

ELEANOR   Art thou gone too? All comfort go with thee,
For none abides with me: my joy is death:

90   Death, at whose name I oft have been afeared,
Because I wished this world's eternity.
Stanley, I prithee go, and take me hence:
I care not whither, for I beg no favour,
Only convey me where thou art commanded.

95   STANLEY   Why, madam, that is to the Isle of Man,
There to be used according to your state.

ELEANOR   That's bad enough, for I am but reproach:
And shall I then be used reproachfully?

STANLEY   Like to a duchess, and Duke Humphrey's lady:

100   According to that state you shall be used.

---

72 Holden to be held   **Bury** Bury St. Edmunds, a town in Suffolk   **74 close dealing** secretive
business, plotting   **76 commission** orders, authorization   **77 stays** ends   **80 protect** take
custody of   **82 Entreat** treat   **90 afeared** afraid   **91 this world's eternity** eternal enjoyment
of this world   **96 used** treated   **state** rank (Eleanor develops the sense of "condition of
shame")   **97 reproach** disgrace itself

ELEANOR	Sheriff, farewell, and better than I fare,
	Although thou hast been conduct of my shame.
SHERIFF	It is my office; and, madam, pardon me.
ELEANOR	Ay, ay, farewell, thy office is discharged:

105 Come, Stanley, shall we go?

STANLEY   Madam, your penance done, throw off this sheet,
And go we to attire you for our journey.

ELEANOR   My shame will not be shifted with my sheet:
No, it will hang upon my richest robes

110 And show itself, attire me how I can.
Go, lead the way: I long to see my prison.   *Exeunt*

[Act 3 Scene 1]   *running scene 9*

*Sound a sennet. Enter King [Henry VI], Queen [Margaret], Cardinal,
Suffolk, York, Buckingham, Salisbury and Warwick to the parliament
[with Attendants]*

KING HENRY VI   I muse my lord of Gloucester is not come:
'Tis not his wont to be the hindmost man,
Whate'er occasion keeps him from us now.

QUEEN MARGARET   Can you not see? Or will ye not observe

5 The strangeness of his altered countenance?
With what a majesty he bears himself,
How insolent of late he is become,
How proud, how peremptory, and unlike himself?
We know the time since he was mild and affable,

10 And if we did but glance a far-off look,
Immediately he was upon his knee,
That all the court admired him for submission.
But meet him now, and be it in the morn,

101 better . . . fare may you fare better than I   102 conduct conductor, guide   103 office job, duty   104 is discharged has been carried out   107 attire clothe   108 shifted moved, altered (puns on the sense of "changed as an undergarment or 'shift'")   3.1 *Location: Bury St. Edmunds*   1 muse wonder   2 wont usual practice   hindmost last (to arrive) 5 strangeness aloof, distant nature   7 insolent haughty, arrogant   8 peremptory overbearing   9 know remember   since when   10 far-off distant   12 admired him for marveled at his

When everyone will give the time of day,

15   He knits his brow and shows an angry eye,
And passeth by with stiff unbowèd knee,
Disdaining duty that to us belongs.
Small curs are not regarded when they grin,
But great men tremble when the lion roars,
20   And Humphrey is no little man in England.
First note that he is near you in descent,
And should you fall, he is the next will mount.
Meseemeth then it is no policy,
Respecting what a rancorous mind he bears,
25   And his advantage following your decease,
That he should come about your royal person
Or be admitted to your highness' Council.
By flattery hath he won the commons' hearts:
And when he please to make commotion,
30   'Tis to be feared they all will follow him.
Now 'tis the spring, and weeds are shallow-rooted:
Suffer them now, and they'll o'ergrow the garden
And choke the herbs for want of husbandry.
The reverent care I bear unto my lord
35   Made me collect these dangers in the duke.
If it be fond, call it a woman's fear:
Which fear, if better reasons can supplant,
I will subscribe and say I wronged the duke.
My lord of Suffolk, Buckingham and York,
40   Reprove my allegation, if you can,
Or else conclude my words effectual.

SUFFOLK   Well hath your highness seen into this duke:
And had I first been put to speak my mind,

14 give . . . day greet one another   15 knits his brow frowns   16 stiff unbowèd knee a
respectful bow involved bending the knee   17 duty i.e. dutiful gestures of respect   18 curs
dogs   grin bare their teeth, snarl   23 Meseemeth it seems to me   no policy not expedient,
imprudent   24 Respecting considering   rancorous malicious, bitter   26 come about
frequent, be in contact with   29 commotion rebellion, riot   31 shallow-rooted i.e. easily
pulled up   32 Suffer allow   33 want lack   husbandry cultivation   35 collect gather
(information about)/conclude, deduce   36 fond foolish   37 supplant uproot, overthrow,
replace   38 subscribe give in, concede   40 Reprove refute, disprove   41 effectual
pertinent, valid   43 put obliged, called upon

I think I should have told your grace's tale.
45 The duchess, by his subornation,
Upon my life, began her devilish practices:
Or if he were not privy to those faults,
Yet by reputing of his high descent,
As next the king he was successive heir,
50 And such high vaunts of his nobility,
Did instigate the bedlam brain-sick duchess
By wicked means to frame our sovereign's fall.
Smooth runs the water where the brook is deep:
And in his simple show he harbours treason.
55 The fox barks not when he would steal the lamb.—
No, no, my sovereign, Gloucester is a man   *To King Henry*
Unsounded yet and full of deep deceit.

CARDINAL   Did he not, contrary to form of law,   *To King Henry*
Devise strange deaths for small offences done?

60 YORK   And did he not, in his Protectorship,   *To King Henry*
Levy great sums of money through the realm
For soldiers' pay in France, and never sent it,
By means whereof the towns each day revolted?

BUCKINGHAM   Tut, these are petty faults to faults unknown,
65 Which time will bring to light in smooth Duke Humphrey.

KING HENRY VI   My lords, at once: the care you have of us
To mow down thorns that would annoy our foot
Is worthy praise: but shall I speak my conscience,
Our kinsman Gloucester is as innocent
70 From meaning treason to our royal person
As is the sucking lamb or harmless dove:
The duke is virtuous, mild and too well given
To dream on evil or to work my downfall.

---

45 **subornation** incitement (to do wrong)   46 **practices** plots   47 **privy to** privately aware of
48 **reputing** boasting/thinking proudly   49 **the** to the   50 **vaunts** boasts   51 **bedlam brain-sick** insane and foolish   52 **frame** organize, devise   54 **simple show** innocent appearance
57 **Unsounded** unfathomed, not probed or measured   59 **strange** i.e. cruel or illegal
61 **Levy** raise   63 **By means whereof** as a result of which   64 **to** compared to   65 **smooth** glib, apparently amiable   66 **at once** in answer to you all/without further ado/once and for all   67 **annoy** injure   68 **shall I** if I   72 **given** disposed, inclined

QUEEN MARGARET   Ah, what's more dangerous than this fond
        affiance?
75   Seems he a dove? His feathers are but borrowed,
        For he's disposèd as the hateful raven.
        Is he a lamb? His skin is surely lent him,
        For he's inclined as is the ravenous wolves.
        Who cannot steal a shape that means deceit?
80   Take heed, my lord, the welfare of us all
        Hangs on the cutting short that fraudful man.
Enter Somerset
SOMERSET   All health unto my gracious sovereign.
KING HENRY VI   Welcome, Lord Somerset. What news from
        France?
SOMERSET   That all your interest in those territories
85   Is utterly bereft you: all is lost.
KING HENRY VI   Cold news, Lord Somerset: but God's will be
        done.
YORK   Cold news for me: for I had hope of France   *Aside*
        As firmly as I hope for fertile England.
        Thus are my blossoms blasted in the bud
90   And caterpillars eat my leaves away:
        But I will remedy this gear ere long,
        Or sell my title for a glorious grave.
Enter Gloucester
GLOUCESTER   All happiness unto my lord the king:
        Pardon, my liege, that I have stayed so long.
95   SUFFOLK   Nay, Gloucester, know that thou art come too soon,
        Unless thou wert more loyal than thou art:
        I do arrest thee of high treason here.
GLOUCESTER   Well, Suffolk, thou shalt not see me blush
        Nor change my countenance for this arrest:

---

74 fond affiance misguided trust/foolish affinity   **76 disposèd as** of the disposition of
raven a bird of ill omen   **78 inclined** of the same disposition   **wolves** i.e. who proverbially
wear sheep's clothing   **79 steal a shape** adopt a disguise   **means** intends   **81 Hangs**
depends   **cutting short** plays on the idea of beheading   **fraudful** treacherous, fraudulent
84 interest legal claim   **85 bereft** deprived   **89 blasted** blighted, withered   **91 gear**
business   **94 stayed** delayed, been absent

100   A heart unspotted is not easily daunted.
       The purest spring is not so free from mud
       As I am clear from treason to my sovereign.
       Who can accuse me? Wherein am I guilty?

YORK   'Tis thought, my lord, that you took bribes of
       France,
105   And, being Protector, stayed the soldiers' pay,
       By means whereof his highness hath lost France.

GLOUCESTER   Is it but thought so? What are they that think it?
       I never robbed the soldiers of their pay,
       Nor ever had one penny bribe from France.
110   So help me God, as I have watched the night,
       Ay, night by night, in studying good for England,
       That doit that e'er I wrested from the king,
       Or any groat I hoarded to my use,
       Be brought against me at my trial day!
115   No: many a pound of mine own proper store,
       Because I would not tax the needy commons,
       Have I disbursèd to the garrisons,
       And never asked for restitution.

CARDINAL   It serves you well, my lord, to say so much.

120 GLOUCESTER   I say no more than truth, so help me God.

YORK   In your Protectorship you did devise
       Strange tortures for offenders, never heard of,
       That England was defamed by tyranny.

GLOUCESTER   Why, 'tis well known that whiles I was Protector,
125   Pity was all the fault that was in me:
       For I should melt at an offender's tears,
       And lowly words were ransom for their fault:
       Unless it were a bloody murderer,
       Or foul felonious thief that fleeced poor passengers,

---

104 of from   **105 stayed** withheld   **107 What** who   **110 watched the night** stayed awake
111 studying pursuing/meditating on   **112 That** may that   **doit** small coin of little value
113 groat coin worth four old pence   **115 proper store** personal wealth   **117 disbursèd**
paid out   **123 That** so that   **was defamed by** became infamous for   **124 whiles** while
127 lowly . . . fault humble words of repentance were payment enough for the crime
129 felonious wicked, criminal   **fleeced** plundered, robbed   **passengers** travelers

130   I never gave them condign punishment.
         Murder indeed, that bloody sin, I tortured
         Above the felon or what trespass else.
         SUFFOLK   My lord, these faults are easy, quickly answered:
         But mightier crimes are laid unto your charge,
135   Whereof you cannot easily purge yourself.
         I do arrest you in his highness' name,
         And here commit you to my lord cardinal
         To keep until your further time of trial.
         KING HENRY VI   My lord of Gloucester, 'tis my special hope
140   That you will clear yourself from all suspense:
         My conscience tells me you are innocent.
         GLOUCESTER   Ah, gracious lord, these days are dangerous:
         Virtue is choked with foul ambition
         And charity chased hence by rancour's hand:
145   Foul subornation is predominant
         And equity exiled your highness' land.
         I know their complot is to have my life:
         And if my death might make this island happy,
         And prove the period of their tyranny,
150   I would expend it with all willingness.
         But mine is made the prologue to their play:
         For thousands more, that yet suspect no peril,
         Will not conclude their plotted tragedy.
         Beaufort's red sparkling eyes blab his heart's malice,
155   And Suffolk's cloudy brow his stormy hate:
         Sharp Buckingham unburdens with his tongue
         The envious load that lies upon his heart:
         And doggèd York, that reaches at the moon,
         Whose overweening arm I have plucked back,

---

130 **condign** fitting, appropriate   **132 Above . . . else** more severely than other types of offense   **133 easy** slight, small   **138 keep** guard, detain   **further** subsequent   **140 suspense** suspicion   **145 subornation** incitement to wrongdoing, bribery   **predominant** in the ascendant (astronomical term)   **146 equity** justice   **147 complot** plot, conspiracy   **149 period** end   **150 expend it** pay the price (of death)   **151 mine** i.e. my death   **154 blab** reveal, betray   **156 Sharp** merciless, severe   **157 envious** malicious   **158 doggèd** doglike, ill-tempered, stubborn   **159 overweening** overreaching, presumptuous

160   By false accuse doth level at my life.—
       And you, my sovereign lady, with the rest,   *To Queen Margaret*
       Causeless have laid disgraces on my head,
       And with your best endeavour have stirred up
       My liefest liege to be mine enemy:
165   Ay, all of you have laid your heads together —
       Myself had notice of your conventicles —
       And all to make away my guiltless life.
       I shall not want false witness to condemn me,
       Nor store of treasons to augment my guilt:
170   The ancient proverb will be well effected:
       'A staff is quickly found to beat a dog.'

       CARDINAL   My liege, his railing is intolerable.
       If those that care to keep your royal person
       From treason's secret knife and traitors' rage
175   Be thus upbraided, chid and rated at,
       And the offender granted scope of speech,
       'Twill make them cool in zeal unto your grace.

       SUFFOLK   Hath he not twit our sovereign lady here
       With ignominious words, though clerkly couched,
180   As if she had subornèd some to swear
       False allegations to o'erthrow his state?

       QUEEN MARGARET   But I can give the loser leave to chide.

       GLOUCESTER   Far truer spoke than meant: I lose indeed:
       Beshrew the winners, for they played me false,
185   And well such losers may have leave to speak.

       BUCKINGHAM   He'll wrest the sense and hold us here all day.
       Lord Cardinal, he is your prisoner.

       CARDINAL   Sirs, take away the duke, and guard him sure.

       GLOUCESTER   Ah, thus King Henry throws away his crutch
190   Before his legs be firm to bear his body.

---

160 **accuse** accusation   **level** aim   162 **Causeless** without cause   164 **liefest liege** dearest
sovereign   166 **conventicles** secret meetings   168 **want** lack   169 **store** abundance
172 **railing** ranting, complaining   175 **chid** rebuked   **rated at** berated   176 **scope** range,
opportunity   177 **zeal** loyalty, devotion   178 **twit** taunted, reproached   179 **clerkly
couched** skillfully expressed   180 **subornèd** bribed   181 **state** authority, high position
184 **Beshrew** curse   **played me false** cheated, deceived me   186 **wrest the sense** twist the
meaning   188 **sure** securely

Thus is the shepherd beaten from thy side,
And wolves are gnarling who shall gnaw thee first.
Ah, that my fear were false: ah, that it were:
For, good King Henry, thy decay I fear.

Exit Gloucester [guarded]

195 KING HENRY VI   My lords, what to your wisdoms seemeth best,
Do or undo, as if ourself were here.

QUEEN MARGARET   What, will your highness leave the
parliament?

KING HENRY VI   Ay, Margaret: my heart is drowned with grief,
Whose flood begins to flow within mine eyes:
200 My body round engirt with misery:
For what's more miserable than discontent?—
Ah, uncle Humphrey, in thy face I see
The map of honour, truth and loyalty:
And yet, good Humphrey, is the hour to come
205 That e'er I proved thee false or feared thy faith.
What louring star now envies thy estate,
That these great lords and Margaret our queen
Do seek subversion of thy harmless life?
Thou never didst them wrong, nor no man wrong:
210 And as the butcher takes away the calf,
And binds the wretch, and beats it when it strays,
Bearing it to the bloody slaughterhouse,
Even so remorseless have they borne him hence:
And as the dam runs lowing up and down,
215 Looking the way her harmless young one went,
And can do naught but wail her darling's loss,
Even so myself bewails good Gloucester's case
With sad unhelpful tears, and with dimmed eyes
Look after him, and cannot do him good:

---

192 gnarling snarling, growling   **194 decay** ruin, downfall   **200 engirt** encircled   **203 map**
image   **205 proved thee false** found you disloyal   **feared thy faith** doubted your loyalty
206 envies thy estate feels malice toward your position   **208 subversion** the destruction,
overthrow   **211 strays** a problematic image as the calf is bound, unless this means loosely
leashed about the neck or penned in—possibly **and** functions more like "or" as Henry lists the
things a butcher might do to a calf; many editors emend to "strains"   **214 dam** mother

220   So mighty are his vowèd enemies.
      His fortunes I will weep, and 'twixt each groan
      Say 'Who's a traitor? Gloucester he is none.'

                    Exit [*with Buckingham, Salisbury and Warwick*]

      QUEEN MARGARET   Free lords, cold snow melts with the sun's
         hot beams:
      Henry my lord is cold in great affairs,
225   Too full of foolish pity: and Gloucester's show
      Beguiles him as the mournful crocodile
      With sorrow snares relenting passengers,
      Or as the snake rolled in a flow'ring bank,
      With shining chequered slough, doth sting a child
230   That for the beauty thinks it excellent.
      Believe me, lords, were none more wise than I—
      And yet herein I judge mine own wit good—
      This Gloucester should be quickly rid the world,
      To rid us from the fear we have of him.
235   CARDINAL   That he should die is worthy policy:
      But yet we want a colour for his death:
      'Tis meet he be condemned by course of law.
      SUFFOLK   But, in my mind, that were no policy:
      The king will labour still to save his life,
240   The commons haply rise, to save his life:
      And yet we have but trivial argument,
      More than mistrust, that shows him worthy death.
      YORK   So that, by this, you would not have him die.
      SUFFOLK   Ah, York, no man alive so fain as I.
245   YORK   'Tis York that hath more reason for his
         death.—   *Aside*

---

220 vowèd avowed, sworn   **221 'twixt** in between   **223 Free** noble, honorable   **224 cold** indifferent, passive   **225 show** false appearance, deceptive behavior   **226 Beguiles** deceives, distracts   **crocodile . . . passengers** crocodiles were believed to shed tears as a means of enticing victims   **227 relenting** pitying   **229 chequered slough** patterned, multicolored outer skin   **232 wit** intellect, reasoning   **233 rid** removed from   **235 worthy** sensible, shrewd   **236 colour** pretext, excuse (picks up on **die**/dye to pun on the sense of "hue"; also puns on "collar"—i.e. hangman's noose)   **237 meet** appropriate, fitting   **238 were** would be **policy** clever strategy   **239 still** continually   **240 haply rise** may perhaps rebel   **241 trivial argument** scant evidence, slight grounds   **242 More than mistrust** except for suspicion **243 by this** on the strength of this reasoning   **244 fain** willing

But, my lord cardinal, and you my lord of Suffolk,   *Aloud*
Say as you think, and speak it from your souls:
Were't not all one, an empty eagle were set
To guard the chicken from a hungry kite,

250 As place Duke Humphrey for the king's Protector?
QUEEN MARGARET   So the poor chicken should be sure of death.
SUFFOLK   Madam, 'tis true: and were't not madness then
To make the fox surveyor of the fold,
Who being accused a crafty murderer,

255 His guilt should be but idly posted over,
Because his purpose is not executed?
No: let him die, in that he is a fox,
By nature proved an enemy to the flock,
Before his chaps be stained with crimson blood,

260 As Humphrey, proved by reasons, to my liege.
And do not stand on quillets how to slay him:
Be it by gins, by snares, by subtlety,
Sleeping or waking, 'tis no matter how,
So he be dead: for that is good deceit

265 Which mates him first that first intends deceit.
QUEEN MARGARET   Thrice-noble Suffolk, 'tis resolutely spoke.
SUFFOLK   Not resolute, except so much were done:
For things are often spoke and seldom meant:
But that my heart accordeth with my tongue,

270 Seeing the deed is meritorious,
And to preserve my sovereign from his foe,
Say but the word, and I will be his priest.
CARDINAL   But I would have him dead, my lord of Suffolk,
Ere you can take due orders for a priest:

248 all one the same (if)   empty hungry   249 kite bird of prey   253 surveyor . . . fold
keeper of the sheepfold   255 idly posted over foolishly ignored   256 Because . . . executed
simply because he had yet to kill one of the sheep   259 chaps jaws   260 proved . . . liege
has been demonstrated through reasoned argument to be a threat to Henry   261 stand
insist   quillets fine distinctions, quibbles   262 gins, by snares two types of traps for
catching game   subtlety cunning, crafty strategy   264 So provided   265 mates
checkmates, catches out   267 except unless   269 that to show that   accordeth is in
accordance with   270 meritorious worthy, deserving of God's reward   272 be his priest
preside over his death like a priest administering the last rites (i.e. kill him)   274 Ere . . . priest
before you have time to be ordained as a priest/to arrange for a priest to be there

275   Say you consent and censure well the deed,
And I'll provide his executioner,
I tender so the safety of my liege.

SUFFOLK   Here is my hand, the deed is worthy doing.

QUEEN MARGARET   And so say I.

280   YORK   And I: and now we three have spoke it,
It skills not greatly who impugns our doom.

Enter a Post

POST   Great lords, from Ireland am I come amain
To signify that rebels there are up
And put the Englishmen unto the sword.

285   Send succours, lords, and stop the rage betime,
Before the wound do grow uncurable:
For, being green, there is great hope of help.

CARDINAL   A breach that craves a quick expedient stop!
What counsel give you in this weighty cause?

290   YORK   That Somerset be sent as regent thither:
'Tis meet that lucky ruler be employed:
Witness the fortune he hath had in France.

SOMERSET   If York, with all his far-fet policy,
Had been the regent there instead of me,

295   He never would have stayed in France so long.

YORK   No, not to lose it all, as thou hast done.
I rather would have lost my life betimes
Than bring a burden of dishonour home
By staying there so long till all were lost.

300   Show me one scar charactered on thy skin:
Men's flesh preserved so whole do seldom win.

QUEEN MARGARET   Nay, then, this spark will prove a raging fire
If wind and fuel be brought to feed it with:
No more, good York: sweet Somerset, be still:

---

275 **censure** approve   277 **tender so** hold so dear   281 **skills . . . doom** does not make
much difference who questions our judgment   *Post* messenger   282 **amain** in haste
283 **signify** inform, report   **up** up in arms   285 **succours** assistance   **betime** rapidly, at an
early stage   287 **green** fresh   288 **breach** gash, hole/uprising, rebellion   289 **weighty
cause** pressing circumstance, important matter   291 **meet** appropriate   **lucky . . . France**
York is being sarcastic and insulting toward Somerset   293 **far-fet** far-fetched, devious
297 **betimes** early   300 **charactered** inscribed, written   301 **Men's flesh** men whose flesh is

305   Thy fortune, York, hadst thou been regent there,
Might happily have proved far worse than his.

YORK   What, worse than naught? Nay, then a shame
take all!

SOMERSET   And, in the number, thee that wishest shame.

CARDINAL   My lord of York, try what your fortune is:

310   The uncivil kerns of Ireland are in arms
And temper clay with blood of Englishmen.
To Ireland will you lead a band of men,
Collected choicely, from each county some,
And try your hap against the Irishmen?

315 YORK   I will, my lord, so please his majesty.

SUFFOLK   Why, our authority is his consent,
And what we do establish he confirms:
Then, noble York, take thou this task in hand.

YORK   I am content: provide me soldiers, lords,

320   Whiles I take order for mine own affairs.

SUFFOLK   A charge, Lord York, that I will see performed.
But now return we to the false Duke Humphrey.

CARDINAL   No more of him: for I will deal with him
That henceforth he shall trouble us no more:

325   And so break off: the day is almost spent.
Lord Suffolk, you and I must talk of that event.

YORK   My lord of Suffolk, within fourteen days
At Bristol I expect my soldiers,
For there I'll ship them all for Ireland.

330 SUFFOLK   I'll see it truly done, my lord of York.

Exeunt [leaving] York

YORK   Now, York, or never, steel thy fearful thoughts,
And change misdoubt to resolution:
Be that thou hop'st to be, or what thou art
Resign to death: it is not worth th'enjoying:

---

306 happily perhaps   **308 in the number** among them   **309 try** put to the test   **310 uncivil** uncivilized, rebellious   **kerns** lightly armed Irish foot soldiers   **311 temper clay** soften, mix earth   **313 Collected choicely** carefully selected   **314 hap** luck, fortune   **320 take order** make arrangements   **332 misdoubt** mistrust, uncertainty   **333 that** that which

335   Let pale-faced fear keep with the mean-born man,
And find no harbour in a royal heart.
Faster than springtime showers comes thought on thought,
And not a thought but thinks on dignity.
My brain, more busy than the labouring spider,
340   Weaves tedious snares to trap mine enemies.
Well, nobles, well: 'tis politicly done,
To send me packing with an host of men:
I fear me you but warm the starvèd snake,
Who, cherished in your breasts, will sting your hearts.
345   'Twas men I lacked and you will give them me:
I take it kindly: yet be well assured
You put sharp weapons in a madman's hands.
Whiles I in Ireland nourish a mighty band,
I will stir up in England some black storm
350   Shall blow ten thousand souls to heaven or hell:
And this fell tempest shall not cease to rage
Until the golden circuit on my head,
Like to the glorious sun's transparent beams,
Do calm the fury of this mad-bred flaw.
355   And for a minister of my intent,
I have seduced a headstrong Kentishman,
John Cade of Ashford,
To make commotion, as full well he can,
Under the title of John Mortimer.
360   In Ireland have I seen this stubborn Cade
Oppose himself against a troop of kerns,
And fought so long, till that his thighs with darts
Were almost like a sharp-quilled porcupine:

---

335 keep dwell, remain   **mean-born** lowborn, humble   **336 harbour** dwelling, shelter
338 dignity honor, high rank, kingship   **340 tedious** laborious, painstakingly intricate
341 politicly strategically, cunningly   **343 fear me** fear   **warm . . . hearts** refers to the
proverbial cautionary tale of the man who warms a frozen snake against his chest, only to have
it revive and bite him   **starvèd** stiff from cold   **348 nourish** generate, support   **350 Shall** that
shall   **351 fell** fierce, cruel   **352 circuit** i.e. crown   **354 mad-bred** created by madness   **flaw**
squall, blast   **355 minister . . . intent** agent of my intentions   **357 Ashford** town in Kent,
south of Canterbury   **358 make commotion** rouse rebellion   **359 John Mortimer** like York, a
member of the Mortimer family, who were descended from Edward III's third son Lionel, Duke
of Clarence, and could thus claim entitlement to the throne   **362 till that** until   **darts** arrows

And in the end, being rescued, I have seen
365　Him caper upright like a wild Morisco,
Shaking the bloody darts as he his bells.
Full often, like a shag-haired crafty kern,
Hath he conversèd with the enemy,
And, undiscovered, come to me again
370　And given me notice of their villainies.
This devil here shall be my substitute:
For that John Mortimer, which now is dead,
In face, in gait, in speech, he doth resemble.
By this I shall perceive the commons' mind,
375　How they affect the house and claim of York.
Say he be taken, racked and torturèd,
I know no pain they can inflict upon him
Will make him say I moved him to those arms.
Say that he thrive, as 'tis great like he will,
380　Why then from Ireland come I with my strength
And reap the harvest which that rascal sowed.
For Humphrey being dead, as he shall be,
And Henry put apart, the next for me.　　　　　*Exit*

[Act 3 Scene 2]

*Enter two or three [Murderers] running over the stage, from the
murder of Duke Humphrey [Gloucester]*

FIRST MURDERER　Run to my lord of Suffolk: let him know
We have dispatched the duke, as he commanded.
SECOND MURDERER　O, that it were to do! What have we done?
Didst ever hear a man so penitent?

---

365 caper perform a leaping, nimble dance　**Morisco** morris dancer　**366 he** the morris
dancer　**bells** traditionally tied to the dancer's legs　**367 Full** very　**shag-haired** shaggy-
haired, wild-haired　**370 notice** information　**372 John . . . dead** Mortimer was executed in
1424　**373 gait** bearing　**374 commons'** common people's, public's　**375 affect** favor,
incline to　**376 taken** arrested　**racked** tortured by being strapped upon a frame and having
the limbs stretched　**378 moved** persuaded　**379 great like** very likely　**381 rascal** lowborn
man/rogue　**383 put apart** ousted, put aside (perhaps with murderous suggestion)
3.2　2 dispatched done away with, killed (Suffolk shifts the sense to "managed, carried out")
3 to do still to be done (i.e. that we had not done it)

Enter Suffolk

5   FIRST MURDERER   Here comes my lord.

SUFFOLK   Now, sirs, have you dispatched this thing?

FIRST MURDERER   Ay, my good lord, he's dead.

SUFFOLK   Why, that's well said. Go, get you to my house:
I will reward you for this venturous deed:

10   The king and all the peers are here at hand.
Have you laid fair the bed? Is all things well,
According as I gave directions?

FIRST MURDERER   'Tis, my good lord.

SUFFOLK   Away! Be gone.   *Exeunt [Murderers]*
Sound trumpets. Enter the King [Henry VI], the Queen [Margaret],
Cardinal, Somerset, with Attendants

15   KING HENRY VI   Go call our uncle to our presence straight:
Say we intend to try his grace today
If he be guilty, as 'tis publishèd.

SUFFOLK   I'll call him presently, my noble lord.   *Exit*

KING HENRY VI   Lords, take your places: and, I pray you all,

20   Proceed no straiter gainst our uncle Gloucester
Than from true evidence of good esteem
He be approved in practice culpable.

QUEEN MARGARET   God forbid any malice should prevail,
That faultless may condemn a noble man:

25   Pray God he may acquit him of suspicion!

KING HENRY VI   I thank thee, Meg: these words content me much.
Enter Suffolk
How now? Why look'st thou pale? Why tremblest thou?
Where is our uncle? What's the matter, Suffolk?

SUFFOLK   Dead in his bed, my lord: Gloucester is dead.

30   QUEEN MARGARET   Marry, God forfend!

CARDINAL   God's secret judgement: I did dream tonight
The duke was dumb and could not speak a word.

---

9 venturous risky   **11 laid fair** tidied, straightened up   **15 straight** straightaway   **17 If** (to
determine) whether   **publishèd** declared   **20 straiter** more harshly   **21 of good esteem**
worthy of belief   **22 approved in** proved guilty of   **practice culpable** guilty plotting,
wrongful conspiracy   **24 faultless . . . man** may condemn an innocent and noble man
25 acquit him clear himself   **30 forfend** forbid   **31 tonight** last night

King [Henry VI] swoons

QUEEN MARGARET   How fares my lord?— Help, lords, the king
    is dead!

SOMERSET   Rear up his body: wring him by the nose.

35   QUEEN MARGARET   Run, go, help, help! O Henry, ope thine eyes!

SUFFOLK   He doth revive again: madam, be patient.

KING HENRY VI   O heavenly God!

QUEEN MARGARET   How fares my gracious lord?

SUFFOLK   Comfort, my sovereign: gracious Henry, comfort.

40   KING HENRY VI   What, doth my lord of Suffolk comfort me?
    Came he right now to sing a raven's note,
    Whose dismal tune bereft my vital powers:
    And thinks he that the chirping of a wren,
    By crying comfort from a hollow breast,
45   Can chase away the first-conceivèd sound?
    Hide not thy poison with such sugared words:
    Lay not thy hands on me: forbear I say,
    Their touch affrights me as a serpent's sting.
    Thou baleful messenger, out of my sight:
50   Upon thy eyeballs murderous tyranny
    Sits in grim majesty, to fright the world.
    Look not upon me, for thine eyes are wounding:
    Yet do not go away: come, basilisk,
    And kill the innocent gazer with thy sight:
55   For in the shade of death I shall find joy:
    In life, but double death, now Gloucester's dead.

QUEEN MARGARET   Why do you rate my lord of Suffolk thus?
    Although the duke was enemy to him,
    Yet he most Christian-like laments his death:
60   And for myself, foe as he was to me,
    Might liquid tears, or heart-offending groans,
    Or blood-consuming sighs recall his life,

---

34 Rear up raise, support   **wring** twist, squeeze (to restore circulation)   **41 raven's note**
proverbially ominous and associated with death   **42 dismal** fatal, ominous   **bereft** robbed
me of   **44 hollow** empty, insincere   **45 first-conceivèd** original, first perceived   **48 affrights**
frightens   **49 baleful** deadly   **53 basilisk** mythological reptile whose gaze had the power to
kill   **57 rate** berate   **61 heart-offending** heart-wounding (each groan or sigh was thought to
deprive the heart of a drop of blood)

I would be blind with weeping, sick with groans,
Look pale as primrose with blood-drinking sighs,
65   And all to have the noble duke alive.
What know I how the world may deem of me?
For it is known we were but hollow friends:
It may be judged I made the duke away.
So shall my name with slander's tongue be wounded,
70   And princes' courts be filled with my reproach:
This get I by his death: ay me, unhappy,
To be a queen, and crowned with infamy.

KING HENRY VI   Ah, woe is me for Gloucester, wretched man!

QUEEN MARGARET   Be woe for me, more wretched than he is.
75   What, dost thou turn away and hide thy face?
I am no loathsome leper: look on me.
What, art thou, like the adder, waxen deaf?
Be poisonous too and kill thy forlorn queen.
Is all thy comfort shut in Gloucester's tomb?
80   Why, then, Dame Margaret was ne'er thy joy.
Erect his statue and worship it,
And make my image but an ale-house sign.
Was I for this nigh wracked upon the sea
And twice by awkward wind from England's bank
85   Drove back again unto my native clime?
What boded this, but well forewarning wind
Did seem to say 'Seek not a scorpion's nest,
Nor set no footing on this unkind shore'?
What did I then, but cursed the gentle gusts
90   And he that loosed them forth their brazen caves,
And bid them blow towards England's blessèd shore,
Or turn our stern upon a dreadful rock?

---

66 deem judge, think   **67 hollow** shallow, insincere   **70 reproach** censure, disgrace
74 woe sorry   **77 adder, waxen deaf** in order to resist snake charmers, the adder supposedly
blocked one ear with its tail and placed the other to the ground   **waxen** grown   **78 forlorn**
wretched, neglected, outcast   **83 nigh** nearly   **84 awkward** adverse, unfavorable   **bank**
shore   **85 clime** land, region   **86 but** unless (the)   **88 unkind** hostile, unnatural
89 gentle kindly (i.e. in relation to what follows)   **90 he** i.e. **Aeolus**   **forth** forth from
brazen strong (as brass); in classical mythology, Aeolus' island is described as being
surrounded by bronze walls

Yet Aeolus would not be a murderer,
But left that hateful office unto thee.
95   The pretty vaulting sea refused to drown me,
Knowing that thou wouldst have me drowned on shore
With tears as salt as sea, through thy unkindness.
The splitting rocks cowered in the sinking sands,
And would not dash me with their ragged sides,
100   Because thy flinty heart, more hard than they,
Might in thy palace perish Margaret.
As far as I could ken thy chalky cliffs,
When from thy shore the tempest beat us back,
I stood upon the hatches in the storm,
105   And when the dusky sky began to rob
My earnest-gaping sight of thy land's view,
I took a costly jewel from my neck —
A heart it was, bound in with diamonds —
And threw it towards thy land. The sea received it,
110   And so I wished thy body might my heart:
And even with this, I lost fair England's view,
And bid mine eyes be packing with my heart,
And called them blind and dusky spectacles,
For losing ken of Albion's wishèd coast.
115   How often have I tempted Suffolk's tongue,
The agent of thy foul inconstancy,
To sit and witch me as Ascanius did,
When he to madding Dido would unfold
His father's acts commenced in burning Troy.
120   Am I not witched like her? Or thou not false like him?

---

93 Aeolus in Greek mythology, the ruler of the winds   **95 pretty** artful/clever/charming
vaulting leaping   **98 splitting** vicious, jagged, capable of splitting ships   **sinking sands** sands
capable of sinking ships   **100 Because** so that   **101 perish** destroy   **102 ken** see, make out
104 hatches deck   **106 earnest-gaping** eagerly gazing   **108 bound in with** surrounded by
112 packing gone   **heart** i.e. the **jewel** (plays on the sense of "affections, desires")
114 wishèd longed for, desired   **116 agent** i.e. as Henry's deputy   **117 witch** bewitch
Ascanius son of Aeneas, in whose form Cupid disguised himself so that he could enchant **Dido**
with tales of Aeneas' bravery in the battle of **Troy**, and make her fall in love with the boy's
father; Aeneas responded to Dido's passion, but eventually deserted her   **118 madding**
frantic, maddened by love   **120 false** inconstant, disloyal

Ay me, I can no more: die, Margaret,

For Henry weeps that thou dost live so long.

Noise within. Enter Warwick, [Salisbury] and many Commons

WARWICK   It is reported, mighty sovereign,

That good Duke Humphrey traitorously is murdered

125   By Suffolk and the Cardinal Beaufort's means:

The commons, like an angry hive of bees

That want their leader, scatter up and down

And care not who they sting in his revenge.

Myself have calmed their spleenful mutiny,

130   Until they hear the order of his death.

KING HENRY VI   That he is dead, good Warwick, 'tis too true:

But how he died, God knows, not Henry:

Enter his chamber, view his breathless corpse,

And comment then upon his sudden death.

135   WARWICK   That shall I do, my liege.— Stay, Salisbury,

With the rude multitude till I return.

                    [*Exeunt Warwick, Salisbury and Commons*]

KING HENRY VI   O, thou that judgest all things, stay my

       thoughts:

My thoughts, that labour to persuade my soul

Some violent hands were laid on Humphrey's life:

140   If my suspect be false, forgive me, God,

For judgement only doth belong to thee:

Fain would I go to chafe his paly lips

With twenty thousand kisses, and to drain

Upon his face an ocean of salt tears,

145   To tell my love unto his dumb deaf trunk,

And with my fingers feel his hand unfeeling:

But all in vain are these mean obsequies;   *Bed put forth*

And to survey his dead and earthy image:

What were it but to make my sorrow greater?

---

121 **can no more** cannot go on   *Commons* commoners   127 **want** lack   128 **his revenge**
payment for his death   129 **spleenful** enraged   130 **order** nature, circumstances
134 **comment then upon** explain   136 **rude** rough, ignorant   137 **stay** stop, restrain
140 **suspect** suspicion   142 **Fain** gladly   **chafe** restore warmth to   **paly** bloodless, pale
145 **trunk** body   147 **mean obsequies** meager funeral rites

[Enter Warwick to reveal Gloucester's body in his bed]

150   WARWICK   Come hither, gracious sovereign, view this body.

KING HENRY VI   That is to see how deep my grave is made,

For with his soul fled all my worldly solace:

For seeing him, I see my life in death.

WARWICK   As surely as my soul intends to live

155   With that dread king that took our state upon him

To free us from his father's wrathful curse,

I do believe that violent hands were laid

Upon the life of this thrice-famèd duke.

SUFFOLK   A dreadful oath, sworn with a solemn tongue:

160   What instance gives Lord Warwick for his vow?

WARWICK   See how the blood is settled in his face.

Oft have I seen a timely-parted ghost,

Of ashy semblance, meagre, pale and bloodless,

Being all descended to the labouring heart,

165   Who in the conflict that it holds with death,

Attracts the same for aidance gainst the enemy,

Which with the heart there cools, and ne'er returneth

To blush and beautify the cheek again.

But see, his face is black and full of blood:

170   His eyeballs further out than when he lived,

Staring full ghastly like a strangled man:

His hair upreared, his nostrils stretched with struggling:

His hands abroad displayed, as one that grasped

And tugged for life and was by strength subdued.

175   Look, on the sheets his hair, you see, is sticking.

His well-proportioned beard, made rough and rugged,

Like to the summer's corn by tempest lodged:

Enter . . . bed i.e. the curtains are drawn to reveal the discovery space, a sizable alcove at the back of the stage   **153 my . . . death** an image of my own death   **155 dread** revered, awe-inspiring   **king** i.e. Christ   **158 thrice-famèd** well-renowned, much honored   **160 instance** evidence   **161 settled** congealed, not flowing   **162 timely-parted ghost** corpse of a person who has died naturally, at their right time   **163 meagre** emaciated   **164 Being** (the blood) having   **166 aidance** assistance   **167 Which** i.e. the blood   **172 upreared** standing on end   **173 abroad displayed** spread out widely   **176 well-proportioned** well-shaped   **rugged** shaggy, disheveled   **177 lodged** flattened

It cannot be but he was murdered here:
The least of all these signs were probable.

180 SUFFOLK   Why, Warwick, who should do the duke to death?
Myself and Beaufort had him in protection,
And we, I hope, sir, are no murderers.

WARWICK   But both of you were vowed Duke Humphrey's foes,
And you, forsooth, had the good duke to keep:

185 'Tis like you would not feast him like a friend,
And 'tis well seen he found an enemy.

QUEEN MARGARET   Then you, belike, suspect these noblemen
As guilty of Duke Humphrey's timeless death.

WARWICK   Who finds the heifer dead and bleeding fresh,

190 And sees fast by a butcher with an axe,
But will suspect 'twas he that made the slaughter?
Who finds the partridge in the puttock's nest,
But may imagine how the bird was dead,
Although the kite soar with unbloodied beak?

195 Even so suspicious is this tragedy.

QUEEN MARGARET   Are you the butcher, Suffolk? Where's your
knife?
Is Beaufort termed a kite? Where are his talons?

SUFFOLK   I wear no knife to slaughter sleeping men:
But here's a vengeful sword, rusted with ease,

200 That shall be scoured in his rancorous heart
That slanders me with murder's crimson badge.
Say, if thou dar'st, proud Lord of Warwickshire,
That I am faulty in Duke Humphrey's death.

[*Exeunt Cardinal and Somerset*]

WARWICK   What dares not Warwick, if false Suffolk dare him?

205 QUEEN MARGARET   He dares not calm his contumelious spirit,
Nor cease to be an arrogant controller,
Though Suffolk dare him twenty thousand times.

---

179 probable sufficient evidence   **184 keep** guard, protect   **185 like** likely   **feast** entertain
186 well seen obvious   **187 belike** perhaps   **188 timeless** untimely   **192 puttock** bird of
prey, especially the **kite**   **199 ease** disuse   **200 scoured** cleaned (often with a thrusting
action)   **201 badge** insignia, sign of allegiance   **203 faulty** guilty   **205 contumelious**
contemptuous, insolent   **206 controller** critic

WARWICK   Madam, be still: with reverence may I say,
          For every word you speak in his behalf
210   Is slander to your royal dignity.

SUFFOLK   Blunt-witted lord, ignoble in demeanour,
          If ever lady wronged her lord so much,
          Thy mother took into her blameful bed
          Some stern untutored churl: and noble stock
215   Was graft with crab-tree slip, whose fruit thou art,
          And never of the Nevilles' noble race.

WARWICK   But that the guilt of murder bucklers thee,
          And I should rob the deathsman of his fee,
          Quitting thee thereby of ten thousand shames,
220   And that my sovereign's presence makes me mild,
          I would, false murd'rous coward, on thy knee
          Make thee beg pardon for thy passèd speech,
          And say it was thy mother that thou meant'st,
          That thou thyself was born in bastardy:
225   And after all this fearful homage done,
          Give thee thy hire and send thy soul to hell,
          Pernicious bloodsucker of sleeping men!

SUFFOLK   Thou shalt be waking while I shed thy blood,
          If from this presence thou dar'st go with me.

230 WARWICK   Away even now, or I will drag thee hence:
          Unworthy though thou art, I'll cope with thee,
          And do some service to Duke Humphrey's ghost.

                              Exeunt [*Suffolk and Warwick*]

KING HENRY VI   What stronger breastplate than a heart
              untainted?
          Thrice is he armed that hath his quarrel just:

---

214 stern untutored churl coarse ignorant peasant   **stock** tree trunk/family tree   **215 graft**
united (horticultural image from the practice of grafting a cutting of one plant or tree onto the
trunk of another, usually a stronger but coarser tree that allowed the superior cutting to
flourish)   **crab-tree slip** cutting of a wild apple tree (**slip** plays on the sense of "moral lapse")
217 bucklers shields (a buckler is a small round shield)   **218 And . . . fee** i.e. by killing you
myself rather than you being executed for the murder of Gloucester   **deathsman** executioner
219 Quitting ridding   **220 makes me mild** makes me restrain myself   **222 passèd** recently
uttered   **225 fearful homage** timorous servility   **226 hire** payment (i.e. death)
227 Pernicious destructive, wicked   **229 presence** royal presence   **231 cope** fight,
encounter   **234 just** justified, with righteousness on his side

235   And he but naked, though locked up in steel,
    Whose conscience with injustice is corrupted.

A noise within

QUEEN MARGARET   What noise is this?

Enter Suffolk and Warwick, with their weapons drawn

KING HENRY VI   Why, how now, lords? Your wrathful weapons drawn
    Here in our presence? Dare you be so bold?
240   Why, what tumultuous clamour have we here?

SUFFOLK   The trait'rous Warwick with the men of Bury
    Set all upon me, mighty sovereign.

Enter Salisbury [from the Commons, within]

SALISBURY   Sirs, stand apart: the king shall know   *To the*
    your mind.—   *Commons*
    Dread lord, the commons send you word by me,   *To King Henry*
245   Unless Lord Suffolk straight be done to death,
    Or banishèd fair England's territories,
    They will by violence tear him from your palace,
    And torture him with grievous ling'ring death.
    They say, by him the good Duke Humphrey died:
250   They say, in him they fear your highness' death:
    And mere instinct of love and loyalty,
    Free from a stubborn opposite intent,
    As being thought to contradict your liking,
    Makes them thus forward in his banishment.
255   They say, in care of your most royal person,
    That if your highness should intend to sleep
    And charge that no man should disturb your rest
    In pain of your dislike, or pain of death,
    Yet, notwithstanding such a strait edict,
260   Were there a serpent seen, with forkèd tongue,
    That slyly glided towards your majesty,
    It were but necessary you were waked:

---

235 **steel** i.e. armor   238 **weapons . . . presence** it was a punishable offense to draw a sword in the presence of the king   251 **mere** pure, absolute   252 **opposite** hostile, opposing   253 **As . . . liking** which might be thought to be opposed to your wishes   254 **forward in** insistent in demanding   257 **charge** order   258 **In** on   259 **strait** strict

Lest, being suffered in that harmful slumber,
The mortal worm might make the sleep eternal.

265 And therefore do they cry, though you forbid,
That they will guard you, whe'er you will or no,
From such fell serpents as false Suffolk is,
With whose envenomèd and fatal sting,
Your loving uncle, twenty times his worth,

270 They say, is shamefully bereft of life.

COMMONS   An answer from the king, my lord of
    Salisbury!   *Within*

SUFFOLK   'Tis like the commons, rude unpolished hinds,
Could send such message to their sovereign:
But you, my lord, were glad to be employed,

275 To show how quaint an orator you are.
But all the honour Salisbury hath won
Is that he was the Lord Ambassador
Sent from a sort of tinkers to the king.

COMMONS   An answer from the king, or we will all
    break in.   *Within*

280 KING HENRY VI   Go, Salisbury, and tell them all from me
I thank them for their tender loving care:
And had I not been cited so by them,
Yet did I purpose as they do entreat:
For sure, my thoughts do hourly prophesy

285 Mischance unto my state by Suffolk's means.
And therefore by his majesty I swear,
Whose far unworthy deputy I am,
He shall not breathe infection in this air
But three days longer, on the pain of death.   [*Exit Salisbury*]

290 QUEEN MARGARET   O Henry, let me plead for gentle Suffolk.

KING HENRY VI   Ungentle queen, to call him gentle Suffolk.
No more, I say: if thou dost plead for him,

---

263 **suffered** allowed to remain   264 **mortal worm** fatal snake   266 **whe'er** whether   267 **fell** dangerous, destructive   272 **like** likely (sarcastic)   **hinds** peasants   275 **quaint** skillful, cunning   278 **sort** gang   **tinkers** menders of metal pots and kettles (also applied to beggars or thieves)   282 **cited** urged, incited   283 **purpose** intend (to do)   285 **Mischance** calamity, misfortune   **state** kingly status   286 **his** i.e. God's   288 **breathe infection in** contaminate   289 **But** any more than   290 **gentle** noble   291 **Ungentle** discourteous, unkind

Thou wilt but add increase unto my wrath.
Had I but said, I would have kept my word:
295   But when I swear, it is irrevocable:
If after three days' space thou here be'st found
On any ground that I am ruler of,
The world shall not be ransom for thy life.
Come, Warwick, come, good Warwick, go with me:
300   I have great matters to impart to thee.

Exeunt [all but Queen Margaret and Suffolk]

QUEEN MARGARET   Mischance and sorrow go along with you!
Heart's discontent and sour affliction
Be playfellows to keep you company!
There's two of you, the devil make a third,
305   And threefold vengeance tend upon your steps.

SUFFOLK   Cease, gentle queen, these execrations,
And let thy Suffolk take his heavy leave.

QUEEN MARGARET   Fie, coward woman and soft-hearted wretch!
Hast thou not spirit to curse thine enemies?

310   SUFFOLK   A plague upon them! Wherefore should I curse
them?
Could curses kill, as doth the mandrake's groan,
I would invent as bitter-searching terms,
As curst, as harsh and horrible to hear,
Delivered strongly through my fixèd teeth,
315   With full as many signs of deadly hate,
As lean-faced envy in her loathsome cave.
My tongue should stumble in mine earnest words:
Mine eyes should sparkle like the beaten flint:
Mine hair be fixed on end, as one distract:
320   Ay, every joint should seem to curse and ban,
And even now my burdened heart would break
Should I not curse them. Poison be their drink!

---

296 be'st be   **305 tend** attend   **306 execrations** curses   **307 heavy** sorrowful
311 mandrake plant with forked roots that resembled the human form; it was said to shriek
when pulled from the ground, causing madness or death in any who heard it   **312 bitter-**
searching sharp, piercing, probing   **314 fixèd** gritted, clenched   **318 beaten flint** this stone
gives off sparks when it is struck   **319 fixed on end** standing upright   **distract** frenzied, mad
320 ban curse

Gall, worse than gall, the daintiest that they taste:
Their sweetest shade, a grove of cypress trees:
325 Their chiefest prospect, murd'ring basilisks:
Their softest touch, as smart as lizards' stings:
Their music, frightful as the serpent's hiss,
And boding screech-owls make the consort full!
All the foul terrors in dark-seated hell—

330 QUEEN MARGARET   Enough, sweet Suffolk, thou torment'st
thyself,
And these dread curses, like the sun gainst glass,
Or like an overchargèd gun, recoil,
And turn the force of them upon thyself.

SUFFOLK   You bade me ban, and will you bid me leave?
335 Now by the ground that I am banished from,
Well could I curse away a winter's night,
Though standing naked on a mountain top,
Where biting cold would never let grass grow,
And think it but a minute spent in sport.

340 QUEEN MARGARET   O, let me entreat thee cease: give me thy hand,
That I may dew it with my mournful tears:
Nor let the rain of heaven wet this place,
To wash away my woeful monuments.   *She kisses his hand*
O, could this kiss be printed in thy hand,
345 That thou mightst think upon these by the seal,
Through whom a thousand sighs are breathed for thee.
So get thee gone, that I may know my grief:
'Tis but surmised whiles thou art standing by,
As one that surfeits thinking on a want:
350 I will repeal thee, or, be well assured,
Adventure to be banishèd myself:

323 **Gall** bile   **daintiest** most refined thing   324 **cypress trees** often planted in graveyards,
they were associated with death   325 **prospect** view   **basilisks** mythical reptiles that could
kill with a look   326 **smart** painful, sharp   **lizards** these reptiles were often confused with
snakes and thought to be poisonous   328 **boding** ominous   **consort** group of musicians
332 **overchargèd** overloaded   334 **leave** stop   339 **sport** entertainment, diversion
343 **monuments** memorials, mementos   345 **these . . . seal** these lips by the imprint they left
on your hand   347 **know** feel, realize the extent of   348 **surmised** guessed at, imagined
349 **surfeits** overindulges and grows sick   **want** deprivation   350 **repeal** recall from exile
351 **Adventure** venture, hazard

And banishèd I am, if but from thee.

Go, speak not to me: even now be gone.

O, go not yet. Even thus two friends condemned

355   Embrace, and kiss, and take ten thousand leaves,

Loather a hundred times to part than die:

Yet now farewell, and farewell life with thee.

SUFFOLK   Thus is poor Suffolk ten times banishèd:

Once by the king, and three times thrice by thee.

360   'Tis not the land I care for, wert thou thence:

A wilderness is populous enough,

So Suffolk had thy heavenly company:

For where thou art, there is the world itself,

With every several pleasure in the world:

365   And where thou art not, desolation.

I can no more: live thou to joy thy life:

Myself no joy in naught but that thou liv'st.

Enter Vaux

QUEEN MARGARET   Whither goes Vaux so fast? What news, I
prithee?

VAUX   To signify unto his majesty

370   That Cardinal Beaufort is at point of death:

For suddenly a grievous sickness took him,

That makes him gasp, and stare, and catch the air,

Blaspheming God and cursing men on earth.

Sometimes he talks as if Duke Humphrey's ghost

375   Were by his side: sometime he calls the king,

And whispers to his pillow, as to him,

The secrets of his overchargèd soul;

And I am sent to tell his majesty

That even now he cries aloud for him.

380   QUEEN MARGARET   Go tell this heavy message to the
king.   *Exit [Vaux]*

Ay me! What is this world? What news are these?

---

354 **friends** plays on the sense of "lovers"   356 **Loather** more reluctant   360 **wert thou
thence** if you were not in it   362 **So** provided   364 **several** various   366 **joy** enjoy
372 **catch the** gasp for   376 **as** as if   377 **overchargèd** overburdened   380 **heavy** sorrowful

But wherefore grieve I at an hour's poor loss,
Omitting Suffolk's exile, my soul's treasure?
Why only, Suffolk, mourn I not for thee,
385   And with the southern clouds contend in tears?
Theirs for the earth's increase, mine for my sorrows.
Now get thee hence: the king, thou know'st, is coming:
If thou be found by me, thou art but dead.

SUFFOLK   If I depart from thee, I cannot live:
390   And in thy sight to die, what were it else
But like a pleasant slumber in thy lap?
Here could I breathe my soul into the air,
As mild and gentle as the cradle-babe
Dying with mother's dug between its lips.
395   Where, from thy sight, I should be raging mad,
And cry out for thee to close up mine eyes,
To have thee with thy lips to stop my mouth,
So shouldst thou either turn my flying soul,   *He kisses her*
Or I should breathe it so into thy body,
400   And then it lived in sweet Elysium.
To die by thee were but to die in jest:
From thee to die were torture more than death:
O let me stay, befall what may befall!

QUEEN MARGARET   Away: though parting be a fretful corrosive,
405   It is applièd to a deathful wound.
To France, sweet Suffolk: let me hear from thee:
For wheresoe'er thou art in this world's globe,
I'll have an Iris that shall find thee out.

SUFFOLK   I go.

410   QUEEN MARGARET   And take my heart with thee.   *She kisses him*

---

382 an . . . loss i.e. the cardinal's old age would mean he did not have long to live in any event
383 Omitting disregarding   **385 southern clouds** rain was thought to come chiefly from the
south   **contend in** compete for   **388 by** near   **but** as good as   **390 die** plays on the sense of
"have an orgasm"   **391 lap** plays on the sense of "vagina"   **392 breathe . . . air** i.e. die
394 dug nipple   **395 Where** whereas   **from** away from   **398 turn** turn back, return
400 lived would live   **Elysium** heaven or paradise of Greek mythology   **401 but . . . jest** not
really to die at all/to play at dying (with sexual connotations)   **404 fretful** abrasive,
aggravating   **405 deathful** deadly, fatal   **408 Iris** in Greek mythology, goddess of the rainbow
and the messenger of Juno, queen of the gods (plays on the sense of "part of the eye")

SUFFOLK   A jewel, locked into the woefull'st cask
That ever did contain a thing of worth:
Even as a splitted bark, so sunder we:
This way fall I to death.

415   QUEEN MARGARET   This way for me.   *Exeunt [severally]*

[Act 3 Scene 3]   *running scene 11*

*Enter the King [Henry VI], Salisbury and Warwick, to the Cardinal
in bed*

KING HENRY VI   How fares my lord? Speak, Beaufort, to thy
sovereign.

CARDINAL   If thou be'st death, I'll give thee England's treasure,
Enough to purchase such another island,
So thou wilt let me live, and feel no pain.

5   KING HENRY VI   Ah, what a sign it is of evil life,
Where death's approach is seen so terrible.

WARWICK   Beaufort, it is thy sovereign speaks to thee.

CARDINAL   Bring me unto my trial when you will.
Died he not in his bed? Where should he die?

10   Can I make men live, whe'er they will or no?
O torture me no more, I will confess.
Alive again? Then show me where he is:
I'll give a thousand pound to look upon him.
He hath no eyes, the dust hath blinded them.

15   Comb down his hair: look, look, it stands upright,
Like lime-twigs set to catch my wingèd soul:
Give me some drink, and bid the apothecary
Bring the strong poison that I bought of him.

KING HENRY VI   O, thou eternal mover of the heavens,

20   Look with a gentle eye upon this wretch:
O beat away the busy meddling fiend

411 cask casket   413 bark ship   sunder we we are split in two, we separate   *severally*
separately   3.3   *Location: the cardinal's bedchamber*   4 So if   6 is seen appears
9 he i.e. Gloucester   14 dust i.e. to which all bodies return   16 lime-twigs twigs smeared
with birdlime, a sticky substance used to catch birds   18 of from   21 fiend the devil

That lays strong siege unto this wretch's soul,
And from his bosom purge this black despair.

WARWICK   See how the pangs of death do make him grin.

25 SALISBURY   Disturb him not: let him pass peaceably.

KING HENRY VI   Peace to his soul, if God's good pleasure be.
Lord Card'nal, if thou think'st on heaven's bliss,
Hold up thy hand, make signal of thy hope.   *Cardinal dies*
He dies and makes no sign: O God, forgive him.

30 WARWICK   So bad a death argues a monstrous life.

KING HENRY VI   Forbear to judge, for we are sinners all.
Close up his eyes and draw the curtain close,
And let us all to meditation.   *Exeunt*

[Act 4 Scene 1]   *running scene 12*

Alarum. Fight at sea. Ordnance goes off. Enter [a] Lieutenant,
[a Master, a Master's Mate, Walter Whitmore; with] Suffolk [disguised
and two Gentlemen as their prisoners] and others

LIEUTENANT   The gaudy, blabbing and remorseful day
Is crept into the bosom of the sea:
And now loud-howling wolves arouse the jades
That drag the tragic melancholy night:

5 Who, with their drowsy, slow and flagging wings
Clip dead men's graves, and from their misty jaws
Breathe foul contagious darkness in the air:
Therefore bring forth the soldiers of our prize,
For whilst our pinnace anchors in the Downs,

10 Here shall they make their ransom on the sand,
Or with their blood stain this discoloured shore.

---

24 grin grimace   **30 argues** testifies to, suggests   **32 close** tightly   **33 meditation** reflection
and prayer   **4.1** *Location: the coast of Kent*   **Ordnance** cannon   **Master** officer in
charge of sailing a ship   **1 gaudy** bright   **blabbing** revealing, telltale   **3 arouse** awaken
jades worn-out horses, but here dragons (who drew the chariot of Hecate, Greek goddess of
the night)   **5 flagging** drooping   **6 Clip** strike glancingly, skim/embrace, clasp   **8 prize**
captured vessel   **9 pinnace** small two-masted boat   **Downs** an anchorage off the coast of
Kent   **11 discoloured** i.e. which will be discolored

Master, this prisoner freely give I thee, *Pointing to First Gentleman*

And thou that art his mate, make boot of this: *Pointing to Second*

The other, Walter Whitmore, is thy share. *Gentleman*

15 FIRST GENTLEMAN   What is my ransom, master, let *Pointing to Suffolk*

me know? *To the Master*

MASTER   A thousand crowns, or else lay down your head.

MATE   And so much shall you give, or off goes

yours. *To Second Gentleman*

LIEUTENANT   What, think you much to pay two thousand

crowns, *To both Gentlemen*

And bear the name and port of gentlemen?

20 WHITMORE   Cut both the villains' throats, for die you shall:

The lives of those which we have lost in fight

Be counterpoised with such a petty sum.

FIRST GENTLEMAN   I'll give it, sir, and therefore *To the Master*

spare my life.

SECOND GENTLEMAN   And so will I, and write home *To the Mate*

for it straight.

25 WHITMORE   I lost mine eye in laying the prize aboard, *To Suffolk*

And therefore to revenge it, shalt thou die,

And so should these, if I might have my will.

LIEUTENANT   Be not so rash: take ransom: let him live.

SUFFOLK   Look on my George: I am a gentleman:

30 Rate me at what thou wilt, thou shalt be paid.

WHITMORE   And so am I: my name is Walter Whitmore.

How now? Why starts thou? What, doth death affright?

SUFFOLK   Thy name affrights me, in whose sound is death:

A cunning man did calculate my birth

35 And told me that by water I should die:

Yet let not this make thee be bloody-minded:

Thy name is Gualtier, being rightly sounded.

---

13 make boot take advantage, make profit   **18 much** it too much   **19 port** social position
22 counterpoised compensated, offset   **25 laying . . . aboard** boarding the captured ship
29 George badge or emblem of Saint George, patron saint of England; part of the insignia of
the knightly Order of the Garter   **30 Rate** value   **31 Walter** pronounced like "water"
32 affright frighten you   **34 cunning man** one skilled in magic and fortune-telling   **calculate
my birth** cast my horoscope   **36 bloody-minded** intent on murder/think on my death
37 sounded pronounced

WHITMORE   Gualtier or Walter, which it is, I care not:
Never yet did base dishonour blur our name,
40   But with our sword we wiped away the blot.
Therefore, when merchant-like I sell revenge,
Broke be my sword, my arms torn and defaced,
And I proclaimed a coward through the world.

SUFFOLK   Stay, Whitmore, for thy prisoner is a prince,
45   The Duke of Suffolk, William de la Pole.

WHITMORE   The Duke of Suffolk muffled up in rags?

SUFFOLK   Ay, but these rags are no part of the duke:
Jove sometimes went disguised, and why not I?

LIEUTENANT   But Jove was never slain as thou shalt be,
50   Obscure and lousy swain, King Henry's blood!

SUFFOLK   The honourable blood of Lancaster
Must not be shed by such a jaded groom:
Hast thou not kissed thy hand and held my stirrup?
Bare-headed plodded by my foot-cloth mule
55   And thought thee happy when I shook my head?
How often hast thou waited at my cup,
Fed from my trencher, kneeled down at the board,
When I have feasted with Queen Margaret?
Remember it, and let it make thee crest-fall'n,
60   Ay, and allay this thy abortive pride:
How in our voiding lobby hast thou stood
And duly waited for my coming forth?
This hand of mine hath writ in thy behalf,
And therefore shall it charm thy riotous tongue.

---

41 **sell revenge** i.e. ransom prisoners   42 **arms** coat of arms   48 **Jove** Roman king of the
gods   50 **Obscure** lowly, insignificant   **lousy** despicable, louse-infested   **swain** rustic, yokel
52 **jaded** contemptible (language in the next line picks up a play on "jades," i.e. worn-out
horses)   **groom** servant/servant who tended to horses   53 **kissed thy hand** a gesture of
respect   54 **Bare-headed** servants did not wear hats in deference to their masters   **foot-
cloth mule** mule used to carry (or possibly wearing) the stately ornamental cloth used to drape
a nobleman's horse   55 **happy** fortunate   **shook my head** nodded in approval/gave the
slightest sign of acknowledgment   56 **waited . . . cup** served me drink   57 **Fed . . .
trencher** acted as my taster/been supported by my household   **trencher** plate   **kneeled . . .
board** bowed, served deferentially at the table (**board**)   59 **crest-fall'n** humbled   61 **voiding
lobby** antechamber or lobby for those leaving the main chamber   64 **charm** i.e. silence (with
a spell)

65	WHITMORE	Speak, captain, shall I stab the forlorn swain?
	LIEUTENANT	First let my words stab him, as he hath me.
	SUFFOLK	Base slave, thy words are blunt and so art thou.
	LIEUTENANT	Convey him hence and on our longboat's side
		Strike off his head.
70	SUFFOLK	Thou dar'st not for thy own.
	LIEUTENANT	Pole—
	SUFFOLK	Pole?
	LIEUTENANT	Ay, kennel, puddle, sink, whose filth and dirt

Troubles the silver spring where England drinks:
75 Now will I dam up this thy yawning mouth
For swallowing the treasure of the realm.
Thy lips that kissed the queen shall sweep the ground:
And thou that smiled'st at good Duke Humphrey's death,
Against the senseless winds shalt grin in vain,
80 Who in contempt shall hiss at thee again.
And wedded be thou to the hags of hell,
For daring to affy a mighty lord
Unto the daughter of a worthless king,
Having neither subject, wealth, nor diadem:
85 By devilish policy art thou grown great,
And like ambitious Sylla, overgorged
With gobbets of thy mother's bleeding heart.
By thee Anjou and Maine were sold to France,
The false revolting Normans thorough thee

---

65 **forlorn swain** wretched fellow/neglected lover (of Queen Margaret; or Whitmore mocks the idea of the servant-master relationship Suffolk has just elaborated on)   67 **blunt** forthright/ unthreatening, lacking sharpness   68 **longboat** the largest boat belonging to a sailing vessel, presumably used to bring the men ashore   70 **for thy own** for fear of losing your own head 72 **Pole?** Suffolk reacts to the insolent use of his family name by an inferior; in his ensuing speech, the Lieutenant puns on "pool"   73 **kennel** gutter   **sink** sewer   74 **Troubles** stirs up, muddies   75 **yawning** gaping   77 **sweep the ground** either as the body kneels with its head bowed for execution or as the decapitated head falls to the ground, its lips against the dirt 79 **Against** exposed to   **senseless** unfeeling   **grin** grimace   80 **Who** i.e. the **winds**   **again** in response   81 **hags of hell** the three Furies of classical mythology   82 **affy** betroth, engage **mighty . . . king** i.e. Henry VI to Margaret   84 **subject** subjects   85 **policy** cunning, strategy 86 **Sylla** Sulla (138–78 BC), notoriously cruel Roman dictator who drew up a list of his enemies who were to be killed   **overgorged** stuffed, glutted   87 **gobbets** chunks of raw flesh **mother's** i.e. native country's   89 **revolting** rebellious   **thorough** through, because of

90   Disdain to call us lord, and Picardy
     Hath slain their governors, surprised our forts,
     And sent the ragged soldiers wounded home.
     The princely Warwick, and the Nevilles all,
     Whose dreadful swords were never drawn in vain,
95   As hating thee, are rising up in arms:
     And now the House of York, thrust from the crown
     By shameful murder of a guiltless king
     And lofty proud encroaching tyranny,
     Burns with revenging fire, whose hopeful colours
100 Advance our half-faced sun, striving to shine,
     Under the which is writ '*Invitis nubibus*'.
     The commons here in Kent are up in arms,
     And, to conclude, reproach and beggary
     Is crept into the palace of our king,
105 And all by thee.— Away, convey him hence.
     SUFFOLK   O, that I were a god, to shoot forth thunder
     Upon these paltry, servile, abject drudges:
     Small things make base men proud. This villain here,
     Being captain of a pinnace, threatens more
110 Than Bargulus the strong Illyrian pirate.
     Drones suck not eagles' blood, but rob beehives:
     It is impossible that I should die
     By such a lowly vassal as thyself.
     Thy words move rage and not remorse in me:

90 **Picardy** region of northern France   91 **surprised** seized   95 **As hating** in hate of
97 **murder . . . king** i.e. Richard II, who was deposed by Bullingbrook (Henry IV), thus
establishing the ascendancy of the house of Lancaster   98 **encroaching** grasping
(wrongfully)   99 **whose** i.e. the **House of York**   **colours** military banners (of the House of
York)   100 **Advance** raise, hold up   **half-faced sun** the emblem of Edward III and Richard II
consisted of the sun's rays emerging above clouds   101 '***Invitis nubibus***' "In spite of clouds"
(Latin)   102 **commons** common people   106 **god . . . thunder** Jove (Jupiter), the Roman
king of the gods, was traditionally armed with a thunderbolt   107 **drudges** base servants
109 **pinnace** i.e. relatively small boat, often in attendance on a larger   110 **Bargulus . . .**
pirate a pirate mentioned in Cicero's *De Officiis*, a standard text in Elizabethan schools
111 **Drones . . . beehives** nonworking male bees (whose sole purpose is to impregnate the
queen) were thought to eat the honey other bees had made; equally inaccurate was the belief
that beetles sucked eagles' blood   113 **vassal** servant, slave

115   I go of message from the queen to France:
    I charge thee waft me safely cross the Channel.

LIEUTENANT   Walter—

WHITMORE   Come, Suffolk, I must waft thee to thy death.

SUFFOLK   *Paene gelidus timor occupat artus*: it is thee I fear.

120 WHITMORE   Thou shalt have cause to fear before I leave thee.
    What, are ye daunted now? Now will ye stoop?

FIRST GENTLEMAN   My gracious lord, entreat him, speak him fair.

SUFFOLK   Suffolk's imperial tongue is stern and rough:
    Used to command, untaught to plead for favour.
125   Far be it we should honour such as these
    With humble suit: no, rather let my head
    Stoop to the block than these knees bow to any,
    Save to the God of heaven and to my king:
    And sooner dance upon a bloody pole
130   Than stand uncovered to the vulgar groom.
    True nobility is exempt from fear:
    More can I bear than you dare execute.

LIEUTENANT   Hale him away, and let him talk no more.

SUFFOLK   Come, soldiers, show what cruelty ye can,
135   That this my death may never be forgot.
    Great men oft die by vile Besonians:
    A Roman sworder and banditto slave
    Murdered sweet Tully: Brutus' bastard hand
    Stabbed Julius Caesar: savage islanders
140   Pompey the Great: and Suffolk dies by pirates.

              Exit Walter [Whitmore] with Suffolk

---

115 **of** with a   116 **waft** guide, convey   119 *Paene . . . artus* "Cold fear almost entirely
seizes my limbs" (Latin)   122 **fair** courteously   123 **imperial** commanding   125 **we** Suffolk
uses the royal pronoun   126 **suit** entreaty   129 **bloody pole** the heads of traitors were
mounted on spikes and displayed on London Bridge; **pole** puns on Suffolk's family name
130 **uncovered** hatless (a mark of deference)   133 **Hale** haul, drag   136 **vile** low,
contemptible   **Besonians** beggars, base men   137 **sworder** assassin   **banditto** bandit,
lawless   138 **sweet** sweet-voiced, rhetorically masterful   **Tully** Cicero, famous Roman orator
and statesman of the first century BC; in fact, he was killed by a centurion and a tribune,
though Thomas Nashe refers to his murder by "slaves"   **Brutus' bastard** rumor had it that
Brutus was **Julius** Caesar's illegitimate son   140 **Pompey the Great** famous Roman general of
the first century BC; he was killed in Egypt, but a play by George Chapman depicted his death
on the Greek island of Lesbos

LIEUTENANT   And as for these whose ransom we have set,
It is our pleasure one of them depart:
Therefore come you with us and let him go.

        Exit Lieutenant, and the rest [leaving] the First Gentleman
Enter Whitmore with the body [of Suffolk]

WHITMORE   There let his head and lifeless body lie,
145   Until the queen his mistress bury it.   *Exit*

FIRST GENTLEMAN   O, barbarous and bloody spectacle!
His body will I bear unto the king:
If he revenge it not, yet will his friends:
So will the queen, that living held him dear.

        [Exit with the body]

[Act 4 Scene 2]   *running scene 13*

Enter [George] Bevis and John Holland [with long staves]

BEVIS   Come and get thee a sword, though made of a lath:
they have been up these two days.

HOLLAND   They have the more need to sleep now then.

BEVIS   I tell thee, Jack Cade the clothier means to dress the
5   commonwealth, and turn it, and set a new nap upon it.

HOLLAND   So he had need, for 'tis threadbare. Well, I say it was
never merry world in England since gentlemen came up.

BEVIS   O miserable age: virtue is not regarded in
handicraftsmen.

10 HOLLAND   The nobility think scorn to go in leather aprons.

BEVIS   Nay more, the King's Council are no good workmen.

---

145 mistress "female master," but here predominantly "lover"   **4.2   *Location: Kent***
[*George*] . . . *Holland* probably the names of the actors Shakespeare had in mind as he wrote
this scene; John Holland is known to have been an actor at the time   ***staves*** staffs used as
weapons   **1 lath** thin strip of wood; a dagger of lath was the conventional weapon of the Vice
character in morality plays   **2 up** in rebellion, up in arms   **4 clothier** cloth worker, who dealt
with cloth after it had been woven   **dress** clothe/reform   **5 turn it** turn it inside out (as a
means of renewing it and prolonging its use)/turn it upside down socially   **set . . . it** give it a
smooth finish   **nap** projecting fibers, surface texture   **7 merry world** like the good old days
up into fashion   **8 regarded** noticed, valued   **10 think scorn** disdain, consider it lowly
leather aprons the typical clothing of an artisan

HOLLAND   True: and yet it is said, 'Labour in thy vocation': which is as much to say as, 'Let the magistrates be labouring men', and therefore should we be magistrates.

15 BEVIS   Thou hast hit it: for there's no better sign of a brave mind than a hard hand.

HOLLAND   I see them! I see them! There's Best's son, the tanner of Wingham.

BEVIS   He shall have the skins of our enemies to make
20   dog's leather of.

HOLLAND   And Dick the Butcher.

BEVIS   Then is sin struck down like an ox, and iniquity's throat cut like a calf.

HOLLAND   And Smith the weaver.

25 BEVIS   Argo, their thread of life is spun.

HOLLAND   Come, come, let's fall in with them.

Drum. Enter Cade, Dick [the] Butcher, Smith the Weaver, and a Sawyer, with infinite numbers [with long staves]

CADE   We, John Cade, so termed of our supposed father—

DICK   Or rather of stealing a cade of herrings.   *Aside*

CADE   For our enemies shall fail before us, inspired with
30   the spirit of putting down kings and princes.— Command silence.

DICK   Silence!

CADE   My father was a Mortimer—

DICK   He was an honest man, and a good bricklayer.   *Aside*

35 CADE   My mother a Plantagenet—

DICK   I knew her well, she was a midwife.   *Aside*

CADE   My wife descended of the Lacys—

---

12 'Labour . . . vocation' proverbial, i.e. each man must walk in his own calling
13 labouring working (manually)   15 hit it got it, hit the nail on the head   brave fine
16 hard hardened, toughened (through manual labor)   17 Best's . . . tanner the son of Best, the tanner (leather worker)   18 Wingham village near Canterbury, in Kent   20 dog's leather used for glove making   25 Argo i.e. *ergo*—"therefore" (Latin)   thread . . . spun in classical mythology, the three Fates spun, measured out, and cut the thread of a person's life   26 fall in join   *Sawyer* workman who saws timber   *infinite numbers* i.e. a large group of people   27 We Cade uses the royal pronoun   termed of named after   28 of for   cade barrel   29 fail some editors emend to "fall," thus generating a possible play on Cade's name as *cadere* is Latin for "to fall"   34 bricklayer puns on Mortimer/mortarer   37 Lacys the family name of the earls of Lincoln

DICK   She was indeed a pedlar's daughter, and   *Aside*
sold many laces.

40   SMITH   But now of late, not able to travel with her   *Aside*
furred pack, she washes bucks here at home.

CADE   Therefore am I of an honourable house.

DICK   Ay, by my faith, the field is honourable, and   *Aside*
there was he born, under a hedge: for his father had never a
45   house but the cage.

CADE   Valiant I am—

SMITH   A must needs, for beggary is valiant.   *Aside*

CADE   I am able to endure much—

DICK   No question of that: for I have seen him   *Aside*
50   whipped three market days together.

CADE   I fear neither sword nor fire—

SMITH   He need not fear the sword, for his coat is of   *Aside*
proof.

DICK   But methinks he should stand in fear of   *Aside*
55   fire, being burnt i'th'hand for stealing of sheep.

CADE   Be brave, then, for your captain is brave, and vows
reformation. There shall be in England seven halfpenny
loaves sold for a penny: the three-hooped pot shall have ten
hoops, and I will make it felony to drink small beer. All the
60   realm shall be in common, and in Cheapside shall my palfrey
go to grass: and when I am king, as king I will be—

ALL   God save your majesty!

CADE   I thank you, good people. There shall be no money:
all shall eat and drink on my score, and I will apparel them

39 laces puns on **Lacys**   **40 travel** puns on "travail" (work, labor/have sex, as a roaming whore)   **41 furred pack** pedlar's pack (made of or trimmed with fur)/vagina covered with pubic hair   **washes bucks** washes laundry/has sex with lecherous men   **43 field** may play on the sense of "background of a coat of arms"   **44 under a hedge** proverbial birthplace for the very lowly   **45 cage** prison for petty criminals and vagabonds   **47 A must needs** he must be **valiant** sturdy, capable of work   **50 whipped** the standard punishment for vagabonds   **53 proof** tried resistance (i.e. old, much worn; usually applied to impenetrable armor)   **54 stand** remain   **55 burnt** branded (with a "T" for "Thief")   **58 the . . . hoops** wooden drinking vessels had hoops around them as a means of measuring their contents; a **three-hooped pot** contained two pints, so Cade's suggestion means that a drinker would get considerably more for his money   **59 small** weak   **60 be in common** become common land, available to all   **Cheapside** market area of London   **palfrey** a horse for riding (as opposed to a warhorse)   **61 grass** graze   **64 score** account, expense   **apparel** dress

65   all in one livery, that they may agree like brothers, and
worship me their lord.

DICK   The first thing we do, let's kill all the lawyers.

CADE   Nay, that I mean to do. Is not this a lamentable
thing, that of the skin of an innocent lamb should be made
70   parchment? That parchment, being scribbled o'er, should
undo a man? Some say the bee stings, but I say, 'tis the bee's
wax: for I did but seal once to a thing, and I was never mine
own man since. How now? Who's there?

Enter [some, bringing forward] a Clerk [of Chartham]

SMITH   The Clerk of Chartham: he can write and read and
75   cast account.

CADE   O, monstrous.

SMITH   We took him setting of boys' copies.

CADE   Here's a villain!

SMITH   H'as a book in his pocket with red letters in't.

80   CADE   Nay, then he is a conjurer.

DICK   Nay, he can make obligations, and write court hand.

CADE   I am sorry for't: the man is a proper man, of mine
honour: unless I find him guilty, he shall not die. Come
hither, sirrah, I must examine thee: what is thy name?

85   CLERK   Emmanuel.

DICK   They use to write it on the top of letters: 'twill go
hard with you.

CADE   Let me alone.— Dost thou use to write   *To the Clerk*
thy name? Or hast thou a mark to thyself, like an honest
90   plain-dealing man?

---

65 livery servants' uniform   **agree** match/get on   **72 wax** sealing wax, used on official
documents   **seal** agree, put my name (plays on the sense of "have sex")   **thing** i.e. document
(plays on the sense of "vagina")   **Clerk** parish clerk with secretarial responsibilities as scribe
or notary   **Chartham** a village near Canterbury, in Kent   **75 cast account** do arithmetic,
add up accounts   **76 monstrous** unnatural (a lack of literacy and numeracy was very
common among country folk)   **77 took** found, encountered/arrested, captured   **setting . . .
copies** preparing written exercises for schoolboys   **79 red letters** in almanacs, the saints'
days were printed in red as were the capital letters in school primers   **80 conjurer** magician
(using an almanac to make predictions)   **81 make obligations** draw up legal bonds   **court
hand** the script used in official, legal documents   **82 proper** fine/handsome   **85 Emmanuel**
meaning "God with us," a phrase often found at the heads of letters or deeds   **86 go hard with**
be the worse   **88 Dost . . . to** do you usually   **89 mark to thyself** illiterate people "signed"
their name by making a mark such as an "X"   **90 plain-dealing** simple, straightforward

CLERK   Sir, I thank God, I have been so well brought up that
I can write my name.

ALL   He hath confessed: away with him: he's a villain
and a traitor.

95 CADE   Away with him, I say: hang him with his pen and
inkhorn about his neck.   *Exit one with the Clerk*

Enter Michael

MICHAEL   Where's our general?

CADE   Here I am, thou particular fellow.

MICHAEL   Fly, fly, fly! Sir Humphrey Stafford and his brother
100   are hard by, with the king's forces.

CADE   Stand, villain, stand, or I'll fell thee down: he shall
be encountered with a man as good as himself. He is but a
knight, is a?

MICHAEL   No.

105 CADE   To equal him I will make myself a knight
presently.   *Kneels*

Rise up Sir John Mortimer.   *Rises*

Now have at him!

*Enter Sir Humphrey Stafford and his brother, with Drum, [Herald] and
Soldiers*

STAFFORD   Rebellious hinds, the filth and scum of Kent,
Marked for the gallows: lay your weapons down:
110   Home to your cottages: forsake this groom.
The king is merciful, if you revolt.

STAFFORD'S BROTHER   But angry, wrathful, and inclined to blood,
If you go forward: therefore yield, or die.

CADE   As for these silken-coated slaves, I pass not:
115   It is to you, good people, that I speak,
Over whom, in time to come, I hope to reign:
For I am rightful heir unto the crown.

---

96 inkhorn portable inkwell   **98 particular** private (playing on opposite of **general**)   **100 hard**
close   **102 encountered** i.e. in combat   **103 a** he   **104 No** i.e. no, nothing but a knight
105 presently immediately   *Drum* drummer   **108 hinds** peasants   **110 groom** servant (i.e.
Cade)   **111 revolt** turn back (to your former allegiance)   **114 pass** care

STAFFORD   Villain, thy father was a plasterer,
And thou thyself a shearman, art thou not?

120   CADE   And Adam was a gardener.

STAFFORD'S BROTHER   And what of that?

CADE   Marry, this: Edmund Mortimer, Earl of March,
married the Duke of Clarence' daughter, did he not?

STAFFORD   Ay, sir.

125   CADE   By her he had two children at one birth.

STAFFORD'S BROTHER   That's false.

CADE   Ay, there's the question: but I say 'tis true:
The elder of them, being put to nurse,
Was by a beggar-woman stol'n away,

130   And, ignorant of his birth and parentage,
Became a bricklayer when he came to age.
His son am I: deny it if you can.

DICK   Nay, 'tis too true: therefore he shall be king.

SMITH   Sir, he made a chimney in my father's house, and the
135   bricks are alive at this day to testify it: therefore deny it not.

STAFFORD   And will you credit this base drudge's words,
That speaks he knows not what?

ALL   Ay, marry, will we: therefore get ye gone.

STAFFORD'S BROTHER   Jack Cade, the Duke of York hath taught
140   you this.

CADE   He lies, for I invented it myself.—   *Aside*
Go to, sirrah, tell the king from me, that for his father's sake,
Henry the Fifth, in whose time boys went to   *Aloud*
span-counter for French crowns, I am content he shall reign:
145   but I'll be Protector over him.

---

119 **shearman** one who shears excess fiber from woolen cloth as it is made   120 **Adam** in the
Bible, the first man; he looked after the Garden of Eden   125 **two . . . birth** i.e. twins
127 **question** problem   128 **put to nurse** given to a wet-nurse to be breastfed (noble women
did not generally breastfeed their own babies)   135 **alive** still there   142 **Go to** expression of
impatient dismissal   144 **span-counter** game in which a player tried to throw a counter or
coin as close to that of his opponent as possible (and within the distance of the span of a hand)
French crowns coins/syphilitic baldness/monarch's crowns (refers to the campaigns against
the French under Henry V)   145 **Protector** legal and political guardian

DICK   And furthermore, we'll have the lord Saye's head for
selling the dukedom of Maine.

CADE   And good reason: for thereby is England mained,
and fain to go with a staff, but that my puissance holds it up.
150   Fellow kings, I tell you that that Lord Saye hath gelded the
commonwealth, and made it an eunuch: and more than
that, he can speak French, and therefore he is a traitor.

STAFFORD   O gross and miserable ignorance!

CADE   Nay, answer if you can: the Frenchmen are our
155   enemies: go to, then, I ask but this: can he that speaks with
the tongue of an enemy be a good counsellor, or no?

ALL   No, no, and therefore we'll have his head.

STAFFORD'S BROTHER   Well, seeing gentle words will not prevail,
Assail them with the army of the king.

160   STAFFORD   Herald, away, and throughout every town
Proclaim them traitors that are up with Cade,
That those which fly before the battle ends
May, even in their wives' and children's sight,
Be hanged up for example at their doors:
165   And you that be the king's friends, follow me.

Exeunt [*Stafford, Stafford's brother and Soldiers*]

CADE   And you that love the commons, follow me:
Now show yourselves men, 'tis for liberty.
We will not leave one lord, one gentleman:
Spare none but such as go in clouted shoon,
170   For they are thrifty honest men, and such
As would, but that they dare not, take our parts.

DICK   They are all in order and march toward us.

CADE   But then are we in order when we are most out of
order. Come, march forward.   [*Exeunt*]

---

148 mained maimed (puns on **Maine**)   **149 fain to go** obliged to walk   **puissance** power
150 gelded castrated   **153 miserable** contemptible, pitiable   **156 tongue** language
158 gentle peaceable   **161 up** up in arms   **162 That** so that   **164 for** as   **169 clouted**
shoon patched or hobnailed shoes (i.e. workingmen's footwear)   **170 thrifty** respectable,
worthy   **172 order** battle formation   **173 out of order** rebellious

[Act 4 Scene 3]   *running scene 13 continues*

Alarums to the fight, wherein both the Staffords [Stafford and
Stafford's brother] are slain. Enter Cade and the rest

CADE   Where's Dick, the butcher of Ashford?

DICK   Here, sir.

CADE   They fell before thee like sheep and oxen, and thou
behaved'st thyself as if thou hadst been in thine own
5   slaughter-house: therefore thus will I reward thee: the Lent
shall be as long again as it is, and thou shalt have a licence to
kill for a hundred lacking one.

DICK   I desire no more.

CADE   And, to speak truth, thou deserv'st no less. This
10   monument of the victory will I bear, and the   *Putting on*
bodies shall be dragged at my horse heels till   *Stafford's*
I do come to London, where we will have the   *brigandine*
Mayor's sword borne before us.

DICK   If we mean to thrive and do good, break open the
15   jails and let out the prisoners.

CADE   Fear not that, I warrant thee. Come, let's march
towards London.   *Exeunt*

[Act 4 Scene 4]   *running scene 14*

Enter the King [Henry VI] with a supplication, and the Queen
[Margaret] with Suffolk's head, the Duke of Buckingham and the Lord
Saye

QUEEN MARGARET   Oft have I heard that grief softens   *Aside*
the mind,
And makes it fearful and degenerate:
Think therefore on revenge and cease to weep.

4.3   **5 Lent . . . one** during Lent, the forty-day period before Easter when Christians were to
eat fish rather than meat, butchers required a special license to slaughter animals; Cade
promises to double the length of Lent and grants Dick the right to kill ninety-nine animals/
supply ninety-nine customers/hold a license for ninety-nine years   **10 monument** memorial
trophy   *brigandine* body armor   **16 Fear** doubt   **warrant** assure   **4.4** ***Location: the***
royal court, London   **supplication** formal petition

But who can cease to weep and look on this?

5   Here may his head lie on my throbbing breast:

But where's the body that I should embrace?

BUCKINGHAM   What answer makes your grace to   *To the King*

the rebels' supplication?

KING HENRY VI   I'll send some holy bishop to entreat:

For God forbid so many simple souls

10   Should perish by the sword. And I myself,

Rather than bloody war shall cut them short,

Will parley with Jack Cade their general.

But stay, I'll read it over once again.

QUEEN MARGARET   Ah, barbarous villains! Hath   *Aside to*

this lovely face   *Suffolk's head*

15   Ruled like a wandering planet over me,

And could it not enforce them to relent,

That were unworthy to behold the same?

KING HENRY VI   Lord Saye, Jack Cade hath sworn to have thy

head.

SAYE   Ay, but I hope your highness shall have his.

20   **KING HENRY VI**   How now, madam?

Still lamenting and mourning for Suffolk's death?

I fear me, love, if that I had been dead,

Thou wouldst not have mourned so much for me.

QUEEN MARGARET   No, my love, I should not mourn, but die for

thee.

Enter a Messenger

25   **KING HENRY VI**   How now? What news? Why com'st thou in

such haste?

MESSENGER   The rebels are in Southwark: fly, my lord!

Jack Cade proclaims himself Lord Mortimer,

Descended from the Duke of Clarence' house,

And calls your grace usurper, openly,

30   And vows to crown himself in Westminster.

His army is a ragged multitude

---

12 parley negotiate   **15 wandering** unfixed, having its own motion   **17 That** who
26 Southwark area just south of the Thames, on the outskirts of the City

Of hinds and peasants, rude and merciless:
Sir Humphrey Stafford and his brother's death
Hath given them heart and courage to proceed:
35   All scholars, lawyers, courtiers, gentlemen,
They call false caterpillars, and intend their death.

KING HENRY VI   O, graceless men: they know not what they do.

BUCKINGHAM   My gracious lord, retire to Killingworth,
Until a power be raised to put them down.

40   QUEEN MARGARET   Ah, were the Duke of Suffolk now alive,
These Kentish rebels would be soon appeased.

KING HENRY VI   Lord Saye, the traitors hateth thee,
Therefore away with us to Killingworth.

SAYE   So might your grace's person be in danger.
45   The sight of me is odious in their eyes:
And therefore in this city will I stay
And live alone as secret as I may.

Enter another Messenger

SECOND MESSENGER   Jack Cade hath gotten London Bridge.
The citizens fly and forsake their houses:
50   The rascal people, thirsting after prey,
Join with the traitor, and they jointly swear
To spoil the city and your royal court.

BUCKINGHAM   Then linger not, my lord, away, take horse.

KING HENRY VI   Come, Margaret: God, our hope, will succour us.

55   QUEEN MARGARET   My hope is gone now Suffolk is
deceased.   *Aside*

KING HENRY VI   Farewell, my lord: trust not the Kentish
rebels.   *To Saye*

BUCKINGHAM   Trust nobody, for fear you be betrayed.

SAYE   The trust I have is in mine innocence,
And therefore am I bold and resolute.   *Exeunt*

---

36 **false caterpillars** treacherous parasites   37 **graceless** rough, ignorant/lacking divine
grace   **they . . . do** echoes Christ's words from the cross (Luke 23:34)   38 **Killingworth**
Kenilworth Castle, near Coventry in Warwickshire   39 **power** army   41 **appeased** pacified
44 **So** then   50 **rascal people** rabble   52 **spoil** plunder, loot

[Act 4 Scene 5]   *running scene 15*

Enter Lord Scales upon the Tower walking. Then enters two or three
Citizens below

SCALES   How now? Is Jack Cade slain?

FIRST CITIZEN   No, my lord, nor likely to be slain: for they have
won the bridge, killing all those that withstand them: the
Lord Mayor craves aid of your honour from the Tower to
5   defend the city from the rebels.

SCALES   Such aid as I can spare you shall command,
But I am troubled here with them myself:
The rebels have assayed to win the Tower.
But get you to Smithfield, and gather head,
10   And thither I will send you Matthew Gough.
Fight for your king, your country, and your lives:
And so, farewell, for I must hence again.   *Exeunt*

[Act 4 Scene 6]   *running scene 16*

Enter Jack Cade and the rest, and strikes his staff on London Stone

CADE   Now is Mortimer lord of this city, and here sitting
upon London Stone, I charge and command that, of the
city's cost, the Pissing Conduit run nothing but claret wine
this first year of our reign. And now henceforward it shall be
5   treason for any that calls me other than Lord Mortimer.

Enter a Soldier running

SOLDIER   Jack Cade! Jack Cade!

CADE   Knock him down there.   *They kill him*

SMITH   If this fellow be wise, he'll never call ye Jack Cade
more: I think he hath a very fair warning.

10   DICK   My lord, there's an army gathered together in
Smithfield.

4.5 *Location: the Tower of London*   **3 the bridge** i.e. London Bridge   **4 craves**
requests/begs   **9 gather head** raise an army   **10 Matthew Gough** historically a very
experienced soldier   **4.6** *Location: Cannon Street, London*   **London Stone** central City
landmark located in Cannon Street   **2 of** at   **3 Pissing Conduit** the nickname for Little
Conduit, a water fountain used by the lower-class Londoners

CADE   Come then, let's go fight with them: but first, go and set London Bridge on fire, and, if you can, burn down the Tower too. Come, let's away.   *Exeunt all*

[Act 4 Scene 7]   *running scene 17*

Alarums. Matthew Gough is slain, and all the rest [of his followers with him]. Then enter Jack Cade, with his company [including Dick, Smith and Holland]

CADE   So, sirs: now go some and pull down the Savoy: others to the Inns of Court: down with them all.

DICK   I have a suit unto your lordship.

CADE   Be it a lordship, thou shalt have it for that word.

5   DICK   Only that the laws of England may come out of your mouth.

HOLLAND   Mass, 'twill be sore law, then; for he was   *Aside*
thrust in the mouth with a spear, and 'tis not whole yet.

SMITH   Nay, John, it will be stinking law, for his   *Aside*
10   breath stinks with eating toasted cheese.

CADE   I have thought upon it: it shall be so. Away, burn all the records of the realm: my mouth shall be the Parliament of England.

HOLLAND   Then we are like to have biting statutes,   *Aside*
15   unless his teeth be pulled out.

CADE   And henceforward all things shall be in common.

Enter a Messenger

MESSENGER   My lord, a prize, a prize! Here's the Lord Saye which sold the towns in France. He that made us pay one and twenty fifteens, and one shilling to the pound, the last subsidy.

Enter George [Bevis], with the Lord Saye

4.7   *Location: Smithfield, London*   1 Savoy the London residence of the Duke of Lancaster   **2 Inns of Court** series of buildings west of the City where young men studied law   **4 lordship** title and estate of a lord   **8 whole** healed, healthy   **14 biting** severe/gnawed, bitten with teeth   **18 towns** i.e. Anjou and Maine   **pay . . . fifteens** a tax of 140 percent on each person's assets   **19 subsidy** levying of taxation to meet a special requirement, e.g. war

20 CADE   Well, he shall be beheaded for it ten times.— *To Saye*
Ah, thou say, thou serge, nay, thou buckram lord! Now art
thou within point-blank of our jurisdiction regal. What canst
thou answer to my majesty for giving up of Normandy unto
Mounsieur Basimecu, the Dauphin of France? Be it known
25 unto thee by these presence, even the presence of Lord
Mortimer, that I am the besom that must sweep the court
clean of such filth as thou art: thou hast most traitorously
corrupted the youth of the realm in erecting a grammar
school: and whereas before, our forefathers had no other
30 books but the score and the tally, thou hast caused printing
to be used, and contrary to the king, his crown, and dignity,
thou hast built a paper-mill. It will be proved to thy face that
thou hast men about thee that usually talk of a noun and a
verb, and such abominable words as no Christian ear can
35 endure to hear. Thou hast appointed justices of peace, to
call poor men before them about matters they were not able
to answer. Moreover, thou hast put them in prison, and
because they could not read, thou hast hanged them, when,
indeed, only for that cause they have been most worthy to
40 live. Thou dost ride on a foot-cloth, dost thou not?

SAYE   What of that?

CADE   Marry, thou ought'st not to let thy horse wear a
cloak, when honester men than thou go in their hose and
doublets.

45 DICK   And work in their shirt too, as myself, for example,
that am a butcher.

---

21 say fine part-silk fabric (puns on **Saye**)   **serge** hard-wearing woolen fabric   **buckram**
coarse linen   **22 point-blank** direct range   **24 Basimecu** i.e. *baise mon cul*, French for "kiss
my ass"   **Be . . . presence** the standard legal phrase used at the beginning of a document
(where "these presents" refers to the document) is confused with the royal "presence"
26 besom broom (puns on "basimecu")   **30 score . . . tally** means of keeping accounts where
sticks were scored, or notched, with a total, then split into halves (tallies) so that debtor and
creditor had one each   **printing . . . paper-mill** an anachronism: the printing press (1476)
and the paper mill (1495) were not established in England until the late fifteenth century
33 usually habitually   **39 only . . . live** if a criminal could prove that he could read Latin he
could claim "benefit of clergy" and avoid being hanged   **40 foot-cloth** stately ornamental
cloth draped over the back of a horse   **42 Marry** by the Virgin Mary   **43 hose and doublets**
breeches and jackets (with no outer garment)

	SAYE	You men of Kent—
	DICK	What say you of Kent?
	SAYE	Nothing but this: 'tis '*bona terra, mala gens*'.
50	CADE	Away with him, away with him! He speaks Latin.
	SAYE	Hear me but speak, and bear me where you will:

Kent, in the commentaries Caesar writ,
Is termed the civil'st place of this isle:
Sweet is the country, because full of riches:
The people liberal, valiant, active, wealthy:
Which makes me hope you are not void of pity.
I sold not Maine, I lost not Normandy,
Yet to recover them would lose my life.
Justice with favour have I always done:
Prayers and tears have moved me, gifts could never.
When have I aught exacted at your hands,
Kent to maintain, the king, the realm and you?
Large gifts have I bestowed on learnèd clerks,
Because my book preferred me to the king.
And seeing ignorance is the curse of God,
Knowledge the wing wherewith we fly to heaven.
Unless you be possessed with devilish spirits,
You cannot but forbear to murder me:
This tongue hath parleyed unto foreign kings
For your behoof—

	CADE	Tut, when struck'st thou one blow in the field?
	SAYE	Great men have reaching hands: oft have I struck

Those that I never saw and struck them dead.

	BEVIS	O monstrous coward! What, to come behind folks?
75	SAYE	These cheeks are pale for watching for your good.

---

49 'bona . . . gens' "a good land, bad people" (Italian catchphrase used of England and the English)   **51 bear** (then) take   **52 commentaries Caesar writ** Julius Caesar's *Commentarii de Bello Gallico* describes his campaigns from 58 to 52 BC; in Golding's 1564 translation the people of Kent are described as the "civilest" in England   **55 liberal** generous   **59 favour** leniency, compassion   **61 aught** anything   **exacted** enforced (payment of taxes)   **63 clerks** scholars   **64 book** learning, education   **preferred me** gained me preferment, recommended me   **68 forbear** desist, refrain   **69 parleyed unto** negotiated with   **70 behoof** benefit, advantage   **71 field** battlefield   **72 reaching** far-reaching, influential   **74 come behind** a dishonorable way to attack an enemy   **75 watching** remaining awake, on guard

CADE   Give him a box o'th'ear and that will make 'em red
    again.

SAYE   Long sitting to determine poor men's causes
    Hath made me full of sickness and diseases.

80   CADE   Ye shall have a hempen caudle, then, and the help
    of hatchet.

DICK   Why dost thou quiver, man?

SAYE   The palsy, and not fear, provokes me.

CADE   Nay, he nods at us, as who should say, 'I'll be even
85   with you.' I'll see if his head will stand steadier on a pole, or
    no: take him away, and behead him.

SAYE   Tell me: wherein have I offended most?
    Have I affected wealth or honour? Speak.
    Are my chests filled up with extorted gold?
90   Is my apparel sumptuous to behold?
    Whom have I injured, that ye seek my death?
    These hands are free from guiltless bloodshedding,
    This breast from harbouring foul deceitful thoughts.
    O, let me live!

95   CADE   I feel remorse in myself with his words: but   *Aside*
    I'll bridle it: he shall die, an it be but for pleading so well for
    his life.— Away with him: he has a familiar under   *Aloud*
    his tongue: he speaks not a God's name. Go, take him away, I
    say, and strike off his head presently, and then break into his
100   son-in-law's house, Sir James Cromer, and strike off his head,
    and bring them both upon two poles hither.

ALL   It shall be done.

SAYE   Ah, countrymen, if when you make your prayers,
    God should be so obdurate as yourselves,
105   How would it fare with your departed souls?
    And therefore yet relent, and save my life.

---

78 sitting i.e. as a judge   **determine** settle, decide   **causes** lawsuits, cases   **80 hempen
caudle** i.e. hangman's rope   **caudle** strengthening medicinal gruel   **81 hatchet** the
executioner's axe   **83 palsy** illness characterized by trembling   **84 who** one who   **even** fair,
forthright/steady, unwavering   **88 affected** loved, aimed at   **92 guiltless bloodshedding** the
shedding of innocent blood   **95 remorse** pity   **96 bridle** restrain   **an . . . but** if only
97 familiar attendant spirit, demon   **98 a** in   **104 obdurate** unyielding

CADE   Away with him, and do as I command ye.

Exeunt one or two with the Lord Saye

The proudest peer in the realm shall not wear a head on his shoulders, unless he pay me tribute: there shall not a maid
110 be married, but she shall pay to me her maidenhead ere they have it: men shall hold of me *in capite*. And we charge and command that their wives be as free as heart can wish or tongue can tell.

DICK   My lord, when shall we go to Cheapside and take up
115 commodities upon our bills?

CADE   Marry, presently.

ALL   O, brave!

Enter one with the heads [of Saye and Cromer on poles]

CADE   But is not this braver? Let them kiss one another, for they loved well when they were alive. Now   *The heads are*
120 part them again, lest they consult about the   *made to kiss* giving up of some more towns in France. Soldiers, defer the spoil of the city until night: for with these borne before us, instead of maces, will we ride through the streets, and at every corner have them kiss. Away!   *Exeunt*

[Act 4 Scene 8]   *running scene 17 continues*

Alarum and retreat. Enter again Cade and all his rabblement

CADE   Up Fish Street, down St Magnus' Corner, kill and knock down: throw them into Thames!

Sound a parley

---

109 **tribute** payment made to a monarch as an act of homage   110 **pay . . . it** alludes to the "droit de seigneur," the right of a feudal lord to have sex with the bride of a vassal on her wedding night   **maidenhead** virginity   111 **hold** hold property   *in capite* directly from the crown (legal term); puns on Latin *caput*, i.e. "head/maidenhead"   112 **free** sexually available   114 **take . . . bills** acquire goods on credit or by means of force/spear decapitated heads on our weapons/spear   115 **bills** financial accounts/long-handled bladed weapons/penises   117 **brave** marvelous, fine   122 **spoil** looting, plunder   123 **maces** staffs of office   **4.8** *Location: near London Bridge, on the north side of the River Thames* **rabblement** riotous followers   1 **Fish Street** on the north side of London Bridge, across the river from Southwark   **St Magnus' Corner** site of St. Magnus' Church, by London Bridge at the bottom of Fish Street   *parley* trumpet summons for negotiation between opposing sides, during which fighting was to stop

What noise is this I hear? Dare any be so bold to sound
retreat or parley, when I command them kill?

Enter Buckingham and old Clifford

5   BUCKINGHAM   Ay, here they be that dare and will disturb thee:
Know, Cade, we come ambassadors from the king
Unto the commons whom thou hast misled,
And here pronounce free pardon to them all
That will forsake thee and go home in peace.

10   CLIFFORD   What say ye, countrymen? Will ye relent
And yield to mercy whilst 'tis offered you,
Or let a rabble lead you to your deaths?
Who loves the king and will embrace his pardon,
Fling up his cap, and say 'God save his majesty!'

15   Who hateth him, and honours not his father,
Henry the Fifth, that made all France to quake,
Shake he his weapon at us and pass by.

ALL   God save the king! God save the king!

CADE   What, Buckingham and Clifford, are ye so brave?—

20   And you, base peasants, do ye believe him? Will   *To the rabble*
you needs be hanged with your pardons about your necks?
Hath my sword therefore broke through London gates, that
you should leave me at the White Hart in Southwark? I
thought ye would never have given out these arms till you

25   had recovered your ancient freedom. But you are all recreants
and dastards, and delight to live in slavery to the nobility. Let
them break your backs with burdens, take your houses over
your heads, ravish your wives and daughters before your
faces. For me, I will make shift for one, and so God's curse

30   light upon you all.

ALL   We'll follow Cade, we'll follow Cade!   *They run to Cade*

CLIFFORD   Is Cade the son of Henry the Fifth,   *again*
That thus you do exclaim you'll go with him?

---

8 **pronounce** formally declare, proclaim   13 **Who** whoever   17 **Shake he** let him shake (in
defiance)   19 **brave** audacious   23 **White Hart** an inn on Borough High Street in
Southwark, south of the Thames, at which Cade had lodged; its name plays on the sense of
"coward"   24 **out** up   25 **recreants** deserters   26 **dastards** cowards   28 **ravish** rape
29 **make . . . one** look out for myself

Will he conduct you through the heart of France,
35   And make the meanest of you earls and dukes?
Alas, he hath no home, no place to fly to:
Nor knows he how to live but by the spoil,
Unless by robbing of your friends and us.
Were't not a shame, that whilst you live at jar,
40   The fearful French, whom you late vanquishèd,
Should make a start o'er seas and vanquish you?
Methinks already in this civil broil
I see them lording it in London streets,
Crying '*Villiago!*' unto all they meet.
45   Better ten thousand base-born Cades miscarry
Than you should stoop unto a Frenchman's mercy.
To France, to France, and get what you have lost:
Spare England, for it is your native coast:
Henry hath money, you are strong and manly:
50   God on our side, doubt not of victory.

ALL   A Clifford, a Clifford! We'll follow the king and Clifford.

CADE   Was ever feather so lightly blown to and fro as this
multitude? The name of Henry the Fifth hales them to an
hundred mischiefs, and makes them leave me desolate. I see
55   them lay their heads together to surprise me. My sword make
way for me, for here is no staying: in despite of the devils and
hell, have through the very middest of you: and heavens and
honour be witness, that no want of resolution in me, but
only my followers' base and ignominious treasons, makes
60   me betake me to my heels.   *Exit*

BUCKINGHAM   What, is he fled? Go, some, and follow him,
And he that brings his head unto the king
Shall have a thousand crowns for his reward.
                                              Exeunt some of them

---

35 **meanest** lowliest, most humble   37 **the spoil** looting, plunder   39 **at jar** in discord
40 **fearful** frightened   41 **start** sudden invasion   42 **broil** turmoil, battle   44 **'Villiago!'**
version of the Italian (here generally "foreign") word for coward, *vigliacco*   45 **miscarry**
perish, come to harm   51 **A** to   53 **hales** hauls, drags   55 **surprise** capture   56 **despite**
spite   57 **have through** here I come through   60 **betake me** take

Follow me, soldiers: we'll devise a mean
65   To reconcile you all unto the king.   *Exeunt all*

[Act 4 Scene 9]   *running scene 18*

Sound Trumpets. Enter King [Henry VI], Queen [Margaret] and
Somerset on the terrace [above]

KING HENRY VI   Was ever king that joyed an earthly throne,
And could command no more content than I?
No sooner was I crept out of my cradle
But I was made a king at nine months old.
5   Was never subject longed to be a king
As I do long and wish to be a subject.

Enter Buckingham and Clifford

BUCKINGHAM   Health and glad tidings to your majesty.

KING HENRY VI   Why, Buckingham, is the traitor Cade surprised?
Or is he but retired to make him strong?

Enter [below] Multitudes with halters about their necks

10   CLIFFORD   He is fled, my lord, and all his powers do yield,
And humbly thus with halters on their necks,
Expect your highness' doom of life or death.

KING HENRY VI   Then, heaven, set ope thy everlasting gates,
To entertain my vows of thanks and praise.
15   Soldiers, this day have you redeemed your lives,
And showed how well you love your prince and country:
Continue still in this so good a mind,
And Henry, though he be infortunate,
Assure yourselves, will never be unkind:
20   And so, with thanks and pardon to you all,
I do dismiss you to your several countries.

ALL   God save the king! God save the king!

64 **mean** way, means   **4.9** *Location: unspecified, presumably Kenilworth Castle*
terrace i.e. the upper staging level or gallery   1 **joyed** enjoyed   8 **surprised** seized   9 **retired**
retreated   ***halters*** nooses   10 **powers** forces, soldiers   12 **Expect** await   **doom** judgment,
sentence   13 **ope** open   14 **entertain** receive   18 **infortunate** unfortunate   21 **several**
countries various regions

Enter a Messenger

MESSENGER   Please it your grace to be advertisèd
        The Duke of York is newly come from Ireland,
25   And with a puissant and a mighty power
        Of galloglasses and stout kerns
        Is marching hitherward in proud array,
        And still proclaimeth, as he comes along,
        His arms are only to remove from thee
30   The Duke of Somerset, whom he terms a traitor.
KING HENRY VI   Thus stands my state, 'twixt Cade and York
            distressed,
        Like to a ship that, having scaped a tempest,
        Is straightway calmed and boarded with a pirate.
        But now is Cade driven back, his men dispersed,
35   And now is York in arms to second him.
        I pray thee, Buckingham, go and meet him,
        And ask him what's the reason of these arms:
        Tell him I'll send Duke Edmund to the Tower,
        And, Somerset, we will commit thee thither,
40   Until his army be dismissed from him.
SOMERSET   My lord,
        I'll yield myself to prison willingly,
        Or unto death, to do my country good.
KING HENRY VI   In any case, be not too rough in terms,
45   For he is fierce and cannot brook hard language.
BUCKINGHAM   I will, my lord, and doubt not so to deal
        As all things shall redound unto your good.
KING HENRY VI   Come, wife, let's in, and learn to govern better,
        For yet may England curse my wretched reign.

                                    Flourish. Exeunt

---

23 **advertisèd** warned   24 **newly** recently, just   25 **puissant** powerful   26 **galloglasses**
Irish soldiers armed with axes   **stout** bold, hardy   **kerns** lightly armed Irish foot soldiers
27 **array** readiness for combat   28 **still** continually   31 **state** situation/country/kingship
distressed afflicted with adversity   33 **calmed** becalmed   35 **second** support, reinforce
37 **of** for   38 **Duke Edmund** i.e. Somerset   44 **rough in terms** harsh in your choice of
language   45 **brook** tolerate   46 **deal** negotiate   47 **redound unto** turn out for   49 **yet** so
far, up until now

[Act 4 Scene 10]   *running scene 19*

Enter Cade

CADE   Fie on ambitions: fie on myself, that have a sword,
and yet am ready to famish. These five days have I hid me in
these woods and durst not peep out, for all the country is laid
for me: but now am I so hungry that if I might have a lease of
5   my life for a thousand years I could stay no longer. Wherefore
o'er a brick wall have I climbed into this garden, to see if I can
eat grass, or pick a sallet another while, which is not amiss to
cool a man's stomach this hot weather: and I think this word
'sallet' was born to do me good: for many a time, but for a
10   sallet, my brain-pan had been cleft with a brown bill: and
many a time when I have been dry and bravely marching, it
hath served me instead of a quart pot to drink in: and now
the word 'sallet' must serve me to feed on.

Enter Iden [and his Men]

IDEN   Lord, who would live turmoiled in the court,
15   And may enjoy such quiet walks as these?
This small inheritance my father left me
Contenteth me, and worth a monarchy.
I seek not to wax great by others' waning,
Or gather wealth I care not with what envy:
20   Sufficeth that I have maintains my state
And sends the poor well pleasèd from my gate.

CADE   Here's the lord of the soil come to seize me for a
stray, for entering his fee-simple without leave. Ah, villain,
thou wilt betray me, and get a thousand crowns of the king

4.10   *Location: Iden's garden, Kent*   **1 Fie** expression of angry impatience   **2 famish**
starve   **3 durst** dared   **laid** set with traps   **5 stay** wait, delay   **7 sallet** salad (leaves and
vegetables)   **while** time   **8 stomach** appetite   **word** possible pun on "wort," i.e. edible herb
or vegetable   **10 sallet** light helmet   **brain-pan** skull   **brown bill** long-handled weapon with
an axe-like blade, either painted or varnished brown, or stained with dried blood   **11 dry**
thirsty   **14 turmoiled** harried, in a state of upheaval   **18 wax** grow   **waning** diminishing,
loss   **19 I . . . envy** regardless of others' envy or malice   **20 Sufficeth that** it is enough that
what   **21 well pleasèd** i.e. with plenty of food   **22 lord . . . soil** i.e. owner of the estate
23 stray trespasser   **fee-simple** land or property that is owned outright, and may be passed
on to heirs in such a condition   **24 of** from

25   by carrying my head to him: but I'll make thee eat iron like
        an ostrich, and swallow my sword like a great pin ere thou
        and I part.

IDEN   Why, rude companion, whatsoe'er thou be,
        I know thee not: why, then, should I betray thee?
30   Is't not enough to break into my garden,
        And, like a thief, to come to rob my grounds,
        Climbing my walls in spite of me the owner,
        But thou wilt brave me with these saucy terms?

CADE   Brave thee? Ay, by the best blood that ever was
35   broached, and beard thee too. Look on me well: I have eat no
        meat these five days, yet come thou and thy five men, and if I
        do not leave you all as dead as a doornail, I pray God I may
        never eat grass more.

IDEN   Nay, it shall ne'er be said, while England stands,
40   That Alexander Iden, an esquire of Kent,
        Took odds to combat a poor famished man.
        Oppose thy steadfast gazing eyes to mine,
        See if thou canst outface me with thy looks:
        Set limb to limb, and thou art far the lesser:
45   Thy hand is but a finger to my fist,
        Thy leg a stick comparèd with this truncheon:
        My foot shall fight with all the strength thou hast,
        And if mine arm be heavèd in the air,
        Thy grave is digged already in the earth:
50   As for words, whose greatness answers words,
        Let this my sword report what speech forbears.

CADE   By my valour, the most complete champion that
        ever I heard. Steel, if thou turn the edge, or cut not out the

---

25 eat . . . ostrich it was popularly thought that ostriches did so; Cade means that he will
stab Iden   **28 rude companion** lowly, rough fellow   **33 brave** defy   **saucy** insolent
35 broached shed   **beard** defy (literally, pull insultingly by the beard)   **eat** eaten   **36 meat**
food   **40 esquire** a gentleman ranking below a knight   **41 Took odds** accepted such an
unequal challenge   **43 outface** defy   **46 truncheon** thick staff, i.e. Iden's leg   **48 if . . . earth**
i.e. if I but raise my arm, you are as good as dead   **50 whose . . . words** either "whose power is
only inflicted upon mere words" or "the power of this (my sword) answers them"
51 forbears refrains from, cannot express   **52 complete** consummate, accomplished
champion defender of a person or cause   **53 turn the edge** fail to cut

burly-boned clown in chines of beef ere thou sleep in thy
55   sheath, I beseech Jove on my knees thou mayst be turned to
hobnails.

Here they fight. [*Cade falls*]

      O, I am slain! Famine and no other hath slain me: let ten
thousand devils come against me, and give me but the ten
meals I have lost, and I'd defy them all. Wither, garden, and
60   be henceforth a burying place to all that do dwell in this
house, because the unconquered soul of Cade is fled.

IDEN   Is't Cade that I have slain, that monstrous traitor?
Sword, I will hallow thee for this thy deed,
And hang thee o'er my tomb when I am dead.
65   Ne'er shall this blood be wipèd from thy point,
But thou shalt wear it as a herald's coat,
To emblaze the honour that thy master got.

CADE   Iden, farewell, and be proud of thy victory. Tell Kent
from me, she hath lost her best man, and exhort all the world
70   to be cowards: for I that never feared any, am vanquished by
famine, not by valour.   *Dies*

IDEN   How much thou wrong'st me, heaven be my judge:
Die, damnèd wretch, the curse of her that bare thee:
And as I thrust thy body in with my sword,
75   So wish I I might thrust thy soul to hell.
Hence will I drag thee headlong by the heels
Unto a dunghill which shall be thy grave,
And there cut off thy most ungracious head,
Which I will bear in triumph to the king,
80   Leaving thy trunk for crows to feed upon.

Exeunt [*with Cade's body*]

---

54 **chines** joints   55 **turned to hobnails** melted down and turned into the nails used in boots
62 **monstrous** unnatural   63 **hallow** consecrate, bless   66 **herald's coat** heraldic device
67 **emblaze** set forth by means of a heraldic device   73 **bare** bore, gave birth to
74 **thrust . . . sword** thrust my sword into your body   78 **ungracious** lacking divine grace
80 **trunk** body

[Act 5 Scene 1]   *running scene 20*

Enter York, and his army of Irish, with Drum and Colours

YORK   From Ireland thus comes York to claim his right,
              And pluck the crown from feeble Henry's head.
              Ring, bells, aloud: burn, bonfires, clear and bright,
              To entertain great England's lawful king.
5   Ah, *sancta majestas!* Who would not buy thee dear?
              Let them obey that knows not how to rule.
              This hand was made to handle naught but gold.
              I cannot give due action to my words,
              Except a sword or sceptre balance it.
10   A sceptre shall it have, have I a soul,
              On which I'll toss the flower-de-luce of France.

Enter Buckingham

              Whom have we here? Buckingham to disturb me?   *Aside*
              The king hath sent him sure: I must dissemble.

BUCKINGHAM   York, if thou meanest well, I greet thee well.

15   YORK   Humphrey of Buckingham, I accept thy greeting.
              Art thou a messenger, or come of pleasure?

BUCKINGHAM   A messenger from Henry, our dread liege,
              To know the reason of these arms in peace:
              Or why thou, being a subject as I am,
20   Against thy oath and true allegiance sworn,
              Should raise so great a power without his leave,
              Or dare to bring thy force so near the court.

     YORK   Scarce can I speak, my choler is so great.   *Aside*
              O, I could hew up rocks and fight with flint,
25   I am so angry at these abject terms.
              And now, like Ajax Telamonius,

5.1   *Location: St. Albans   Drum* drummer   *Colours* flagbearers   4 entertain welcome
5 *sancta majestas* "sacred majesty" (Latin)   **7 gold** i.e. the official regalia of kingship
9 Except unless   **10 have I** as sure as I have   **11 toss** impale   **flower-de-luce** fleur-de-lis,
the heraldic lily of the French royal coat of arms   **13 dissemble** deceive, disguise the truth
16 of pleasure on your own initiative, to please yourself   **23 choler** anger   **25 abject** lowly,
despicable   **26 Ajax Telamonius** a hero of the Trojan war, Ajax, son of Telamon, flew into a
mad fit of rage when the armor of Achilles was awarded to Odysseus rather than himself; in
his frenzy he slaughtered a flock of **sheep**, thinking they were his enemies

On sheep or oxen could I spend my fury.
I am far better born than is the king:
More like a king, more kingly in my thoughts.
30   But I must make fair weather yet a while,
Till Henry be more weak and I more strong.—
Buckingham, I prithee pardon me,   *Aloud*
That I have given no answer all this while:
My mind was troubled with deep melancholy.
35   The cause why I have brought this army hither
Is to remove proud Somerset from the king,
Seditious to his grace and to the state.

BUCKINGHAM   That is too much presumption on thy part:
But if thy arms be to no other end,
40   The king hath yielded unto thy demand:
The Duke of Somerset is in the Tower.

YORK   Upon thine honour, is he prisoner?

BUCKINGHAM   Upon mine honour, he is prisoner.

YORK   Then, Buckingham, I do dismiss my powers.
45   Soldiers, I thank you all: disperse yourselves:
Meet me tomorrow in St George's Field,
You shall have pay and everything you wish.
And let my sovereign, virtuous Henry,
Command my eldest son, nay, all my sons,
50   As pledges of my fealty and love,
I'll send them all as willing as I live:
Lands, goods, horse, armour, anything I have,
Is his to use, so Somerset may die.

BUCKINGHAM   York, I commend this kind submission:
55   We twain will go into his highness' tent.

Enter King [Henry VI] and Attendants

KING HENRY VI   Buckingham, doth York intend no harm to us,
That thus he marcheth with thee arm in arm?

27 **spend** expend   28 **better born** i.e. have a superior claim to the throne   30 **make fair weather** pretend to be agreeable   46 **St George's Field** area between Southwark and Lambeth on the south side of the Thames   49 **Command** demand, send for   50 **fealty** loyalty   53 **so** provided that   54 **kind** proper, noble   55 **twain** two

YORK   In all submission and humility
York doth present himself unto your highness.

60   KING HENRY VI   Then what intends these forces thou dost bring?

YORK   To heave the traitor Somerset from hence,
And fight against that monstrous rebel Cade,
Who since I heard to be discomfited.

Enter Iden with Cade's head

IDEN   If one so rude and of so mean condition
65   May pass into the presence of a king,
Lo, I present your grace a traitor's head,
The head of Cade, whom I in combat slew.

KING HENRY VI   The head of Cade? Great God, how just art thou!
O, let me view his visage, being dead,
70   That living wrought me such exceeding trouble.
Tell me, my friend, art thou the man that slew him?

IDEN   I was, an't like your majesty.

KING HENRY VI   How art thou called? And what is thy degree?

IDEN   Alexander Iden, that's my name:
75   A poor esquire of Kent, that loves his king.

BUCKINGHAM   So please it you, my lord, 'twere not amiss
He were created knight for his good service.

KING HENRY VI   Iden, kneel down.   *Iden kneels and is knighted*
                     Rise up a knight.   *He rises*
We give thee for reward a thousand marks,
80   And will that thou henceforth attend on us.

IDEN   May Iden live to merit such a bounty,
And never live but true unto his liege.   [*Exit*]

Enter Queen [Margaret] and Somerset

KING HENRY VI   See, Buckingham, Somerset comes wi'th'queen:
Go bid her hide him quickly from the duke.

85   QUEEN MARGARET   For thousand Yorks he shall not hide his head,
But boldly stand and front him to his face.

YORK   How now? Is Somerset at liberty?
Then, York, unloose thy long-imprisoned thoughts,

---

63 discomfited defeated   **64 rude . . . condition** ignorant and of such low rank   **70 wrought** created for   **72 an't like** if it please   **73 degree** rank   **79 marks** a mark was an accounting unit, rather than a coin, worth two thirds of a pound   **80 will** desire   **86 front** confront

And let thy tongue be equal with thy heart.
90   Shall I endure the sight of Somerset?
False king, why hast thou broken faith with me,
Knowing how hardly I can brook abuse?
King did I call thee? No, thou art not king:
Not fit to govern and rule multitudes,
95   Which dar'st not, no, nor canst not rule a traitor.
That head of thine doth not become a crown:
Thy hand is made to grasp a palmer's staff,
And not to grace an awful princely sceptre.
That gold must round engirt these brows of mine,
100   Whose smile and frown, like to Achilles' spear,
Is able with the change to kill and cure.
Here is a hand to hold a sceptre up,
And with the same to act controlling laws:
Give place: by heaven, thou shalt rule no more
105   O'er him whom heaven created for thy ruler.

SOMERSET   O monstrous traitor! I arrest thee, York,
Of capital treason gainst the king and crown:
Obey, audacious traitor, kneel for grace.

YORK   Wouldst have me kneel? First let me ask of these,
110   If they can brook I bow a knee to man.
Sirrah, call in my sons to be my bail;   [*Exit Attendant*]
I know, ere they will have me go to ward,
They'll pawn their swords for my enfranchisement.

QUEEN MARGARET   Call hither Clifford: bid him come amain,
115   To say if that the bastard boys of York
Shall be the surety for their traitor father.

[*Exit Buckingham*]

---

92 **how hardly** with what difficulty   **brook abuse** tolerate deception, abide insult   95 **Which** who   96 **become** befit   97 **palmer's** pilgrim's; carrying a **staff** signaled that one had visited the Holy Land   98 **awful** awe-inspiring   99 **engirt** encircle   100 **Achilles' spear** having received a fatal wound from the spear of the Greek hero, Telephus was able to cure it with rust from the same weapon   103 **act** enact, bring about   **controlling** i.e. firm, effective   107 **capital** punishable by death   109 **these** may refer to attendants/sons/weapons   110 **brook** permit   **man** any man   112 **ward** custody   113 **enfranchisement** liberty   114 **amain** quickly   115 **if that** whether

YORK   O blood-bespotted Neapolitan,
              Outcast of Naples, England's bloody scourge!
              The sons of York, thy betters in their birth,
120   Shall be their father's bail, and bane to those
              That for my surety will refuse the boys.

Enter Edward and Richard

              See where they come: I'll warrant they'll make it good.

Enter Clifford [and his son Young Clifford]

QUEEN MARGARET   And here comes Clifford to deny their bail.

CLIFFORD   Health and all happiness to my lord the
              king.   *Kneeling to Henry, then rising*

125 YORK   I thank thee, Clifford: say, what news with thee?
              Nay, do not fright us with an angry look:
              We are thy sovereign, Clifford, kneel again:
              For thy mistaking so, we pardon thee.

CLIFFORD   This is my king, York, I do not mistake:
130   But thou mistakes me much to think I do:
              To Bedlam with him! Is the man grown mad?

KING HENRY VI   Ay, Clifford, a bedlam and ambitious humour
              Makes him oppose himself against his king.

CLIFFORD   He is a traitor: let him to the Tower,
135   And chop away that factious pate of his.

QUEEN MARGARET   He is arrested, but will not obey:
              His sons, he says, shall give their words for him.

YORK   Will you not, sons?

EDWARD   Ay, noble father, if our words will serve.

140 RICHARD   And if words will not, then our weapons shall.

CLIFFORD   Why, what a brood of traitors have we here?

YORK   Look in a glass, and call thy image so.
              I am thy king, and thou a false-heart traitor:
              Call hither to the stake my two brave bears,

---

117 **blood-bespotted** warmongering, bloodthirsty   **Neapolitan** Margaret was the daughter of
Reignier, the titular King of Naples   118 **scourge** punishment, whip   120 **bane** destruction,
poison   131 **Bedlam** the hospital of Saint Mary of Bethlehem in London, an institution for
the insane   132 **bedlam** mad   **humour** mood, temperament   134 **to** be sent to
135 **factious pate** rebellious head   142 **glass** mirror   143 **false-heart** treacherous, disloyal
144 **stake . . . bears** an image from bear-baiting, a popular entertainment at which a bear was
chained to a stake and set upon by dogs

145   That with the very shaking of their chains
       They may astonish these fell-lurking curs:
       Bid Salisbury and Warwick come to me.

Enter the Earls of Warwick and Salisbury

CLIFFORD   Are these thy bears? We'll bait thy bears to death,
       And manacle the bearherd in their chains,
150   If thou dar'st bring them to the baiting place.

RICHARD   Oft have I seen a hot o'erweening cur
       Run back and bite, because he was withheld:
       Who, being suffered with the bear's fell paw,
       Hath clapped his tail between his legs and cried:
155   And such a piece of service will you do,
       If you oppose yourselves to match Lord Warwick.

CLIFFORD   Hence, heap of wrath, foul indigested lump,
       As crooked in thy manners as thy shape!

YORK   Nay, we shall heat you thoroughly anon.

160   CLIFFORD   Take heed, lest by your heat you burn yourselves.

KING HENRY VI   Why, Warwick, hath thy knee forgot to bow?
       Old Salisbury, shame to thy silver hair,
       Thou mad misleader of thy brainsick son!
       What, wilt thou on thy death-bed play the ruffian,
165   And seek for sorrow with thy spectacles?
       O, where is faith? O, where is loyalty?
       If it be banished from the frosty head,
       Where shall it find a harbour in the earth?
       Wilt thou go dig a grave to find out war,
170   And shame thine honourable age with blood?
       Why art thou old and want'st experience,
       Or wherefore dost abuse it if thou hast it?

---

146 astonish terrify   **fell-lurking curs** fierce dogs waiting to attack   **149 bearherd** bear
keeper, handler (i.e. York)   **150 baiting place** bear pit   **151 o'erweening** overexcited,
presumptuous   **152 Run . . . bite** i.e. twist round and bite the dog handler   **153 suffered**
released/hurt   **fell** savage, fierce   **155 piece of service** sort of action   **156 oppose**
yourselves set yourselves in opposition   **match** fight/equal the strength of   **157 lump**
possibly continues bear imagery as newborn cubs were popularly supposed to be licked into
shape by their mother   **158 crooked . . . shape** Richard is famed for a hunched back and
various other physical deformities or ailments   **159 heat you** make things hot for you/make
you hot from fighting   **165 spectacles** eyes/eyeglasses (suggests the failing eyesight of
Salisbury's old age)   **167 frosty** i.e. white-haired   **168 harbour** refuge

For shame in duty bend thy knee to me,
That bows unto the grave with mickle age.

175 SALISBURY   My lord, I have considered with myself
The title of this most renownèd duke,
And in my conscience do repute his grace
The rightful heir to England's royal seat.

KING HENRY VI   Hast thou not sworn allegiance unto me?

180 SALISBURY   I have.

KING HENRY VI   Canst thou dispense with heaven for such an
oath?

SALISBURY   It is great sin to swear unto a sin:
But greater sin to keep a sinful oath:
Who can be bound by any solemn vow
185 To do a murd'rous deed, to rob a man,
To force a spotless virgin's chastity,
To reave the orphan of his patrimony,
To wring the widow from her customed right,
And have no other reason for this wrong
190 But that he was bound by a solemn oath?

QUEEN MARGARET   A subtle traitor needs no sophister.

KING HENRY VI   Call Buckingham, and bid him arm himself.

YORK   Call Buckingham, and all the friends thou hast,
I am resolved for death or dignity.

195 CLIFFORD   The first I warrant thee, if dreams prove true.

WARWICK   You were best to go to bed and dream again,
To keep thee from the tempest of the field.

CLIFFORD   I am resolved to bear a greater storm
Than any thou canst conjure up today:
200 And that I'll write upon thy burgonet,
Might I but know thee by thy household badge.

---

174 **mickle** great   177 **repute** consider   181 **dispense with** obtain dispensation from/
disregard, do without   187 **reave** rob   188 **wring** force   **customed right** legally sanctioned
rights of inheritance   191 **subtle** cunning, skillful   **sophister** one who makes skillful use of
false logic, a specious reasoner   194 **dignity** honor, high rank, kingship   197 **field** battlefield
200 **burgonet** light helmet, often bearing a crest   201 **know** recognize, identify   **household
badge** family crest

WARWICK   Now by my father's badge, old Neville's crest,
The rampant bear chained to the ragged staff,
This day I'll wear aloft my burgonet,
205   As on a mountain top the cedar shows
That keeps his leaves in spite of any storm,
Even to affright thee with the view thereof.

CLIFFORD   And from thy burgonet I'll rend thy bear
And tread it under foot with all contempt,
210   Despite the bearherd that protects the bear.

YOUNG CLIFFORD   And so to arms, victorious father,
To quell the rebels and their complices.

RICHARD   Fie, charity, for shame! Speak not in spite,
For you shall sup with Jesu Christ tonight.

215   YOUNG CLIFFORD   Foul stigmatic, that's more than thou canst
tell.

RICHARD   If not in heaven, you'll surely sup in hell.

Exeunt [severally]

[Act 5 Scene 2]

running scene 21

[Alarums to the battle.] Enter Warwick

WARWICK   Clifford of Cumberland, 'tis Warwick calls:
And if thou dost not hide thee from the bear,
Now, when the angry trumpet sounds alarum
And dead men's cries do fill the empty air,
5   Clifford, I say, come forth and fight with me:
Proud northern lord, Clifford of Cumberland,
Warwick is hoarse with calling thee to arms.

Enter York

How now, my noble lord? What, all afoot?

YORK   The deadly-handed Clifford slew my steed:
10   But match to match I have encountered him

---

202 **father's** father-in-law's   203 **rampant** rearing, on hind legs   **ragged** rough-hewn
204 **aloft** mounted on   **burgonet** visored helmet   205 **shows** is visible, shows itself
208 **rend** tear, rip   212 **complices** accomplices   215 **stigmatic** criminal who has been
branded, i.e. deformed one   **5.2   4 dead** dying   **8 afoot** on foot

And made a prey for carrion kites and crows
Even of the bonny beast he loved so well.

Enter Clifford

WARWICK   Of one or both of us the time is come.

YORK   Hold, Warwick: seek thee out some other chase,

15 For I myself must hunt this deer to death.

WARWICK   Then, nobly, York: 'tis for a crown thou fight'st:—
As I intend, Clifford, to thrive today,
It grieves my soul to leave thee unassailed.   *Exit Warwick*

CLIFFORD   What seest thou in me, York? Why dost thou pause?

20 YORK   With thy brave bearing should I be in love,
But that thou art so fast mine enemy.

CLIFFORD   Nor should thy prowess want praise and esteem,
But that 'tis shown ignobly and in treason.

YORK   So let it help me now against thy sword

25 As I in justice and true right express it.

CLIFFORD   My soul and body on the action both!

YORK   A dreadful lay! Address thee
instantly.   *They fight, and Clifford falls*

CLIFFORD   *La fin couronne les oeuvres.*   *Dies*

YORK   Thus war hath given thee peace, for thou art still.

30 Peace with his soul, heaven, if it be thy will.   [*Exit*]

Enter Young Clifford

YOUNG CLIFFORD   Shame and confusion, all is on the rout!
Fear frames disorder, and disorder wounds
Where it should guard. O war, thou son of hell,
Whom angry heavens do make their minister,

35 Throw in the frozen bosoms of our part
Hot coals of vengeance. Let no soldier fly.
He that is truly dedicate to war
Hath no self-love: nor he that loves himself

---

11 carrion kites birds of prey that feed on dead flesh   **13 Of** for   **14 chase** prey   **16 nobly**
i.e. may you fight nobly   **21 fast** firmly   **25 it** i.e. my **prowess**   **26 on . . . both** I lay upon the
outcome of the action   **27 lay** wager, bet   **Address** prepare   **28 La . . . oeuvres** "The end
crowns the works" (French)   **31 confusion** overthrow, ruin   **on the rout** in disorderly retreat
32 frames creates   **35 frozen** inactive, frozen with fear   **part** party, side   **36 fly** flee
37 dedicate dedicated   **38 self-love** self-interest, concern for preserving himself

Hath not essentially but by circumstance
40   The name of valour.— O, let the vile world end,   *Seeing his*
And the premised flames of the last day   *dead father*
Knit earth and heaven together.
Now let the general trumpet blow his blast,
Particularities and petty sounds
45   To cease. Wast thou ordainèd, dear father,
To lose thy youth in peace, and to achieve
The silver livery of advisèd age,
And in thy reverence and thy chair-days, thus
To die in ruffian battle? Even at this sight
50   My heart is turned to stone: and while 'tis mine,
It shall be stony. York not our old men spares:
No more will I their babes: tears virginal
Shall be to me even as the dew to fire,
And beauty that the tyrant oft reclaims
55   Shall to my flaming wrath be oil and flax:
Henceforth I will not have to do with pity.
Meet I an infant of the House of York,
Into as many gobbets will I cut it
As wild Medea young Absyrtus did.
60   In cruelty will I seek out my fame.
Come, thou new ruin of old Clifford's house:
As did Aeneas old Anchises bear,
So bear I thee upon my manly shoulders:
But then Aeneas bare a living load,
65   Nothing so heavy as these woes of mine.

                              [*Exit with Clifford's body*]

39 essentially inherently   **circumstance** accident, chance events   **41 premised** preordained
last day Judgment Day   **42 Knit** unite, join   **43 general trumpet** the trumpet sounding
doomsday to all men   **44 Particularities** individual trifles   **45 ordainèd** Folio reads
"ordain'd"—final syllable may or may not be sounded   **46 lose** spend   **47 livery** i.e. hair
advisèd cautious/experienced, prudent   **48 chair-days** infirm or inactive old age   **52 tears
virginal** virgins' tears   **53 dew to fire** it was thought that dew encouraged fire to burn more
fiercely   **54 reclaims** calms, subdues   **55 oil and flax** both highly flammable   **58 gobbets**
chunks of raw flesh   **59 Medea young Absyrtus** daughter of the King of Colchis, Medea fell
in love with Jason, and ran away with him; to delay her father's pursuit, she killed her brother
Absyrtus and scattered pieces of his body in her wake   **62 Aeneas . . . bear** in Virgil's *Aeneid*,
Aeneas carried his elderly father, **Anchises**, on his back as they escaped from burning Troy
64 bare bore   **65 heavy** sorrowful/weighty

Enter Richard and Somerset to fight. [Somerset is killed]

RICHARD   So lie thou there:

For underneath an ale-house' paltry sign,

The Castle in St Albans, Somerset

Hath made the wizard famous in his death:

70   Sword, hold thy temper: heart, be wrathful still:

Priests pray for enemies, but princes kill.   [*Exit*]

*Fight. Excursions. Enter King [Henry VI], Queen [Margaret] and
others*

QUEEN MARGARET   Away, my lord, you are slow: for shame, away!

KING HENRY VI   Can we outrun the heavens? Good Margaret,
      stay.

QUEEN MARGARET   What are you made of? You'll nor fight nor
      fly:

75   Now is it manhood, wisdom and defence,

To give the enemy way, and to secure us

By what we can, which can no more but fly.   *Alarum afar off*

If you be ta'en, we then should see the bottom

Of all our fortunes: but if we haply scape,

80   As well we may, if not through your neglect,

We shall to London get, where you are loved

And where this breach now in our fortunes made

May readily be stopped.

Enter [Young] Clifford

YOUNG CLIFFORD   But that my heart's on future mischief set,

85   I would speak blasphemy ere bid you fly:

But fly you must: uncurable discomfit

Reigns in the hearts of all our present parts.

Away, for your relief, and we will live

---

69 **wizard** Roger Bullingbrook, who raised a spirit that predicted that Somerset would die
"where castles mounted stand" (Act 1 Scene 4)   70 **temper** hardness   **still** always
Excursions bouts of fighting across the stage   73 **stay** wait   74 **nor** neither   75 **is it** it is
76 **secure us** save ourselves   77 **what** whatever (means)   78 **ta'en** captured   79 **haply**
scape by chance escape   82 **breach** hole (literally, gap in defensive fortifications)
84 **mischief** harm (to the enemy)   85 **ere** before I would, rather than   86 **discomfit**
discouragement, defeat   87 **present parts** surviving forces   88 **relief** safety

To see their day and them our fortune give.

90   Away, my lord, away!   *Exeunt*

[Act 5 Scene 3]   *running scene 21 continues*

Alarum. Retreat. Enter York, Richard, Warwick and Soldiers, with
Drum and Colours

YORK   Of Salisbury, who can report of him,
That winter lion, who in rage forgets
Agèd contusions and all brush of time,
And, like a gallant in the brow of youth,
5   Repairs him with occasion? This happy day
Is not itself, nor have we won one foot,
If Salisbury be lost.

RICHARD   My noble father:
Three times today I holp him to his horse,
10   Three times bestrid him: thrice I led him off,
Persuaded him from any further act:
But still where danger was, still there I met him,
And like rich hangings in a homely house,
So was his will in his old feeble body.
15   But noble as he is, look where he comes.

Enter Salisbury

SALISBURY   Now, by my sword, well hast thou fought today:
By th'mass, so did we all. I thank you, Richard.
God knows how long it is I have to live:
And it hath pleased him that three times today
20   You have defended me from imminent death.
Well, lords, we have not got that which we have:

---

89 **their . . . give** a day of victory like theirs and to make them suffer our misfortunes
5.3   2 winter i.e. aged   **3 Agèd contusions** the bruises of old age   **brush** hostile
encounters, collisions   **4 gallant** fashionable young man   **brow** i.e. height, prime
5 Repairs . . . occasion restores himself with opportunity (for action)   **6 foot** i.e. of ground
9 holp helped   **10 bestrid him** stood over him to defend him when he was down   **12 still**
always   **13 hangings** wall hangings, tapestries   **homely** humble   **21 got . . . have** secured
what we in essence possess (refers either to the gains of the battle or to York's kingship)

'Tis not enough our foes are this time fled,
Being opposites of such repairing nature.

YORK   I know our safety is to follow them,
For, as I hear, the king is fled to London,
To call a present court of parliament:
Let us pursue him ere the writs go forth.
What says Lord Warwick, shall we after them?

WARWICK   After them? Nay, before them, if we can:
Now by my hand, lords, 'twas a glorious day.
St Albans battle won by famous York
Shall be eternized in all age to come.
Sound drum and trumpets, and to London all,
And more such days as these to us befall!   *Exeunt*

---

23 **Being . . . nature** since they are enemies who can recover swiftly (**repairing** plays on the sense of "returning")   24 **safety** best means of safeguard   26 **a present** an immediate
27 **writs** summons to parliament   32 **eternized** immortalized

TEXTUAL NOTES

Q = First Quarto text of 1594
Q2 = Second Quarto text of 1600
Q3 = Third Quarto text of 1619
F = First Folio text of 1623
F2 = a correction introduced in the Second Folio text of 1632
F4 = a correction introduced in the Fourth Folio text of 1685
Ed = a correction introduced by a later editor
SD = stage direction
SH = speech heading (i.e. speaker's name)

List of parts = Ed

THE . . . HUMPHREY = F. *Printed as* The First Part of the Contention
betwixt the two famous Houses of York and Lancaster, with the death of
the good Duke Humphrey *in* Q, Q2, *and* Q3
1.1.24–31 Great . . . minister Q *has the following alternative lines (all
alternative Q passages are here edited and modernized):*
    Th'excessive love I bear unto your grace
    Forbids me to be lavish of my tongue,
    Lest I should speak more than beseems a woman:
    Let this suffice: my bliss is in your liking,
    And nothing can make poor Margaret miserable,
    Unless the frown of mighty England's King.
  50 SD Lets . . . fall *derived from* Q's *direction:* Duke *Humphrey* lets it
fall **92 had** = Ed. F = hath **100 Razing** = Ed. F = Racing **131 SH
GLOUCESTER** = Ed. F = *Hum./Glo. (throughout)* **168 hoist** *spelled*
hoyse *in* F **177 Protector** = Q. F = Protectors **255 in my** = Ed. F = in in
my **256 grapple** = F, Q3. Q = graffle, *although there is no record of it in
the* OED
1.2.19 thought = F. Ed = hour **22 dreams** = F (dreames). Ed = dream
38 are = Q. F = wer **75 witch** = F. Q = witch of Ely. Q3 = witch of Rye.
Ed = witch of Eye
1.3.6 SH FIRST PETITIONER = F4. F = *Peter. In agreement with the Textual
Companion that the First Petitioner must have pushed forward to warrant
his apology, "Peter" and "Petitioner" being easily confused; other editors
defend* F **30 master** = Ed. F = Mistresse **31 usurper** = F. Q = usurer
66 haughty = F (haughtie). F2 = haught **88 the** = F. Ed = their **99** *At
this point* F *has an exit direction for Suffolk, yet he contributes to the*

following discussion; therefore his exit direction has been removed
102 denied = Ed. F = denay'd   **123 dauphin** = Ed. F = Dolphin
140 I'd = Q. F = I could   **148 fury** = Ed. F = Fume. *However, the
emendation better fits the meter and the mistake can be explained as a
minim error*   **185 SH HORNER** = Ed. F = *Armorer*   **202 judge** = F. Ed =
judge by case   **216–18 Away . . . away** = F. *The following alternative
lines are spoken by Gloucester in Q, where the action takes place before
Queen Margaret drops her glove (as opposed to F's fan):*

> The law my lord is this by case, it rests suspicious
> That a day of combat be appointed
> And there to try each other's right or wrong
> Which shall be on the thirtieth of this month,
> With Eben staves and standbags combatting
> In Smithfield before your royal majesty.

*The reference to "Eben staves" and "standbags" might refer to the remembered
performance of the scene*
1.4.23 SH ASNATH = Ed. F = *Spirit*   **24 SH MARGARET JORDAN** = Ed. F =
Witch   **39–40 Descend . . . avoid** = F. *Q has the following longer alternative:*

> Then down, I say, unto the damnèd pool,
> Where Pluto in his fiery wagon sits
> Riding, amidst the singed and parchèd smokes,
> The road of Ditis by the River Styx.
> There howl and burn for ever in those flames.
> Rise, Jordan, rise, and stay thy charming spells.
> Zounds, we are betrayed!

59–60 The . . . death *some editors move the reading aloud of the prophecies
to the next scene, following Q, which also assigns them to King Henry*
2.1.27 such = F. Ed = some   **52 SH CARDINAL . . . you.** = Ed. F = Cardinall,
I am with you. *F presents the line as a continuation of Gloucester's speech
rather than a response from the cardinal*   **65 SH TOWNSMAN** = Ed. F =
One   **138 his** = Q. F = it,
2.2.35 Philippa = Ed. F = *Phillip*   **46–47 who . . . son** = Ed. F*'s lines are
considered unmetrical and nonsensical:*

> Who was to Edmond Langley,
> Edward the thirds fift Sonnes Sonne;

2.3.3 sins = Ed. F = sinne   **68** *After the First Prentice Q inserts a third prentice
who speaks the following line:* Here, Peter, here's a pint of claret wine for
thee. *Q also adds the following extra line at the beginning of* F's *"Second"
Prentice's line:* And here's a quart for me.
3.1.0 SD Enter . . . parliament = F. *Q has the following stage direction, which
may reflect contemporary performance:*

> Enter to the parliament. Enter two heralds before, then the Duke of
> Buckingham, and the Duke of Suffolk, and then the Duke of York,

and the Cardinal of Winchester, and then the King and the Queen,
and then the Earl of Salisbury, and the Earl of Warwick.

78 wolves = F. Ed = wolf **117 disbursèd** = Ed. F = dis-pursed *which is
now archaic* **264 deceit** = F. Ed = conceit **329 For** = F. Ed = From
3.2.0 SD *Enter . . . Humphrey* = F. Q = Then the curtains being drawn,
Duke Humphrey is discovered in his bed, and two men lying on his
breast and smothering him in his bed. And then enter the Duke of
Suffolk to them. **14 Away . . . gone** = F. Q = Then draw the curtains
again and get you gone. Ed = Then draw the curtains close; away, be
gone! **SD *Sound . . . Attendants*** F's *original direction includes an entry
for Suffolk, who is already onstage, and is therefore omitted here* **26 Meg** =
Ed. F = *Nell* **76 leper** = Ed. F = Leaper **80 Dame** = F. Ed = Queen
Margaret = Ed. F = *Elianor* **101 Margaret** = Ed. F = *Elianor* **117 witch** =
Ed. F = watch **121 Margaret** = Ed. F = *Elinor* **203 SD [*Exeunt . . .
Somerset*]** *the direction "Exit Cardinal" is found in Q; editors add an exit
direction for Somerset here because he has no further activity in the scene*
232 SD *Exeunt . . . Warwick* *based on Q's direction:* Warwick pulls him
out. Exit Warwick and Suffolk. F = *Exeunt Q's stage direction continues:*
and then all the Commons within, cries, 'Down with Suffolk, down with
Suffolk'. *This presumably represents original performance, and it is on this
basis that some editors have decided to insert stage directions and/or spoken
lines for Commons* **279 SH COMMONS** = Ed. *Not in F* **309 enemies** = Q.
F = enemy. *Privileging Q over F results in agreement with "them" in the
following line* **311 Could** = Q. F = Would. *Emendation directed by the
editorial tradition in response to the repeated use of "would" in the following
line* **319 Mine** = F. Q = My **on** = Ed. F = an **333 turn** = Ed. F = turnes
335 the = F. Q = this **345 these** = F. Ed = these lips **410 SD [*She kisses
him*]** = Q. *Not in F* **415 SD *severally*** = Q. *Not in F*
3.3.0 SD *to . . . bed* = F. Q = *and then the curtains be drawn, and the Cardinal
is discovered in his bed, raving and staring as if he were mad*
4.1.0 SD *a Master . . . prisoners* *based on Q's stage direction:* Alarms within,
and the chambers be discharged, like as it were a fight at sea. And then
enter the Captain of the ship and the Master, and the Master's Mate, and
the Duke of Suffolk disguised, and others with him, and Walter
Whickmore **1 SH LIEUTENANT** = F. Q = *Captain* **6 Clip** = Ed. F =
Cleape **20 SH WHITMORE** = Ed. *In F these lines continue the Lieutenant's
speech* **32 death** = F. Ed = thee **48 Jove . . . I** = Q. *Not in F; justified by
the Lieutenant's following line* **50 Obscure . . . blood** = F. *Editors often
reassign this line to Suffolk, arguing that he is distinguishing between himself
and the Lieutenant. However, F's reading can be supported as a slight on
Suffolk by the Lieutenant, and by Whitmore's subsequent line in response to
Suffolk's speech where he refers directly to Suffolk as "swain"* **lousy** = F
(lowsie). Ed = lowly **72 SH SUFFOLK** = Ed. F = Sir; *presumed compositor*

misreading of "Suf" or "S" or "Su"   **73 SH LIEUTENANT** = Ed. F = Lord;
presumed compositor misreading of "Lieu" or "L"   **79 shalt** = Q. F = shall
87 mother's bleeding = Ed. F = Mother-bleeding   **95 are** = Ed. F = and
114 Thy . . . me Q *has an extra line at this point attributed to the "Captain,"*
F's *Lieutenant:* Ay, but my deeds shall stay thy fury soon. *Some editions*
print the following: But my deeds, Suffolk, soon shall stay thy rage.
134 SH SUFFOLK = Ed. *In* F *this line is spoken by the Lieutenant, but*
Suffolk's "That" appears to refer to it as his own
4.2.0, 26 SD with long staves = Q. *Not in* F   **28 SH DICK** = Ed. F = But.
29 fail = F. Ed = fall, *on the grounds that Cade is punning on his name, Latin*
"cadere" *meaning "to fall"*   **40 SH SMITH** = Ed. F = *Weaver*   **74 SD**
Chartham = Ed. Q = *Chattam. Both are places in the southeast of England*
89 an = F2. F = a   **97 SD Michael** = F. Q = *Tom.* Ed = a messenger
106 Mortimer *at this point in* Q *Cade also knights Dick the butcher*
4.4.21 mourning for = F. Q. Ed = mourning   **42 traitors** = F. Ed = trait'rous
rabble   **48 hath** = F. Q = hath almost   **57 be betrayed** = F2. F = betraid
4.6.8 SH SMITH = Ed. F = *But.*
4.7.7 SH HOLLAND = Ed. F = Iohn. *In this edition the character labelled*
"John" is identified as "John Holland" and therefore assigned the speech
heading "Holland," rather than identifying him as a new character, as in other
editions   **40 on** = Q. F = in   **50 Away . . . Latin** = F. *In place of this* Q *has*
the following lines:

CADE   'Bonum terrum'. Zounds, what is that?

DICK   He speaks French.

WILL   No, 'tis Dutch.

NICK   No, 'tis Outalian: I know it well enough.

62 Kent = F. Ed = But   **80 caudle** = F4. F = Candle   **help of** = F. Ed =
health o'th'   **99** *At this point* Q *adds the following detail taken from the*
Chronicles: *to the Standard in Cheapside*   **100** Q *again adds the following*
detail, again present in the Chronicles: *go to Mile End Green*   **111 men** = F.
Q = Married men   **113** *At this point* Q *has the following additional lines,*
thought to be an authorial addition to the promptbook by some editors:

Enter Robin

ROBIN   O captain, London Bridge is afire!

CADE   Run to Billingsgate and fetch pitch and flax and
           squench it.

Enter Dick and a Sergeant

SERGEANT   Justice, justice, I pray you, sir, let me have justice of
           this fellow here.

CADE   Why, what has he done?

SERGEANT   Alas, sir, he has ravished my wife.

BUTCHER   Why, my lord, he would have 'rested me and I went
           and entered my action in his wife's paper house.

CADE   Dick, follow thy suit in her common place. You
whoreson villain, you are a sergeant — you'll take any
man by the throat for twelvepence, and 'rest a man when
he's at dinner, and have him to prison ere the meat be out
of his mouth. Go, Dick, take him hence: cut out his tongue
for cogging, hough him for running, and, to conclude,
brave him with his own mace.

                                   Exit [*Butcher*] *with the Sergeant*

116 *Additional lines at this point in* Q *for Cade:* He that will lustily stand to
it shall go with me and take up these commodities following: item, a
gown, a kirtle, a petticoat, and a smock.

[Act 4 Scene 8] *there is no scene break at this point in* Q. *Some editors explain
the apparent scene break in* F *as necessary in order to waste space at the end of
the page due to incorrectly cast-off copy.*

4.18.12 rabble = F. Ed = rebel **31 SD** *They . . . again* = Q. *Not in* F
4.9.33 calmed = F4. F = calme **34 dispersed** = Ed. F = dispierc'd
4.10.6 o'er = Ed. F = on **18 waning** = Ed. F = warning **55 Jove** = F. Q =
God
5.1.10 soul = F. Ed = sword **30–1 But . . . strong** = F. *In place of these lines* Q
has the following:

   But York dissemble, till thou meet thy sons,
   Who now in arms expect their father's sight,
   And not far hence I know they cannot be.

70 trouble Q *adds the following lines:*

   A visage stern, coal-black his curlèd locks,
   Deep trenchèd furrows in his frowning brow,
   Presageth warlike humours in his life.

83 wi'th'queen = Ed. F = with th'Queen **109 these** = Ed. F = thee
111 sons = Q. F = sonne **113 for** = F2. F = of **149 bearherd** = Ed. F =
Berard **194 or** = Ed. F = and **201 household** = Q. F = housed. F2 =
house's **210 bearherd** = Ed. F = Bearard
5.2.0 SD [Alarums . . . battle] = Q. *Not in* F **62–5 As . . . mine** = F. Q
includes a confrontation between Young Clifford and Richard in place of F's
lines:

   [YOUNG CLIFFORD]   And thus as old Anchises' son did bear
               His agèd father on his manly back,
               And fought with him against the bloody Greeks,
               Even so will I. But stay, here's one of them,
               To whom my soul hath sworn immortal hate.
   Enter RICHARD, and then [YOUNG] *CLIFFORD lays down his father,
   fights with him, and Richard flies away again.*
               Out, crookback villain, get thee from my sight,
               But I will after thee, and once again

When I have borne my father to his tent,
I'll try my fortune better with thee yet.

                              Exit Young Clifford with his father

5.3.1 SH YORK *York has four lines in Q which precede his speech in* F:
How now, boys: fortunate this fight hath been,
I hope to us and ours, for England's good,
And our great honour, that so long we lost
Whilst faint-heart Henry did usurp our rights:

HENRY VI PART III:
KEY FACTS

MAJOR PARTS: (*with percentage of lines/number of speeches/scenes onstage*) Edward, Earl of March/King Edward IV (15%/132/18), Earl of Warwick (15%/99/12), Richard/Duke of Gloucester (14%/108/17), King Henry VI (12%/71/7), Queen Margaret (10%/53/7), Richard, Duke of York (6%/37/3), Lord Clifford (5%/35/6), George/Duke of Clarence (4%/39/12), Lady Elizabeth Grey/Queen Elizabeth (3%/31/4), King Lewis XI (2%/21/1), Edward, Prince of Wales (2%/16/6).

LINGUISTIC MEDIUM: 100% verse.

DATE: 1591? York's line "O, tiger's heart wrapt in a woman's hide!" is parodied in *Greene's Groatsworth of Wit* (a pamphlet prepared for the press—entered for publication September 1592—by Henry Chettle, perhaps based in part on the papers of the late dramatist Robert Greene), where Shakespeare is described as an "upstart crow, beautified with our feathers, that with his *Tiger's heart wrapped in a player's hide,* supposes he is as well able to bombast out a blank verse as the best of you." Pembroke's Men, who played the Octavo version, were active in 1592. The possibility of an earlier pre-Shakespearean version and a later Shakespearean revision cannot be ruled out.

SOURCES: Based primarily on Edward Hall, *The Union of the Two Noble and Illustre Famelies of Lancastre and Yorke* (1548) and the second (1587) edition of Holinshed's *Chronicles*. In some details, the Octavo text seems to follow Hall and the Folio Holinshed, which may support the theory of revision (see below).

TEXT: A short version was published in Octavo form in 1595, entitled *The true Tragedie of Richard Duke of Yorke, and the death of good King Henrie the Sixt, with the whole contention betweene the two Houses*

Lancaster and Yorke, as it was sundrie times acted by the Right Honourable the Earle of Pembrooke his seruants, reprinted in Quarto in 1600 and, with attribution to Shakespeare and title combined with that of the previous play, 1619 (*The Whole Contention betweene the two Famous Houses, Lancaster and Yorke*). The Octavo text is a reconstruction of a playing version, but there is much dispute over whether it is a short and often poorly remembered version of the play that is preserved in full in the Folio or the text of an early version (not by Shakespeare? partly by Shakespeare?) that Shakespeare then revised into the play that was printed in the Folio. It is equally unclear whether the linguistic signs of a non-Shakespearean hand (or hands) in the Folio text are vestiges of an older version or the result of active collaboration/coauthorship. We use the Folio text, which has the authority of Hemings and Condell, though the nature of the copy from which it was set is disputed. The Octavo remains valuable for certain details of staging.

THE THIRD PART OF HENRY THE SIXTH, WITH THE DEATH OF THE DUKE OF YORK

Lancastrians

KING HENRY VI

QUEEN MARGARET

PRINCE EDWARD, their son

Lord CLIFFORD

Duke of EXETER

Duke of SOMERSET, adherent of both Lancaster and York

Earl of NORTHUMBERLAND

Earl of WESTMORLAND

Earl of OXFORD

Henry, Earl of Richmond, the future King Henry VII

Mayor of Coventry

SOMERVILLE

A FATHER who has killed his son in battle, while fighting for Lancaster

A HUNTSMAN

Yorkists

Richard Plantagenet, Duke of YORK

EDWARD, Earl of March, his eldest son, later KING EDWARD IV

GEORGE, his second son, later Duke of CLARENCE

RICHARD, his third son, later Duke of GLOUCESTER, the future King Richard III

Edmund, his youngest son, Earl of RUTLAND

TUTOR to Rutland

Duke of NORFOLK

Earl of WARWICK

MONTAGUE, brother to Warwick

Earl of PEMBROKE

Lord STAFFORD

Lord HASTINGS

Sir JOHN MORTIMER

Sir Hugh Mortimer

Sir William STANLEY

Sir John MONTGOMERY

Elizabeth, LADY GREY, later QUEEN ELIZABETH

Lord RIVERS, her brother (adherent first of Lancaster, then of York)

Prince Edward, infant son of Edward IV and Lady Grey

MAYOR of York

LIEUTENANT of the Tower of London

A SON who has killed his father in battle, while fighting for York

NURSE of Prince Edward of York

NOBLEMAN

Three WATCHMEN

The French   MESSENGERS

KING LEWIS XI of France   POSTS

Lady BONA of Savoy   Two Aldermen of York

Lord Bourbon   Soldiers, Drummers, Trumpeters,

Others   Colours (military flagbearers),
                                         Attendants
TWO GAMEKEEPERS

Act 1 Scene 1   *running scene 1*

Alarum. Enter Plantagenet, [the Duke of York,] Edward, Richard,
Norfolk, Montague, Warwick [with white roses in their hats,] and
Soldiers

WARWICK   I wonder how the king escaped our hands.

YORK   While we pursued the horsemen of the north,
          He slyly stole away and left his men:
          Whereat the great lord of Northumberland,
5   Whose warlike ears could never brook retreat,
          Cheered up the drooping army, and himself,
          Lord Clifford and Lord Stafford, all abreast,
          Charged our main battle's front, and breaking in,
          Were by the swords of common soldiers slain.

10 EDWARD   Lord Stafford's father, Duke of Buckingham,
          Is either slain or wounded dangerous.
          I cleft his beaver with a downright blow.
          That this is true, father, behold his blood.

    MONTAGUE   And, brother, here's the Earl of Wiltshire's blood,
15   Whom I encountered as the battles joined.

1.1   *Location: the Parliament House at Westminster, London   Alarum* trumpet call to
arms   ***white roses*** emblems of the House of York   **5 brook retreat** tolerate the sound of a
trumpet call signaling retreat   **6 drooping** flagging, spiritless   **8 battle's** army's, battalion's
11 dangerous dangerously, potentially fatally   **12 cleft** split   **beaver** face-guard, helmet
visor   **downright** directed from above, straight down   **14 brother** historically, Montague was
Warwick's brother; his father was York's brother-in-law   **15 encountered** fought with

RICHARD   Speak thou for me and tell them what I
    did.   *Shows Somerset's*

YORK   Richard hath best deserved of all my sons.—   *head*
    But is your grace dead, my lord of Somerset?

NORFOLK   Such hope have all the line of John of Gaunt.

20 RICHARD   Thus do I hope to shake King Henry's head.

WARWICK   And so do I.— Victorious Prince of York,
    Before I see thee seated in that throne
    Which now the house of Lancaster usurps,
    I vow by heaven these eyes shall never close.
25   This is the palace of the fearful king,
    And this the regal seat: possess it, York,
    For this is thine and not King Henry's heirs'.

YORK   Assist me, then, sweet Warwick, and I will,
    For hither we have broken in by force.

30 NORFOLK   We'll all assist you, he that flies shall die.

YORK   Thanks, gentle Norfolk.— Stay by me, my lords,
    And soldiers, stay and lodge by me this night.
                            They go up [to the throne]

WARWICK   And when the king comes, offer him no violence,
    Unless he seek to thrust you out perforce.

35 YORK   The queen this day here holds her parliament,
    But little thinks we shall be of her council.
    By words or blows here let us win our right.

RICHARD   Armed as we are, let's stay within this house.

WARWICK   The bloody parliament shall this be called,
40   Unless Plantagenet, Duke of York, be king,
    And bashful Henry deposed, whose cowardice
    Hath made us bywords to our enemies.

YORK   Then leave me not, my lords: be resolute.
    I mean to take possession of my right.

45 WARWICK   Neither the king, nor he that loves him best,
    The proudest he that holds up Lancaster,

---

16 thou Richard addresses Somerset's head   **19 Such . . . Gaunt** may all the descendants of Gaunt have such a fate   **22 Before** until   **25 fearful** anxious, frightened   **26 possess** sit in (literally)/seize (metaphorically)   **31 gentle** noble   **33 offer** attempt, start   **34 perforce** by force   **41 bashful** timorous   **42 bywords** proverbial   **46 holds up** supports

Dares stir a wing, if Warwick shake his bells.

I'll plant Plantagenet, root him up who dares.

Resolve thee, Richard: claim the English crown.

Flourish. Enter King Henry, Clifford, Northumberland, Westmorland,
Exeter [with red roses in their hats,] and the rest

50 KING HENRY VI   My lords, look where the sturdy rebel sits,

Even in the chair of state: belike he means,

Backed by the power of Warwick, that false peer,

To aspire unto the crown and reign as king.

Earl of Northumberland, he slew thy father,

55 And thine, Lord Clifford, and you both have vowed revenge

On him, his sons, his favourites and his friends.

NORTHUMBERLAND   If I be not, heavens be revenged on me!

CLIFFORD   The hope thereof makes Clifford mourn in steel.

WESTMORLAND   What, shall we suffer this? Let's pluck him
    down.

60 My heart for anger burns. I cannot brook it.

KING HENRY VI   Be patient, gentle Earl of Westmorland.

CLIFFORD   Patience is for poltroons, such as he.

He durst not sit there had your father lived.

My gracious lord, here in the parliament

65 Let us assail the family of York.

NORTHUMBERLAND   Well hast thou spoken, cousin: be it so.

KING HENRY VI   Ah, know you not the city favours them,

And they have troops of soldiers at their beck?

WESTMORLAND   But when the duke is slain, they'll quickly fly.

70 KING HENRY VI   Far be the thought of this from Henry's heart,

To make a shambles of the parliament house.—

Cousin of Exeter, frowns, words and threats

---

47 shake his bells i.e. move, make to swoop on (an image from falconry: bells attached to the bird's legs served to terrify its prey)   **48 plant** establish, install (puns on **Plantagenet**)
Flourish trumpet fanfare signaling the arrival of a person of authority   *red roses* emblems of the House of Lancaster   **50 sturdy** uncompromising, obstinate, defiant   **51 chair of state** throne   **belike** presumably, probably   **52 false peer** disloyal lord   **57 be not** i.e. be not avenged   **58 steel** armor (rather than the traditional black cloth; i.e. ready for revenge)
59 suffer allow   **60 brook** endure   **62 poltroons** cowards, worthless men   **63 durst not** would not have dared   **65 assail** attack, assault   **66 cousin** kinsman; a common form of address among the nobility   **67 city** i.e. citizens of London   **68 beck** command, call
71 shambles slaughterhouse

Shall be the war that Henry means to use.—
Thou factious Duke of York, descend my throne,
75　And kneel for grace and mercy at my feet.
I am thy sovereign.

YORK　I am thine.

EXETER　For shame, come down. He made thee Duke of York.

YORK　It was my inheritance, as the earldom was.

80　**EXETER**　Thy father was a traitor to the crown.

WARWICK　Exeter, thou art a traitor to the crown
In following this usurping Henry.

CLIFFORD　Whom should he follow but his natural king?

WARWICK　True, Clifford, that's Richard Duke of York.

85　**KING HENRY VI**　And shall I stand, and thou sit in my throne?

YORK　It must and shall be so. Content thyself.

WARWICK　Be Duke of Lancaster, let him be king.　*To King Henry*

WESTMORLAND　He is both king and Duke of Lancaster,
And that the Lord of Westmorland shall maintain.

90　**WARWICK**　And Warwick shall disprove it. You forget
That we are those which chased you from the field
And slew your fathers, and with colours spread
Marched through the city to the palace gates.

NORTHUMBERLAND　Yes, Warwick, I remember it to my grief.
95　And by his soul, thou and thy house shall rue it.

WESTMORLAND　Plantagenet, of thee and these thy sons,
Thy kinsmen and thy friends, I'll have more lives
Than drops of blood were in my father's veins.

CLIFFORD　Urge it no more, lest that instead of words,
100　I send thee, Warwick, such a messenger
As shall revenge his death before I stir.

WARWICK　Poor Clifford, how I scorn his worthless threats.

---

74 factious rebellious, generator of division　**78 He . . . York** in *1 Henry VI* (Act 3 Scene 1),
Henry restores Richard to a noble title (previously denied him because his father had been
executed for treason)　**79 earldom** York inherited the earldom of March through his mother,
through whom he claimed a right to the throne　**80 traitor . . . crown** the Earl of Cambridge,
York's father, was executed for treason (*Henry V*, Act 2 Scene 2)　**86 Content thyself** accept it
89 maintain defend, support　**91 field** battlefield　**92 colours** military flags　**95 his** i.e.
Northumberland's father, slain in the battle　**99 Urge** claim, insist on　**100 messenger**
perhaps Clifford means an avenging angel

YORK Will you we show our title to the crown?
If not, our swords shall plead it in the field.

105 KING HENRY VI What title hast thou, traitor, to the crown?
Thy father was, as thou art, Duke of York:
Thy grandfather, Roger Mortimer, Earl of March:
I am the son of Henry the Fifth,
Who made the dauphin and the French to stoop
110 And seized upon their towns and provinces.

WARWICK Talk not of France, sith thou hast lost it all.

KING HENRY VI The Lord Protector lost it and not I:
When I was crowned, I was but nine months old.

RICHARD You are old enough now, and yet, methinks, you
lose.—
115 Father, tear the crown from the usurper's head.

EDWARD Sweet father, do so, set it on your head.

MONTAGUE Good brother, as thou lov'st and honourest arms,
Let's fight it out and not stand cavilling thus.

RICHARD Sound drums and trumpets, and the king will fly.

120 YORK Sons, peace!

KING HENRY VI Peace, thou, and give King Henry leave to speak.

WARWICK Plantagenet shall speak first: hear him, lords,
And be you silent and attentive too,
For he that interrupts him shall not live.

125 KING HENRY VI Think'st thou that I will leave my kingly throne,
Wherein my grandsire and my father sat?
No: first shall war unpeople this my realm;
Ay, and their colours, often borne in France,
And now in England to our heart's great sorrow,
130 Shall be my winding-sheet. Why faint you, lords?
My title's good, and better far than his.

WARWICK Prove it, Henry, and thou shalt be king.

---

103 Will you we do you want me to   **104 plead** make a case for   **106 father . . . York**
historically, York inherited the title from his uncle Edward, his father's elder brother
109 dauphin title of the French king's eldest son, heir to the throne   **stoop** submit, bow down
111 sith since   **112 Lord Protector** Duke of Gloucester, murdered in *2 Henry VI*; the Protector
ruled on behalf of a monarch who was too young to do so   **114 yet** still   **118 cavilling**
disputing over details   **121 leave** permission, opportunity   **127 unpeople** depopulate
130 winding-sheet burial shroud   **faint you** do you lose heart

KING HENRY VI   Henry the Fourth by conquest got the crown.

YORK   'Twas by rebellion against his king.

135 KING HENRY VI   I know not what to say, my title's weak.—   *Aside*

Tell me, may not a king adopt an heir?

YORK   What then?

KING HENRY VI   An if he may, then am I lawful king,

For Richard, in the view of many lords,

140 Resigned the crown to Henry the Fourth,

Whose heir my father was, and I am his.

YORK   He rose against him, being his sovereign,

And made him to resign his crown perforce.

WARWICK   Suppose, my lords, he did it unconstrained,

145 Think you 'twere prejudicial to his crown?

EXETER   No, for he could not so resign his crown,

But that the next heir should succeed and reign.

KING HENRY VI   Art thou against us, Duke of Exeter?

EXETER   His is the right, and therefore pardon me.

150 YORK   Why whisper you, my lords, and answer not?

EXETER   My conscience tells me he is lawful king.

KING HENRY VI   All will revolt from me and turn to him.   *Aside?*

NORTHUMBERLAND   Plantagenet, for all the claim thou   *To York*

lay'st,

Think not that Henry shall be so deposed.

155 WARWICK   Deposed he shall be, in despite of all.

NORTHUMBERLAND   Thou art deceived. 'Tis not thy southern

power,

Of Essex, Norfolk, Suffolk, nor of Kent,

Which makes thee thus presumptuous and proud,

Can set the duke up in despite of me.

160 CLIFFORD   King Henry, be thy title right or wrong,

Lord Clifford vows to fight in thy defence:

---

134 his king i.e. Richard II, whom Henry IV deposed   **138 An if** if   **142 him, being**
Richard II, who was   **144 unconstrained** voluntarily   **145 'twere . . . crown** it would
invalidate his right (or that of his descendants) to the throne   **147 heir** i.e. heir who is next in
line or has been specifically nominated (by Richard)   **149 His** i.e. York's   **155 despite** spite
156 deceived mistaken   **power** army, forces   **159 up** i.e. on the throne

May that ground gape and swallow me alive,

Where I shall kneel to him that slew my father!

KING HENRY VI   O Clifford, how thy words revive my heart!

165   YORK   Henry of Lancaster, resign thy crown.

What mutter you, or what conspire you, lords?

WARWICK   Do right unto this princely Duke of York,

Or I will fill the house with armèd men,

And over the chair of state, where now he sits,

170   Write up his title with usurping blood.

He stamps with his foot and the Soldiers show themselves

KING HENRY VI   My lord of Warwick, hear me but one word:

Let me for this my lifetime reign as king.

YORK   Confirm the crown to me and to mine heirs,

And thou shalt reign in quiet while thou liv'st.

175   KING HENRY VI   I am content. Richard Plantagenet,

Enjoy the kingdom after my decease.

CLIFFORD   What wrong is this unto the prince your son!

WARWICK   What good is this to England and himself!

WESTMORLAND   Base, fearful and despairing Henry!

180   CLIFFORD   How hast thou injured both thyself and us!

WESTMORLAND   I cannot stay to hear these articles.

NORTHUMBERLAND   Nor I.

CLIFFORD   Come, cousin, let us tell the queen these news.   *To*

WESTMORLAND   Farewell, faint-hearted and   *Northumberland*

degenerate king,

185   In whose cold blood no spark of honour bides.

NORTHUMBERLAND   Be thou a prey unto the House of York,

And die in bands for this unmanly deed.

CLIFFORD   In dreadful war mayst thou be overcome,

Or live in peace abandoned and despised.

[*Exeunt Northumberland, Clifford and Westmorland*]

190   WARWICK   Turn this way, Henry, and regard them not.

EXETER   They seek revenge and therefore will not yield.

---

170 usurping blood i.e. the blood of Henry VI   **179 Base** dishonorable, unworthy
181 articles conditions, terms of agreement   **185 cold** weak, cowardly, unnatural
187 bands bonds, chains

KING HENRY VI   Ah, Exeter.

WARWICK   Why should you sigh, my lord?

KING HENRY VI   Not for myself, Lord Warwick, but my son,

195   Whom I unnaturally shall disinherit.

But be it as it may.— I here entail   *To York*

The crown to thee and to thine heirs for ever,

Conditionally, that here thou take an oath

To cease this civil war, and, whilst I live,

200   To honour me as thy king and sovereign,

And neither by treason nor hostility

To seek to put me down and reign thyself.

YORK   This oath I willingly take and will perform.

WARWICK   Long live King Henry!— Plantagenet embrace him.

205   KING HENRY VI   And long live thou and these thy forward sons!

YORK   Now York and Lancaster are reconciled.

EXETER   Accursed be he that seeks to make them foes.

Sennet. Here they come down

YORK   Farewell, my gracious lord, I'll to my castle.

[Exeunt York, his sons and their Soldiers]

WARWICK   And I'll keep London with my soldiers.   *[Exit]*

210   NORFOLK   And I to Norfolk with my followers.   *[Exit]*

MONTAGUE   And I unto the sea from whence I came.   *[Exit]*

KING HENRY VI   And I with grief and sorrow to the court.

Enter the Queen [Margaret, with Prince Edward]

EXETER   Here comes the queen, whose looks bewray her
   anger.

I'll steal away.   *Starts to leave*

215   KING HENRY VI   Exeter, so will I.

QUEEN MARGARET   Nay, go not from me, I will follow thee.

KING HENRY VI   Be patient, gentle queen, and I will stay.

---

196 entail bequeath as a legally untransferable possession   **198 Conditionally** on the
condition   **202 put me down** depose/murder me   **205 forward** precocious, promising/
presumptuous, demanding   ***Sennet*** trumpet call signaling a procession   ***down*** i.e. from the
throne, or a dais on which it sits   **209 keep** remain in/guard   **211 unto the sea** meaning
obscure, since Montague did not have any particular connection with the sea; Shakespeare
may be confusing him with Falconbridge   **213 bewray** betray, reveal

QUEEN MARGARET   Who can be patient in such extremes?
Ah, wretched man, would I had died a maid
220   And never seen thee, never borne thee son,
Seeing thou hast proved so unnatural a father.
Hath he deserved to lose his birthright thus?
Hadst thou but loved him half so well as I,
Or felt that pain which I did for him once,
225   Or nourished him as I did with my blood,
Thou wouldst have left thy dearest heart-blood there,
Rather than have made that savage duke thine heir
And disinherited thine only son.

PRINCE EDWARD   Father, you cannot disinherit me:
230   If you be king, why should not I succeed?

KING HENRY VI   Pardon me, Margaret.— Pardon me, sweet son.
The Earl of Warwick and the duke enforced me.

QUEEN MARGARET   Enforced thee? Art thou king, and wilt be
   forced?
I shame to hear thee speak. Ah, timorous wretch,
235   Thou hast undone thyself, thy son and me,
And given unto the House of York such head
As thou shalt reign but by their sufferance.
To entail him and his heirs unto the crown,
What is it, but to make thy sepulchre
240   And creep into it far before thy time?
Warwick is chancellor and the lord of Calais,
Stern Falconbridge commands the narrow seas,
The duke is made protector of the realm,
And yet shalt thou be safe? Such safety finds
245   The trembling lamb environèd with wolves.
Had I been there, which am a silly woman,
The soldiers should have tossed me on their pikes

---

219 would I wish   **maid** a virgin, unmarried   **224 pain** i.e. of labor   **225 blood** i.e. breast milk, thought to be converted from blood, and popularly supposed to convey to the child some of the mother's temperament (another sense of "blood")   **235 undone** ruined   **236 head** free reign   **237 sufferance** permission, tolerance   **239 sepulchre** tomb   **242 narrow seas** i.e. the English Channel   **243 duke** i.e. of York   **245 environèd** surrounded   **246 silly** helpless, defenseless   **247 tossed** impaled   **pikes** spears

Before I would have granted to that act.
But thou preferr'st thy life before thine honour.
250 And seeing thou dost, I here divorce myself
Both from thy table, Henry, and thy bed,
Until that act of parliament be repealed
Whereby my son is disinherited.
The northern lords that have forsworn thy colours
255 Will follow mine, if once they see them spread:
And spread they shall be, to thy foul disgrace
And utter ruin of the House of York.
Thus do I leave thee.— Come, son, let's away.
Our army is ready; come, we'll after them.

260 KING HENRY VI   Stay, gentle Margaret, and hear me speak.

QUEEN MARGARET   Thou hast spoke too much already. Get thee
gone.

KING HENRY VI   Gentle son Edward, thou wilt stay with me?

QUEEN MARGARET   Ay, to be murdered by his enemies.

PRINCE EDWARD   When I return with victory from the field
265 I'll see your grace: till then I'll follow her.

QUEEN MARGARET   Come, son, away. We may not linger thus.

[*Exeunt Queen Margaret and Prince Edward*]

KING HENRY VI   Poor queen, how love to me and to her son
Hath made her break out into terms of rage.
Revenged may she be on that hateful duke,
270 Whose haughty spirit, wingèd with desire,
Will cost my crown, and like an empty eagle
Tire on the flesh of me and of my son.
The loss of those three lords torments my heart:
I'll write unto them and entreat them fair.
275 Come, cousin you shall be the messenger.

EXETER   And I, I hope, shall reconcile them all.

Flourish.   Exeunt

---

248 granted agreed   **250 I . . . bed** legally, a type of divorce known as *mensa et thoro*, in which partners were free from the duty to cohabit, but not permitted to remarry   **254 forsworn** rejected their oaths to serve under   **271 cost** cost me, deprive me of/accost, attack   **empty** hungry   **272 Tire** feed voraciously   **274 fair** courteously

[Act 1 Scene 2]   *running scene 2*

Enter Richard, Edward and Montague

RICHARD   Brother, though I be youngest, give me leave.

EDWARD   No, I can better play the orator.

MONTAGUE   But I have reasons strong and forcible.

Enter the Duke of York

YORK   Why, how now, sons and brother, at a strife?

5   What is your quarrel? How began it first?

EDWARD   No quarrel, but a slight contention.

YORK   About what?

RICHARD   About that which concerns your grace and us:
            The crown of England, father, which is yours.

10   YORK   Mine boy? Not till King Henry be dead.

RICHARD   Your right depends not on his life or death.

EDWARD   Now you are heir: therefore enjoy it now.
            By giving the House of Lancaster leave to breathe,
            It will outrun you, father, in the end.

15   YORK   I took an oath that he should quietly reign.

EDWARD   But for a kingdom any oath may be broken:
            I would break a thousand oaths to reign one year.

RICHARD   No: God forbid your grace should be forsworn.

YORK   I shall be, if I claim by open war.

20   RICHARD   I'll prove the contrary, if you'll hear me speak.

YORK   Thou canst not, son: it is impossible.

RICHARD   An oath is of no moment, being not took
            Before a true and lawful magistrate,
            That hath authority over him that swears.

25   Henry had none, but did usurp the place.
            Then, seeing 'twas he that made you to depose,
            Your oath, my lord, is vain and frivolous.
            Therefore to arms: and, father, do but think

1.2   Location: the Duke of York's castle (historically Sandal Castle in Yorkshire,
northern England)   1 leave permission (to speak)   **3 forcible** compelling   **13 breathe** rest,
recover itself   **14 outrun** escape, elude   **15 quietly** peacefully   **18 forsworn** guilty of perjury,
an oath breaker   **22 moment** significance   **26 depose** take an oath   **27 vain** worthless
frivolous paltry

How sweet a thing it is to wear a crown,
30 Within whose circuit is Elysium
And all that poets feign of bliss and joy.
Why do we linger thus? I cannot rest
Until the white rose that I wear be dyed
Even in the lukewarm blood of Henry's heart.

35 YORK   Richard, enough: I will be king or die.
Brother, thou shalt to London presently,
And whet on Warwick to this enterprise.
Thou, Richard, shalt to the Duke of Norfolk,
And tell him privily of our intent.
40 You Edward, shall unto my lord Cobham,
With whom the Kentishmen will willingly rise.
In them I trust, for they are soldiers,
Witty, courteous, liberal, full of spirit.
While you are thus employed, what resteth more,
45 But that I seek occasion how to rise,
And yet the king not privy to my drift,
Nor any of the House of Lancaster?

Enter a Messenger

But stay. What news? Why com'st thou in such post?
MESSENGER   The queen with all the northern earls and lords
50 Intend here to besiege you in your castle.
She is hard by with twenty thousand men,
And therefore fortify your hold, my lord.   [*Exit*]
YORK   Ay, with my sword. What, think'st thou that we
    fear them?
Edward and Richard, you shall stay with me,
55 My brother Montague shall post to London.
Let noble Warwick Cobham and the rest,
Whom we have left protectors of the king,

---

30 **circuit** circumference   **Elysium** in Greek mythology, a paradise inhabited by the good or distinguished after death   31 **feign** conjure up, imagine (plays on "fain," i.e. to make glad, rejoice in)   33 **dyed** puns on "died"   36 **presently** immediately   37 **whet on** encourage, sharpen the inclination of   39 **privily** privately, secretly   41 **rise** rebel, rise up in arms   43 **Witty** intelligent   **liberal** generous hearted   **spirit** courage, vigor   44 **resteth more** else remains   45 **occasion** opportunity   46 **privy . . . drift** aware of my intentions   48 **stay** wait **post** haste   51 **hard** close   52 **hold** stronghold, fortress   55 **post** ride swiftly

With powerful policy strengthen themselves,
And trust not simple Henry nor his oaths.

60   MONTAGUE   Brother, I go: I'll win them, fear it not.
And thus most humbly I do take my leave.   *Exit*

Enter [John] Mortimer and his brother [Hugh]

YORK   Sir John and Sir Hugh Mortimer, mine uncles,
You are come to Sandal in a happy hour.
The army of the queen mean to besiege us.

65   JOHN MORTIMER   She shall not need: we'll meet her in the field.

YORK   What, with five thousand men?

RICHARD   Ay, with five hundred, father, for a need.
A woman's general: what should we fear?   *A march afar off*

EDWARD   I hear their drums: let's set our men in order,

70   And issue forth and bid them battle straight.

YORK   Five men to twenty: though the odds be great,
I doubt not, uncle, of our victory.
Many a battle have I won in France,
Whenas the enemy hath been ten to one.

75   Why should I not now have the like success?

Alarum. Exeunt

[Act 1 Scene 3]   *running scene 3*

Enter Rutland and his Tutor

RUTLAND   Ah, whither shall I fly to scape their hands?
Ah, tutor, look where bloody Clifford comes.

Enter Clifford [and Soldiers]

CLIFFORD   Chaplain, away, thy priesthood saves thy life.
As for the brat of this accursèd duke,

5   Whose father slew my father, he shall die.

TUTOR   And I, my lord, will bear him company.

CLIFFORD   Soldiers, away with him.

---

58 policy strategy/cunning   **59 simple** foolish   **63 happy** fortunate   **65 need** need to
67 for a need if necessary   **70 straight** straightaway   **74 Whenas** when, although   **75 like**
same   **1.3**   *Location: the battlefield, near Sandal Castle, Yorkshire*   **1 scape** escape
2 bloody bloodthirsty, warmongering   **4 duke** i.e. York, who killed Clifford's father in *2 Henry
VI* (Act 5 Scene 2)

TUTOR   Ah, Clifford, murder not this innocent child,
Lest thou be hated both of God and man.

Exit [dragged off by Soldiers]

10   CLIFFORD   How now? Is he dead already? Or is it fear
That makes him close his eyes? I'll open them.

RUTLAND   So looks the pent-up lion o'er the wretch
That trembles under his devouring paws:
And so he walks, insulting o'er his prey,
15   And so he comes, to rend his limbs asunder.
Ah, gentle Clifford, kill me with thy sword,
And not with such a cruel threat'ning look.
Sweet Clifford, hear me speak before I die:
I am too mean a subject for thy wrath.
20   Be thou revenged on men, and let me live.

CLIFFORD   In vain thou speak'st, poor boy. My father's blood
Hath stopped the passage where thy words should enter.

RUTLAND   Then let my father's blood open it again.
He is a man, and, Clifford, cope with him.

25   CLIFFORD   Had I thy brethren here, their lives and thine
Were not revenge sufficient for me.
No, if I digged up thy forefathers' graves
And hung their rotten coffins up in chains,
It could not slake mine ire, nor ease my heart.
30   The sight of any of the house of York
Is as a fury to torment my soul,
And till I root out their accursèd line
And leave not one alive, I live in hell.
Therefore—   *Raises his rapier*

35   RUTLAND   O, let me pray before I take my death!
To thee I pray: sweet Clifford, pity me!   *Kneels?*

CLIFFORD   Such pity as my rapier's point affords.

RUTLAND   I never did thee harm: why wilt thou slay me?

---

9 of by   **12 So** thus   **pent-up** caged (furious and ravenous)   **14 insulting** exulting
scornfully   **15 rend** tear   **asunder** apart   **19 mean** unworthy, small, young   **22 the . . .
enter** i.e. the route to compassion   **24 cope** fight   **29 slake** reduce, abate   **31 fury** avenging
spirit (in classical mythology, the Furies were the goddesses of vengeance)   **37 rapier** light
sharp-pointed sword

	CLIFFORD	Thy father hath.
40	RUTLAND	But 'twas ere I was born.

Thou hast one son, for his sake pity me,
Lest in revenge thereof, sith God is just,
He be as miserably slain as I.
Ah, let me live in prison all my days,
And when I give occasion of offence,
Then let me die, for now thou hast no cause.

CLIFFORD   No cause?
Thy father slew my father: therefore, die.   *Stabs him*

RUTLAND   *Di faciant laudis summa sit ista tuae!*   *Dies*

CLIFFORD   Plantagenet, I come, Plantagenet!
And this thy son's blood cleaving to my blade
Shall rust upon my weapon, till thy blood,
Congealed with this, do make me wipe off both.   *Exit*

[Act 1 Scene 4]   *running scene 3 continues*

Alarum. Enter Richard, Duke of York

YORK   The army of the queen hath got the field.
My uncles both are slain in rescuing me;
And all my followers to the eager foe
Turn back and fly, like ships before the wind,
Or lambs pursued by hunger-starvèd wolves.
My sons, God knows what hath bechancèd them:
But this I know, they have demeaned themselves
Like men born to renown by life or death.
Three times did Richard make a lane to me,
And thrice cried 'Courage, father, fight it out!'
And full as oft came Edward to my side,
With purple falchion, painted to the hilt

---

40 ere before   **42 sith** since   **45 occasion** instance/cause   **49 *Di . . . tuae!*** (Latin) "The gods
grant that this may be the height of your glory" (Ovid, *Heroides* 2.66)   **1.4   1 got** won
2 uncles i.e. Sir John and Sir Hugh Mortimer   **3 to** compared to/faced with   **eager** fierce,
savage/impatient   **6 bechancèd** happened to   **7 demeaned** behaved   **9 lane** path, passage
11 full as oft just as frequently   **12 purple** bloodied, bloodred   **falchion** curved sword

In blood of those that had encountered him.
And when the hardiest warriors did retire,

15   Richard cried 'Charge, and give no foot of ground!'
And cried 'A crown, or else a glorious tomb,
A sceptre, or an earthly sepulchre!'
With this we charged again, but, out, alas,
We bodged again, as I have seen a swan

20   With bootless labour swim against the tide
And spend her strength with overmatching waves.

A short alarum within

Ah, hark, the fatal followers do pursue,
And I am faint and cannot fly their fury.
And were I strong, I would not shun their fury.

25   The sands are numbered that makes up my life.
Here must I stay, and here my life must end.

*Enter the Queen, Clifford, Northumberland, the young Prince and
Soldiers*

Come, bloody Clifford, rough Northumberland,
I dare your quenchless fury to more rage:
I am your butt, and I abide your shot.

30   NORTHUMBERLAND   Yield to our mercy, proud Plantagenet.

CLIFFORD   Ay, to such mercy as his ruthless arm,
With downright payment, showed unto my father.
Now Phaethon hath tumbled from his car,
And made an evening at the noontide prick.

35   YORK   My ashes, as the phoenix, may bring forth
A bird that will revenge upon you all.
And in that hope I throw mine eyes to heaven,

---

13 **encountered** fought with   14 **hardiest** boldest   18 **out, alas** exclamation of dismay
19 **bodged** budged, gave way/botched, bungled   20 **bootless** pointless   21 **spend** expend,
use up   **overmatching** overwhelming, more powerful   22 **fatal** death-bringing   25 **sands**
i.e. grains of sand in an hourglass   29 **butt** target (archery term)   **abide** await, will endure
32 **payment** dealing out of death   33 **Phaethon . . . car** in Greek mythology, Phaethon was
the son of the sun god Apollo/Phoebus; he drove his father's sun-chariot (**car**), but could not
control it, burned part of the earth, and was killed with a thunderbolt hurled by Zeus
34 **noontide prick** mark of noon on a sundial   35 **phoenix** mythical Arabian **bird** that was
consumed by fire every five hundred years, then resurrected from the **ashes**; only one existed at
a time   36 **bird** i.e. child

Scorning whate'er you can afflict me with.
Why come you not? What, multitudes and fear?

40   CLIFFORD   So cowards fight when they can fly no further,
So doves do peck the falcon's piercing talons,
So desperate thieves, all hopeless of their lives,
Breathe out invectives gainst the officers.

YORK   O Clifford, but bethink thee once again,

45   An in thy thought o'er-run my former time:
An if thou canst for blushing, view this face,
And bite thy tongue that slanders him with cowardice
Whose frown hath made thee faint and fly ere this!

CLIFFORD   I will not bandy with thee word for word,

50   But buckler with thee blows, twice two for one.

QUEEN MARGARET   Hold, valiant Clifford, for a thousand causes
I would prolong awhile the traitor's life.—
Wrath makes him deaf; speak thou, Northumberland.

NORTHUMBERLAND   Hold, Clifford, do not honour him so much

55   To prick thy finger, though to wound his heart.
What valour were it, when a cur doth grin,
For one to thrust his hand between his teeth,
When he might spurn him with his foot away?
It is war's prize to take all vantages,

60   And ten to one is no impeach of valour.   *They seize York, who*

CLIFFORD   Ay, ay, so strives the woodcock with the gin.   *struggles*

NORTHUMBERLAND   So doth the cony struggle in the net.

YORK   So triumph thieves upon their conquered booty,
So true men yield, with robbers so o'ermatched.

65   NORTHUMBERLAND   What would your grace have done unto him
now?

QUEEN MARGARET   Brave warriors, Clifford and Northumberland,
Come, make him stand upon this molehill here,

---

39 fear still afraid   **44 bethink thee** remind yourself/think   **45 o'er-run** recollect, go over
46 for in spite of   **49 bandy** exchange (insults)   **50 buckler** fight at close quarters/ward off
(blows)   **51 Hold** wait, desist   **causes** reasons   **55 though to** even though it   **56 cur doth
grin** dog bears its teeth   **58 spurn** kick   **59 prize** benefit, privilege   **vantages** advantages,
opportunities   **60 ten . . . valour** for ten men to attack one is no disgrace   **61 woodcock** a
proverbially stupid, and easily captured, bird   **gin** trap   **62 cony** rabbit   **64 true** honest
o'ermatched outnumbered

That raught at mountains with outstretchèd arms,
Yet parted but the shadow with his hand.—

70 What, was it you that would be England's king?   *To York*
Was't you that revelled in our parliament,
And made a preachment of your high descent?
Where are your mess of sons to back you now,
The wanton Edward and the lusty George?

75 And where's that valiant crook-back prodigy,
Dicky, your boy, that with his grumbling voice
Was wont to cheer his dad in mutinies?
Or with the rest, where is your darling Rutland?
Look, York, I stained this napkin with the blood

80 That valiant Clifford, with his rapier's point,
Made issue from the bosom of the boy.
And if thine eyes can water for his death,
I give thee this to dry thy cheeks withal.
Alas poor York, but that I hate thee deadly,

85 I should lament thy miserable state.
I prithee grieve to make me merry, York.
What, hath thy fiery heart so parched thine entrails
That not a tear can fall for Rutland's death?
Why art thou patient, man? Thou shouldst be mad.

90 And I, to make thee mad, do mock thee thus.
Stamp, rave and fret, that I may sing and dance.
Thou wouldst be fee'd, I see, to make me sport.
York cannot speak unless he wear a crown.
A crown for York! And, lords, bow low to him.

95 Hold you his hands, whilst I do set it on.   *Puts a paper crown*
Ay, marry, sir, now looks he like a king.   *on his head*
Ay, this is he that took King Henry's chair,

---

68 That raught he who reached   **69 parted** took as his share/divided (as he reached for
something illusory)   **71 revelled** made merry   **72 preachment** sermon   **73 mess** group of
four   **74 wanton** wild/lascivious   **lusty** vigorous, lively/lustful   **75 prodigy** monster,
abnormal child (considered ominous)   **76 grumbling** growling, deep/discontented   **77 wont**
accustomed   **79 napkin** handkerchief   **81 issue** flow, spring forth   **83 withal** with   **84 but**
were it not   **86 prithee** beg, pray you   **87 parched** dried up, shriveled   **entrails** insides,
intestines   **91 fret** rage   **92 fee'd** paid   **sport** entertainment   **96 marry** by the Virgin Mary
97 chair throne

And this is he was his adopted heir.
But how is it that great Plantagenet
100   Is crowned so soon and broke his solemn oath?
As I bethink me, you should not be king
Till our King Henry had shook hands with death.
And will you pale your head in Henry's glory,
And rob his temples of the diadem,
105   Now in his life, against your holy oath?
O, 'tis a fault too too unpardonable!
Off with the crown, and with the crown his head.
And whilst we breathe, take time to do him dead.

CLIFFORD   That is my office, for my father's sake.

110   QUEEN MARGARET   Nay, stay, let's hear the orisons he makes.

YORK   She-wolf of France, but worse than wolves of
France,
Whose tongue more poisons than the adder's tooth!
How ill-beseeming is it in thy sex
To triumph, like an Amazonian trull,
115   Upon their woes whom fortune captivates!
But that thy face is vizard-like, unchanging,
Made impudent with use of evil deeds,
I would assay, proud queen, to make thee blush.
To tell thee whence thou cam'st, of whom derived,
120   Were shame enough to shame thee, wert thou not
shameless.
Thy father bears the type of King of Naples,
Of both the Sicils and Jerusalem,
Yet not so wealthy as an English yeoman.
Hath that poor monarch taught thee to insult?
125   It needs not, nor it boots thee not, proud queen,

---

103 pale encircle   **104 diadem** crown   **108 breathe** pause for breath   **109 office** duty, task
110 orisons prayers   **113 ill-beseeming** unbecoming   **114 triumph** exult (literally, return
home in great ceremony, displaying one's captives)   **Amazonian** the Amazons were a
mythical race of female warriors   **trull** whore   **115 captivates** captures   **116 vizard-like**
masklike, expressionless   **117 impudent** shameless   **use** habitual practice   **118 assay**
attempt   **119 whence** from where   **derived** descended   **121 type** title   **122 both the Sicils**
i.e. Naples and Sicily   **123 yeoman** man who owns property but is not a gentleman
124 insult be insolent, scornful   **125 boots** profits

Unless the adage must be verified,
That beggars mounted run their horse to death.
'Tis beauty that doth oft make women proud,
But, God he knows, thy share thereof is small.

130   'Tis virtue that doth make them most admired,
The contrary doth make thee wondered at.
'Tis government that makes them seem divine,
The want thereof makes thee abominable.
Thou art as opposite to every good

135   As the Antipodes are unto us,
Or as the south to the Septentrion.
O, tiger's heart wrapt in a woman's hide!
How couldst thou drain the life-blood of the child,
To bid the father wipe his eyes withal,

140   And yet be seen to bear a woman's face?
Women are soft, mild, pitiful and flexible;
Thou stern, obdurate, flinty, rough, remorseless.
Bid'st thou me rage? Why, now thou hast thy wish.
Wouldst have me weep? Why, now thou hast thy will.

145   For raging wind blows up incessant showers,
And when the rage allays, the rain begins.
These tears are my sweet Rutland's obsequies,
And every drop cries vengeance for his death,
Gainst thee, fell Clifford, and thee, false Frenchwoman.

150   NORTHUMBERLAND   Beshrew me, but his passions moves me so
That hardly can I check my eyes from tears.

YORK   That face of his the hungry cannibals
Would not have touched, would not have stained with
blood.

---

126 **adage** maxim, saying   127 **mounted** on horseback/socially elevated   131 **wondered**
marveled   132 **government** self-control   133 **want** lack   **abominable** loathsome (often
popularly "inhuman, unnatural")   135 **Antipodes** the other side of the world
136 **Septentrion** i.e. the north (literally, the seven stars that make up the Plough or Big Dipper
constellation)   139 **withal** with it (the handkerchief stained with Rutland's blood)
141 **pitiful** full of pity, compassionate   **flexible** yielding, easily moved   142 **obdurate**
stubborn, unmovable   **flinty** hard, stony   **rough** violent, harsh   147 **obsequies** funeral
rites   149 **fell** cruel, savage   **false** treacherous   150 **Beshrew** curse   151 **check** restrain

But you are more inhuman, more inexorable,
155   O, ten times more, than tigers of Hyrcania.
See, ruthless queen, a hapless father's tears.
This cloth thou dipped'st in blood of my sweet boy,
And I with tears do wash the blood away.
Keep thou the napkin, and go boast of this,
160   And if thou tell'st the heavy story right,
Upon my soul, the hearers will shed tears.
Yea, even my foes will shed fast-falling tears,
And say 'Alas, it was a piteous deed!'
There, take the crown, and with the crown, my curse.
165   And in thy need such comfort come to thee
As now I reap at thy too cruel hand.
Hard-hearted Clifford, take me from the world:
My soul to heaven, my blood upon your heads.

NORTHUMBERLAND   Had he been slaughterman to all my kin,
170   I should not for my life but weep with him,
To see how inly sorrow gripes his soul.

QUEEN MARGARET   What, weeping-ripe, my lord
            Northumberland?
Think but upon the wrong he did us all,
And that will quickly dry thy melting tears.

175   CLIFFORD   Here's for my oath, here's for my father's
            death.   *Stabs him twice*

QUEEN MARGARET   And here's to right our gentle-hearted
            king.   *Stabs him*

YORK   Open thy gate of mercy, gracious God.
My soul flies through these wounds to seek out thee.   *Dies*

QUEEN MARGARET   Off with his head and set it on York gates,
180   So York may overlook the town of York.

                        Flourish.   Exeunt [with the body]

---

155 **Hyrcania** in ancient times the region south of the Caspian Sea; its **tigers** were proverbially
fierce   156 **hapless** unfortunate   160 **heavy** sorrowful, terrible   163 **piteous** worthy of
pity   171 **inly** inward   **gripes** grips   172 **weeping-ripe** on the verge of tears   176 **gentle-
hearted** noble-hearted/tender-hearted

[Act 2 Scene 1]   *running scene 4*

A march. Enter Edward, Richard and their power

EDWARD   I wonder how our princely father scaped,
              Or whether he be scaped away or no
              From Clifford's and Northumberland's pursuit?
              Had he been ta'en, we should have heard the news:
5   Had he been slain, we should have heard the news:
              Or had he scaped, methinks we should have heard
              The happy tidings of his good escape.
              How fares my brother? Why is he so sad?

RICHARD   I cannot joy, until I be resolved
10   Where our right valiant father is become.
              I saw him in the battle range about
              And watched him how he singled Clifford forth.
              Methought he bore him in the thickest troop
              As doth a lion in a herd of neat,
15   Or as a bear encompassed round with dogs,
              Who having pinched a few and made them cry,
              The rest stand all aloof, and bark at him.
              So fared our father with his enemies,
              So fled his enemies my warlike father.
20   Methinks, 'tis prize enough to be his son.   *Three suns appear*
              See how the morning opes her golden gates,
              And takes her farewell of the glorious sun.
              How well resembles it the prime of youth,
              Trimmed like a younker prancing to his love.

25   EDWARD   Dazzle mine eyes, or do I see three suns?

     RICHARD Three glorious suns, each one a perfect sun,
              Not separated with the racking clouds,

2.1   *Location: the borders of Wales*   *power* army   4 ta'en taken, captured   **9 resolved**
satisfied, informed   **10 Where . . . become** what has become of our very valiant father
11 range move, wander   **12 forth** out   **13 bore him** conducted himself   **14 neat** cattle
16 pinched bitten, tormented   **17 aloof** at a distance   **20 prize** privilege, reward   **21 opes**
opens   **24 Trimmed** adorned, decked out   **younker** fashionable young man   **prancing**
posturing, nimbly dancing for   **25 suns** the emblem of Edward III and Richard II consisted of
the sun's rays emerging above clouds   **27 racking** drifting, scudding

But severed in a pale clear-shining sky.
See, see: they join, embrace, and seem to kiss,
30   As if they vowed some league inviolable.
Now are they but one lamp, one light, one sun.
In this the heaven figures some event.

EDWARD   'Tis wondrous strange, the like yet never heard of.
I think it cites us, brother, to the field,
35   That we, the sons of brave Plantagenet,
Each one already blazing by our meeds,
Should notwithstanding join our lights together
And overshine the earth, as this the world.
Whate'er it bodes, henceforward will I bear
40   Upon my target three fair-shining suns.

RICHARD   Nay, bear three daughters: by your leave, I speak it,
You love the breeder better than the male.

Enter one [a Messenger] blowing

But what art thou, whose heavy looks foretell
Some dreadful story hanging on thy tongue?

45   MESSENGER   Ah, one that was a woeful looker-on
Whenas the noble Duke of York was slain,
Your princely father and my loving lord!

EDWARD   O, speak no more, for I have heard too much.

RICHARD   Say how he died, for I will hear it all.

50   MESSENGER   Environèd he was with many foes,
And stood against them, as the hope of Troy
Against the Greeks that would have entered Troy.
But Hercules himself must yield to odds,
And many strokes, though with a little axe,
55   Hews down and fells the hardest-timbered oak.
By many hands your father was subdued,
But only slaughtered by the ireful arm

---

28 severed separate   **32 figures** foretells, prefigures   **34 cites** summons   **36 meeds** merits
38 overshine illuminate, shine on/outshine, surpass   **this** this phenomenon   **40 target**
shield   **41 daughters** Richard plays on **suns**/"sons"   **42 breeder** woman   *blowing* out of
breath   **43 heavy** serious, sad   **46 Whenas** when   **50 Environèd** surrounded   **51 hope of
Troy** Hector, the mighty warrior who defended the city of Troy against the invasion of the
Greeks   **53 Hercules** semidivine hero of classical mythology, famed for his strength

Of unrelenting Clifford and the queen,
Who crowned the gracious duke in high despite,
60   Laughed in his face, and when with grief he wept,
The ruthless queen gave him to dry his cheeks
A napkin steepèd in the harmless blood
Of sweet young Rutland, by rough Clifford slain.
And after many scorns, many foul taunts,
65   They took his head, and on the gates of York
They set the same, and there it doth remain,
The saddest spectacle that e'er I viewed.   [*Exit*]

EDWARD   Sweet Duke of York, our prop to lean upon,
Now thou art gone, we have no staff, no stay.
70   O Clifford, boist'rous Clifford, thou hast slain
The flower of Europe for his chivalry,
And treacherously hast thou vanquished him,
For hand to hand he would have vanquished thee.
Now my soul's palace is become a prison.
75   Ah, would she break from hence, that this my body
Might in the ground be closèd up in rest,
For never henceforth shall I joy again:
Never, O, never, shall I see more joy!

RICHARD   I cannot weep, for all my body's moisture
80   Scarce serves to quench my furnace-burning heart.
Nor can my tongue unload my heart's great burden,
For selfsame wind that I should speak withal
Is kindling coals that fires all my breast,
And burns me up with flames that tears would quench.
85   To weep is to make less the depth of grief:
Tears then for babes; blows and revenge for me.
Richard, I bear thy name, I'll venge thy death,
Or die renownèd by attempting it.

EDWARD   His name that valiant duke hath left with thee:
90   His dukedom and his chair with me is left.

---

59 despite contempt, scorn, mockery   **62 harmless** innocent   **63 rough** cruel, violent
69 stay support   **70 boist'rous** brutal   **74 soul's palace** i.e. body   **75 she** i.e. his soul
78 more joy joy anymore   **82 wind** breath   **87 venge** avenge   **90 chair** seat of authority as
duke; also, claim to the throne

RICHARD   Nay, if thou be that princely eagle's bird,
Show thy descent by gazing gainst the sun.
For chair and dukedom, throne and kingdom say,
Either that is thine, or else thou wert not his.

March. Enter Warwick, Marquis [of] Montague and their army

95 WARWICK   How now, fair lords? What fare? What news
abroad?

RICHARD   Great Lord of Warwick, if we should recount
Our baleful news, and at each word's deliverance
Stab poniards in our flesh till all were told,
The words would add more anguish than the wounds.
100   O, valiant lord, the Duke of York is slain!

EDWARD   O Warwick, Warwick, that Plantagenet
Which held thee dearly as his soul's redemption,
Is by the stern Lord Clifford done to death.

WARWICK   Ten days ago I drowned these news in tears,
105   And now, to add more measure to your woes,
I come to tell you things sith then befall'n.
After the bloody fray at Wakefield fought,
Where your brave father breathed his latest gasp,
Tidings, as swiftly as the posts could run,
110   Were brought me of your loss and his depart.
I, then in London, keeper of the king,
Mustered my soldiers, gathered flocks of friends,
Marched toward St Albans to intercept the queen,
Bearing the king in my behalf along.
115   For by my scouts I was advisèd
That she was coming with a full intent
To dash our late decree in parliament
Touching King Henry's oath and your succession.

---

91 eagle's . . . sun eagles were thought to be able to gaze unblinkingly at the sun and to test
their young by making them do so   94 that the sun (i.e. kingship)   95 What fare? What is
the state of things?   abroad in the world   97 baleful deadly   98 poniards daggers
103 stern cruel   105 measure quantity   106 sith since   107 Wakefield town in West
Yorkshire   108 latest last   109 posts messengers   110 depart death   111 keeper guard
113 St Albans town about twenty-five miles north of London   114 in my behalf for my own
interests   115 advisèd notified, warned   117 dash overturn   late recent
118 Touching regarding

Short tale to make, we at St Albans met
120 Our battles joined, and both sides fiercely fought.
But whether 'twas the coldness of the king,
Who looked full gently on his warlike queen,
That robbed my soldiers of their heated spleen,
Or whether 'twas report of her success,
125 Or more than common fear of Clifford's rigour,
Who thunders to his captives blood and death,
I cannot judge: but to conclude with truth,
Their weapons like to lightning came and went,
Our soldiers' like the night-owl's lazy flight,
130 Or like an idle thresher with a flail,
Fell gently down, as if they struck their friends.
I cheered them up with justice of our cause,
With promise of high pay and great rewards,
But all in vain: they had no heart to fight,
135 And we in them no hope to win the day,
So that we fled. The king unto the queen,
Lord George your brother, Norfolk and myself,
In haste, post-haste, are come to join with you,
For in the marches here we heard you were,
140 Making another head to fight again.

EDWARD   Where is the Duke of Norfolk, gentle Warwick?
And when came George from Burgundy to England?

WARWICK   Some six miles off the duke is with the soldiers,
And for your brother, he was lately sent
145 From your kind aunt, Duchess of Burgundy,
With aid of soldiers to this needful war.

RICHARD   'Twas odds, belike, when valiant Warwick fled;
Oft have I heard his praises in pursuit,
But ne'er till now his scandal of retire.

---

120 battles armies   **121 coldness** indifference, apathy   **122 full** very, extremely   **123 heated spleen** fiery passion   **125 rigour** cruelty, severity   **128 like to** like   **130 flail** instrument used to thresh corn, consisting of a staff from which a shorter pole swings   **139 marches** borders of Wales   **140 Making another head** raising another army   **145 aunt . . . Burgundy** this granddaughter of John of Gaunt was in fact a distant cousin   **146 needful** needing reinforcements   **147 'Twas odds, belike** the odds were probably very unfavorable   **148 in pursuit** for pursuing the enemy   **149 scandal of retire** notoriety for retreating

150 WARWICK   Nor now my scandal, Richard, dost thou hear,
     For thou shalt know this strong right hand of mine
     Can pluck the diadem from faint Henry's head,
     And wring the awful sceptre from his fist,
     Were he as famous and as bold in war
155 As he is famed for mildness, peace, and prayer.
     RICHARD   I know it well, Lord Warwick, blame me not.
     'Tis love I bear thy glories make me speak.
     But in this troublous time, what's to be done?
     Shall we go throw away our coats of steel,
160 And wrap our bodies in black mourning gowns,
     Numb'ring our Ave Maries with our beads?
     Or shall we on the helmets of our foes
     Tell our devotion with revengeful arms?
     If for the last, say ay, and to it, lords.
165 WARWICK   Why, therefore Warwick came to seek you out,
     And therefore comes my brother Montague.
     Attend me, lords: the proud insulting queen,
     With Clifford and the haught Northumberland,
     And of their feather many more proud birds,
170 Have wrought the easy-melting king like wax.
     He swore consent to your succession,
     His oath enrollèd in the parliament.
     And now to London all the crew are gone,
     To frustrate both his oath and what beside
175 May make against the house of Lancaster.
     Their power, I think, is thirty thousand strong.
     Now, if the help of Norfolk and myself,
     With all the friends that thou, brave Earl of March,
     Amongst the loving Welshmen canst procure,

---

153 wring wrench   **awful** awe-inspiring   **161 Numb'ring** counting   **Ave Maries** Hail
Marys, prayers frequently recited over a rosary   **beads** rosary (beads used as prompts in the
reciting of prayers)   **163 Tell** proclaim/count (with sword strokes rather than prayers)
165 therefore for that reason   **167 Attend** listen, pay attention to   **168 haught** haughty,
arrogant   **170 wrought** worked, molded   **172 enrollèd** officially recorded   **173 crew**
body of men, gang   **174 frustrate** annul   **what beside** anything else   **175 make** work, be
used

180   Will but amount to five-and-twenty thousand,
    Why, *via*, to London will we march,
    And once again bestride our foaming steeds,
    And once again cry 'Charge!' upon our foes,
    But never once again turn back and fly.

185   RICHARD   Ay, now methinks I hear great Warwick speak;
    Ne'er may he live to see a sunshine day,
    That cries 'Retire!' if Warwick bid him stay.

  EDWARD   Lord Warwick, on thy shoulder will I lean,
    And when thou fail'st — as God forbid the hour —

190   Must Edward fall, which peril heaven forfend!

  WARWICK   No longer Earl of March, but Duke of York:
    The next degree is England's royal throne.
    For King of England shalt thou be proclaimed
    In every borough as we pass along.

195   And he that throws not up his cap for joy
    Shall for the fault make forfeit of his head.
    King Edward, valiant Richard, Montague,
    Stay we no longer, dreaming of renown,
    But sound the trumpets, and about our task.

200   RICHARD   Then, Clifford, were thy heart as hard as steel,
    As thou hast shown it flinty by thy deeds,
    I come to pierce it or to give thee mine.

  EDWARD   Then strike up drums. God and Saint George for us!

Enter a Messenger

  WARWICK   How now? What news?

205   MESSENGER   The Duke of Norfolk sends you word by me,
    The queen is coming with a puissant host,
    And craves your company for speedy counsel.

  WARWICK   Why then it sorts, brave warriors, let's away.

                                          Exeunt

---

181 *via* "onward" (Italian)   **182 bestride** straddle   **187 'Retire!'** Withdraw!   **190 forfend** forbid   **192 degree** rank/step   **203 Saint George** patron saint of England   **206 puissant host** powerful army   **207 craves** requests   **208 sorts** arranges itself

[Act 2 Scene 2]   *running scene 5*

*Flourish. Enter the King, the Queen, Clifford, Northum[berland] and
young Prince, with Drum and Trumpets*   *York's head is set
above the city gates*

QUEEN MARGARET   Welcome, my lord, to this brave town
    of York.
    Yonder's the head of that arch-enemy
    That sought to be encompassed with your crown:
    Doth not the object cheer your heart, my lord?
5   KING HENRY VI   Ay, as the rocks cheer them that fear their wreck:
    To see this sight, it irks my very soul.
    Withhold revenge, dear God! 'tis not my fault,
    Nor wittingly have I infringed my vow.
    CLIFFORD   My gracious liege, this too much lenity
10   And harmful pity must be laid aside.
    To whom do lions cast their gentle looks?
    Not to the beast that would usurp their den.
    Whose hand is that the forest bear doth lick?
    Not his that spoils her young before her face.
15   Who scapes the lurking serpent's mortal sting?
    Not he that sets his foot upon her back.
    The smallest worm will turn being trodden on,
    And doves will peck in safeguard of their brood.
    Ambitious York doth level at thy crown,
20   Thou smiling while he knit his angry brows:
    He, but a duke, would have his son a king,
    And raise his issue, like a loving sire;
    Thou, being a king, blest with a goodly son,
    Didst yield consent to disinherit him,
25   Which argued thee a most unloving father.
    Unreasonable creatures feed their young;

2.2   Location: outside the city walls of York   Drum and Trumpets drummer and
trumpeters   **1 brave** splendid   **5 wreck** shipwreck   **6 irks** distresses, troubles   **9 lenity**
mildness   **14 spoils** slaughters, destroys   **19 level** aim   **20 knit** furrows   **22 raise** promote
(the rank of; plays on the sense of "conceive, bring into existence")   **issue** offspring   **sire**
father   **23 goodly** fine, excellent   **25 argued thee** demonstrated, suggested that you were
26 Unreasonable brute, not endowed with reason

And though man's face be fearful to their eyes,
Yet, in protection of their tender ones,
Who hath not seen them, even with those wings
30   Which sometime they have used with fearful flight,
Make war with him that climbed unto their nest,
Offering their own lives in their young's defence?
For shame, my liege, make them your precedent!
Were it not pity that this goodly boy
35   Should lose his birthright by his father's fault,
And long hereafter say unto his child,
'What my great-grandfather and his grandsire got
My careless father fondly gave away'?
Ah, what a shame were this! Look on the boy;
40   And let his manly face, which promiseth
Successful fortune, steel thy melting heart
To hold thine own and leave thine own with him.

KING HENRY VI   Full well hath Clifford played the orator,
Inferring arguments of mighty force:
45   But, Clifford, tell me, didst thou never hear
That things ill-got had ever bad success?
And happy always was it for that son
Whose father for his hoarding went to hell?
I'll leave my son my virtuous deeds behind,
50   And would my father had left me no more:
For all the rest is held at such a rate
As brings a thousand-fold more care to keep
Than in possession any jot of pleasure.
Ah, cousin York, would thy best friends did know
55   How it doth grieve me that thy head is here!

QUEEN MARGARET   My lord, cheer up your spirits: our foes are
      nigh,

---

27 fearful frightening   **28 tender** young/vulnerable   **33 precedent** example   **34 pity** a disaster, a shame   **38 fondly** foolishly   **39 shame** disgrace, dishonor   **41 melting** i.e. soft, compassionate   **44 Inferring** offering, adducing   **46 ill-got** wrongfully gained   **success** outcome   **47 happy** fortunate (i.e. in his inheritance)   **48 hoarding** i.e. of goods, money   **51 rate** cost   **52 care** troubles, burdensome responsibilities   **keep** maintain, defend, protect   **56 nigh** near

And this soft courage makes your followers faint.
You promised knighthood to our forward son:
Unsheathe your sword, and dub him presently.

60   Edward, kneel down.

KING HENRY VI   Edward Plantagenet, arise a knight;
And learn this lesson, draw thy sword in right.

PRINCE EDWARD   My gracious father, by your kingly leave,
I'll draw it as apparent to the crown,

65   And in that quarrel use it to the death.

CLIFFORD   Why, that is spoken like a toward prince.

Enter a Messenger

MESSENGER   Royal commanders, be in readiness:
For with a band of thirty thousand men
Comes Warwick, backing of the Duke of York;

70   And in the towns, as they do march along,
Proclaims him king, and many fly to him.
Deraign your battle, for they are at hand.   [*Exit*]

CLIFFORD   I would your highness would depart the field:
The queen hath best success when you are absent.

75   QUEEN MARGARET   Ay, good my lord, and leave us to our fortune.

KING HENRY VI   Why, that's my fortune too: therefore I'll stay.

NORTHUMBERLAND   Be it with resolution then to fight.

PRINCE EDWARD   My royal father, cheer these noble lords
And hearten those that fight in your defence.

80   Unsheathe your sword, good father, cry 'Saint George!'

March. Enter Edward, Warwick, Richard, Clarence [George], Norfolk,
Montague and Soldiers

EDWARD   Now, perjured Henry, wilt thou kneel for grace,
And set thy diadem upon my head,
Or bide the mortal fortune of the field?

---

57 faint lose heart   **58 forward** promising, precocious   **59 dub** create a knight (by touching
the shoulders with a sword while the knight kneeled before the monarch)   **presently**
immediately   **62 right** righteousness, a just cause   **64 apparent** heir   **66 toward** bold,
promising   **69 backing of** supporting   **72 Deraign** set in order, prepare   **battle** army
Clarence [George] George is not in fact made Duke of Clarence until Act 2 Scene 6   **83 bide**
undergo/await   **mortal** fatal

QUEEN MARGARET   Go, rate thy minions, proud insulting boy.

85 Becomes it thee to be thus bold in terms

Before thy sovereign and thy lawful king?

EDWARD   I am his king, and he should bow his knee:

I was adopted heir by his consent.

Since when, his oath is broke, for as I hear,

90 You that are king, though he do wear the crown,

Have caused him, by new act of parliament,

To blot out me and put his own son in.

CLIFFORD   And reason too:

Who should succeed the father but the son?

95 RICHARD   Are you there, butcher? O, I cannot speak!

CLIFFORD   Ay, crookback, here I stand to answer thee,

Or any he, the proudest of thy sort.

RICHARD   'Twas you that killed young Rutland, was it not?

CLIFFORD   Ay, and old York, and yet not satisfied.

100 RICHARD   For God's sake, lords, give signal to the fight.

WARWICK   What say'st thou, Henry, wilt thou yield the crown?

QUEEN MARGARET   Why, how now, long-tongued

Warwick, dare you speak?

When you and I met at St Albans last,

105 Your legs did better service than your hands.

WARWICK   Then 'twas my turn to fly, and now 'tis thine.

CLIFFORD   You said so much before and yet you fled.

WARWICK   'Twas not your valour, Clifford, drove me thence.

NORTHUMBERLAND   No, nor your manhood that durst make you

stay.

110 RICHARD   Northumberland, I hold thee reverently.

Break off the parley, for scarce I can refrain

The execution of my big-swol'n heart

Upon that Clifford, that cruel child-killer.

CLIFFORD   I slew thy father. Call'st thou him a child?

---

84 rate rebuke, berate   **minions** favorites/servants   **97 he** man   **sort** gang   **102 long-tongued** i.e. prattling   **105 legs . . . hands** i.e. in fleeing rather than fighting   **109 durst** dared   **110 reverently** in great esteem, in respect   **111 parley** conversation, exchange/negotiation between opposing sides   **refrain** hold back   **112 execution** carrying out, enacting (of feelings; plays on sense of "putting to death")   **big-swol'n** i.e. with anger, grief, revenge

115 RICHARD   Ay, like a dastard and a treacherous coward,
As thou didst kill our tender brother Rutland.
But ere sunset, I'll make thee curse the deed.

KING HENRY VI   Have done with words, my lords, and hear me
speak.

QUEEN MARGARET   Defy them then, or else hold close thy lips.

120 KING HENRY VI   I prithee, give no limits to my tongue:
I am a king and privileged to speak.

CLIFFORD   My liege, the wound that bred this meeting here
Cannot be cured by words: therefore be still.

RICHARD   Then, executioner, unsheathe thy sword:

125   By him that made us all, I am resolved
That Clifford's manhood lies upon his tongue.

EDWARD   Say, Henry, shall I have my right or no?
A thousand men have broke their fasts today,
That ne'er shall dine unless thou yield the crown.

130 WARWICK   If thou deny, their blood upon thy head,
For York in justice puts his armour on.

PRINCE EDWARD   If that be right which Warwick says is right,
There is no wrong, but everything is right.

RICHARD   Whoever got thee, there thy mother stands,

135   For well I wot, thou hast thy mother's tongue.

QUEEN MARGARET   But thou art neither like thy sire nor dam,
But like a foul misshapen stigmatic,
Marked by the destinies to be avoided,
As venom toads or lizards' dreadful stings.

140 RICHARD   Iron of Naples hid with English gilt,
Whose father bears the title of a king
As if a channel should be called the sea

---

115 dastard coward   **116 tender** young   **123 still** silent   **125 him . . . all** i.e. God   **resolved** convinced, satisfied   **126 lies** plays on the sense of "deceives"   **upon his tongue** i.e. only in his words   **128 broke their fasts** breakfasted, i.e. started the day   **130 deny** refuse   **134 got** begot, conceived, fathered   **135 wot** know   **136 dam** mother   **137 stigmatic** one marked with a physical deformity or blemish   **138 Marked** branded   **destinies** i.e. fate (in classical mythology, the three Fates who controlled the birth, life, and death of all)   **139 venom** poisonous   **140 Naples** Margaret was the daughter of Reignier, the titular King of Naples   **gilt** gold veneer (i.e. marriage to an Englishman); puns on "guilt"   **142 channel** stream/gutter

Sham'st thou not, knowing whence thou art extraught,
To let thy tongue detect thy base-born heart?

145   EDWARD   A wisp of straw were worth a thousand crowns,
To make this shameless callet know herself.
Helen of Greece was fairer far than thou,
Although thy husband may be Menelaus;
And ne'er was Agamemnon's brother wronged
150   By that false woman, as this king by thee.
His father revelled in the heart of France,
And tamed the king, and made the dauphin stoop.
And had he matched according to his state,
He might have kept that glory to this day.
155   But when he took a beggar to his bed,
And graced thy poor sire with his bridal-day,
Even then that sunshine brewed a shower for him,
That washed his father's fortunes forth of France,
And heaped sedition on his crown at home.
160   For what hath broached this tumult but thy pride?
Hadst thou been meek, our title still had slept,
And we, in pity of the gentle king,
Had slipped our claim until another age.

    GEORGE   But when we saw our sunshine made thy spring,
165   And that thy summer bred us no increase,
We set the axe to thy usurping root.
And though the edge hath something hit ourselves,
Yet, know thou, since we have begun to strike,

---

143 **Sham'st thou not** are you not ashamed   **extraught** descended   144 **detect** reveal
145 **wisp of straw** scolds (verbally abusive women) were traditionally made to wear a straw
garland as a means of publicly shaming them   146 **callet** scold/whore   147 **Helen . . .
Menelaus** Helen of Troy was allegedly the most beautiful woman in the world; she betrayed
her husband, **Menelaus**, King of Sparta and **Agamemnon's brother**, when Paris carried her off
and provoked the Trojan war   149 **Agamemnon's brother** Menelaus   151 **His father** i.e.
Henry V   **revelled** made merry, had his will   153 **he** i.e. Henry VI   **matched** married
state social standing, rank   156 **graced . . . sire** honored your impoverished father   **his** i.e.
Henry VI's   158 **forth** out   159 **sedition** turbulence, violence, rebellion   160 **broached** set
flowing, initiated   161 **title** claim to the throne   **still** always   163 **slipped** passed over, left
unasserted   164 **our . . . spring** i.e. that we were not benefiting from your prosperity/that our
favor was making you successful rather than ourselves   165 **increase** harvest, yield
167 **something** somewhat, to some extent

We'll never leave till we have hewn thee down,

170   Or bathed thy growing with our heated bloods.

EDWARD   And in this resolution, I defy thee,

Not willing any longer conference,

Since thou denied'st the gentle king to speak.

Sound trumpets, let our bloody colours wave,

175   And either victory or else a grave!

QUEEN MARGARET   Stay, Edward.

EDWARD   No, wrangling woman, we'll no longer stay.

These words will cost ten thousand lives this day.   *Exeunt*

[Act 2 Scene 3]   *running scene 5 continues*

Alarum. Excursions. Enter Warwick

WARWICK   Forspent with toil, as runners with a race,

I lay me down a little while to breathe,

For strokes received, and many blows repaid

Have robbed my strong-knit sinews of their strength,

5   And spite of spite needs must I rest awhile.

Enter Edward running

EDWARD   Smile, gentle heaven, or strike, ungentle death,

For this world frowns, and Edward's sun is clouded.

WARWICK   How now, my lord, what hap? What hope of good?

Enter Clarence [George]

GEORGE   Our hap is loss, our hope but sad despair,

10   Our ranks are broke, and ruin follows us.

What counsel give you? Whither shall we fly?

EDWARD   Bootless is flight, they follow us with wings,

And weak we are and cannot shun pursuit.

Enter Richard

RICHARD   Ah, Warwick, why hast thou withdrawn thyself?

15   Thy brother's blood the thirsty earth hath drunk,

---

173 denied'st forbade, refused to allow   2.3   *Location: the battlefield, near York*
Excursions bouts of fighting across the stage   1 Forspent exhausted   2 breathe rest, draw
breath   5 spite of spite come what may   8 hap fortune   12 Bootless pointless, useless
15 brother's i.e. Warwick's illegitimate half brother, Thomas Neville

Broached with the steely point of Clifford's lance,
And in the very pangs of death he cried,
Like to a dismal clangour heard from far,
'Warwick, revenge! Brother, revenge my death!'
20 So, underneath the belly of their steeds,
That stained their fetlocks in his smoking blood,
The noble gentleman gave up the ghost.

WARWICK   Then let the earth be drunken with our blood.
I'll kill my horse, because I will not fly.
25 Why stand we like soft-hearted women here,
Wailing our losses, whiles the foe doth rage,
And look upon, as if the tragedy
Were played in jest by counterfeiting actors?
Here on my knee, I vow to God above,   *Kneels*
30 I'll never pause again, never stand still,
Till either death hath closed these eyes of mine
Or fortune given me measure of revenge.

EDWARD   O Warwick, I do bend my knee with thine,
And in this vow do chain my soul to thine.
35 And, ere my knee rise from the earth's cold face,
I throw my hands, mine eyes, my heart to thee,
Thou setter-up and plucker-down of kings,
Beseeching thee, if with thy will it stands
That to my foes this body must be prey,
40 Yet that thy brazen gates of heaven may ope,
And give sweet passage to my sinful soul.
Now, lords, take leave until we meet again,
Where'er it be, in heaven or in earth.

RICHARD   Brother, give me thy hand, and, gentle Warwick,
45 Let me embrace thee in my weary arms.

---

18 Like to like   **dismal** ominous   **clangour** ringing, reverberation   **21 fetlocks** the parts of
a horse's legs just above the hooves   **27 upon** on   **28 played in jest** pretend, make-believe,
performed for entertainment   **counterfeiting** imitating, pretending   **32 measure** due
proportion, full quantity   **36 throw** i.e. give over, dedicate   **thee** i.e. God   **38 stands** agrees
40 brazen strong (as brass)   **ope** open

I, that did never weep, now melt with woe
That winter should cut off our springtime so.

WARWICK   Away, away! Once more, sweet lords farewell.

GEORGE   Yet let us all together to our troops,
50   And give them leave to fly that will not stay,
And call them pillars that will stand to us.
And, if we thrive, promise them such rewards
As victors wear at the Olympian games.
This may plant courage in their quailing breasts,
55   For yet is hope of life and victory.
Forslow no longer, make we hence amain.   *Exeunt*

[Act 2 Scene 4]   *running scene 5 continues*

Excursions. Enter Richard and Clifford

RICHARD   Now, Clifford, I have singled thee alone.
Suppose this arm is for the Duke of York,
And this for Rutland, both bound to revenge,
Wert thou environed with a brazen wall.
5   CLIFFORD   Now, Richard, I am with thee here alone.
This is the hand that stabbed thy father York,
And this the hand that slew thy brother Rutland,
And here's the heart that triumphs in their death
And cheers these hands that slew thy sire and brother
10   To execute the like upon thyself.
And so, have at thee!   *They fight*
Warwick comes [and rescues Richard], Clifford flies

RICHARD   Nay Warwick, single out some other chase,
For I myself will hunt this wolf to death.   *Exeunt*

---

51 to by   52 thrive succeed/live   53 Olympian games held every four years in honor of the
supreme Greek god Zeus; winners were honored with olive garlands   56 Forslow delay
amain speedily   2.4   1 singled thee alone isolated you from the rest (hunting term for
separating a deer from the herd)   4 Wert thou were you, even if you were   11 have at thee
i.e. here I come (standard utterance at the opening of a fight)   12 chase prey

[Act 2 Scene 5]   *running scene 5 continues*

Alarum. Enter King Henry alone

KING HENRY VI   This battle fares like to the morning's war,
When dying clouds contend with growing light,
What time the shepherd, blowing of his nails,
Can neither call it perfect day nor night.

5   Now sways it this way, like a mighty sea
Forced by the tide to combat with the wind.
Now sways it that way, like the selfsame sea
Forced to retire by fury of the wind.
Sometime the flood prevails, and then the wind,

10   Now one the better, then another best;
Both tugging to be victors, breast to breast,
Yet neither conqueror nor conquerèd:
So is the equal poise of this fell war.
Here on this molehill will I sit me down.

15   To whom God will, there be the victory.
For Margaret my queen, and Clifford too,
Have chid me from the battle, swearing both
They prosper best of all when I am thence.
Would I were dead, if God's good will were so;

20   For what is in this world but grief and woe?
O, God! Methinks it were a happy life,
To be no better than a homely swain,
To sit upon a hill, as I do now,
To carve out dials quaintly, point by point,

25   Thereby to see the minutes how they run:
How many makes the hour full complete,
How many hours brings about the day,
How many days will finish up the year,
How many years a mortal man may live.

2.5   3 What that   **blowing . . . nails** i.e. warming his hands by blowing on them/having
nothing much to do   **of** on   **4 perfect** complete   **9 flood** sea   **13 poise** balance   **fell**
fierce, cruel   **17 chid** driven with rebukes   **22 homely swain** simple rustic   **24 dials**
sundials   **quaintly** skillfully, intricately   **27 brings about** conclude

30   When this is known, then to divide the times:
      So many hours must I tend my flock,
      So many hours must I take my rest,
      So many hours must I contemplate,
      So many hours must I sport myself,
35   So many days my ewes have been with young,
      So many weeks ere the poor fools will ean,
      So many years ere I shall shear the fleece.
      So minutes, hours, days, months and years,
      Passed over to the end they were created,
40   Would bring white hairs unto a quiet grave.
      Ah, what a life were this! How sweet! How lovely!
      Gives not the hawthorn bush a sweeter shade
      To shepherds looking on their silly sheep,
      Than doth a rich embroidered canopy
45   To kings that fear their subjects' treachery?
      O, yes, it doth; a thousand-fold it doth.
      And to conclude, the shepherd's homely curds,
      His cold thin drink out of his leather bottle,
      His wonted sleep under a fresh tree's shade,
50   All which secure and sweetly he enjoys,
      Is far beyond a prince's delicates,
      His viands sparkling in a golden cup,
      His body couchèd in a curious bed,
      When care, mistrust and treason waits on him.

      Alarum. Enter a Son that has killed his father, at one door, and a Father
      that hath killed his son at another door [*with their bodies*]
55 SON   Ill blows the wind that profits nobody.
      This man, whom hand to hand I slew in fight,
      May be possessèd with some store of crowns,
      And I, that haply take them from him now,

---

34 sport enjoy, entertain   **35 with young** pregnant   **36 ean** give birth   **39 they** for which
they   **43 silly** simple/helpless   **44 canopy** i.e. one above a bed, throne, or carried over the
king in a procession   **47 curds** cheeselike foodstuff made from coagulated milk   **49 wonted**
usual, accustomed   **50 secure** carefree, safe   **51 delicates** luxuries, delicacies   **52 viands**
food   **53 curious** finely, skillfully made   **54 care** anxiety, troubles   **waits on** attends (like a
servant)/lies in wait for   **57 possessèd with** in possession of   **crowns** gold coins   **58 haply**
by chance/with luck

May yet ere night yield both my life and them
60   To some man else, as this dead man doth me.
Who's this? O, God! It is my father's face,
Whom in this conflict I unwares have killed.
O heavy times, begetting such events!
From London by the king was I pressed forth.
65   My father, being the Earl of Warwick's man,
Came on the part of York, pressed by his master.
And I, who at his hands received my life,
Have by my hands of life bereavèd him.
Pardon me, God, I knew not what I did.
70   And pardon, father, for I knew not thee.
My tears shall wipe away these bloody marks,
And no more words till they have flowed their fill.

KING HENRY VI   O, piteous spectacle! O, bloody times!
Whiles lions war and battle for their dens,
75   Poor harmless lambs abide their enmity.
Weep, wretched man: I'll aid thee tear for tear,
And let our hearts and eyes, like civil war,
Be blind with tears and break o'ercharged with grief.

              [*The*] *Father* [*steps forward*], *bearing of his Son*

FATHER   Thou that so stoutly hath resisted me,
80   Give me thy gold, if thou hast any gold,
For I have bought it with an hundred blows.
But let me see: is this our foeman's face?
Ah, no, no, no, it is mine only son!
Ah, boy, if any life be left in thee,
85   Throw up thine eye! See, see what showers arise,
Blown with the windy tempest of my heart,
Upon thy wounds, that kills mine eye and heart.
O, pity, God, this miserable age!
What stratagems, how fell, how butcherly,
90   Erroneous, mutinous and unnatural,

---

62 unwares unknowingly, unintentionally   **63 heavy** sorrowful   **64 pressed** conscripted,
enlisted compulsorily   **65 man** servant   **66 part** side   **75 abide** endure   **78 o'ercharged**
overburdened   **79 stoutly** bravely   **85 Throw up** open   **89 stratagems** violent, bloody deeds
90 Erroneous wrongful, criminal

This deadly quarrel daily doth beget!
O boy, thy father gave thee life too soon,
And hath bereft thee of thy life too late!

KING HENRY VI   Woe above woe! Grief more than common grief!
95   O, that my death would stay these ruthful deeds!
O, pity, pity, gentle heaven, pity!
The red rose and the white are on his face,
The fatal colours of our striving houses:
The one his purple blood right well resembles,
100   The other his pale cheeks, methinks, presenteth.
Wither one rose, and let the other flourish.
If you contend, a thousand lives must wither.

SON   How will my mother for a father's death
Take on with me and ne'er be satisfied!

105 FATHER   How will my wife for slaughter of my son
Shed seas of tears and ne'er be satisfied!

KING HENRY VI   How will the country for these woeful chances
Misthink the king and not be satisfied!

SON   Was ever son so rued a father's death?
110 FATHER   Was ever father so bemoaned his son?
KING HENRY VI   Was ever king so grieved for subjects' woe?
Much is your sorrow; mine ten times so much.

SON   I'll bear thee hence, where I may weep my fill.

[*Exit with the body*]

FATHER   These arms of mine shall be thy winding-sheet,
115   My heart, sweet boy, shall be thy sepulchre,
For from my heart thine image ne'er shall go.
My sighing breast shall be thy funeral bell;
And so obsequious will thy father be,
E'en for the loss of thee, having no more,
120   As Priam was for all his valiant sons.

---

93 late recently, early   **95 stay** stop, prevent   **ruthful** piteous, lamentable   **97 on his face** in
his complexion   **99 purple** deep red   **100 presenteth** represents, imitates   **102 contend**
compete, fight   **104 Take on with** rage against, cry out on   **107 chances** fortunes, events
108 Misthink think badly of   **109 rued** regretted, lamented   **114 winding-sheet** burial
shroud   **118 obsequious** dutiful in performing funeral rites   **120 Priam . . . sons** Priam,
King of Troy, had fifty sons, all of whom were killed in the Trojan war

I'll bear thee hence; and let them fight that will,
For I have murdered where I should not kill.

Exit [with the body]

KING HENRY VI   Sad-hearted men, much overgone with care,
Here sits a king more woeful than you are.

Alarums. Excursions. Enter the Queen, the Prince and Exeter

125 PRINCE EDWARD   Fly, father, fly! For all your friends are fled,
And Warwick rages like a chafèd bull:
Away, for death doth hold us in pursuit.

QUEEN MARGARET   Mount you, my lord, towards Berwick post
amain.
Edward and Richard, like a brace of greyhounds
130 Having the fearful flying hare in sight,
With fiery eyes sparkling for very wrath,
And bloody steel grasped in their ireful hands,
Are at our backs, and therefore hence amain.

EXETER   Away, for vengeance comes along with them.
135 Nay, stay not to expostulate, make speed,
Or else come after. I'll away before.

KING HENRY VI   Nay, take me with thee, good sweet Exeter:
Not that I fear to stay, but love to go
Whither the queen intends. Forward, away!   *Exeunt*

[Act 2 Scene 6]

running scene 5 continues

A loud alarum. Enter Clifford wounded

CLIFFORD   Here burns my candle out; ay, here it dies,
Which whiles it lasted gave King Henry light.
O Lancaster, I fear thy overthrow
More than my body's parting with my soul!
5 My love and fear glued many friends to thee,
And now I fall. Thy tough commixtures melts,

---

123 **overgone** overcome, worn out   126 **chafèd** provoked, angered   128 **Berwick** Berwick-upon-Tweed, town on the Scotland-England border   **post amain** ride with extreme haste
129 **brace** pair   131 **very** absolute   133 **hence amain** leave quickly   135 **expostulate** remonstrate, debate (the matter)   **2.6**   5 **My . . . fear** love for and fear of me
6 **commixtures** compounds (produced by love and fear)

Impairing Henry, strength'ning misproud York,
The common people swarm like summer flies,
And whither fly the gnats but to the sun?
10 And who shines now but Henry's enemies?
O Phoebus, hadst thou never given consent
That Phaethon should check thy fiery steeds,
Thy burning car never had scorched the earth!
And, Henry, hadst thou swayed as kings should do,
15 Or as thy father and his father did,
Giving no ground unto the House of York,
They never then had sprung like summer flies;
I and ten thousand in this luckless realm
Had left no mourning widows for our death,
20 And thou this day hadst kept thy chair in peace.
For what doth cherish weeds but gentle air?
And what makes robbers bold but too much lenity?
Bootless are plaints, and cureless are my wounds.
No way to fly, nor strength to hold out flight.
25 The foe is merciless, and will not pity,
For at their hands I have deserved no pity.
The air hath got into my deadly wounds,
And much effuse of blood doth make me faint.
Come, York and Richard, Warwick and the rest:
30 I stabbed your fathers' bosoms; split my breast. *Faints*

Alarum and retreat. Enter Edward, Warwick, Richard and Soldiers,
Montague and Clarence [George]

EDWARD   Now breathe we, lords. Good fortune bids us pause,
And smooth the frowns of war with peaceful looks.
Some troops pursue the bloody-minded queen,
That led calm Henry, though he were a king,
35 As doth a sail, filled with a fretting gust,

---

7 misproud wrongfully proud, treacherously arrogant   **9 sun** i.e. Edward's emblem
11 Phoebus the sun god   **12 Phaethon . . . earth** Phoebus' son, who was unable to control
(**check**) the horses that drew his father's sun-chariot (**car**), burned part of the earth and was
killed   **14 swayed** ruled   **16 ground** advantage   **20 chair** throne   **21 cherish** nurture
23 Bootless are plaints laments are useless   **28 effuse** loss, effusion   *retreat* trumpet or
drum call signaling retreat   **31 breathe** rest, pause   **35 fretting** sporadic, blustery/impatient,
nagging

Command an argosy to stem the waves.
But think you, lords, that Clifford fled with them?

WARWICK   No, 'tis impossible he should escape,
For, though before his face I speak the words,
40   Your brother Richard marked him for the grave,
And wheresoe'er he is, he's surely dead.

Clifford groans [and dies]

RICHARD   Whose soul is that which takes her heavy leave?
A deadly groan, like life and death's departing.

EDWARD   See who it is. And now the battle's ended,
45   If friend or foe, let him be gently used.

RICHARD   Revoke that doom of mercy. for 'tis Clifford,
Who not contented that he lopped the branch
In hewing Rutland when his leaves put forth,
But set his murd'ring knife unto the root
50   From whence that tender spray did sweetly spring,
I mean our princely father, Duke of York.

WARWICK   From off the gates of York fetch down the head,
Your father's head, which Clifford placèd there,
Instead whereof let this supply the room:
55   Measure for measure must be answerèd.

EDWARD   Bring forth that fatal screech-owl to our house,
That nothing sung but death to us and ours:
Now death shall stop his dismal threat'ning sound,
And his ill-boding tongue no more shall speak.

60   WARWICK   I think his understanding is bereft.
Speak, Clifford, dost thou know who speaks to thee?
Dark cloudy death o'ershades his beams of life,
And he nor sees nor hears us what we say.

---

36 **Command** compel, force   **argosy** large merchant ship   **stem** cut through   39 **his** may
refer to either Clifford or Richard   40 **marked** destined/wounded   42 **heavy** sorrowful
43 **departing** separation, parting   45 **gently used** treated honorably   46 **doom** judgment,
sentence   50 **spray** branch, offshoot   54 **this . . . room** Clifford's head fill the place
55 **Measure** due proportion/retribution/justice   56 **fatal screech-owl** owl (i.e. Clifford)
whose cry foretold death to our family   **house** family   57 **nothing sung** has sung nothing
58 **dismal** ominous   59 **ill-boding** evil-predicting, ominous   60 **bereft** gone   62 **beams**
eye-beams (thought to radiate from the eyes and enable sight)   63 **nor** neither

RICHARD   O, would he did, and so perhaps he doth.

65   'Tis but his policy to counterfeit,
Because he would avoid such bitter taunts
Which in the time of death he gave our father.

GEORGE   If so thou think'st, vex him with eager words.

RICHARD   Clifford, ask mercy and obtain no grace.

70 EDWARD   Clifford, repent in bootless penitence.

WARWICK   Clifford, devise excuses for thy faults.

GEORGE   While we devise fell tortures for thy faults.

RICHARD   Thou didst love York, and I am son to York.

EDWARD   Thou pitied'st Rutland, I will pity thee.

75 GEORGE   Where's Captain Margaret to fence you now?

WARWICK   They mock thee, Clifford: swear as thou wast wont.

RICHARD   What, not an oath? Nay, then the world goes hard
When Clifford cannot spare his friends an oath.
I know by that he's dead, and, by my soul,

80   If this right hand would buy two hours' life,
That I in all despite might rail at him,
This hand should chop it off, and with the issuing blood
Stifle the villain whose unstanchèd thirst
York and young Rutland could not satisfy.

85 WARWICK   Ay, but he's dead. Off with the traitor's head,
And rear it in the place your father's stands.
And now to London with triumphant march,
There to be crownèd England's royal king:
From whence shall Warwick cut the sea to France,

90   And ask the lady Bona for thy queen.
So shalt thou sinew both these lands together,
And having France thy friend, thou shalt not dread
The scattered foe that hopes to rise again,
For though they cannot greatly sting to hurt,

---

65 policy strategy, cunning   **68 eager** sharp, biting   **71 faults** crimes   **75 fence** protect
76 wast wont used to do, were accustomed to   **77 goes hard** is harsh, tough   **81 despite**
malice, anger   **rail** rant, insult   **82 This** i.e. the other   **83 Stifle** choke   **unstanchèd**
insatiable   **86 rear** raise   **89 cut** cross   **90 ask** ask for   **lady Bona** daughter of the Duke of
Savoy; her sister was married to King Louis XI of France   **91 sinew** unite, tie closely

95   Yet look to have them buzz to offend thine ears.

First will I see the coronation,

And then to Brittany I'll cross the sea,

To effect this marriage, so it please my lord.

EDWARD   Even as thou wilt, sweet Warwick, let it be,

100   For in thy shoulder do I build my seat,

And never will I undertake the thing

Wherein thy counsel and consent is wanting.

Richard, I will create thee Duke of Gloucester,

And George, of Clarence; Warwick, as ourself,

105   Shall do and undo as him pleaseth best.

RICHARD   Let me be Duke of Clarence, George of Gloucester,

For Gloucester's dukedom is too ominous.

WARWICK   Tut, that's a foolish observation.

Richard, be Duke of Gloucester. Now to London,

110   To see these honours in possession.   *Exeunt*

[Act 3 Scene 1]

running scene 6

Enter two Keepers with crossbows in their hands

FIRST KEEPER   Under this thick-grown brake we'll shroud
ourselves,

For through this laund anon the deer will come,

And in this covert will we make our stand,

Culling the principal of all the deer.

5   SECOND KEEPER   I'll stay above the hill, so both may shoot.

FIRST KEEPER   That cannot be. The noise of thy crossbow

Will scare the herd, and so my shoot is lost.

Here stand we both, and aim we at the best,

And, for the time shall not seem tedious,

---

95 buzz spread rumors, agitate   **99 Even** just   **100 in thy shoulder** i.e. relying on your
support   **seat** throne   **102 wanting** lacking   **107 ominous** the three previous dukes of
Gloucester had all met violent deaths   **3.1**   *Location: a forest in northern England, near
the Scottish border*   **Keepers** gamekeepers   **1 brake** thicket, bush   **2 laund** clearing,
glade   **anon** soon   **3 covert** concealed spot   **stand** hiding place from which to shoot
4 principal superior, best   **7 shoot** shot   **9 for** so

10   I'll tell thee what befell me on a day
        In this self-place where now we mean to stand.

SECOND KEEPER   Here comes a man. Let's stay till he be past.

Enter the King, [disguised,] with a prayer-book

KING HENRY VI   From Scotland am I stol'n, even of pure love,
        To greet mine own land with my wishful sight.

15   No, Harry, Harry, 'tis no land of thine:
        Thy place is filled, thy sceptre wrung from thee,
        Thy balm washed off wherewith thou wast anointed.
        No bending knee will call thee Caesar now,
        No humble suitors press to speak for right,

20   No, not a man comes for redress of thee.
        For how can I help them, and not myself?

FIRST KEEPER   Ay, here's a deer whose skin's a keeper's fee:
        This is the quondam king; let's seize upon him.

KING HENRY VI   Let me embrace the sour adversaries,

25   For wise men say it is the wisest course.

SECOND KEEPER   Why linger we? Let us lay hands upon him.

FIRST KEEPER   Forbear awhile, we'll hear a little more.

KING HENRY VI   My queen and son are gone to France for aid,
        And, as I hear, the great commanding Warwick

30   Is thither gone, to crave the French king's sister
        To wife for Edward. If this news be true,
        Poor queen and son, your labour is but lost,
        For Warwick is a subtle orator,
        And Lewis a prince soon won with moving words.

35   By this account then Margaret may win him,
        For she's a woman to be pitied much:
        Her sighs will make a batt'ry in his breast,
        Her tears will pierce into a marble heart,
        The tiger will be mild whiles she doth mourn;

---

11 **self-place** same place   13 **of** out of   14 **wishful** longing   17 **balm** consecrated oil with
which the monarch was anointed at coronation   18 **Caesar** emperor, ruler   19 **speak for
right** ask for justice   20 **redress of** aid from   22 **keeper's fee** the horns and skin of a slain
deer were customarily given to the park's gamekeeper   23 **quondam** former   27 **Forbear**
desist   30 **crave** ask for   **sister** sister-in-law   33 **subtle** skillful, cunning   34 **Lewis**
Louis XI   37 **batt'ry** assault, bombardment/breach, entry

40   And Nero will be tainted with remorse,
        To hear and see her plaints, her brinish tears.
        Ay, but she's come to beg, Warwick to give:
        She on his left side, craving aid for Henry,
        He on his right, asking a wife for Edward.
45   She weeps, and says her Henry is deposed,
        He smiles, and says his Edward is installed;
        That she, poor wretch, for grief can speak no more,
        Whiles Warwick tells his title, smooths the wrong,
        Inferreth arguments of mighty strength,
50   And in conclusion wins the king from her,
        With promise of his sister, and what else,
        To strengthen and support King Edward's place.
        O Margaret, thus 'twill be, and thou, poor soul,
        Art then forsaken, as thou went'st forlorn.
55   SECOND KEEPER   Say, what art thou that talk'st of kings and
            queens?
        KING HENRY VI   More than I seem, and less than I was born to:
        A man at least, for less I should not be.
        And men may talk of kings, and why not I?
        SECOND KEEPER   Ay, but thou talk'st as if thou wert a king.
60   KING HENRY VI   Why, so I am, in mind, and that's enough.
        SECOND KEEPER   But, if thou be a king, where is thy crown?
        KING HENRY VI   My crown is in my heart, not on my head,
        Not decked with diamonds and Indian stones,
        Nor to be seen: my crown is called content.
65   A crown it is that seldom kings enjoy.
        SECOND KEEPER   Well, if you be a king crowned with content,
        Your crown content and you must be contented
        To go along with us, for, as we think,
        You are the king King Edward hath deposed,

---

40 Nero notoriously cruel Roman emperor   **tainted** tinged, touched (unnaturally in such a
cruel man)   **41 plaints** laments, pleas   **brinish** salty   **48 tells his title** recounts the
rightfulness of Edward's claims to the throne   **smooths** glosses over   **49 Inferreth** presents,
adduces   **arguments** evidence   **51 what** whatever   **54 forlorn** neglected, destitute
63 stones jewels

70   And we his subjects sworn in all allegiance
      Will apprehend you as his enemy.
KING HENRY VI   But did you never swear and break an oath?
SECOND KEEPER   No, never such an oath, nor will not now.
KING HENRY VI   Where did you dwell when I was King of
      England?
75 **SECOND KEEPER**   Here in this country, where we now remain.
KING HENRY VI   I was anointed king at nine months old.
      My father and my grandfather were kings,
      And you were sworn true subjects unto me:
      And tell me, then, have you not broke your oaths?
80 **FIRST KEEPER**   No,
      For we were subjects but while you were king.
KING HENRY VI   Why? Am I dead? Do I not breathe a man?
      Ah, simple men, you know not what you swear.
      Look, as I blow this feather from my face,
85   And as the air blows it to me again,
      Obeying with my wind when I do blow,
      And yielding to another when it blows,
      Commanded always by the greater gust,
      Such is the lightness of you, common men.
90   But do not break your oaths, for of that sin
      My mild entreaty shall not make you guilty.
      Go where you will, the king shall be commanded,
      And be you kings, command, and I'll obey.
FIRST KEEPER   We are true subjects to the king, King Edward.
95 **KING HENRY VI**   So would you be again to Henry,
      If he were seated as King Edward is.
FIRST KEEPER   We charge you, in God's name and the king's,
      To go with us unto the officers.
KING HENRY VI   In God's name, lead. Your king's name be obeyed,
100   And what God will, that let your king perform,
      And what he will, I humbly yield unto.   *Exeunt*

---

71 apprehend arrest   **75 country** region   **81 but** only   **82 a** as a   **83 simple** foolish
86 Obeying with obeying, following   **wind** breath   **89 lightness** lack of weight/fickleness
97 charge order

[Act 3 Scene 2]   *running scene 7*

*Enter King Edward, [Richard, now Duke of] Gloucester, [George, now
Duke of] Clarence, Lady Grey*   *Richard is henceforth known as
                                        Gloucester, George as Clarence*

KING EDWARD IV   Brother of Gloucester, at St Alban's field

This lady's husband, Sir Richard Grey, was slain,

His land then seized on by the conqueror.

Her suit is now to repossess those lands,

5   Which we in justice cannot well deny,

Because in quarrel of the House of York

The worthy gentleman did lose his life.

GLOUCESTER   Your highness shall do well to grant her suit:

It were dishonour to deny it her.

10   KING EDWARD IV   It were no less, but yet I'll make a

pause.   *Gloucester and Clarence speak aside throughout*

GLOUCESTER   Yea, is it so?

I see the lady hath a thing to grant,

Before the king will grant her humble suit.

CLARENCE   He knows the game. How true he keeps the wind!

15   GLOUCESTER   Silence!

KING EDWARD IV   Widow, we will consider of your suit,

And come some other time to know our mind.

LADY GREY   Right gracious lord, I cannot brook delay.

May it please your highness to resolve me now,

20   And what your pleasure is, shall satisfy me.

GLOUCESTER   Ay, widow? Then I'll warrant you all your lands,

An if what pleases him shall pleasure you.

Fight closer, or good faith, you'll catch a blow.

CLARENCE   I fear her not, unless she chance to fall.

3.2   Location: the royal court, London   1 field battlefield   **2 Richard** historically John
4 suit petition, entreaty   **repossess** regain possession of   **6 of** on behalf of   **12 thing** plays
on the sense of "vagina"   **14 game** animal being hunted/woman being pursued sexually
true . . . wind determinedly he remains downwind of the prey (so that it cannot scent him)
18 brook endure   **19 resolve** answer   **20 pleasure** will (plays on the sense of "sexual
desire")   **satisfy** content (plays on the sense of "satisfy sexually")   **21 warrant** guarantee,
assure   **22 An if** if   **23 closer** closer to the enemy, so as to contain and avoid his thrusts (with
sexual suggestion)   **blow** hit/sexual thrust   **24 fear her not** do not fear for her   **fall** stumble
in the fight/succumb sexually/become pregnant

25   GLOUCESTER   God forbid that, for he'll take vantages.

KING EDWARD IV   How many children hast thou, widow? Tell me.

CLARENCE   I think he means to beg a child of her.

GLOUCESTER   Nay, then, whip me: he'll rather give her two.

LADY GREY   Three, my most gracious lord.

30   GLOUCESTER   You shall have four, if you'll be ruled by him.

KING EDWARD IV   'Twere pity they should lose their father's lands.

LADY GREY   Be pitiful, dread lord, and grant it then.

KING EDWARD IV   Lords, give us leave: I'll try this widow's wit.

GLOUCESTER   Ay, good leave have you, for you will have leave,

35   Till youth take leave and leave you to the crutch.

KING EDWARD IV   Now tell me, madam, do you love your
    children?

LADY GREY   Ay, full as dearly as I love myself.

KING EDWARD IV   And would you not do much to do them good?

LADY GREY   To do them good, I would sustain some harm.

40   KING EDWARD IV   Then get your husband's lands, to do them
    good.

LADY GREY   Therefore I came unto your majesty.

KING EDWARD IV   I'll tell you how these lands are to be got.

LADY GREY   So shall you bind me to your highness' service.

KING EDWARD IV   What service wilt thou do me, if I give them?

45   LADY GREY   What you command, that rests in me to do.

KING EDWARD IV   But you will take exceptions to my boon.

LADY GREY   No, gracious lord, except I cannot do it.

KING EDWARD IV   Ay, but thou canst do what I mean to ask.

LADY GREY   Why, then I will do what your grace commands.

50   GLOUCESTER   He plies her hard, and much rain wears the
    marble.

CLARENCE   As red as fire! Nay, then her wax must melt.

---

25 vantages superior position in fighting/sexual opportunity   **27 beg . . . her** request legal
guardianship of one of her children (this could generate financial profit for the guardian)/get
her pregnant   **28 whip me** a mild oath   **32 dread** revered   **33 give us leave** give us privacy
try test   **wit** intellect (probably also "genitals")   **34 good . . . leave** enjoy your privacy for you
will take liberties   **35 the crutch** i.e. old age (puns on "crotch")   **41 Therefore** for that reason
44 service i.e. as a subject/sexually   **45 rests in me** is in my power   **46 boon** request
47 except unless   **48 do** plays on the sense of "perform sexually"   **50 plies her hard** works
on her persistently/works on her sexually with an erect penis   **51 red** hot

LADY GREY   Why stops my lord? Shall I not hear my task?

KING EDWARD IV   An easy task, 'tis but to love a king.

LADY GREY   That's soon performed, because I am a subject.

55 KING EDWARD IV   Why, then, thy husband's lands I freely give
thee.

LADY GREY   I take my leave with many thousand thanks.

GLOUCESTER   The match is made: she seals it with a curtsy.

KING EDWARD IV   But stay thee, 'tis the fruits of love I mean.

LADY GREY   The fruits of love I mean, my loving liege.

60 KING EDWARD IV   Ay, but, I fear me, in another sense.
What love, think'st thou, I sue so much to get?

LADY GREY   My love till death, my humble thanks, my prayers,
That love which virtue begs and virtue grants.

KING EDWARD IV   No, by my troth, I did not mean such love.

65 LADY GREY   Why, then you mean not as I thought you did.

KING EDWARD IV   But now you partly may perceive my mind.

LADY GREY   My mind will never grant what I perceive
Your highness aims at, if I aim aright.

KING EDWARD IV   To tell thee plain, I aim to lie with thee.

70 LADY GREY   To tell you plain, I had rather lie in prison.

KING EDWARD IV   Why, then thou shalt not have thy husband's
lands.

LADY GREY   Why, then mine honesty shall be my dower,
For by that loss I will not purchase them.

KING EDWARD IV   Therein thou wrong'st thy children mightily.

75 LADY GREY   Herein your highness wrongs both them and me.
But, mighty lord, this merry inclination
Accords not with the sadness of my suit.
Please you dismiss me either with 'Ay' or 'No'.

KING EDWARD IV   Ay, if thou wilt say 'Ay' to my request;

80 No if thou dost say 'No' to my demand.

LADY GREY   Then, no, my lord. My suit is at an end.

---

53 task duty, job/sexual action   **57 match** agreement/sexual encounter   **58 fruits of love**
i.e. sex (Lady Grey understands "the obedience and devotion of a subject")   **61 sue** entreat,
beg/woo   **64 troth** faith   **68 aim aright** guess correctly   **69 lie with** have sex with
72 honesty chastity, virtue   **dower** widow's portion (of her husband's estate)   **73 that loss**
the loss of it (**honesty**)   **76 inclination** attitude, disposition   **77 sadness** seriousness

GLOUCESTER   The widow likes him not, she knits her brows.

CLARENCE   He is the bluntest wooer in Christendom.

KING EDWARD IV   Her looks do argue her replete with   *Aside*
    modesty,

85   Her words doth show her wit incomparable,
    All her perfections challenge sovereignty.
    One way or other, she is for a king,
    And she shall be my love, or else my queen.—
    Say that King Edward take thee for his queen?   *To her*

90   LADY GREY   'Tis better said than done, my gracious lord:
    I am a subject fit to jest withal,
    But far unfit to be a sovereign.

KING EDWARD IV   Sweet widow, by my state I swear to thee,
    I speak no more than what my soul intends,

95   And that is, to enjoy thee for my love.

LADY GREY   And that is more than I will yield unto:
    I know I am too mean to be your queen
    And yet too good to be your concubine.

KING EDWARD IV   You cavil, widow: I did mean, my queen.

100   LADY GREY   'Twill grieve your grace my sons should call you
    father.

KING EDWARD IV   No more than when my daughters call thee
    mother.
    Thou art a widow, and thou hast some children,
    And, by God's mother, I, being but a bachelor,
    Have other some. Why, 'tis a happy thing

105   To be the father unto many sons.
    Answer no more, for thou shalt be my queen.

GLOUCESTER   The ghostly father now hath done his shrift.

CLARENCE   When he was made a shriver, 'twas for shift.

KING EDWARD IV   Brothers, you muse what chat we two have had.

---

82 knits her brows frowns   **83 bluntest** most unceremonious, plainspoken   **84 argue her**
demonstrate her to be   **86 challenge** call for, lay claim to   **88 love** lover   **93 state** majesty,
royal status   **97 mean** humble   **99 cavil** quibble over details   **104 other some** some others,
i.e. illegitimate children   **107 ghostly father** priest   **ghostly** holy, spiritual   **done his shrift**
heard confession (plays on the sense of "had sex")   **108 shriver** confessor, priest/sexually
active man   **for shift** out of strategy, a trick/to get at women's undergarments (puns on **shrift**)
109 muse wonder/speculate

110 GLOUCESTER   The widow likes it not, for she looks   *To Edward*
                    very sad.

KING EDWARD IV   You'll think it strange if I should marry her.

CLARENCE   To who, my lord?

KING EDWARD IV   Why, Clarence, to myself.

GLOUCESTER   That would be ten days' wonder at the least.

115 CLARENCE   That's a day longer than a wonder lasts.

GLOUCESTER   By so much is the wonder in extremes.

KING EDWARD IV   Well, jest on, brothers. I can tell you both
                    Her suit is granted for her husband's lands.

Enter a Nobleman

NOBLEMAN   My gracious lord, Henry your foe is taken,
120   And brought your prisoner to your palace gate.

KING EDWARD IV   See that he be conveyed unto the Tower,
                    And go we, brothers, to the man that took him,
                    To question of his apprehension.—
                    Widow, go you along.— Lords, use her honourably.

                    Exeunt. Richard [of Gloucester] remains

125 GLOUCESTER   Ay, Edward will use women honourably.
                    Would he were wasted, marrow, bones and all,
                    That from his loins no hopeful branch may spring,
                    To cross me from the golden time I look for.
                    And yet, between my soul's desire and me —
130   The lustful Edward's title burièd —
                    Is Clarence, Henry, and his son young Edward,
                    And all the unlooked for issue of their bodies,
                    To take their rooms, ere I can place myself.
                    A cold premeditation for my purpose.
135   Why, then, I do but dream on sovereignty,
                    Like one that stands upon a promontory,

---

114 ten . . . lasts proverbial: "a wonder lasts but nine days"   **116 in extremes** excessive, much greater   **119 taken** captured   **123 question . . . apprehension** ask about his arrest   **124 use** treat (Gloucester shifts the sense to "employ sexually")   **126 wasted** consumed with disease (particularly syphilis, which eats at the **bones**)   **marrow** bone marrow/semen   **127 branch** i.e. offspring, child (also with phallic connotations)   **128 cross** thwart, hinder   **golden time** i.e. kingship, the crown   **130 The . . . burièd** i.e. once Edward is dead   **132 unlooked for** unwanted/unforeseeable   **issue** children, offspring   **133 rooms** places, positions   **134 cold premeditation** discouraging prospect   **136 promontory** headland jutting into the sea

And spies a far-off shore where he would tread,
Wishing his foot were equal with his eye,
And chides the sea that sunders him from thence,
140 Saying, he'll lade it dry to have his way:
So do I wish the crown, being so far off,
And so I chide the means that keeps me from it,
And so I say, I'll cut the causes off,
Flattering me with impossibilities.
145 My eye's too quick, my heart o'erweens too much,
Unless my hand and strength could equal them.
Well, say there is no kingdom then for Richard:
What other pleasure can the world afford?
I'll make my heaven in a lady's lap,
150 And deck my body in gay ornaments,
And witch sweet ladies with my words and looks.
O, miserable thought, and more unlikely
Than to accomplish twenty golden crowns.
Why, love forswore me in my mother's womb,
155 And, for I should not deal in her soft laws,
She did corrupt frail nature with some bribe,
To shrink mine arm up like a withered shrub,
To make an envious mountain on my back,
Where sits deformity to mock my body;
160 To shape my legs of an unequal size,
To disproportion me in every part,
Like to a chaos or an unlicked bear-whelp,
That carries no impression like the dam.
And am I then a man to be beloved?
165 O, monstrous fault, to harbour such a thought.

---

138 **were equal with** could reach as far as   139 **chides** chastises   **sunders** separates
140 **lade** drain, empty   141 **wish** wish for   142 **means** obstacle   143 **cut . . . off** murder
those in my way   144 **Flattering me** deluding myself   145 **o'erweens** is arrogant,
presumptuous   150 **deck** adorn   **gay ornaments** bright, ostentatious attire   151 **witch**
bewitch, seduce   153 **accomplish** get hold of   154 **forswore** rejected   155 **for** so that
deal in have dealings with (plays on the sense of "have sex according to")   158 **envious**
spiteful, malicious   162 **chaos** shapeless mass   **unlicked bear-whelp** bear cubs were
thought to be licked into shape by their mothers   163 **impression . . . dam** shape like that of
the mother   165 **monstrous** unnatural, deformed   **fault** mistake

Then, since this earth affords no joy to me,
But to command, to check, to o'erbear such
As are of better person than myself,
I'll make my heaven to dream upon the crown,
170   And whiles I live, t'account this world but hell,
Until my misshaped trunk that bears this head
Be round impalèd with a glorious crown.
And yet I know not how to get the crown,
For many lives stand between me and home,
175   And I — like one lost in a thorny wood,
That rents the thorns and is rent with the thorns,
Seeking a way and straying from the way,
Not knowing how to find the open air,
But toiling desperately to find it out —
180   Torment myself to catch the English crown:
And from that torment I will free myself,
Or hew my way out with a bloody axe.
Why, I can smile, and murder whiles I smile,
And cry 'Content' to that which grieves my heart,
185   And wet my cheeks with artificial tears,
And frame my face to all occasions.
I'll drown more sailors than the mermaid shall,
I'll slay more gazers than the basilisk,
I'll play the orator as well as Nestor,
190   Deceive more slyly than Ulysses could,
And, like a Sinon, take another Troy.
I can add colours to the chameleon,
Change shapes with Proteus for advantages,

---

167 check rebuke   **o'erbear** dominate   **168 person** appearance   **170 t'account** to consider
171 trunk body   **172 impalèd** surrounded, enclosed   **174 home** my target   **176 rents** tears
apart   **180 catch** seize   **186 frame** fashion, adapt   **187 mermaid** the siren of classical
mythology was said to sing sweetly in order to draw sailors onto rocks where they would
drown   **188 basilisk** mythical reptile whose gaze had the power to kill   **189 Nestor** Greek
leader who fought at Troy; famed for his wisdom and eloquence   **190 Ulysses** King of Ithaca
and hero of Homer's *Odyssey*; noted for his cunning   **191 Sinon** in Virgil's *Aeneid*, the man
who pretended to desert the Greeks and persuaded King Priam of Troy to admit the wooden
horse into the city, as a result of which Troy was destroyed   **193 Proteus** the sea god
Neptune's herdsman who had the ability to change shape at will

And set the murderous Machevil to school.

195   Can I do this, and cannot get a crown?

Tut, were it further off, I'll pluck it down.   *Exit*

[Act 3 Scene 3]   *running scene 8*

Flourish. Enter Lewis the French King, his sister Bona, his Admiral called Bourbon, Prince Edward, Queen Margaret and the Earl of Oxford. Lewis sits and riseth up again

KING LEWIS   Fair Queen of England, worthy Margaret,

Sit down with us. It ill befits thy state

And birth, that thou shouldst stand while Lewis doth sit.

QUEEN MARGARET   No, mighty King of France: now Margaret

5   Must strike her sail and learn awhile to serve

Where kings command. I was, I must confess,

Great Albion's queen in former golden days,

But now mischance hath trod my title down

And with dishonour laid me on the ground,

10   Where I must take like seat unto my fortune,

And to my humble seat conform myself.

KING LEWIS   Why, say, fair queen, whence springs this deep despair?

QUEEN MARGARET   From such a cause as fills mine eyes with tears

And stops my tongue, while heart is drowned in cares.

15   KING LEWIS   Whate'er it be, be thou still like thyself,

And sit thee by our side: *Seats her by him*

Yield not thy neck

To fortune's yoke, but let thy dauntless mind

Still ride in triumph over all mischance.

---

194 set . . . school teach Machiavelli a few things   **Machevil** an intriguer, an unscrupulous schemer (from Niccolò Machiavelli's *The Prince*, a sixteenth-century treatise perceived as advocating ruthless political cunning)   **3.3** *Location: the royal court, France*   **2 state** rank   **5 strike her sail** humble herself (literally, lower a ship's sail in deference to a vessel of greater importance)   **7 Albion's** England's   **8 mischance** misfortune   **10 like seat unto** a place befitting   **15 be . . . thyself** always behave in a manner that befits your position

Be plain, Queen Margaret, and tell thy grief:

20   It shall be eased, if France can yield relief.

QUEEN MARGARET   Those gracious words revive my drooping
     thoughts

And give my tongue-tied sorrows leave to speak.

Now therefore be it known to noble Lewis,

That Henry, sole possessor of my love,

25   Is, of a king, become a banished man,

And forced to live in Scotland a forlorn;

While proud ambitious Edward, Duke of York,

Usurps the regal title and the seat

Of England's true-anointed lawful king.

30   This is the cause that I, poor Margaret,

With this my son, Prince Edward, Henry's heir,

Am come to crave thy just and lawful aid.

And if thou fail us, all our hope is done.

Scotland hath will to help, but cannot help,

35   Our people and our peers are both misled,

Our treasures seized, our soldiers put to flight,

And, as thou see'st, ourselves in heavy plight.

KING LEWIS   Renownèd queen, with patience calm the storm,

While we bethink a means to break it off.

40   QUEEN MARGARET   The more we stay, the stronger grows our foe.

KING LEWIS   The more I stay, the more I'll succour thee.

QUEEN MARGARET   O, but impatience waiteth on true sorrow.

And see where comes the breeder of my sorrow!

Enter Warwick

KING LEWIS   What's he approacheth boldly to our presence?

45   QUEEN MARGARET   Our Earl of Warwick, Edward's greatest
     friend.

KING LEWIS   Welcome, brave Warwick! What brings thee to
     France?

He descends. She ariseth

---

20 France i.e. the King of France   **25 of** from   **26 forlorn** destitute, abandoned person
37 heavy burdensome/sorrowful   **38 storm** i.e. of grief, passion   **40 stay** wait, delay
41 stay plays on the sense of "support"   **succour** help   **42 waiteth on** attends, accompanies
descends i.e. from the throne, or dais on which it sits

QUEEN MARGARET   Ay, now begins a second storm to rise,
For this is he that moves both wind and tide.

WARWICK   From worthy Edward, King of Albion,

50   My lord and sovereign, and thy vowèd friend,
I come, in kindness and unfeignèd love,
First, to do greetings to thy royal person,
And then to crave a league of amity,
And lastly, to confirm that amity

55   With nuptial knot, if thou vouchsafe to grant
That virtuous Lady Bona, thy fair sister,
To England's king in lawful marriage.

QUEEN MARGARET   If that go forward, Henry's hope   *Aside?*
      is done.

WARWICK   And, gracious madam, in our king's behalf,

                                                  Speaking to Bona

60   I am commanded, with your leave and favour,
Humbly to kiss your hand, and with my tongue
To tell the passion of my sovereign's heart;
Where fame, late ent'ring at his heedful ears,
Hath placed thy beauty's image and thy virtue.

65   QUEEN MARGARET   King Lewis and Lady Bona, hear me speak,
Before you answer Warwick. His demand
Springs not from Edward's well-meant honest love,
But from deceit bred by necessity.
For how can tyrants safely govern home,

70   Unless abroad they purchase great alliance?
To prove him tyrant this reason may suffice,
That Henry liveth still: but were he dead,
Yet here Prince Edward stands, King Henry's son.
Look, therefore, Lewis, that by this league and marriage

75   Thou draw not on thy danger and dishonour,
For though usurpers sway the rule awhile,
Yet heav'ns are just, and time suppresseth wrongs.

WARWICK   Injurious Margaret.

---

55 vouchsafe permit, consent   **59 in** on   **63 fame** report   **late** recently   **heedful** attentive
69 tyrants usurpers   **74 Look** beware   **75 draw . . . thy** do not bring on yourself   **76 sway**
the rule wield power   **78 Injurious** slanderous, offensive

PRINCE EDWARD   And why not queen?

80   WARWICK   Because thy father Henry did usurp,
And thou no more art prince than she is queen.

OXFORD   Then Warwick disannuls great John of Gaunt,
Which did subdue the greatest part of Spain;
And, after John of Gaunt, Henry the Fourth,
85   Whose wisdom was a mirror to the wisest,
And after that wise prince, Henry the Fifth,
Who by his prowess conquerèd all France:
From these our Henry lineally descends.

WARWICK   Oxford, how haps it, in this smooth discourse,
90   You told not how Henry the Sixth hath lost
All that which Henry Fifth had gotten?
Methinks these peers of France should smile at that.
But for the rest, you tell a pedigree
Of threescore and two years, a silly time
95   To make prescription for a kingdom's worth.

OXFORD   Why, Warwick, canst thou speak against thy liege,
Whom thou obeyed'st thirty-and-six years,
And not bewray thy treason with a blush?

WARWICK   Can Oxford, that did ever fence the right,
100   Now buckler falsehood with a pedigree?
For shame, leave Henry and call Edward king.

OXFORD   Call him my king by whose injurious doom
My elder brother, the lord Aubrey Vere,
Was done to death? And more than so, my father,
105   Even in the downfall of his mellowed years,
When nature brought him to the door of death?

---

82 disannuls cancels, ignores   **John of Gaunt** father of **Henry the Fourth**, great-grandfather of Henry VI; he features in *Richard II*   **83 Which** who   **85 mirror** i.e. image, model   **89 haps** happens, chances   **smooth** plausible, glib   **93 tell** recount   **94 threescore . . . years** i.e. the sixty-two years between 1399, when Henry IV deposed Richard II, and 1461, when Edward IV deposed Henry VI   **silly** meager, trifling   **95 prescription** a claim founded on long use (legal term)   **97 thirty-and-six years** a period that corresponds more fittingly to Warwick's age (he was born in 1428) rather than his allegiance, as he had joined the Yorkists in 1455
98 bewray betray, reveal   **99 fence** protect   **100 buckler** defend   **102 injurious doom** wrongful judgment, sentence   **103 Aubrey Vere** he and his **father**, the Earl of Oxford, were executed for treason by Edward IV in 1462   **104 more than so** furthermore   **105 downfall** decline   **mellowed** ripened

No, Warwick, no: while life upholds this arm,
This arm upholds the House of Lancaster.

WARWICK   And I the House of York.

110   KING LEWIS   Queen Margaret, Prince Edward, and Oxford,
Vouchsafe, at our request, to stand aside,
While I use further conference with Warwick.

They stand aloof

QUEEN MARGARET   Heavens grant that Warwick's words
bewitch him not.

KING LEWIS   Now Warwick, tell me, even upon thy conscience,
115   Is Edward your true king? For I were loath
To link with him that were not lawful chosen.

WARWICK   Thereon I pawn my credit and mine honour.

KING LEWIS   But is he gracious in the people's eye?

WARWICK   The more that Henry was unfortunate.

120   KING LEWIS   Then further, all dissembling set aside,
Tell me for truth the measure of his love
Unto our sister Bona.

WARWICK   Such it seems
As may beseem a monarch like himself.
125   Myself have often heard him say and swear
That this his love was an external plant,
Whereof the root was fixed in virtue's ground,
The leaves and fruit maintained with beauty's sun,
Exempt from envy, but not from disdain,
130   Unless the lady Bona quit his pain.

KING LEWIS   Now, sister, let us hear your firm resolve.

BONA   Your grant, or your denial, shall be mine.—
Yet I confess that often ere this day,   *Speaks to Warwick*
When I have heard your king's desert recounted,
135   Mine ear hath tempted judgement to desire.

---

112 use engage in   **conference** discussion   *aloof* aside   **114 even** justly, fully   **117 pawn**
pledge, stake   **credit** reputation   **118 gracious** esteemed, popular   **119 more that** more so
because   **120 dissembling** duplicity, pretense   **121 for truth** truly   **measure** extent
124 beseem befit   **126 external** visible; some editors prefer Octavo's "eternal"   **129 envy**
malice   **disdain** (Bona's possible) loathing, scorn   **130 quit** end   **132 grant** consent   **mine**
the decision I make—i.e. I will agree with whatever you think fit   **134 desert** merits

KING LEWIS Then, Warwick, thus: our sister shall be Edward's.
And now forthwith shall articles be drawn
Touching the jointure that your king must make,
Which with her dowry shall be counterpoised.—

140 Draw near, Queen Margaret, and be a witness
That Bona shall be wife to the English king.

PRINCE EDWARD To Edward, but not to the English king.

QUEEN MARGARET Deceitful Warwick, it was thy device
By this alliance to make void my suit.

145 Before thy coming Lewis was Henry's friend.

KING LEWIS And still is friend to him and Margaret.
But if your title to the crown be weak,
As may appear by Edward's good success,
Then 'tis but reason that I be released

150 From giving aid which late I promisèd.
Yet shall you have all kindness at my hand
That your estate requires and mine can yield.

WARWICK Henry now lives in Scotland at his ease,
Where having nothing, nothing can he lose.

155 And as for you yourself, our quondam queen,
You have a father able to maintain you,
And better 'twere you troubled him than France.

QUEEN MARGARET Peace, impudent and shameless Warwick,
Proud setter-up and puller-down of kings.

160 I will not hence, till with my talk and tears —
Both full of truth — I make King Lewis behold
Thy sly conveyance and thy lord's false love,

Post blowing a horn within

For both of you are birds of selfsame feather.

KING LEWIS Warwick, this is some post to us or thee.

Enter the Post

---

137 articles terms, conditions   **drawn** drawn up   **138 Touching** regarding   **jointure**
marriage settlement provided for the wife by the husband   **139 counterpoised** matched,
equaled   **143 device** plot, strategy   **148 success** fortune/outcome (plays on the sense of
"succession to the throne")   **150 late** recently   **152 estate** status   **155 quondam** former
160 hence go from here   **162 conveyance** trickery, cunning   *Post* messenger

165   POST   My lord ambassador, these letters are for you,

Speaks to Warwick

Sent from your brother, Marquis Montague.—

These from our king unto your majesty.—   *To Lewis*

And, madam, these for you, from whom I know not.

To Margaret

They all read their letters

OXFORD   I like it well that our fair queen and mistress

170   Smiles at her news, while Warwick frowns at his.

PRINCE EDWARD   Nay, mark how Lewis stamps, as he were
nettled.

I hope all's for the best.

KING LEWIS   Warwick, what are thy news?— And yours, fair
queen?

QUEEN MARGARET   Mine, such as fill my heart with unhoped joys.

175   WARWICK   Mine, full of sorrow and heart's discontent.

KING LEWIS   What? Has your king married the Lady Grey?

And now, to soothe your forgery and his,

Sends me a paper to persuade me patience?

Is this th'alliance that he seeks with France?

180   Dare he presume to scorn us in this manner?

QUEEN MARGARET   I told your majesty as much before:

This proveth Edward's love and Warwick's honesty.

WARWICK   King Lewis, I here protest, in sight of heaven

And by the hope I have of heavenly bliss,

185   That I am clear from this misdeed of Edward's,

No more my king, for he dishonours me,

But most himself, if he could see his shame.

Did I forget that by the house of York

My father came untimely to his death?

190   Did I let pass th'abuse done to my niece?

---

171 as as if   **174 unhoped** unexpected   **177 soothe** smooth over   **forgery** deception
180 scorn insult   **185 clear from** innocent of   **189 untimely . . . death** Warwick's father, the
Earl of Salisbury, was executed after being captured fighting for the Yorkists at the battle of
Wakefield   **untimely** prematurely   **190 th'abuse . . . niece** Holinshed's *Chronicles*, one of
Shakespeare's key sources, reports that Edward tried to "deflower" Warwick's daughter or
niece

Did I impale him with the regal crown?
Did I put Henry from his native right?
And am I guerdoned at the last with shame?
Shame on himself, for my desert is honour.

195 And to repair my honour lost for him,
I here renounce him and return to Henry.—
My noble queen, let former grudges pass,
And henceforth I am thy true servitor.
I will revenge his wrong to Lady Bona,

200 And replant Henry in his former state.

QUEEN MARGARET   Warwick, these words have turned my hate to love,
And I forgive and quite forget old faults,
And joy that thou becom'st King Henry's friend.

WARWICK   So much his friend, ay, his unfeignèd friend,

205 That, if King Lewis vouchsafe to furnish us
With some few bands of chosen soldiers,
I'll undertake to land them on our coast
And force the tyrant from his seat by war.
'Tis not his new-made bride shall succour him.

210 And as for Clarence, as my letters tell me,
He's very likely now to fall from him
For matching more for wanton lust than honour,
Or than for strength and safety of our country.

BONA   Dear brother, how shall Bona be revenged

215 But by thy help to this distressèd queen?

QUEEN MARGARET   Renownèd prince, how shall poor Henry live,
Unless thou rescue him from foul despair?

BONA   My quarrel and this English queen's are one.

WARWICK   And mine, fair Lady Bona, joins with yours.

220 KING LEWIS   And mine with hers, and thine, and Margaret's.
Therefore at last I firmly am resolved
You shall have aid.

---

191 impale him encircle his head   **192 put** force   **193 guerdoned** rewarded   **194 my desert** what I deserve   **198 servitor** servant   **203 joy** rejoice   **204 unfeignèd** sincere, honest   **205 vouchsafe to furnish** will consent to equip   **206 bands** troops   **211 fall from** abandon, turn against   **212 matching** marrying

QUEEN MARGARET   Let me give humble thanks for all at once.

KING LEWIS   Then, England's messenger, return in post

225   And tell false Edward, thy supposèd king,
That Lewis of France is sending over masquers
To revel it with him and his new bride.
Thou see'st what's passed, go fear thy king withal.

BONA   Tell him, in hope he'll prove a widower shortly,

230   I'll wear the willow garland for his sake.

QUEEN MARGARET   Tell him, my mourning weeds are laid aside,
And I am ready to put armour on.

WARWICK   Tell him from me that he hath done me wrong,
And therefore I'll uncrown him ere't be long.

235   There's thy reward. Be gone.   *Gives money*

                                                        Exit Post

KING LEWIS   But, Warwick,
Thou and Oxford, with five thousand men
Shall cross the seas, and bid false Edward battle.
And, as occasion serves, this noble queen

240   And prince shall follow with a fresh supply.
Yet, ere thou go, but answer me one doubt:
What pledge have we of thy firm loyalty?

WARWICK   This shall assure my constant loyalty,
That if our queen and this young prince agree,

245   I'll join mine eldest daughter and my joy
To him forthwith in holy wedlock bands.

QUEEN MARGARET   Yes, I agree, and thank you for your
      motion.—
Son Edward, she is fair and virtuous:
Therefore delay not, give thy hand to Warwick,

250   And, with thy hand, thy faith irrevocable,
That only Warwick's daughter shall be thine.

---

224 post haste   **226 masquers** performers of masques (courtly entertainments involving dancing and elaborate costume; often put on to celebrate aristocratic marriages)   **228 passed** happened   **fear** frighten   **withal** with it   **230 willow garland** token of a forsaken lover   **231 weeds** garments   **234 ere't be** before   **235 reward** payment   **238 bid** challenge (to)   **239 occasion** opportunity/events   **240 supply** reinforcements   **245 eldest daughter** historically Warwick's second daughter, Anne, who was betrothed to Edward, although he died before they married   **246 bands** bonds   **247 motion** suggestion

PRINCE EDWARD   Yes, I accept her, for she well deserves it.
And here, to pledge my vow, I give my hand.

He gives his hand to Warwick

KING LEWIS   Why stay we now? These soldiers shall be levied.—
255   And thou, Lord Bourbon, our High Admiral,
Shall waft them over with our royal fleet.
I long till Edward fall by war's mischance,
For mocking marriage with a dame of France.

Exeunt. Warwick remains

WARWICK   I came from Edward as ambassador,
260   But I return his sworn and mortal foe:
Matter of marriage was the charge he gave me,
But dreadful war shall answer his demand.
Had he none else to make a stale but me?
Then none but I shall turn his jest to sorrow.
265   I was the chief that raised him to the crown,
And I'll be chief to bring him down again,
Not that I pity Henry's misery,
But seek revenge on Edward's mockery.   *Exit*

[Act 4 Scene 1]   *running scene 9*

Enter Richard [of Gloucester], Clarence, Somerset and Montague

GLOUCESTER   Now tell me, brother Clarence, what think you
Of this new marriage with the lady Grey?
Hath not our brother made a worthy choice?
CLARENCE   Alas, you know, 'tis far from hence to France.
5   How could he stay till Warwick made return?
SOMERSET   My lords, forbear this talk: here comes the king.
GLOUCESTER   And his well-chosen bride.
CLARENCE   I mind to tell him plainly what I think.
*Flourish. Enter King Edward, Lady Grey [now Queen Elizabeth],
Pembroke, Stafford, Hastings: four stand on one side and four on the
other*

---

256 waft convey (by water)   **263 stale** fool, mockery (of)   **4.1   *Location:* the royal court,
London   5 stay** wait (spoken in irony)   **8 mind** intend

KING EDWARD IV   Now, brother of Clarence, how like you our
     choice,
10   That you stand pensive, as half malcontent?

CLARENCE   As well as Lewis of France, or the Earl of Warwick,
     Which are so weak of courage and in judgement
     That they'll take no offence at our abuse.

KING EDWARD IV   Suppose they take offence without a cause:
15   They are but Lewis and Warwick. I am Edward,
     Your king and Warwick's, and must have my will.

GLOUCESTER   And shall have your will, because our king.
     Yet hasty marriage seldom proveth well.

KING EDWARD IV   Yea, brother Richard, are you offended too?

20   **GLOUCESTER**   Not I, no:
     God forbid that I should wish them severed
     Whom God hath joined together. Ay, and 'twere pity
     To sunder them that yoke so well together.

KING EDWARD IV   Setting your scorns and your mislike aside,
25   Tell me some reason why the lady Grey
     Should not become my wife and England's queen.—
     And you too, Somerset and Montague,
     Speak freely what you think.

CLARENCE   Then this is mine opinion: that King Lewis
30   Becomes your enemy, for mocking him
     About the marriage of the lady Bona.

GLOUCESTER   And Warwick, doing what you gave in charge,
     Is now dishonoured by this new marriage.

KING EDWARD IV   What if both Lewis and Warwick be appeased
35   By such invention as I can devise?

MONTAGUE   Yet, to have joined with France in such alliance
     Would more have strengthened this our commonwealth
     Gainst foreign storms than any home-bred marriage.

HASTINGS   Why, knows not Montague that of itself
40   England is safe, if true within itself?

---

10 malcontent dissatisfied, discontented   **12 Which** who   **13 abuse** insult   **16 will** wishes
(plays on the sense of "sexual desire")   **23 yoke** are joined, coupled like oxen under a yoke
(plays on the sense of "sexually united")   **24 mislike** displeasure   **32 gave in charge** ordered
35 invention scheme, plan   **40 true** loyal, trustworthy

MONTAGUE   But the safer when 'tis backed with France.

HASTINGS   'Tis better using France than trusting France.
Let us be backed with God and with the seas
Which he hath given for fence impregnable,
45   And with their helps only defend ourselves.
In them, and in ourselves, our safety lies.

CLARENCE   For this one speech, Lord Hastings well deserves
To have the heir of the lord Hungerford.

KING EDWARD IV   Ay, what of that? It was my will and grant,
50   And for this once my will shall stand for law.

GLOUCESTER   And yet methinks your grace hath not done well,
To give the heir and daughter of Lord Scales
Unto the brother of your loving bride;
She better would have fitted me or Clarence,
55   But in your bride you bury brotherhood.

CLARENCE   Or else you would not have bestowed the heir
Of the lord Bonville on your new wife's son,
And leave your brothers to go speed elsewhere.

KING EDWARD IV   Alas, poor Clarence, is it for a wife
60   That thou art malcontent? I will provide thee.

CLARENCE   In choosing for yourself, you showed your
judgement,
Which being shallow, you shall give me leave
To play the broker in mine own behalf.
And to that end, I shortly mind to leave you.

65   KING EDWARD IV   Leave me, or tarry, Edward will be king,
And not be tied unto his brother's will.

LADY GREY   My lords, before it pleased his majesty
To raise my state to title of a queen,
Do me but right, and you must all confess
70   That I was not ignoble of descent,

---

44 fence defense   **45 only** alone   **48 have . . . Hungerford** marry the rich heiress, Mary, daughter of Lord Hungerford; historically, it was Hastings' son who married her   **52 heir . . . bride** the wealthy Lord Scales' daughter, Elizabeth, was married to Lord Anthony Rivers, the new queen's brother   **55 bury** forget   **57 new wife's son** Sir Thomas Grey, married to the heir of Lord Harrington and **Bonville**   **58 speed** get on, fare/succeed   **63 broker** marriage broker, agent   **64 mind** intend   **65 tarry** stay

And meaner than myself have had like fortune.
But as this title honours me and mine,
So your dislikes, to whom I would be pleasing,
Doth cloud my joys with danger and with sorrow.

75 KING EDWARD IV   My love, forbear to fawn upon their frowns.
What danger or what sorrow can befall thee,
So long as Edward is thy constant friend,
And their true sovereign, whom they must obey?
Nay, whom they shall obey, and love thee too,

80 Unless they seek for hatred at my hands,
Which if they do, yet will I keep thee safe,
And they shall feel the vengeance of my wrath.

GLOUCESTER   I hear, yet say not much, but think the   *Aside*
more.

Enter a Post

KING EDWARD IV   Now, messenger, what letters or what news

85 From France?

POST   My sovereign liege, no letters, and few words,
But such as I, without your special pardon,
Dare not relate.

KING EDWARD IV   Go to, we pardon thee: therefore, in brief,

90 Tell me their words as near as thou canst guess them.
What answer makes King Lewis unto our letters?

POST   At my depart, these were his very words:
'Go tell false Edward, thy supposèd king,
That Lewis of France is sending over masquers

95 To revel it with him and his new bride.'

KING EDWARD IV   Is Lewis so brave? Belike he thinks me Henry.
But what said Lady Bona to my marriage?

POST   These were her words, uttered with mild disdain:
'Tell him, in hope he'll prove a widower shortly,

100 I'll wear the willow garland for his sake.'

---

71 **meaner** humbler people, those of lower rank   73 **dislikes** disapproval   **would** wish to
74 **danger** hurt/apprehension   75 **fawn . . . frowns** i.e. try to ingratiate yourself, win them
round   77 **friend** supporter/lover   89 **Go to** expression of impatience   90 **guess**
reconstruct from memory   96 **brave** daring, insolent, defiant

KING EDWARD IV   I blame not her; she could say little less.

She had the wrong.— But what said Henry's queen?

For I have heard that she was there in place.

POST   'Tell him', quoth she, 'my mourning weeds are done,

105   And I am ready to put armour on.'

KING EDWARD IV   Belike she minds to play the Amazon.

But what said Warwick to these injuries?

POST   He, more incensed against your majesty

Than all the rest, discharged me with these words:

110   'Tell him from me that he hath done me wrong,

And therefore I'll uncrown him ere't be long.'

KING EDWARD IV   Ha? Durst the traitor breathe out so proud words?

Well, I will arm me, being thus forewarned.

They shall have wars and pay for their presumption.—

115   But say, is Warwick friends with Margaret?

POST   Ay, gracious sovereign, they are so linked in friendship

That young Prince Edward marries Warwick's daughter.

CLARENCE   Belike the elder; Clarence will have the   *Aside*

younger.—

Now, brother king, farewell, and sit you fast,

120   For I will hence to Warwick's other daughter,

That, though I want a kingdom, yet in marriage

I may not prove inferior to yourself.

You that love me and Warwick, follow me.

Exit Clarence, and Somerset follows

GLOUCESTER   Not I.   *Aside*

125   My thoughts aim at a further matter:

I stay not for the love of Edward, but the crown.

KING EDWARD IV   Clarence and Somerset both gone to Warwick!

Yet am I armed against the worst can happen,

---

103 in place present   **104 done** over with, no longer worn   **106 Amazon** member of a legendary race of female warriors   **107 injuries** insults   **109 discharged** dismissed
118 Belike probably   **119 sit you fast** sit tight, hold on to your throne   **121 want** lack

And haste is needful in this desp'rate case.—

130 Pembroke and Stafford, you in our behalf
Go levy men, and make prepare for war;
They are already, or quickly will be landed.
Myself in person will straight follow you.

Exeunt Pembroke and Stafford

But, ere I go, Hastings and Montague,
135 Resolve my doubt. You twain, of all the rest,
Are near to Warwick by blood and by alliance:
Tell me if you love Warwick more than me?
If it be so, then both depart to him.
I rather wish you foes than hollow friends.
140 But if you mind to hold your true obedience,
Give me assurance with some friendly vow,
That I may never have you in suspect.

MONTAGUE   So God help Montague as he proves true.

HASTINGS   And Hastings as he favours Edward's cause.

145 KING EDWARD IV   Now, brother Richard, will you stand by us?

GLOUCESTER   Ay, in despite of all that shall withstand you.

KING EDWARD IV   Why, so. Then am I sure of victory.
Now therefore let us hence, and lose no hour
Till we meet Warwick with his foreign power.   *Exeunt*

[Act 4 Scene 2]

running scene 10

Enter Warwick and Oxford in England, with French Soldiers

WARWICK   Trust me, my lord, all hitherto goes well.
The common people by numbers swarm to us.

Enter Clarence and Somerset

But see where Somerset and Clarence comes.
Speak suddenly, my lords, are we all friends?

---

129 **needful** necessary   131 **prepare** preparation   133 **straight** straightaway   135 **twain**
two   139 **hollow** insincere   142 **in suspect** under suspicion   146 **withstand** resist
149 **power** army   **4.2** *Location: England (historically, near Warwick)*   1 **hitherto** thus
far   4 **suddenly** immediately

5 CLARENCE   Fear not that, my lord.

WARWICK   Then, gentle Clarence, welcome unto Warwick.—
And welcome, Somerset. I hold it cowardice
To rest mistrustful where a noble heart
Hath pawned an open hand in sign of love;
10 Else might I think that Clarence, Edward's brother,
Were but a feignèd friend to our proceedings.
But welcome, sweet Clarence, my daughter shall be thine.
And now what rests but, in night's coverture,
Thy brother being carelessly encamped,
15 His soldiers lurking in the towns about,
And but attended by a simple guard,
We may surprise and take him at our pleasure?
Our scouts have found the adventure very easy,
That as Ulysses and stout Diomede
20 With sleight and manhood stole to Rhesus' tents,
And brought from thence the Thracian fatal steeds,
So we, well covered with the night's black mantle,
At unawares may beat down Edward's guard
And seize himself. I say not, slaughter him,
25 For I intend but only to surprise him.
You that will follow me to this attempt,
Applaud the name of Henry with your leader.

They all cry, 'Henry!'

Why, then, let's on our way in silent sort,
For Warwick and his friends, God and Saint George!   *Exeunt*

---

8 rest remain   **9 pawned** pledged   **11 proceedings** course of action   **13 in night's coverture** under cover of darkness   **14 carelessly** without concern/without proper military precautions   **15 lurking** idling   **16 but** only   **17 surprise** ambush, seize   **18 the . . . easy** venturing into Edward's camp is simple/there is little hazard   **19 Ulysses . . . steeds** in Homer's *Iliad*, Ulysses and Diomede sneak under cover of night into the camp of the Thracian leader, Rhesus, and steal his horses, an oracle having predicted that Troy would not fall to the Greeks as long as the horses of Rhesus grazed on the plains of Troy   **stout** bold   **20 sleight** cunning   **21 fatal** fated, part of destiny/causing death   **23 At unawares** suddenly, unexpectedly   **28 sort** manner

[Act 4 Scene 3]   *running scene 11*

Enter three Watchmen to guard the King's tent

FIRST WATCHMAN   Come on, my masters, each man take his
        stand.
    The king by this is set him down to sleep.
SECOND WATCHMAN   What, will he not to bed?
FIRST WATCHMAN   Why, no, for he hath made a solemn vow
5   Never to lie and take his natural rest
    Till Warwick or himself be quite suppressed.
SECOND WATCHMAN   Tomorrow then belike shall be the day,
    If Warwick be so near as men report.
THIRD WATCHMAN   But say, I pray, what nobleman is that
10   That with the king here resteth in his tent?
FIRST WATCHMAN   'Tis the lord Hastings, the king's chiefest friend.
THIRD WATCHMAN   O, is it so? But why commands the king
    That his chief followers lodge in towns about him,
    While he himself keeps in the cold field?
15   SECOND WATCHMAN   'Tis the more honour, because more
        dangerous.
THIRD WATCHMAN   Ay, but give me worship and quietness.
    I like it better than a dangerous honour.
    If Warwick knew in what estate he stands,
    'Tis to be doubted he would waken him.
20   FIRST WATCHMAN   Unless our halberds did shut up his passage.
SECOND WATCHMAN   Ay, wherefore else guard we his royal tent,
    But to defend his person from night-foes?
Enter Warwick, Clarence, Oxford, Somerset and French Soldiers,
silent all
WARWICK   This is his tent, and see where stand his guard.
    Courage, my masters: honour now or never:
25   But follow me, and Edward shall be ours.

4.3   *Location: King Edward's camp (historically, near Warwick)*   1 my masters
gentlemen   **stand** post, position   **2 this** this time   **set** sat   **13 about** around   **14 keeps**
lodges, sleeps   **16 worship** dignified ease   **18 estate** situation   **he** i.e. Edward   **19 doubted**
feared   **20 halberds** long-handled weapons with axelike heads   **shut up** prevent, bar
passage progress   **21 wherefore** why   **25 But** only, merely

FIRST WATCHMAN   Who goes there?

SECOND WATCHMAN   Stay, or thou diest!

Warwick and the rest cry all, 'Warwick! Warwick!' and set upon the
guard, who fly, crying, 'Arm! Arm!' Warwick and the rest following
them. The Drum playing and Trumpet sounding, enter Warwick,
Somerset and the rest bringing the King [Edward] out in his gown,
sitting in a chair. Richard and Hastings fly over the stage

SOMERSET   What are they that fly there?

WARWICK   Richard and Hastings. Let them go. Here is

30   The duke.

KING EDWARD IV   The duke? Why, Warwick, when we parted,
Thou called'st me king.

WARWICK   Ay, but the case is altered.
When you disgraced me in my embassade,
35   Then I degraded you from being king,
And come now to create you Duke of York.
Alas, how should you govern any kingdom,
That know not how to use ambassadors,
Nor how to be contented with one wife,
40   Nor how to use your brothers brotherly,
Nor how to study for the people's welfare,
Nor how to shroud yourself from enemies?

KING EDWARD IV   Yea, brother of Clarence, art thou here too?
Nay, then I see that Edward needs must down.—
45   Yet, Warwick, in despite of all mischance,
Of thee thyself and all thy complices,
Edward will always bear himself as king.
Though fortune's malice overthrow my state,
My mind exceeds the compass of her wheel.

50   **WARWICK**   Then, for his mind, be Edward England's king,

Takes off his crown

But Henry now shall wear the English crown,

---

gown dressing gown or nightgown/loose upper garment for men   **28 What** who
34 embassade ambassadorial mission   **35 degraded** lowered in rank   **44 down** fall
46 complices accomplices   **48 fortune's . . . wheel** fortune was traditionally depicted as a
blind woman turning a wheel that raised humans up and cast them down   **state** sovereignty
49 compass range, circumference   **50 for** i.e. in

And be true king indeed, thou but the shadow.—
My lord of Somerset, at my request,
See that forthwith Duke Edward be conveyed
55   Unto my brother, Archbishop of York.
When I have fought with Pembroke and his fellows,
I'll follow you, and tell what answer
Lewis and the lady Bona send to him.—
Now, for awhile farewell, good Duke of York.

They lead him out forcibly

60   KING EDWARD IV   What fates impose, that men must needs abide;
It boots not to resist both wind and tide.

Exeunt [all but Oxford and Warwick]

OXFORD   What now remains, my lords, for us to do
But march to London with our soldiers?
WARWICK   Ay, that's the first thing that we have to do,
65   To free King Henry from imprisonment
And see him seated in the regal throne.   *Exeunt*

[Act 4 Scene 4]   *running scene 12*

Enter Rivers and Lady Grey [Queen Elizabeth]

RIVERS   Madam, what makes you in this sudden change?
LADY GREY   Why brother Rivers, are you yet to learn
What late misfortune is befall'n King Edward?
RIVERS   What? Loss of some pitched battle against
Warwick?
5   LADY GREY   No, but the loss of his own royal person.
RIVERS   Then is my sovereign slain?
LADY GREY   Ay, almost slain, for he is taken prisoner,
Either betrayed by falsehood of his guard
Or by his foe surprised at unawares.

---

60 **abide** endure   61 **boots not** is useless   **4.4** *Location: London*   1 **makes . . . change**
is the reason for your sudden change in mood   4 **pitched** planned, designated   8 **falsehood**
disloyalty, treachery   9 **surprised at** captured

10 And as I further have to understand,
Is new committed to the Bishop of York,
Fell Warwick's brother and by that our foe.

RIVERS These news I must confess are full of grief,
Yet, gracious madam, bear it as you may,
15 Warwick may lose, that now hath won the day.

LADY GREY Till then fair hope must hinder life's decay.
And I the rather wean me from despair
For love of Edward's offspring in my womb.
This is it that makes me bridle passion
20 And bear with mildness my misfortune's cross.
Ay, ay, for this I draw in many a tear
And stop the rising of blood-sucking sighs,
Lest with my sighs or tears I blast or drown
King Edward's fruit, true heir to th'English crown.

25 RIVERS But, madam, where is Warwick then become?

LADY GREY I am informed that he comes towards London,
To set the crown once more on Henry's head.
Guess thou the rest: King Edward's friends must down.
But, to prevent the tyrant's violence —
30 For trust not him that hath once broken faith —
I'll hence forthwith unto the sanctuary,
To save at least the heir of Edward's right.
There shall I rest secure from force and fraud.
Come, therefore, let us fly while we may fly.
35 If Warwick take us we are sure to die.   *Exeunt*

11 to i.e. to the custody of Bishop i.e. Archbishop 12 Fell fierce, cruel by that therefore
16 hinder delay, prevent 19 bridle reign in, restrain passion intense feeling, grief
22 blood-sucking sighs each sigh was thought to drain a drop of blood from the heart
23 blast blight, wither 25 where . . . become what has become of/where is Warwick
28 down fall 29 tyrant's usurper's 31 sanctuary churches and associated Church-owned
buildings provided sanctuary from arrest; the historical sources Shakespeare drew on say that
Elizabeth went to Westminster 32 right title to the throne 33 secure protected fraud
trickery, treachery

[Act 4 Scene 5]

Enter Richard, Lord Hastings and Sir William Stanley [with Soldiers]

GLOUCESTER   Now, my lord Hastings and Sir William Stanley,
Leave off to wonder why I drew you hither,
Into this chiefest thicket of the park.
Thus stands the case: you know our king, my brother,
5   Is prisoner to the bishop here, at whose hands
He hath good usage and great liberty,
And, often but attended with weak guard,
Comes hunting this way to disport himself.
I have advertised him by secret means
10   That if about this hour he make this way
Under the colour of his usual game,
He shall here find his friends with horse and men
To set him free from his captivity.

Enter King Edward and a Huntsman with him

HUNTSMAN   This way, my lord, for this way lies the game.
15   KING EDWARD IV   Nay, this way, man. See where the huntsmen
stand.—
Now, brother of Gloucester, Lord Hastings and the rest,
Stand you thus close, to steal the bishop's deer?
GLOUCESTER   Brother, the time and case requireth haste.
Your horse stands ready at the park-corner.
20   KING EDWARD IV   But whither shall we then?
HASTINGS   To Lynn, my lord,
And shipped from thence to Flanders.
GLOUCESTER   Well guessed, believe me, for that was my
meaning.
KING EDWARD IV   Stanley, I will requite thy forwardness.
25   GLOUCESTER   But wherefore stay we? 'Tis no time to talk.

4.5   *Location: Yorkshire, at hunting grounds belonging to the Archbishop of York*
2 Leave off cease   **3 chiefest** largest, most dense   **park** private hunting ground   **4 case**
circumstances   **6 hath good usage** is well treated   **7 but** only   **8 disport** entertain, amuse
9 advertised informed, alerted   **11 colour** pretext   **game** hunting   **14 game** prey, quarry
17 close concealed   **21 Lynn** King's Lynn, a town on the Norfolk coast   **24 requite** reward
forwardness eagerness, zeal

KING EDWARD IV   Huntsman, what say'st thou? Wilt thou go
　　　along?

HUNTSMAN   Better do so than tarry and be hanged.

GLOUCESTER   Come then, away. Let's ha' no more ado.

KING EDWARD IV   Bishop, farewell. Shield thee from Warwick's
　　　frown,

30　　And pray that I may repossess the crown.　　　　*Exeunt*

[Act 4 Scene 6]

running scene 14

Flourish. Enter King Henry the Sixth, Clarence, Warwick, Somerset,
young Henry [of Richmond], Oxford, Montague and Lieutenant

KING HENRY VI   Master lieutenant, now that God and friends
　　　Have shaken Edward from the regal seat,
　　　And turned my captive state to liberty,
　　　My fear to hope, my sorrows unto joys,

5　　At our enlargement what are thy due fees?

LIEUTENANT   Subjects may challenge nothing of their
　　　sov'reigns,
　　　But if an humble prayer may prevail,
　　　I then crave pardon of your majesty.

KING HENRY VI   For what, lieutenant? For well using me?

10　　Nay, be thou sure I'll well requite thy kindness,
　　　For that it made my imprisonment a pleasure.
　　　Ay, such a pleasure as encagèd birds
　　　Conceive, when after many moody thoughts,
　　　At last, by notes of household harmony,

15　　They quite forget their loss of liberty.
　　　But, Warwick, after God, thou set'st me free,
　　　And chiefly therefore I thank God and thee.
　　　He was the author, thou the instrument.

---

28 ado fuss, time-wasting　　**4.6** *Location: the Tower of London*　　**Lieutenant** the second-in-command at the Tower of London　　**5 enlargement** release　　**due fees** wealthy prisoners could pay for special food or service　　**6 challenge** require, ask　　**11 For that** because
13 Conceive begin to experience　　**moody** melancholy, somber　　**14 notes . . . harmony** filling the house with song, singing in a manner that is harmonious with their domestic environment
18 author creator, originator

Therefore, that I may conquer fortune's spite
20 By living low, where fortune cannot hurt me,
And that the people of this blessèd land
May not be punished with my thwarting stars,
Warwick, although my head still wear the crown,
I here resign my government to thee,
25 For thou art fortunate in all thy deeds.

WARWICK   Your grace hath still been famed for virtuous
And now may seem as wise as virtuous,
By spying and avoiding fortune's malice,
For few men rightly temper with the stars:
30 Yet in this one thing let me blame your grace,
For choosing me when Clarence is in place.

CLARENCE   No, Warwick, thou art worthy of the sway,
To whom the heav'ns in thy nativity
Adjudged an olive branch and laurel crown,
35 As likely to be blest in peace and war.
And therefore I yield thee my free consent.

WARWICK   And I choose Clarence only for Protector.

KING HENRY VI   Warwick and Clarence give me both your hands.
Now join your hands, and with your hands your hearts,
40 That no dissension hinder government.
I make you both protectors of this land,
While I myself will lead a private life
And in devotion spend my latter days,
To sin's rebuke and my creator's praise.

45 WARWICK   What answers Clarence to his sovereign's will?

CLARENCE   That he consents, if Warwick yield consent,
For on thy fortune I repose myself.

---

20 low humbly   **22 thwarting stars** bad fortune   **26 still** always   **famed for** renowned as being   **28 spying** spying out/foreseeing   **29 temper . . . stars** allow themselves to conform to their fate, mold their dispositions to their fate   **31 in place** present   **32 sway** power, influence   **34 Adjudged** awarded   **olive branch** a symbol of peace   **laurel crown** a symbol of victory   **36 yield** grant   **free consent** willing agreement   **37 only** alone   **Protector** one who governs in the absence of the monarch   **40 dissension** dissent, disagreement   **43 devotion** prayer, religious commitment   **latter** last, remaining   **47 repose myself** depend, rely

WARWICK   Why, then, though loath, yet must I be content.
We'll yoke together, like a double shadow
50   To Henry's body, and supply his place,
I mean, in bearing weight of government,
While he enjoys the honour and his ease.
And, Clarence, now then it is more than needful
Forthwith that Edward be pronounced a traitor,
55   And all his lands and goods be confiscate.

CLARENCE   What else? And that succession be determinèd.

WARWICK   Ay, therein Clarence shall not want his part.

KING HENRY VI   But, with the first of all your chief affairs,
Let me entreat, for I command no more,
60   That Margaret your queen and my son Edward
Be sent for, to return from France with speed.
For till I see them here, by doubtful fear
My joy of liberty is half eclipsed.

CLARENCE   It shall be done, my sovereign, with all speed.

65 KING HENRY VI   My lord of Somerset, what youth is that,
Of whom you seem to have so tender care?

SOMERSET   My liege, it is young Henry, Earl of Richmond.

KING HENRY VI   Come hither, England's hope.

Lays his hand on his head
                     If secret powers
Suggest but truth to my divining thoughts,
70   This pretty lad will prove our country's bliss.
His looks are full of peaceful majesty,
His head by nature framed to wear a crown,
His hand to wield a sceptre, and himself
Likely in time to bless a regal throne.
75   Make much of him, my lords, for this is he
Must help you more than you are hurt by me.

Enter a Post

---

49 yoke join   **50 supply** fill   **56 What else?** i.e. "yes, of course"   **57 Clarence . . . part** if the Lancastrian claim were set aside, Edward attainted for treason, and his unborn child disregarded, then Clarence would have a significant claim to the throne   **want** lack
62 doubtful apprehensive   **67 Henry . . . Richmond** Henry Tudor, the future Henry VII, whose kingship put an end to the Wars of the Roses   **69 divining** foreseeing, prophetic
70 pretty fine, handsome

WARWICK   What news, my friend?

POST   That Edward is escapèd from your brother,
And fled, as he hears since, to Burgundy.

80 WARWICK   Unsavoury news! But how made he escape?

POST   He was conveyed by Richard, Duke of Gloucester,
And the Lord Hastings, who attended him
In secret ambush on the forest side
And from the bishop's huntsmen rescued him,

85 For hunting was his daily exercise.

WARWICK   My brother was too careless of his charge.
But let us hence, my sovereign, to provide
A salve for any sore that may betide.

Exeunt. Somerset, Richmond and Oxford remain

SOMERSET   My lord, I like not of this flight of Edward's,

90 For doubtless Burgundy will yield him help,
And we shall have more wars before't be long.
As Henry's late presaging prophecy
Did glad my heart with hope of this young Richmond,
So doth my heart misgive me, in these conflicts

95 What may befall him, to his harm and ours:
Therefore, Lord Oxford, to prevent the worst,
Forthwith we'll send him hence to Brittany,
Till storms be past of civil enmity.

OXFORD   Ay, for if Edward repossess the crown,

100 'Tis like that Richmond with the rest, shall down.

SOMERSET   It shall be so. He shall to Brittany.
Come, therefore, let's about it speedily.   *Exeunt*

[Act 4 Scene 7]

running scene 15

Flourish. Enter Edward, Richard, Hastings and Soldiers

KING EDWARD IV   Now, brother Richard, Lord Hastings and the
rest,

---

78 **brother** i.e. the Archbishop of York   81 **conveyed** carried away in secrecy   82 **attended**
awaited   86 **charge** duty, orders/prisoner   88 **salve** healing ointment   **betide** occur
4.7   *Location*: outside the city gates of York

Yet thus far fortune maketh us amends,
And says that once more I shall interchange
My wanèd state for Henry's regal crown.

5   Well have we passed and now repassed the seas
And brought desirèd help from Burgundy.
What then remains, we being thus arrived
From Ravenspurgh haven before the gates of York,
But that we enter, as into our dukedom?   *Hastings knocks*

10   GLOUCESTER   The gates made fast? Brother, I like not this,
For many men that stumble at the threshold
Are well foretold that danger lurks within.

KING EDWARD IV   Tush, man, abodements must not now
          affright us.
By fair or foul means we must enter in,
15   For hither will our friends repair to us.

HASTINGS   My liege, I'll knock once more to summon
          them.   *Knocks*

Enter [above], on the walls, the Mayor of York and his brethren

MAYOR   My lords, we were forewarned of your coming,
And shut the gates for safety of ourselves;
For now we owe allegiance unto Henry.

20   KING EDWARD IV   But, Master Mayor, if Henry be your king,
Yet Edward, at the least, is Duke of York.

MAYOR   True, my good lord, I know you for no less.

KING EDWARD IV   Why, and I challenge nothing but my dukedom,
As being well content with that alone.

25   GLOUCESTER   But when the fox hath once got in his nose,   *Aside*
He'll soon find means to make the body follow.

HASTINGS   Why, Master Mayor, why stand you in a doubt?
Open the gates, we are King Henry's friends.

MAYOR   Ay, say you so? The gates shall then be opened.
          He descends [with his brethren]

---

3 interchange exchange   **4 wanèd** weakened, diminished   **8 Ravenspurgh** former Yorkshire
port on the River Humber   **haven** harbor   **10 made fast** tightly secured   **12 well foretold**
clearly warned   **13 abodements** omens, premonitions   **affright** frighten   **15 repair** make
their way, return   *above* i.e. on the upper staging level or gallery, conventionally used to
represent city walls   *brethren* members of the town corporation   **23 challenge** demand,
require   **25 got . . . nose** got his nose in

30   GLOUCESTER   A wise stout captain, and soon persuaded.

HASTINGS   The good old man would fain that all were well,
So 'twere not long of him. But being entered,
I doubt not, I, but we shall soon persuade
Both him and all his brothers unto reason.

Enter the Mayor and two Aldermen [below]

35   KING EDWARD IV   So, Master Mayor, these gates must not be shut
But in the night or in the time of war.
What! Fear not, man, but yield me up the keys.

Takes his keys

For Edward will defend the town and thee,
And all those friends that deign to follow me.

March. Enter Montgomery, with Drum and Soldiers

40   GLOUCESTER   Brother, this is Sir John Montgomery,
Our trusty friend, unless I be deceived.

KING EDWARD IV   Welcome, Sir John. But why come you in arms?

MONTGOMERY   To help King Edward in his time of storm,
As every loyal subject ought to do.

45   KING EDWARD IV   Thanks, good Montgomery, but we now forget
Our title to the crown and only claim
Our dukedom, till God please to send the rest.

MONTGOMERY   Then fare you well, for I will hence again.
I came to serve a king and not a duke.—

50   Drummer, strike up and let us march away.

The Drum begins to march

KING EDWARD IV   Nay, stay, Sir John, awhile, and we'll debate
By what safe means the crown may be recovered.

MONTGOMERY   What talk you of debating? In few words,
If you'll not here proclaim yourself our king,

55   I'll leave you to your fortune and be gone
To keep them back that come to succour you.
Why shall we fight, if you pretend no title?

GLOUCESTER   Why, brother, wherefore stand you on nice points?

---

30 stout valiant   **31 fain** be glad   **32 So . . . him** so long as he is not held accountable
Aldermen members of the town council   **36 But** except   **39 deign** are willing   **45 forget**
disregard   **57 pretend** claim, profess   **58 wherefore stand you** why do you dwell, insist on
nice overly precise, particular

KING EDWARD IV   When we grow stronger, then we'll make our
    claim.
60   Till then, 'tis wisdom to conceal our meaning.

HASTINGS   Away with scrupulous wit, now arms must rule.

GLOUCESTER   And fearless minds climb soonest unto crowns.
    Brother, we will proclaim you out of hand.
    The bruit thereof will bring you many friends.

65 KING EDWARD IV   Then be it as you will, for 'tis my right,
    And Henry but usurps the diadem.

MONTGOMERY   Ay, now my sovereign speaketh like himself,
    And now will I be Edward's champion.

HASTINGS   Sound trumpet. Edward shall be here proclaimed.
70   Come, fellow soldier, make thou proclamation.

Flourish. Sound

SOLDIER   'Edward the Fourth, by the grace of God,   *Reads*
    King of England and France, and Lord of Ireland, etc.'

MONTGOMERY   And whosoe'er gainsays King Edward's right,
    By this I challenge him to single fight.

Throws down his gauntlet

75 ALL   Long live Edward the Fourth!

KING EDWARD IV   Thanks, brave Montgomery, and thanks unto
    you all.
    If fortune serve me, I'll requite this kindness.
    Now, for this night, let's harbour here in York,
    And when the morning sun shall raise his car
80   Above the border of this horizon,
    We'll forward towards Warwick and his mates;
    For well I wot that Henry is no soldier.
    Ah, froward Clarence, how evil it beseems thee
    To flatter Henry and forsake thy brother!

---

60 meaning intention   **61 scrupulous wit** quibbling reason, cautious intellect   **63 out of hand** immediately   **64 bruit** news, announcement   **68 champion** defender   *Sound* i.e. trumpets sound   **71 SOLDIER** some editors suppose that this speech heading has been inserted erroneously and that Montgomery should read the proclamation   **73 gainsays** denies   *gauntlet* armored glove, traditionally thrown down as a means of challenging one's enemy to single combat; to pick it up was to accept a challenge to a duel   **76 brave** noble **78 harbour** make our lodging   **79 car** chariot (of the sun god)   **82 wot** know   **83 froward** willful, obstinate, perverse   **beseems** suits, befits

85   Yet, as we may, we'll meet both thee and Warwick.
        Come on, brave soldiers, doubt not of the day,
        And that once gotten, doubt not of large pay.   *Exeunt*

[Act 4 Scene 8]

Flourish. Enter the King, Warwick, Montague, Clarence, Oxford and
Somerset

WARWICK   What counsel, lords? Edward from Belgia,
        With hasty Germans and blunt Hollanders,
        Hath passed in safety through the narrow seas,
        And with his troops doth march amain to London,
5   And many giddy people flock to him.
        KING HENRY VI   Let's levy men and beat him back again.
        CLARENCE   A little fire is quickly trodden out,
        Which, being suffered, rivers cannot quench.
        WARWICK   In Warwickshire I have true-hearted friends,
10   Not mutinous in peace, yet bold in war.
        Those will I muster up, and thou, son Clarence,
        Shalt stir up in Suffolk, Norfolk and in Kent,
        The knights and gentlemen to come with thee.
        Thou, brother Montague, in Buckingham,
15   Northampton and in Leicestershire, shalt find
        Men well inclined to hear what thou command'st.
        And thou, brave Oxford, wondrous well beloved,
        In Oxfordshire shalt muster up thy friends.
        My sovereign, with the loving citizens,
20   Like to his island girt in with the ocean,
        Or modest Dian circled with her nymphs,
        Shall rest in London till we come to him.

---

86 **the day** victory in battle   **4.8**   *Location: London, at the Bishop of London's palace*
1 **Belgia** the Netherlands   2 **hasty** rash, quick-tempered   **blunt** harsh, uncivilized, rough
3 **narrow seas** i.e. the English Channel   4 **amain** speedily   5 **giddy** unstable, fickle, excitable
8 **suffered** tolerated, permitted (to burn)   11 **son** son-in-law   17 **wondrous** extraordinarily
20 **girt in with** surrounded by   21 **Dian** Diana, Roman goddess of the moon, hunting, and
chastity; often portrayed with her attendant virginal **nymphs**   22 **rest** remain

Fair lords, take leave and stand not to reply.
Farewell, my sovereign.

25   KING HENRY VI   Farewell, my Hector, and my Troy's true hope.

CLARENCE   In sign of truth, I kiss your highness' hand.

KING HENRY VI   Well-minded Clarence, be thou fortunate.

MONTAGUE   Comfort, my lord, and so I take my leave.

OXFORD   And thus I seal my truth, and bid adieu.

30   KING HENRY VI   Sweet Oxford, and my loving Montague,
And all at once, once more a happy farewell.

WARWICK   Farewell, sweet lords, let's meet at Coventry.

Exeunt. [King Henry and Exeter remain]

KING HENRY VI   Here at the palace will I rest awhile.
Cousin of Exeter, what thinks your lordship?

35   Methinks the power that Edward hath in field
Should not be able to encounter mine.

EXETER   The doubt is that he will seduce the rest.

KING HENRY VI   That's not my fear. My meed hath got me fame:
I have not stopped mine ears to their demands,

40   Nor posted off their suits with slow delays.
My pity hath been balm to heal their wounds,
My mildness hath allayed their swelling griefs,
My mercy dried their water-flowing tears.
I have not been desirous of their wealth,

45   Nor much oppressed them with great subsidies,
Nor forward of revenge, though they much erred.
Then why should they love Edward more than me?
No, Exeter, these graces challenge grace,
And when the lion fawns upon the lamb,

50   The lamb will never cease to follow him.

Shout within, 'A Lancaster! A Lancaster!'

EXETER   Hark, hark, my lord, what shouts are these?

---

23 stand not do not wait   **25 Hector** the eldest son of Priam, King of Troy, Hector was one of
the great warriors of the Trojan war   **26 truth** faith, loyalty   **27 Well-minded** loyal,
virtuous, well-intentioned   **28 Comfort** be encouraged   **29 thus** Oxford probably also kisses
Henry's hand   **31 at once** together   **happy** propitious, fortunate   **36 encounter** fight and
defeat   **37 doubt** fear   **38 meed** merit, virtue   **39 their demands** the various requests and
appeals of the people   **40 posted off** postponed   **suits** pleas, petitions   **45 subsidies** taxes
46 forward of eager for   **48 graces challenge grace** virtues claim respect and favor

Enter Edward and his Soldiers

KING EDWARD IV   Seize on the shame-faced Henry. Bear him
　　hence,
　　And once again proclaim us King of England.—
　　You are the fount that makes small brooks to flow:
55　　Now stops thy spring, my sea shall suck them dry,
　　And swell so much the higher by their ebb.—
　　Hence with him to the Tower. Let him not speak.

　　　　　　　　　　　　　Exeunt [some] with King Henry

　　And, lords, towards Coventry bend we our course
　　Where peremptory Warwick now remains.
60　　The sun shines hot, and if we use delay,
　　Cold biting winter mars our hoped-for hay.

GLOUCESTER   Away betimes, before his forces join,
　　And take the great-grown traitor unawares.
　　Brave warriors, march amain towards Coventry.　　*Exeunt*

[Act 5 Scene 1]   *running scene 17*

*Enter Warwick, the Mayor of Coventry, two Messengers and others
upon the walls*

WARWICK   Where is the post that came from valiant Oxford?
　　How far hence is thy lord, mine honest fellow?

FIRST MESSENGER   By this at Dunsmore, marching
　　hitherward.　　　　　　　　　　　　　　　*[He may exit]*

WARWICK   How far off is our brother Montague?
5　　Where is the post that came from Montague?

SECOND MESSENGER   By this at Daintry, with a puissant
　　troop.　　　　　　　　　　　　　　　　　*[He may exit]*

Enter Somerville

WARWICK   Say, Somerville, what says my loving son?
　　And, by thy guess, how nigh is Clarence now?

---

52 shame-faced timid, shy, modest　**54 fount** spring, source　**56 ebb** waning, reducing
58 bend direct　**59 peremptory** imperious, overbearing　**61 mars** ruins　**hay** i.e. yield,
harvest　**62 betimes** quickly　**5.1**　*Location: the city walls of Coventry*　**3 this** this
time, now　**Dunsmore** between Coventry and Daventry　**6 Daintry** Daventry　**puissant**
powerful　**7 son** son-in-law

SOMERVILLE   At Southam I did leave him with his forces

10   And do expect him here some two hours hence.   *Drum heard*

WARWICK   Then Clarence is at hand, I hear his drum.

SOMERVILLE   It is not his, my lord, here Southam lies.

     The drum your honour hears marcheth from Warwick.

WARWICK   Who should that be? Belike, unlooked-for friends.

15   SOMERVILLE   They are at hand, and you shall quickly

       know.   [*Exit into the city*]

March. Flourish. Enter Edward, Richard and Soldiers

KING EDWARD IV   Go, trumpet, to the walls, and sound a parle.

GLOUCESTER   See how the surly Warwick mans the wall.

WARWICK   O, unbid spite, is sportful Edward come?

     Where slept our scouts or how are they seduced,

20   That we could hear no news of his repair?

KING EDWARD IV   Now, Warwick, wilt thou ope the city gates,

     Speak gentle words and humbly bend thy knee?

     Call Edward king and at his hands beg mercy,

     And he shall pardon thee these outrages.

25   WARWICK   Nay, rather, wilt thou draw thy forces hence,

     Confess who set thee up and plucked thee down,

     Call Warwick patron and be penitent?

     And thou shalt still remain the Duke of York.

GLOUCESTER   I thought, at least, he would have said the king,

30   Or did he make the jest against his will?

WARWICK   Is not a dukedom, sir, a goodly gift?

GLOUCESTER   Ay, by my faith, for a poor earl to give.

     I'll do thee service for so good a gift.

WARWICK   'Twas I that gave the kingdom to thy brother.

35   KING EDWARD IV   Why then 'tis mine, if but by Warwick's gift.

WARWICK   Thou art no Atlas for so great a weight,

     And weakling, Warwick takes his gift again,

     And Henry is my king, Warwick his subject.

---

9 Southam town about ten miles southeast of Coventry   **12 here** in this direction   **16 parle** parley, a trumpet summons for negotiation between opposing sides, during which fighting was to stop   **17 surly** imperious, arrogant   **18 unbid** unwelcome   **sportful** lecherous   **20 repair** approach   **25 draw** withdraw   **27 patron** protector   **32 earl** lower in rank than a duke   **36 Atlas . . . weight** in classical mythology, the giant Atlas carried the earth on his shoulders

KING EDWARD IV   But Warwick's king is Edward's prisoner.
40   And, gallant Warwick, do but answer this:
        What is the body when the head is off?

GLOUCESTER   Alas, that Warwick had no more forecast,
        But whiles he thought to steal the single ten,
        The king was slyly fingered from the deck.
45   You left poor Henry at the bishop's palace,
        And ten to one you'll meet him in the Tower.

EDWARD   'Tis even so, yet you are Warwick still.

GLOUCESTER   Come, Warwick, take the time, kneel down, kneel
        down.
        Nay, when? Strike now, or else the iron cools.

50   WARWICK   I had rather chop this hand off at a blow,
        And with the other fling it at thy face,
        Than bear so low a sail to strike to thee.

KING EDWARD IV   Sail how thou canst, have wind and tide thy
        friend,
        This hand, fast wound about thy coal-black hair,
55   Shall, whiles thy head is warm and new cut off,
        Write in the dust this sentence with thy blood,
        'Wind-changing Warwick now can change no more.'

Enter Oxford with Drum and Colours

WARWICK   O, cheerful colours, see where Oxford comes!

OXFORD   Oxford, Oxford, for Lancaster!   *He and his forces enter*

60   GLOUCESTER   The gates are open, let us enter too.   *the city*

KING EDWARD IV   So other foes may set upon our backs.
        Stand we in good array, for they no doubt
        Will issue out again and bid us battle;

---

42 forecast forethought, prudence/anticipated   **43 single ten** a mere ten-point card, valuable
but less so than a royal card   **44 fingered** stolen   **47 even** exactly   **are Warwick still** i.e. will
always be yourself, and doubtless will not change your attitude/remain in position, and have
the chance to change your attitude   **48 time** opportunity   **49 Nay, when?** expression of
impatience   **Strike . . . cools** proverbial: "strike while the iron is hot" (Warwick shifts the
sense of **strike** to "lower one's **sail** in submission")   **57 Wind-changing** i.e. changeable, fickle
Colours military flagbearers   **61 set . . . backs** attack our rearguard forces   **62 array**
readiness for combat   **63 bid** challenge

If not, the city being but of small defence,

65   We'll quickly rouse the traitors in the same.   *Oxford appears*

WARWICK   O, welcome, Oxford, for we want thy help.   *on the walls*

Enter Montague with Drum and Colours

MONTAGUE   Montague, Montague, for Lancaster!   *He and his forces*

GLOUCESTER   Thou and thy brother both shall buy   *enter the city*
this treason

Even with the dearest blood your bodies bear.

70   KING EDWARD IV   The harder matched, the greater victory.

My mind presageth happy gain and conquest.

Enter Somerset with Drum and Colours

SOMERSET   Somerset, Somerset, for Lancaster!   *He and his forces*

GLOUCESTER   Two of thy name, both Dukes of   *enter the city*
Somerset,

Have sold their lives unto the house of York,

75   And thou shalt be the third if this sword hold.

Enter Clarence with Drum and Colours

WARWICK   And lo, where George of Clarence sweeps along,

Of force enough to bid his brother battle,

With whom an upright zeal to right prevails

More than the nature of a brother's love.

80   Come, Clarence, come. Thou wilt, if Warwick call.

CLARENCE   Father of Warwick, know you what this
means?   *Takes red rose out of his hat*

Look here, I throw my infamy at thee.   *Throws it at Warwick*

I will not ruinate my father's house,

Who gave his blood to lime the stones together,

85   And set up Lancaster. Why, trowest thou, Warwick,

That Clarence is so harsh, so blunt, unnatural,

To bend the fatal instruments of war

Against his brother and his lawful king?

---

64 of small defence poorly fortified   **65 rouse** draw out (from a lair; a hunting term)
66 want need   **68 buy** pay for   **70 harder matched** greater the enemy   **71 presageth**
foretells   **happy** fortunate   **73 Two . . . name** Edmund, second Duke of Somerset, killed at
the 1455 battle of St. Albans (his head appears in Act 1 Scene 1), and his son Henry, third
duke, beheaded in 1464 for his Lancastrian sympathies   **78 to right** for justice   **79 nature**
natural instinct   **81 Father** father-in-law   **83 ruinate** ruin   **84 lime** stick, join   **85 trowest**
thou do you think   **86 blunt** rough, ignorant   **87 bend** aim, direct

Perhaps thou wilt object my holy oath:
90   To keep that oath were more impiety
Than Jephthah, when he sacrificed his daughter.
I am so sorry for my trespass made
That, to deserve well at my brother's hands,
I here proclaim myself thy mortal foe,
95   With resolution, wheresoe'er I meet thee —
As I will meet thee, if thou stir abroad —
To plague thee for thy foul misleading me.
And so, proud-hearted Warwick, I defy thee,
And to my brother turn my blushing cheeks.—
100   Pardon me, Edward, I will make amends.—
And, Richard, do not frown upon my faults,
For I will henceforth be no more unconstant.

KING EDWARD IV   Now welcome more, and ten times more
        beloved,
Than if thou never hadst deserved our hate.
105 GLOUCESTER   Welcome, good Clarence, this is brotherlike.
WARWICK   O passing traitor, perjured and unjust!
KING EDWARD IV   What, Warwick, wilt thou leave the town and
        fight?
Or shall we beat the stones about thine ears?
WARWICK   Alas, I am not cooped here for defence.
110   I will away towards Barnet presently,
And bid thee battle, Edward, if thou dar'st.
KING EDWARD IV   Yes, Warwick, Edward dares, and leads the
        way.—
Lords, to the field. Saint George and victory!

                Exeunt [King Edward and his company]. March.
                        Warwick and his company follows

---

89 object bring up, urge as an objection   **91 Jephthah . . . daughter** biblical character who
vowed that if the Israelites defeated the Ammonites in battle he would sacrifice the first thing
he saw on his return home, little realizing that it would mean having to kill his own daughter
(Judges 11)   **92 trespass** wrong, crime   **96 abroad** i.e. outside Coventry   **99 blushing** i.e.
in shame   **102 unconstant** changeable, disloyal   **106 passing** surpassing, extreme
109 cooped protectively enclosed   **110 Barnet** town about ten miles north of London
(seventy-five miles southeast of Coventry, but Shakespeare has compressed various historical
events for dramatic purposes; the action between this and the next scene is virtually
continuous)   **presently** immediately

[Act 5 Scene 2]   *running scene 18*

Alarum and excursions. Enter Edward bringing forth Warwick
wounded

KING EDWARD IV   So, lie thou there. Die thou, and die our fear,
For Warwick was a bug that feared us all.
Now, Montague, sit fast: I seek for thee,
That Warwick's bones may keep thine company.   *Exit*

5   WARWICK   Ah, who is nigh? Come to me, friend or foe,
And tell me who is victor, York or Warwick?
Why ask I that? My mangled body shows,
My blood, my want of strength, my sick heart shows,
That I must yield my body to the earth
10   And, by my fall, the conquest to my foe.
Thus yields the cedar to the axe's edge,
Whose arms gave shelter to the princely eagle,
Under whose shade the ramping lion slept,
Whose top-branch overpeered Jove's spreading tree
15   And kept low shrubs from winter's powerful wind.
These eyes, that now are dimmed with death's black veil,
Have been as piercing as the midday sun,
To search the secret treasons of the world.
The wrinkles in my brows, now filled with blood,
20   Were likened oft to kingly sepulchres,
For who lived king, but I could dig his grave?
And who durst smile when Warwick bent his brow?
Lo, now my glory smeared in dust and blood.
My parks, my walks, my manors that I had,
25   Even now forsake me; and of all my lands
Is nothing left me but my body's length.

5.2   *Location: the battlefield, near Barnet, ten miles north of London*   **2 bug**
imaginary terror, bogeyman   **feared** frightened   **3 sit fast** be on guard, secure yourself
4 That so that   **11 cedar** the tallest of evergreen trees was a popular symbol of sovereignty,
like the **eagle** and the **lion**   **12 arms** branches   **13 ramping** rearing fiercely onto its hind legs
14 overpeered peered over/lorded over, outranked   **Jove's spreading tree** the oak, the tree
associated with the Roman king of the gods   **18 search** seek out, discern/probe   **22 bent his**
brow frowned   **24 parks** private hunting grounds   **walks** pathways of garden or park

Why, what is pomp, rule, reign, but earth and dust?
And live we how we can, yet die we must.

Enter Oxford and Somerset

SOMERSET   Ah, Warwick, Warwick, wert thou as we are,
30   We might recover all our loss again.
The queen from France hath brought a puissant power.
Even now we heard the news. Ah, couldst thou fly.

WARWICK   Why, then I would not fly. Ah, Montague,
If thou be there, sweet brother, take my hand
35   And with thy lips keep in my soul awhile.
Thou lov'st me not, for, brother, if thou didst,
Thy tears would wash this cold congealèd blood
That glues my lips and will not let me speak.
Come quickly, Montague, or I am dead.

40   SOMERSET   Ah, Warwick, Montague hath breathed his last,
And to the latest gasp cried out for Warwick
And said 'Commend me to my valiant brother.'
And more he would have said, and more he spoke,
Which sounded like a cannon in a vault,
45   That mought not be distinguished, but at last
I well might hear, delivered with a groan,
'O, farewell, Warwick!'

WARWICK   Sweet rest his soul. Fly, lords, and save yourselves,
For Warwick bids you all farewell to meet in heaven.   *Dies*
50   OXFORD   Away, away, to meet the queen's great power.

Here they bear away his body.   Exeunt

[Act 5 Scene 3]   *running scene 18 continues*

*Flourish. Enter King Edward in triumph, with Richard, Clarence and
the rest*

KING EDWARD IV   Thus far our fortune keeps an upward course,
And we are graced with wreaths of victory.

---

27 pomp splendor, luxury   **31 puissant power** powerful army   **35 with . . . awhile** i.e. kiss
me; at death the soul was thought to escape through the mouth   **45 mought** might
5.3   *triumph* a display of victorious celebration

But, in the midst of this bright-shining day,
I spy a black, suspicious, threat'ning cloud,
5   That will encounter with our glorious sun,
Ere he attain his easeful western bed.
I mean, my lords, those powers that the queen
Hath raised in Gallia have arrived our coast
And, as we hear, march on to fight with us.
10 CLARENCE   A little gale will soon disperse that cloud
And blow it to the source from whence it came.
Thy very beams will dry those vapours up,
For every cloud engenders not a storm.
GLOUCESTER   The queen is valued thirty thousand strong,
15   And Somerset with Oxford fled to her:
If she have time to breathe, be well assured
Her faction will be full as strong as ours.
KING EDWARD IV   We are advertised by our loving friends
That they do hold their course toward Tewkesbury.
20   We, having now the best at Barnet field,
Will thither straight, for willingness rids way,
And as we march, our strength will be augmented
In every county as we go along.
Strike up the drum, cry 'Courage!' and away.   *Exeunt*

[Act 5 Scene 4]   *running scene 19*

*Flourish. March. Enter the Queen, young Edward, Somerset, Oxford
and Soldiers*

QUEEN MARGARET   Great lords, wise men ne'er sit and wail their
    loss,
But cheerly seek how to redress their harms.
What though the mast be now blown overboard,
The cable broke, the holding-anchor lost,

8 **Gallia** France   14 **valued** estimated to be   16 **breathe** rest, gather her strength
18 **advertised** informed   19 **Tewkesbury** town in Gloucestershire   21 **rids way** makes the
journey seem shorter   **5.4   *Location: near Tewkesbury, in Gloucestershire***   2 **cheerly**
cheerfully, optimistically   4 **holding-anchor** i.e. anchor, used to secure a ship by holding fast
to the bottom of the sea

5   And half our sailors swallowed in the flood?
     Yet lives our pilot still. Is't meet that he
     Should leave the helm and like a fearful lad,
     With tearful eyes add water to the sea
     And give more strength to that which hath too much,
10   Whiles, in his moan, the ship splits on the rock,
     Which industry and courage might have saved?
     Ah, what a shame! Ah, what a fault were this!
     Say Warwick was our anchor: what of that?
     And Montague our topmast: what of him?
15   Our slaughtered friends the tackles: what of these?
     Why, is not Oxford here another anchor?
     And Somerset another goodly mast?
     The friends of France our shrouds and tacklings?
     And, though unskilful, why not Ned and I
20   For once allowed the skilful pilot's charge?
     We will not from the helm to sit and weep,
     But keep our course, though the rough wind say no,
     From shelves and rocks that threaten us with wreck.
     As good to chide the waves as speak them fair.
25   And what is Edward but a ruthless sea?
     What Clarence but a quicksand of deceit?
     And Richard but a ragged fatal rock?
     All these the enemies to our poor bark.
     Say you can swim, alas, 'tis but a while:
30   Tread on the sand, why, there you quickly sink,
     Bestride the rock, the tide will wash you off,
     Or else you famish, that's a three-fold death.
     This speak I, lords, to let you understand,
     If case some one of you would fly from us,
35   That there's no hoped-for mercy with the brothers
     More than with ruthless waves, with sands and rocks.

---

5 flood sea   **6 pilot** captain, i.e. Henry   **meet** right, fitting   **10 in his moan** as he laments
11 industry hard work   **15 tackles** rigging   **18 shrouds** ropes that brace and support the
mast   **19 Ned** i.e. Edward, Henry and Margaret's son   **20 charge** responsibility   **21 from**
leave   **23 shelves** sandbanks   **27 ragged** jagged, uneven   **28 bark** ship   **31 Bestride** sit
upon, straddle

Why, courage then: what cannot be avoided
'Twere childish weakness to lament or fear.

PRINCE EDWARD   Methinks a woman of this valiant spirit
40   Should, if a coward heard her speak these words,
Infuse his breast with magnanimity
And make him, naked, foil a man at arms.
I speak not this as doubting any here,
For did I but suspect a fearful man
45   He should have leave to go away betimes,
Lest in our need he might infect another
And make him of like spirit to himself.
If any such be here — as God forbid —
Let him depart before we need his help.

50   OXFORD   Women and children of so high a courage,
And warriors faint: why, 'twere perpetual shame.
O, brave young prince, thy famous grandfather
Doth live again in thee: long mayst thou live
To bear his image and renew his glories!

55   SOMERSET   And he that will not fight for such a hope,
Go home to bed, and like the owl by day,
If he arise, be mocked and wondered at.

QUEEN MARGARET   Thanks, gentle Somerset. Sweet Oxford,
thanks.

PRINCE EDWARD   And take his thanks that yet hath nothing else.

Enter a Messenger

60   MESSENGER   Prepare you, lords, for Edward is at hand.
Ready to fight: therefore be resolute.   [*He may exit*]

OXFORD   I thought no less: it is his policy
To haste thus fast, to find us unprovided.

SOMERSET   But he's deceived: we are in readiness.

65   QUEEN MARGARET   This cheers my heart, to see your
forwardness.

---

41 magnanimity greatness of spirit   **42 naked** unarmed   **foil . . . arms** defeat an armed man
in combat   **45 betimes** at once   **50 Women and children** i.e. Margaret and Edward
52 grandfather i.e. Henry V   **59 his** i.e. Edward's   **that yet** who as yet   **62 policy** stratagem,
cunning   **63 unprovided** unprepared   **65 forwardness** eagerness, readiness

OXFORD   Here pitch our battle, hence we will not budge.

Flourish and march. Enter Edward, Richard, Clarence and Soldiers

KING EDWARD IV   Brave followers, yonder stands the thorny
    wood,

Which by the heavens' assistance and your strength,

Must by the roots be hewn up yet ere night.

70   I need not add more fuel to your fire,

For well I wot ye blaze to burn them out.

Give signal to the fight, and to it, lords!

QUEEN MARGARET   Lords, knights, and gentlemen, what I
    should say

My tears gainsay, for every word I speak,

75   Ye see I drink the water of my eye.

Therefore no more but this: Henry, your sovereign,

Is prisoner to the foe, his state usurped,

His realm a slaughter-house, his subjects slain,

His statutes cancelled and his treasure spent,

80   And yonder is the wolf that makes this spoil.

You fight in justice. Then, in God's name, lords,

Be valiant and give signal to the fight.

        Alarum, retreat, excursions.   Exeunt

[Act 5 Scene 5]   *running scene 19 continues*

*Flourish. Enter Edward, Richard [and] Clarence [with] Queen, Oxford,
Somerset, [prisoners]*

KING EDWARD IV   Now here a period of tumultuous broils.

Away with Oxford to Hames Castle straight.

For Somerset, off with his guilty head.

Go, bear them hence: I will not hear them speak.

5 OXFORD   For my part, I'll not trouble thee with words.

SOMERSET   Nor I, but stoop with patience to my fortune.

        Exeunt [Oxford and Somerset, guarded]

---

66 pitch our battle set up, deploy our army   **71 wot** know   **blaze** burn with zeal,
excitement   **74 gainsay** contradict   **77 state** sovereignty   **80 spoil** destruction, pillage
5.5   1 a period an end   **broils** turmoil, confused fighting   **2 Hames** now Ham, a town on
the River Somme near Calais   **straight** immediately   **6 stoop** submit

QUEEN MARGARET   So part we sadly in this troublous world,
To meet with joy in sweet Jerusalem.

KING EDWARD IV   Is proclamation made that who finds Edward
10   Shall have a high reward, and he his life?

GLOUCESTER   It is, and lo where youthful Edward comes!

Enter [Soldiers with] the Prince

KING EDWARD IV   Bring forth the gallant, let us hear him speak.
What? Can so young a thorn begin to prick?
Edward, what satisfaction canst thou make
15   For bearing arms, for stirring up my subjects,
And all the trouble thou hast turned me to?

PRINCE EDWARD   Speak like a subject, proud ambitious York.
Suppose that I am now my father's mouth.
Resign thy chair, and where I stand kneel thou,
20   Whilst I propose the selfsame words to thee,
Which, traitor, thou wouldst have me answer to.

QUEEN MARGARET   Ah, that thy father had been so resolved!

GLOUCESTER   That you might still have worn the petticoat,
And ne'er have stol'n the breech from Lancaster.

25   PRINCE EDWARD   Let Aesop fable in a winter's night,
His currish riddles sorts not with this place.

GLOUCESTER   By heaven, brat, I'll plague ye for that word.

QUEEN MARGARET   Ay, thou wast born to be a plague to men.

GLOUCESTER   For God's sake, take away this captive scold.

30   PRINCE EDWARD   Nay, take away this scolding crookback rather.

KING EDWARD IV   Peace, wilful boy, or I will charm your tongue.

CLARENCE   Untutored lad, thou art too malapert.

PRINCE EDWARD   I know my duty. You are all undutiful:
Lascivious Edward, and thou perjured George,
35   And thou misshapen Dick, I tell ye all

---

8 Jerusalem i.e. heaven   **9 who** whoever   **10 he** i.e. Edward   **11 lo** look   **12 gallant** fine
young man (usually applied to a fashionable man about town)   **14 satisfaction** amends,
atonement   **19 chair** throne   **24 breech** breeches, trousers   **25 Aesop** the Greek writer of
moral fables concerning animals was a slave and reputedly hunchbacked   **fable** tell tales
26 currish snarling, contemptible, cynical/about animals   **sorts not** are not in keeping
29 scold verbally abusive woman   **31 charm** subdue, silence with a charm   **32 malapert**
impudent   **35 Dick** possibly plays on the sense of "penis"

I am your better, traitors as ye are,
And thou usurp'st my father's right and mine.

KING EDWARD IV   Take that, the likeness of this railer
here.   *Stabs him*

GLOUCESTER   Sprawl'st thou? Take that to end thy agony.
                                          Richard stabs him

40 CLARENCE   And there's for twitting me with perjury.
                                          Clarence stabs him

QUEEN MARGARET   O, kill me too!

GLOUCESTER   Marry, and shall.   *Offers to kill her*

KING EDWARD IV   Hold, Richard, hold, for we have done too
much.

GLOUCESTER   Why should she live to fill the world with words?

45 KING EDWARD IV   What, doth she swoon? Use means for her
recovery.

GLOUCESTER   Clarence, excuse me to the king my brother.
I'll hence to London on a serious matter.
Ere ye come there, be sure to hear some news.

CLARENCE   What? What?

50 GLOUCESTER   Tower, the Tower.   *Exit*

QUEEN MARGARET   O Ned, sweet Ned! Speak to thy mother, boy.
Canst thou not speak? O, traitors, murderers!
They that stabbed Caesar shed no blood at all,
Did not offend, nor were not worthy blame,

55 If this foul deed were by to equal it.
He was a man; this, in respect, a child,
And men ne'er spend their fury on a child.
What's worse than murderer, that I may name it?
No, no, my heart will burst, an if I speak —

60 And I will speak, that so my heart may burst.
Butchers and villains, bloody cannibals!
How sweet a plant have you untimely cropped.

---

38 likeness image   **railer** abusive ranter (i.e. Margaret)   **39 Sprawl'st thou?** Do you thrash,
writhe around?   **40 twitting** taunting/rebuking   **42 Marry, and shall** I shall, by the Virgin
Mary   *Offers* attempts   **48 be sure** expect   **55 by . . . it** there to compare with it
56 respect comparison   **62 untimely** prematurely

You have no children, butchers! If you had,
The thought of them would have stirred up remorse.
65 But if you ever chance to have a child,
Look in his youth to have him so cut off
As, deathmen, you have rid this sweet young prince.

KING EDWARD IV   Away with her: go, bear her hence perforce.

QUEEN MARGARET   Nay, never bear me hence, dispatch me here:
70 Here sheathe thy sword, I'll pardon thee my death.
What, wilt thou not? Then, Clarence, do it thou.

CLARENCE   By heaven, I will not do thee so much ease.

QUEEN MARGARET   Good Clarence, do, sweet Clarence, do thou
do it.

CLARENCE   Didst thou not hear me swear I would not do it?

75 QUEEN MARGARET   Ay, but thou usest to forswear thyself.
'Twas sin before, but now 'tis charity.
What, wilt thou not? Where is that devil's butcher, Richard?
Hard-favoured Richard? Richard, where art thou?
Thou art not here; murder is thy alms-deed:
80 Petitioners for blood thou ne'er put'st back.

KING EDWARD IV   Away, I say: I charge ye, bear her hence.

QUEEN MARGARET   So come to you and yours, as to this prince.

Exit Queen, [dragged out by Soldiers]

KING EDWARD IV   Where's Richard gone?

CLARENCE   To London all in post and, as I guess,
85 To make a bloody supper in the Tower.

KING EDWARD IV   He's sudden if a thing comes in his head.
Now march we hence. Discharge the common sort
With pay and thanks, and let's away to London
And see our gentle queen how well she fares:
90 By this, I hope, she hath a son for me.   *Exeunt*

---

63 **have no** cannot possibly have   64 **remorse** pity   66 **Look** expect   67 **rid** killed
68 **perforce** forcibly   69 **dispatch** kill   70 **Here** i.e. in my body   72 **ease** comfort, release
75 **usest** are accustomed   **forswear thyself** perjure yourself, break your word   78 **Hard-favoured** ugly   79 **alms-deed** act of charity   80 **put'st back** rejected, turned away   82 **So come to** may the same happen to   86 **sudden** swift, impulsive   87 **common sort** ordinary
soldiers

[Act 5 Scene 6]   *running scene 20*

Enter Henry the Sixth and Richard, with the Lieutenant, on the walls

GLOUCESTER   Good day, my lord. What, at your book so hard?

KING HENRY VI   Ay, my good lord — my lord, I should say rather.
'Tis sin to flatter. 'Good' was little better.
'Good Gloucester' and 'good devil' were alike,
5   And both preposterous: therefore, not 'good lord'.

GLOUCESTER   Sirrah, leave us to ourselves: we must confer.

                                              [*Exit Lieutenant*]

KING HENRY VI   So flies the reckless shepherd from the wolf,
So first the harmless sheep doth yield his fleece
And next his throat unto the butcher's knife.
10   What scene of death hath Roscius now to act?

GLOUCESTER   Suspicion always haunts the guilty mind,
The thief doth fear each bush an officer.

KING HENRY VI   The bird that hath been limèd in a bush
With trembling wings misdoubteth every bush;
15   And I, the hapless male to one sweet bird,
Have now the fatal object in my eye
Where my poor young was limed, was caught and killed.

GLOUCESTER   Why, what a peevish fool was that of Crete,
That taught his son the office of a fowl!
20   And yet, for all his wings, the fool was drowned.

KING HENRY VI   I, Daedalus, my poor boy, Icarus,
Thy father, Minos, that denied our course,

5.6   *Location: the Tower of London*   1 book probably prayer book or Bible   **3 better** i.e.
than flattery   **5 preposterous** an inversion of the natural order   **6 Sirrah** sir (used to an
inferior)   **7 reckless** negligent, careless   **10 Roscius** famous first-century Roman actor
11 Suspicion apprehension of something evil   **13 limèd** trapped with birdlime, a sticky
substance spread on branches to snare birds   **14 misdoubteth** suspects, fears   **15 male**
father   **bird** offspring   **16 fatal** deadly/fateful   **object . . . eye** sight, scene in my mind's eye/
thing, person before me (or, conceivably, Gloucester has already drawn the **weapon** Henry goes
on to refer to)   **17 Where** in which/by whom   **18 peevish** foolish, childish   **fool . . . fowl**
Icarus and his father, **Daedalus**, tried to escape imprisonment in Crete using wings Daedalus
had made out of feathers and wax; **Icarus** flew too close to the sun, the wax melted and he fell
to his death   **19 office** function, role   **20 fool** continues the punning on **fowl**   **22 Minos** the
King of Crete, who imprisoned **Daedalus** and **Icarus**   **course** departure

The sun that seared the wings of my sweet boy,
Thy brother Edward, and thyself the sea
25   Whose envious gulf did swallow up his life.
Ah, kill me with thy weapon, not with words!
My breast can better brook thy dagger's point
Than can my ears that tragic history.
But wherefore dost thou come? Is't for my life?

30   GLOUCESTER   Think'st thou I am an executioner?

KING HENRY VI   A persecutor I am sure, thou art,
If murdering innocents be executing,
Why then, thou art an executioner.

GLOUCESTER   Thy son I killed for his presumption.

35   KING HENRY VI   Hadst thou been killed when first thou didst
            presume,
Thou hadst not lived to kill a son of mine.
And thus I prophesy, that many a thousand,
Which now mistrust no parcel of my fear,
And many an old man's sigh and many a widow's,
40   And many an orphan's water-standing eye —
Men for their sons, wives for their husbands,
Orphans for their parents' timeless death —
Shall rue the hour that ever thou wast born.
The owl shrieked at thy birth — an evil sign —
45   The night-crow cried, aboding luckless time,
Dogs howled, and hideous tempest shook down trees,
The raven rooked her on the chimney's top,
And chatt'ring pies in dismal discords sung.
Thy mother felt more than a mother's pain,
50   And yet brought forth less than a mother's hope,
To wit, an indigested and deformèd lump,

23 sun likened here to Edward, the sun alludes to the Yorkist emblem   25 envious malicious,
evil   gulf whirlpool/voracious depths   27 brook endure, take   28 history story
38 mistrust . . . fear apprehend, suspect no part of what I fear (will happen)   40 water-
standing filled, flooded with tears   42 timeless untimely, premature   45 night-crow literary
name for a bird whose nighttime croak was an evil omen   aboding forewarning   47 rooked
her cowered, huddled (perhaps with play on "rook," a type of bird)   48 pies magpies (also
thought to be bad luck)   dismal ominous, sinister   49 pain labor pains   51 To wit that is to
say   indigested shapeless

Not like the fruit of such a goodly tree.
Teeth hadst thou in thy head when thou wast born,
To signify thou cam'st to bite the world.
55 And if the rest be true which I have heard,
Thou cam'st—
GLOUCESTER   I'll hear no more: die, prophet, in thy speech,
For this amongst the rest, was I ordained.   *Stabs him*
KING HENRY VI   Ay, and for much more slaughter after this.
60 O, God forgive my sins and pardon thee!   *Dies*
GLOUCESTER   What? Will the aspiring blood of Lancaster
Sink in the ground? I thought it would have mounted.
See how my sword weeps for the poor king's death.
O, may such purple tears be alway shed
65 From those that wish the downfall of our house.
If any spark of life be yet remaining,
Down, down to hell, and say I sent thee thither,
I, that have neither pity, love, nor fear.   *Stabs him again*
Indeed, 'tis true that Henry told me of,
70 For I have often heard my mother say
I came into the world with my legs forward.
Had I not reason, think ye, to make haste,
And seek their ruin that usurped our right?
The midwife wondered and the women cried
75 'O, Jesus bless us, he is born with teeth!'
And so I was, which plainly signified
That I should snarl and bite and play the dog.
Then, since the heavens have shaped my body so,
Let hell make crook'd my mind to answer it.
80 I have no brother, I am like no brother.
And this word 'love', which greybeards call divine,
Be resident in men like one another
And not in me: I am myself alone.

---

53 Teeth . . . born this was considered abnormal and ominous   **58 ordained** destined
63 weeps i.e. drips blood   **64 purple** blood-colored   **alway** always   **69 that . . . of** what
Henry said about me/what Henry said to me   **71 came . . . forward** i.e. was a breech birth,
where the baby is born feet first   **74 wondered** was amazed   **79 answer** correspond to
81 greybeards wise old men   **82 like** who resemble

Clarence, beware, thou keep'st me from the light,
85   But I will sort a pitchy day for thee,
For I will buzz abroad such prophecies
That Edward shall be fearful of his life,
And then, to purge his fear, I'll be thy death.
King Henry and the prince his son are gone.
90   Clarence, thy turn is next, and then the rest,
Counting myself but bad till I be best.
I'll throw thy body in another room
And triumph, Henry, in thy day of doom.

Exit [with the body]

[Act 5 Scene 7]   *running scene 21*

Flourish. Enter King, Queen, Clarence, Richard, Hastings, Nurse [with the young Prince] and Attendants

KING EDWARD IV   Once more we sit in England's royal throne,
Repurchased with the blood of enemies.
What valiant foemen, like to autumn's corn,
Have we mowed down in tops of all their pride!
5   Three Dukes of Somerset, three-fold renowned
For hardy and undoubted champions,
Two Cliffords, as the father and the son,
And two Northumberlands: two braver men
Ne'er spurred their coursers at the trumpet's sound.
10   With them, the two brave bears, Warwick and Montague,
That in their chains fettered the kingly lion
And made the forest tremble when they roared.
Thus have we swept suspicion from our seat

---

84 light the crown (an image drawn from the Yorkist sun)   **85 sort** arrange/set   **pitchy** black as pitch (a tarlike substance)   **86 buzz abroad** spread rumors in the world   **prophecies** omens, forewarnings   **87 of** for   **91 bad** worthless, contemptible   **93 doom** judgment, i.e. your death   **5.7** *Location: the royal court, London*   **4 in tops** at the height   **6 hardy** bold, resolute   **undoubted** unquestionable/fearless   **champions** warriors, men of valor   **7 as** namely   **9 coursers** powerful horses used in war   **10 bears** refers to Warwick's family emblem, a bear chained to a ragged staff   **11 in** with   **fettered** shackled   **13 suspicion** apprehension, anxiety   **seat** throne

And made our footstool of security.—

15   Come hither, Bess, and let me kiss my boy.—

Young Ned, for thee, thine uncles and myself

Have in our armours watched the winter's night,

Went all afoot in summer's scalding heat,

That thou mightst repossess the crown in peace,

20   And of our labours thou shalt reap the gain.

GLOUCESTER   I'll blast his harvest, if your head were laid,   *Aside*

For yet I am not looked on in the world.

This shoulder was ordained so thick to heave,

And heave it shall some weight, or break my back.

25   Work thou the way, and that shalt execute.

KING EDWARD IV   Clarence and Gloucester, love my lovely queen,

And kiss your princely nephew, brothers both.

CLARENCE   The duty that I owe unto your majesty

I seal upon the lips of this sweet babe.   *Kisses the baby*

30   QUEEN ELIZABETH   Thanks, noble Clarence. Worthy brother,

thanks.

GLOUCESTER   And that I love the tree from whence thou

sprang'st,

Witness the loving kiss I give the fruit.—   *Kisses the baby*

To say the truth, so Judas kissed his master   *Aside*

And cried 'All hail!' whenas he meant all harm.

35   KING EDWARD IV   Now am I seated as my soul delights,

Having my country's peace and brothers' loves.

CLARENCE   What will your grace have done with Margaret?

Reynard, her father, to the King of France

Hath pawned the Sicils and Jerusalem,

40   And hither have they sent it for her ransom.

---

17 watched kept watch, remained awake throughout   **18 all afoot** on foot, as soldiers/all over the place   **21 blast** blight, wither   **head** plays the sense of "head of wheat"   **laid** cut off (maintains the crop image)   **22 looked on** held in high regard   **23 thick** sturdy (referring to his hunched back)   **25 Work** devise (addressed to himself)   **that** i.e. his shoulder   **execute** carry it out (with grim play on the sense of "put to death")   **30 brother** i.e. brother-in-law **31 that** because   **tree** i.e. the family of York, his own stock   **33 Judas . . . master** Judas famously kissed Christ and betrayed him   **34 whenas** although   **38 Reynard . . . Jerusalem** Margaret's father, Reignier, was the titular King of Sicily, Naples (**the Sicils**), and Jerusalem; spelling "Reynard" may imply the craft of a fox   **40 it** i.e. the money raised

KING EDWARD IV   Away with her, and waft her hence to France.
And now what rests but that we spend the time
With stately triumphs, mirthful comic shows,
Such as befits the pleasure of the court.
45   Sound drums and trumpets! Farewell sour annoy,
For here I hope begins our lasting joy.   *Exeunt all*

---

41 waft convey by sea   **43 triumphs** public processions celebrating victory   **45 sour annoy** bitter trouble

TEXTUAL NOTES

O = First Octavo text of 1595
Q3 = Third Quarto text of 1619
F = First Folio text of 1623
F2 = a correction introduced in the Second Folio text of 1632
F3 = a correction introduced in the Third Folio text of 1663–64
Ed = a correction introduced by a later editor
SD = Stage direction
SH = Speech heading (i.e. speaker's names)

List of parts = Ed

1.1.2 SH YORK = O. F = *Pl. or Plat. (throughout)* **106 Thy** = O. F = My
  171 hear me = F3. F = heare **262 with me** = O. F = me **264 from** = O. F =
  to **276 SD** *Flourish* printed as part of the entrance direction to the next scene *in* F
1.2.47 SD *a Messenger* = O. F = *Gabriel (the name of an actor in*
  Shakespeare's company) **49 SH MESSENGER** = O. F = *Gabriel*
2.1.96 recount = F3. F = tecompt **130 an idle** = O. F = a lazie
2.2.89 Since = F2. F = *Cla.* Since *(assigning lines 89–92 to George of Clarence)*
  152 dauphin *spelled* Dolphin *in* F **164 SH GEORGE** = O. F = *Cla.*
2.5.89 stratagems = F3. F = Stragems **90 Erroneous** = F2. F = Erreoneous
  119 E'en = Ed. F = Men
2.6.8 The . . . flies = O. *Not in* F **44 SH EDWARD See . . . is.** = O. *Assigned*
  to Richard in F **60 his** = O. F = is **91 sinew** *spelled* sinow *in* F
3.1.0 SD *two Keepers* = O. F = *Sinklo, and Humfrey (the names of actors in*
  Shakespeare's company) **1 SH FIRST KEEPER** = Ed. F = *Sink. or Sinklo.*
  (throughout) **5 SH SECOND KEEPER** = Ed. F = *Hum. throughout*
  17 wast = F3. F = was **30 Is** = F2. F = I: **55 that** = O. *Not in* F
3.2.8 SH GLOUCESTER F = *Rich.* **18 SH LADY GREY** = Ed. F = *Wid.*
  84 looks do = F2. F = Looks doth **124 honourably** = O. F = honourable
3.3.126 external = F. O = eternall
4.1.93 thy = O. F = the
4.2.15 towns = Ed. F = Towne
4.4.17 wean *spelled* waine *in* F
4.5.4 stands = Ed. F = stand **8 Comes** = Ed. F = Come
5.1.78 an = F2. F = in
5.7.5 renowned = Q3. F = Renowne **30 SH QUEEN ELIZABETH** = O. F =
  Cla. **Thanks** = O. F = Thanke

SYNOPSES OF THE PLOTS OF *HENRY VI PART I, PART II,* AND *PART III*

HENRY VI PART I

ACT 1

Following the death of his father, Henry V, the young Henry VI is proclaimed king under the protectorship of his uncles, the Dukes of Gloucester and Exeter. There is conflict between Gloucester and his long-term rival, the Bishop of Winchester, and their respective supporters. News arrives of renewed war with France, and the king's uncles move to secure and reorganize the kingdom, sending Bedford to the aid of Talbot—a legendary warrior, much feared by the French—the leader of the English forces. In France, the Bastard of Orléans introduces the under-siege dauphin, Charles, to Joan la Pucelle, a maid who claims she has had visions that she must lead the French in battle. He challenges her to single combat and she wins, assuring the dauphin that she will break the siege and defeat the English. In London, Gloucester and Winchester renew their conflict: Winchester bars Gloucester from entering the Tower, and both parties come to blows, finally parted by the Lord Mayor. In France, Talbot is released in exchange for a French lord, and fights with Joan when the French attack. She wins, but spares him, and the French celebrate having Orléans back under their control.

ACT 2

Talbot and other English lords immediately launch a surprise attack and retake the city. The dauphin feels Joan has betrayed him, but she urges him to have more faith in her. The French flee and the English bury their dead lords. A Messenger summons Talbot to the Countess of Auvergne, who has heard of his renown and wants to see him in person. He goes to her castle, where she tells him he has walked into a trap, but he says he is part of a much larger power than she can cope with and his army arrives to rescue him. Richard Plantagenet declares his animosity toward the Duke of Somerset. Each adopts a rose as an emblem for his faction: white for York, red for Lancaster. Richard later visits his uncle, Mortimer, in prison, who tells him of his rightful claim to the English throne through the Mortimer line of his family.

ACT 3

Gloucester and Winchester continue their struggles, this time with both their factions engaging in an open brawl in parliament. The young king implores them to be friends, fearing for the nation's stability if they create civil unrest. Warwick urges Richard Plantagenet's right to be restored to his hereditary titles, which Henry grants, making him Duke of York. All swear amity and part but Exeter sees the falseness of their promises and fears the prophecy that Henry's reign would end in ruin will be too true. In France, Charles the dauphin, fortified by his alliance with the mysterious maid Joan la Pucelle (Joan of Arc), begins to dominate the battles. Talbot attempts to draw the French out of the walled city of Rouen to fight fairly in the field but they refuse. The English attack anyway and win, though Bedford is killed. Joan sees another strategy, and passionately persuades Burgundy, a disgruntled French lord fighting with the English, to come back to the French side, thus strengthening their forces. Henry arrives in France and is greeted by Talbot. Vernon and Basset, of the Houses of York and Lancaster respectively, and also arrived in France with the English party, quarrel bitterly.

ACT 4

Henry is crowned. A letter arrives telling of Burgundy's revolt, and Talbot is sent to deal with him. Richard Duke of York and Somerset come to Henry about the quarrel between their men, Vernon and Basset, asking that they be allowed to fight in open combat. Henry is surprised to hear of the dissension between the two houses, and refuses to take sides and choose one rose over the other, nonetheless taking a red rose of Lancaster, which York privately resents. Exeter again predicts civil war. Talbot marches on Bordeaux and becomes trapped between the city walls and the dauphin's army, which attacks from the rear. As a direct result of the continuing enmity between York and Somerset, both fail to supply reinforcements to Talbot and his troops. Talbot begs his son, John, not to fight but to no avail. The battle ensues and both are killed. Sir William Lucy comes to the French and requests the bodies of the Talbots, taking them away and vowing revenge.

ACT 5

Fortunes turn and Joan is captured and burned. An uneasy peace is concluded between England and France. In light of this, Gloucester engineers a politically astute marriage between Henry and the Earl of Armagnac's daughter. Winchester is created Cardinal. Meanwhile, in France, Suffolk is enchanted by Margaret, daughter of the Duke of Anjou. Suffolk woos her to be Henry's queen and in order to gain her father's consent cedes the newly conquered French territories of Anjou and Maine. Suffolk returns to England and persuades Henry, against opposition from the court, to marry Margaret and make her Queen of England.

HENRY VI PART II

ACT 1

Despite the recently concluded peace between England and France, dissension is rife within the English court. Suffolk brings Margaret to the king with a letter stating that she is to be exchanged for the territories of Anjou and Maine. Henry agrees and makes him Duke of Suffolk. Gloucester confides to the English nobles that he is outraged that the lands so hard won by his brother, Henry V, should be so lightly given back to the French. He prophesies the loss of France and leaves, and Cardinal Beaufort (Winchester), Somerset, and Buckingham, along with Suffolk, unite in their common aim to get rid of him. Salisbury, Warwick, and York unite to undo the powers of Suffolk and the Cardinal. York soliloquizes that the lost lands are his by rights, and opts to bide his time in the alliance he has forged. Gloucester dreams that his staff of office was broken by the Cardinal, and Eleanor, his wife, tells him she dreamed of being queen, which angers him. Eleanor is lured by a priest, John Hume, who is in the pay of Suffolk, to consult a sorcerer about her ambitions. Suffolk's influence, both at court and with the new Queen Margaret, intensifies. Petitioners come to seek Gloucester because one, Peter, accuses his master, Horner, of saying that York is the rightful king. They encounter Margaret and Suffolk, however, and tell them this, believing Suffolk to be Gloucester. Suffolk now knows he has ammunition against York. Henry and his court enter discussing the regency of France. Gloucester suggests York, but changes his mind to Somerset when he hears of the controversy. Margaret attacks Gloucester and Eleanor, questioning Gloucester's continued protectorship and accusing them of having ambitions on the crown. Gloucester orders Peter and Horner to settle the dispute in combat. Later, Eleanor meets the sorcerer Roger Bullingbrook and they raise spirits that give ambiguous answers to her questions about Henry's reign. York and Buckingham burst in on them and Eleanor and Hume are arrested for treason.

ACT 2

Henry and his party meet a man claiming to have been cured of blindness. Henry thinks it is a miracle, but Gloucester reveals the man to be a liar, his worldly wisdom contrasting with Henry's naive faith. York illustrates his claim to the throne to Warwick and Salisbury, and both men swear allegiance to him, convinced of his right. Eleanor is brought to trial and banished. Gloucester resigns his staff of office, allowing Henry to become king in his own right. Peter and Horner fight and Horner loses, confessing his treason as he dies. On her way to banishment, Eleanor warns Gloucester that the other nobles will conspire against him, but he believes his innocence puts him beyond their reach.

ACT 3

Henry meets with his lords and Somerset returns from France with the news of the loss of all English territories. York and others seize this opportunity to implicate Gloucester in the loss of France and to accuse him of treason. Gloucester is arrested and Henry grieves, knowing he is powerless to defend his innocent uncle. Suffolk, Margaret, the Cardinal, and York agree that Gloucester should be murdered. Meanwhile, there is a rebellion in Ireland and York is sent by Suffolk to deal with the crisis. York in soliloquy resolves to move against his enemies and strive for the throne, revealing that he has incited Jack Cade, a clothier posing as Mortimer, to promote further dissension by rebelling in Kent. Gloucester is murdered and the king turns against Suffolk, banishing him. Suffolk and Margaret, plainly in love with each other, share a passionate farewell. Cardinal Beaufort outlives his old enemy by only a few hours, dying in agony of body and soul.

ACT 4

Suffolk is captured at sea and beheaded, killed "by water" as Bullingbrook's prophecy had foretold. Jack Cade's rebellion begins in Kent. Cade speaks to the rabble claiming he will be the next king and will change the laws of England to suit the common man. Stafford and his brother attempt to quell the rebellion but are killed and Cade and his army drag their bodies to London. Margaret mourns over Suffolk's head, and, despite her denials, Henry believes that she loved Suffolk far more than she loves him. Hearing of the rebellion's approach he resolves to leave London for a while. Cade marches on London, and has Lord Saye killed for his encouragement of literacy. Cade and his followers run riot until Buckingham and Clifford arrive to quell the crowds, urging them to remember the glories of England under Henry V. The rabble is swayed and Cade flees, killed by Alexander Iden in Iden's garden in Kent. Henry is told that York has returned at the head of an army to remove Somerset, whom he has deemed a traitor.

ACT 5

York returns to claim the crown, supported by his sons Edward, Richard, and George (Clarence), and by Salisbury and Warwick, though he claims he only wants Somerset imprisoned. He is promised by Buckingham that this has already happened, but, seeing Somerset free, York becomes enraged and accuses Henry of weakness. The two sides take up arms, Henry supported by Margaret, Somerset, Buckingham, and the Cliffords. For the first time, Lancastrians face Yorkists at the battle of St. Albans. The play ends with the king and queen in flight and the Yorkists contemplating the crown.

HENRY VI PART III

ACT 1

Having won the battle of St. Albans and with Richard Plantagenet sitting on the throne of England, the Yorkists confront the Lancastrians. Partly admitting his claim to sovereignty is dubious, King Henry asks York that he be allowed to reign for his lifetime, after which the crown will pass to the House of York. York swears an oath in agreement, though Margaret is furious that Henry has disinherited his own son, Edward, Prince of Wales. Margaret vows to destroy York and his followers. She enlists the support of Clifford and others to raise an army. York and his sons discuss what has happened, all three urging their father to take the crown. York says he has sworn an oath, but Richard quickly talks him out of it. Margaret's forces meet with those of York in battle, during which York's youngest son, Rutland, is killed by Clifford. York is then captured by Margaret, Clifford, and Northumberland, taunted with details of his son's death—even offered a handkerchief dipped in Rutland's blood with which to wipe his tears—and brutally murdered.

ACT 2

Edward and Richard see three suns in the sky and take it as a sign that they, with Clarence, York's three sons, should unite and defeat the Lancastrians. They are informed of their father's murder and swear revenge, uniting with Warwick, who proclaims Edward the new Duke of York. York's head is set upon the gates of his own city, which appalls Henry, though Clifford and Margaret tell him to be without pity in his claim for what is his and his son's: the crown. Henry, however, retorts that "things ill-got had ever bad success." The Yorkists and Lancastrians trade insults and Henry tries to calm them but neither side will listen to him any longer. Both armies fight at Towton, and the fortunes of the battle ebb and flow between them. Richard seeks Clifford to take his revenge. Henry, isolated and all but forsaken, soliloquizes on the miseries of kingship, wishing himself a shepherd that he might live free from the treacherous world of the court. He sees a father who has mistakenly killed his own son and a son his father in the battle and laments that the nation's strife has become so desperate and inhumane. The Yorkists defeat the Lancastrians, and Henry, Margaret, and their son, Edward, are forced to flee to the north. Clifford is killed and his head set on the walls in place of York's. The Yorkists head to London to claim the throne.

ACT 3

Henry, returning to England from Scotland, is captured by two gamekeepers and brought to London, where he is placed in the Tower by the new King Edward. Lady Elizabeth Grey comes to see Edward to ask for her lands to be returned to her. Edward falls in love with her and asks her to marry him. Richard, in a powerful soliloquy, reveals that he has no allegiance to anyone but himself and that he will remove all who stand in his way to the throne. In France, Margaret and Warwick meet at the court of King Lewis. News reaches them that Edward has married Lady Grey, in spite of his earlier betrothal, instigated by Warwick, to King Lewis' sister, Lady Bona. This insult turns both Warwick and Lewis against Edward. Warwick pledges support to Margaret, offering her his daughter, Anne, as wife to her son, Prince Edward. Lewis gives Margaret troops to fight King Edward.

ACT 4

Edward's brothers are unhappy about his match with Lady Grey, not wanting to make enemies of Lewis and Warwick. They learn that Margaret and Warwick have joined forces and Clarence revolts to Warwick's side, seeking to marry Warwick's other daughter. Richard stays, "not for the love of Edward, but the crown." Warwick returns to England and joins with Clarence in support of Henry. They seize upon King Edward and take his crown, imprisoning him at the estate of Warwick's brother, the Archbishop of York. Lady Grey, now Queen Elizabeth, reveals that she is pregnant with Edward's child. Richard and Hastings rescue Edward and send him to Flanders. Warwick and Clarence release Henry from the Tower, and reinstate him as King of England. He asks to be king in name only, and confers the protectorship of the realm upon Warwick and Clarence. Seeing the young Earl of Richmond (also named Henry), Henry prophesies that the youth will prove to be England's savior. Hearing that Edward is in Flanders and fearing he will return to make war, Somerset and Oxford take Richmond to Brittany for his safety. Edward returns and retakes York, proclaiming himself king again. Warwick hears of Edward's approach toward London and leaves to muster his army. Henry is recaptured by Edward and Richard and sent to the Tower.

ACT 5

The forces of Edward and Warwick meet at Barnet, where Edward convinces Clarence to rejoin him. Warwick is killed in the ensuing battle. Margaret arrives in England with reinforcements, and is joined by Warwick's supporters, Somerset and Oxford. Her forces encounter Edward's for the last time at Tewkesbury, where she is defeated. Her son Edward is killed, she imprisoned, and Somerset and Oxford sent to execution. Richard goes to the Tower to murder Henry, who, knowing why he has come, prophesies that Richard will bring untold suffering to the country before the end. Henry taunts Richard, and Richard stabs and kills him in an angry rage. Over Henry's body Richard soliloquizes on his own rejection of all ties of brotherhood and his newly strengthened resolve to do away with Edward and Clarence and take the crown for himself. Edward's son is born and Richard and Clarence join the celebrations, kissing the child, though Richard has multiple asides in which he states that he means "all harm" to it and to his brothers. The play ends with King Edward calling for festivity "as befits the pleasure of the court." The Wars of the Roses seem finally to be over with the House of York victorious at last. Its new enemy, however, will come from within in events dramatized in Shakespeare's *Richard III.*

HENRY VI IN PERFORMANCE: THE RSC AND BEYOND

The best way to understand a Shakespeare play is to see it or ideally to participate in it. By examining a range of productions, we may gain a sense of the extraordinary variety of approaches and interpretations that are possible—a variety that gives Shakespeare his unique capacity to be reinvented and made "our contemporary" four centuries after his death.

We begin with a brief overview of the play's theatrical and cinematic life, offering historical perspectives on how it has been performed. We then analyze in more detail a series of productions staged over the last half-century by the Royal Shakespeare Company. The sense of dialogue between productions that can only occur when a company is dedicated to the revival and investigation of the Shakespeare canon over a long period, together with the uniquely comprehensive archival resource of promptbooks, program notes, reviews, and interviews held on behalf of the RSC at the Shakespeare Birthplace Trust in Stratford-upon-Avon, allows an "RSC stage history" to become a crucible in which the chemistry of the play can be explored.

We then go to the horse's mouth. Modern theater is dominated by the figure of the director. He or she must hold together the whole play, whereas the actor must concentrate on his or her part. The director's viewpoint is therefore especially valuable. Shakespeare's plasticity is wonderfully revealed when we hear the directors of two highly successful productions answering the same questions in very different ways. We also hear from the designer of one of these acclaimed productions about the challenges posed by mounting an ambitious cycle of historical plays.

FOUR CENTURIES OF *HENRY VI*: AN OVERVIEW

The three plays dealing with the reign of *Henry VI* have an unusual performance history. They are rarely revived—almost never individually—and are among the least performed of Shakespeare's canon. Yet when they are mounted, they are often high profile and audacious experiments, spreading several hours of history over a number of sittings. The relative paucity of performances perhaps contributes to the sense of anticipation and event that accompanies productions of the trilogy.

It is probable that the 1592 reference to "harey the vj" in the diary of Philip Henslowe refers to *Henry VI Part I*, and the 1595 octavo of *The True Tragedy of Richard, Duke of York* (*Henry VI Part III*) claims it was performed by the Earl of Pembroke's Men. Current consensus is that *Part II* and *Part III* were staged first, with *Part I* appearing later as a "prequel." We know little of these early stagings, but references in the literature of the period to the exploits of Talbot, as well as the famous reference to Shakespeare in *Greene's Groatsworth of Wit* paraphrasing a line from *Henry VI Part III*, suggest their popularity.[1] The plays are perhaps still most familiar to modern audiences for certain memorable lines quoted in different contexts: Laurence Olivier's seminal film of *Richard III* opens with a soliloquy augmented by lines from *Part III* (Act 3 Scene 2), and Richard Loncraine's *Richard III* similarly used "I can smile . . . and murder while I smile!" as its tagline.

The first performances of which we have a definite record took place in 1680 at Lincoln's Inn Theatre. Thomas Crowne became the first to offer a two-part adaptation, the format most frequently adopted even into the twenty-first century. Entitled *Henry the Sixth; The First Part, with the Murder of Humphrey, Duke of Glocester* [sic] and *The Miseries of Civil-War*, the plays, featuring Thomas Betterton as a heroic Humphrey and Lady Slingsby as Margaret, were a success. Following the action of *Part II* and *Part III*, the first play concentrates on the fall of Humphrey, while the second begins with Cade's rebellion and proceeds to the coronation of Edward. However popular the play, Crowne's own political leanings doomed it to failure:

Crowne, to use his own words, had mixed with the mutilated relics of Shakespeare's play "A little vinegar against the Pope" as well as a very thick coating of sickening sweet loyalty, and this was fatal. The offended Roman Catholics went to the King, who had found or was seeking conciliation with the Pope, and he at once suppressed the "new history play" in the midst of its success.[2]

Crowne appropriated the plays to provide commentary on current political affairs, particularly attacking civil dissension:

> Crowne's most substantial, and most remarkable, addition to the play was a scene involving soldiers who rob a "couple of seditious rogues" (i.e. supporters of civil war) and rape their daughters. The scene was played in the same comic vein as the Simpcox scenes, except this time the punishment for civil disobedience was more extreme. Before hanging them, the soldiers give the rogues a stern lesson on the consequences of rising up against the crown.[3]

Crowne's model was revived in the early eighteenth century. Ambrose Philips' adaptation *Humfrey, Duke of Gloucester* (1723) borrowed characters and situations from Shakespeare, but minimal dialogue. Here, "Gloucester was not just a Protestant hero but a model statesman" and the role of Eleanor was dramatically increased.[4] Even more interestingly, the play was restructured to make York (as an enemy of the Cardinal) the hero. Philips' play ended with Beaufort's death scene and Eleanor's pious forgiveness of her enemy.

Theophilus Cibber provided a continuation of Philips' play with his adaptation of *Part II* (from the Cade rebellion onward) and *Part III* into *The Historical Tragedy of Henry VI*. Intended as a prequel to his uncle Colley Cibber's *Richard III* (which anticipated Olivier in its interpolation of lines from *Henry VI Part III* into Richard's opening soliloquy), Theophilus' play was hampered by attempts to unify the two. The Lady Anne is introduced awkwardly, and the play ends with Henry still alive in the Tower, as Colley had used the murder to begin his *Richard III*. Theophilus shared Philips' interest in condemning civil war, and the two plays enjoyed some success, being revived in 1738 with Delane as Talbot and Mrs. Hallam as Joan of Arc at Covent Garden.

John Herman Merivale adapted the trilogy into a single play as a vehicle for Edmund Kean, which opened in December 1817. Entitled *Richard, Duke of York*, Kean took the title role and the production ended with his death at the hands of Margaret. Joan and Talbot were entirely cut, and John Hamilton Reynolds complained that "missing [Talbot] is like walking among the Elgin Marbles, and seeing an empty place where the Theseus had reclined."[5] Rutter and Hampton-Reeves point out, however, that the recent Napoleonic Wars may have complicated the resonances of Joan and Talbot too much for contemporary audiences.[6] Kean's York was the central concern:

> Kean stands like a tower. He is "all power, passion, self-will." His insinuations flow from his lips as "musical as is Apollo's lute." It is impossible to point out any peculiar and little felici-ties, where the whole piece of acting is of no mingled web. If we were to single a favourite part, we should chuse [i.e. choose] that in which he parts with his son, *Young Rutland*, just before the battle. It was pathetic to oppression. Our hearts swelled with the feeling of tears, which is a deeper feeling than the starting of them in the eye . . . His death was very great . . . The bodily functions wither up, and the mental faculties hold out, till they crack. It is an extinguishment, not a decay. The hand is agonized with death; the lip trembles, with the last breath, as we see the autumn leaf thrill in the cold wind of evening. The very eye-lid dies.[7]

There was little in the other performances to remark upon, however, and the play failed to thrive as a star vehicle when *Richard III* offered far richer opportunities.

The plays appeared individually in their first outings at Stratford-upon-Avon, finally allowing each to be evaluated on its own terms. Oswald Tearle produced *Part I* in 1889, in a heavily cut version that excelled in its historical pageantry and magnificent settings. Most notable was the reluctance to turn Joan into a villain:

By a little clever manipulation of the text, [she] is presented not as the designing adventuress who attempts to save her life at the expense of her fair fame, that Shakespeare drew, but the noble, inspired being that we all prefer to think she was.[8]

Most praise was reserved for Tearle, whose Talbot "realised the grand old battle hero of both Shakespeare and history."[9] A decade later, F. R. Benson mounted *Part II* in isolation, taking the part of Cardinal Beaufort, which allowed him a moving death scene. The text was followed reasonably closely and included the gruesome spectacle of bodies on poles for the rabble scenes. Oscar Asche quickly established Jack Cade as the standout role of this play:

The London street scenes were wonderfully effective, and in Mr. Asche Jack Cade had an appropriate exponent, a burly rebel of independent mind, whose rude but persuasive eloquence swayed the crowd readily.[10]

Also noted were Miss Robertson as the Duchess of Gloucester, who was particularly affecting in her scene of penance, and Mrs. Benson as an imperious and chafing Margaret. In the early years of the play at Stratford, this became the most revived part of the trilogy, appearing again in 1901 with a selection of other history plays. This time the discovery of Humphrey's murder stood out, and Mr. Weir's Apprentice was particularly praised. The variety of incident in the play worked both for and against the play's reputation, entertaining audiences while diminishing the play in comparison to more "significant" histories such as *Richard II* and *Henry V.*

In 1906, Benson became the first modern producer to stage all three parts of the trilogy, taking the role of Talbot himself in *Part I. Part III*, staged for the first time at Stratford and completing the Memorial Theatre's ambition to stage all of Shakespeare's plays, took place on a stage with fixed scenery and continuous action. The strongest scene was York's capture and torture at the hands of Margaret, for which Clarence Derwent's "dignity and patience left nothing to be desired."[11] There were some questionable omissions, such as the scene of the French court, which makes sense of Warwick's change of allegiance, and although Benson himself took the role of Richard in *Part II* and *Part III*, he rearranged the ending for the purposes of closure, bringing on the young Prince Edward to end the play on an optimistic note. While the production was praised, it was not revived, and after one further performance of Benson's *Part II* in 1909, the plays did not return to Stratford until after the founding of the modern RSC.

Perhaps because of the particular association of these plays with ideas of "Englishness," and no doubt in part because of the costs of running a trilogy, the *Henry VI* plays have one of the sparsest international histories of the whole Shakespeare canon. Barring some festival performances in the US and Canada, the plays have struggled to find the same broad audience accorded the *Richard* plays and the *Henry IV–V* cycle. Even in the UK, perhaps as a result of war-weariness, the few productions in the first half of the century failed to make an impression, though Rutter and Hampton-Reeves note that Robert Atkins' production for the Old Vic in 1923 was the first to make a new trilogy out of a two-part *Henry VI* followed by *Richard III*. Atkins' "most significant revision was to do not with war but with gender, for he rewrote Joan's part to make her more sympathetic; in his own words, he 'thought fit to rob St Joan of Arc of all unpleasant lines.' "[12] This was in line with George Bernard Shaw's feelings: in his *St. Joan* of the same year he attempted to answer Shakespeare by recasting Joan as a hero and Warwick as a calculating politician.

The connection between the trilogy and national pride was emphasized by the timing of the next major production, directed by Barry Jackson at Birmingham Repertory Theatre, to coincide with the 1951 Festival of Britain. Opening with *Part II*, and expanding to include the other two parts by 1953, Jackson's production "traded on the irresolution and fracture of a country traumatised by war and victimised by the appalling destructiveness of power politics."[13] Jackson emphasized the carnivalesque elements, including a showstopping turn by Kenneth Williams as a vaudevillian Smith the Weaver in *Part II*. Much was made of Suffolk, with Richard Pasco playing up the character's role as a substitute king, and John Arnott played an ambitious but noble York.

While the Royal Shakespeare Company dominated the play's performance history in the second half of the twentieth century, they did occasionally surface elsewhere. Stuart Vaughan directed a two-part *The Chronicles of Henry VI* in repertory with *Richard III* for the New York Shakespeare Festival in 1970, stressing the action and spectacle, but largely failing to give the characters color. Foster Hirsch praised "Jack Ryland's energetic, crafty Suffolk [who] provided the right contrast to the withdrawn King" and, once again, it was the character of York who provided the strongest through-line for the play.[14] The growing fascination with the later parts of the trilogy meant that reviewers were beginning to pay less attention to Humphrey and Winchester, described here as respectively "bluff" and "unctuous" but peripheral, to the more interesting dynamics governing the later wars.[15]

In 1975–77, the Oregon Shakespeare Festival staged the three parts in succession but as individual plays without cross-casting. Alan C. Dessen reviewed all three, and was particularly disappointed by the decision to provide closure to *Part II* by ending it with the parley between Henry and York from the opening of *Part III*: "By ending the production with the acquiescence of Henry to Richard, [director Jerry] Turner missed completely the open-ended horror of Shakespeare's *Part Two*."[16] Director Will Huddleston prioritized a declamatory style for *Part I*, allowing the formal rhymed couplets between the Talbots to emerge as a high point, while Turner's *Part II* "exploited every opportunity for spectacle, violence, and horror, presenting us with elaborate dumb shows, stirring stage combats, eerie spirits, life-like severed heads (trailing bits of esophagus), swirling mob scenes, and a Suffolk beheaded on stage."[17] Pat Patton directed *Part III* with more attention to character, with an emotional Henry and a polished Edward IV. However, "as figure after figure was swept aside, more room was left for the daemonic energy of Michael Santo's aggressive yet controlled Richard of Gloucester," indicating the primary value of the latter parts of the trilogy was still seen to be the opportunity to glimpse the future tyrant.[18]

The 1980s saw two important reimaginings of the plays that finally brought them to a much wider audience. In 1983, Jane Howell directed the trilogy, along with *Richard III*, in full-text productions for the BBC/Time Life television series. Widely regarded as the best of the series, as well as the least conventional, Howell's approach was to assemble an ensemble cast in a black studio space, with a fixed set of a large-scale children's adventure playground. The trilogy begins with a light touch, including Humphrey and Winchester riding to meet one another on pantomime horses and the French running comically on- and offstage, arguing for the childishness of the squabbles. The initial rose-cutting begins in a spirit of good humor, Somerset and York joking before the more serious dispute begins. As the trilogy continues, however, the tone grows gradually darker. A standout sequence sees the normally cut John Fastolfe making his escape through the carnage, winking and gasping at the camera as bloodied bodies fall around him. Across the later parts, the playground falls into disrepair, deaths become bloodier (notably that of Warwick in *Part III*, played movingly in close-up), and a feeling of weariness and disillusion sets in as Ron Cook's excellent, diminutive Richard of Gloucester becomes more prominent. The decline continues into *Richard III*, culminating in the famous closing image of Richard's mangled body being laid on top of a pile of bloody corpses played by the rest of the ensemble. Doubling is used intelligently throughout to draw links—most notably, Trevor Peacock's heroic Talbot becomes the jaded Jack Cade.

From 1986 to 1989, the English Shakespeare Company toured its seven-part *The Wars of the Roses* under the direction of Michael Bogdanov. The *Henry VI* trilogy was split across two plays, *House of Lancaster* and *House of York*, the first concluding with the death of Suffolk and the second beginning with the Cade rebellion. In *House of York*, special prominence was given to the Father/Son scene, used to close the first half, and the second half of this play was devoted to the rise of Richard. The production design careered through early twentieth-century history, from the Edwardian era through both world wars, emphasizing the timelessness of the civil broils. Within the context of the seven-play cycle, reviewers responded to the state-of-the-nation commentary:

> Mr. Bogdanov's success lies in giving the action a specific context: the original quarrel between the two houses develops

between boozed, black-tied figures emerging from a good Temple dinner. Jack Cade becomes a National Front populist draping himself in the Union Jack and addressing a pathetic crowd straight out of David Edgar's *Destiny* and Edward IV makes a clumsy pass at the widowed Lady Grey to the accompaniment of tinkling cocktail-party music.[19]

In 2001, playing in competition with Michael Boyd's revival for the RSC, Edward Hall's all-male company Propeller toured the UK with a two-part adaptation of the trilogy entitled *Rose Rage*. The irreverent title clued up the focus on the visual fascination with violence, drawing on schlock horror to offer a grimly humorous version of the play:

> We are in the abattoir. The hooks and trusses await the carcasses, rubber gloves are at the ready. The cast are fully gowned and masked. There is the sound of knives being sharpened. Be in no doubt—the slaughter is about to begin . . . The violence is both precise and distanced, scary and macabre. There is a high body count, but Hall applies a grisly comic touch. Every murder is played out in graphic detail but the bodies receive no blows or cuts. Instead animal entrails are sliced and gored, giant cabbages axed and cleaved. Soon a faint, sickening smell of offal pervades the theatre. It is hard to look at what is happening on stage, harder still to avert your eyes.[20]

In a more cynical century, Hall's blackly comic treatment pointed to the futility and cruelty of the almost casual violence.

The critical and popular success of the RSC's 2006–08 Histories Cycle served to bring the plays to a much wider audience, and increasingly small companies are willing to take the risk of staging individual parts. The Young Rep at Birmingham Repertory Theatre staged a surprisingly sophisticated version of *Henry VI Part III* in 2008 which drew heavily on the RSC productions but found its own identity, particularly in contrasting a strong and frustrated Margaret with a weak and indecisive Henry, and in foregrounding Clifford and Warwick as the dominant movers in battle. In May 2011, *Henry VI Part I* finally returned to its original home in the first in-house production at the ruins of the Rose on Bankside. Performed in the massive cavern that houses the submerged remains of the original theater, audiences watched from a viewing platform as soldiers clashed swords in slow-motion in the shadows and Joan strode into the center of a lake to be consumed by smoke and orange light. This evocative production, with a particularly strong performance from Ben Higgins' grizzled Talbot and a compelling conflict between Oliver Lavery's moustache-twirling Gloucester and Morgan Thomas' dignified Winchester, made a powerful case for the play's strength as an independent piece, evoking the spirit of the old theater in order to make a fresh case for the play in the twenty-first century.

AT THE RSC

Three Plays Become One

In its Summer 2000 programme, the Royal Shakespeare Company announced the staging of Shakespeare's two tetralogies as a cycle called *This England*. The programme made a distinctive break with the past by conceding that the plays were "originally conceived by Shakespeare at different times and written in non-chronological order," but, in order to preserve the integrity of the history play cycle, the programme went on to argue that the separate plays together "form a collage of one man's insight into England's history."[21]

Both Peter Hall in 1963 and Adrian Noble in 1988 had the three parts of *Henry VI* edited and rewritten into two plays entitled *Henry VI* and *Edward IV*, and performed as part of a trilogy with *Richard III*. The 1963 script written by John Barton was called *The Wars of the Roses* and the 1988 version, originally adapted by Chris Wood but worked on by the acting company, was known as *The Plantagenets*. Partly to do with finances and the box office bankability of the *Henry VI* plays, and partly so that the entire cycle could be watched in one day as a unique experience for the audience, adaptation was considered essential. Peter Hall also felt that the plays, if performed in an unedited state, would lose their focus for a modern audience.

In many ways, Hall opened the door for directors to stage the plays in a more complete form, by reinstating these neglected works. At the time many critics regretted the fact that Hall and Barton had drastically cut and reworked the text. J. C. Trewin commented: "I regret only that we do not have the plays in full. I cannot really agree with Mr Hall and Mr Barton that, if the trilogy were unadapted, a modern audience would lose the force of its political and human meaning."[22]

The problem of maintaining focus and continuity was solved by rewriting these three very different plays, but it has remained an important issue for all the directors who produced the Henrys as part of a sequence. As a reaction against the Hall/Barton approach, Terry Hands in 1978 presented the plays virtually uncut, and Michael Boyd's staging in 2000 did the same to great critical acclaim: "the result is an awesome day-long event in which the actors' commitment is matched by that of the audience":[23]

this view of history, coloured, distorted and even invented— does make a living experience out of what would otherwise be a colossal dump of dates, battles and rulers. And seeing this living experience through at one sitting does throw an extra dimension of time over even the most superficially drawn characters. For every hour that we watch them they live through a decade and we leave them our feelings bruised by their rude experience of life.[24]

In 2006, this production was reworked for the Complete Works Festival and opened the Courtyard Theatre, the Royal Shakespeare Company's temporary home during the redevelopment of the main Stratford theaters. Michael Boyd had particularly wanted to direct all eight plays of the two historical tetralogies himself. He believed that in this later revival, the ensemble company "found more depth of characterisation" and "had time to be more daring."[25]

These plays which had been rarely performed since Shakespeare's day found a sympathetic audience in postwar Britain: disillusioned, cynical about the nature of men in power and the devastating effect that individual decisions can have on the lives of many, "the plays took on new meanings for a generation facing the aftermath of world war on the one hand, and the failure of the great early twentieth-century ideologies on the other."[26]

In his introduction to the text of his adaptation with John Barton, *The Wars of the Roses*, Peter Hall stated:

> I realised that the mechanism of power had not changed in centuries. We also were in the middle of a blood-soaked century. I was convinced that a presentation of one of the bloodiest and most hypocritical periods in history would teach many lessons to the present.[27]

The contemporary relevance of the plays has prompted passionate and political readings. As a direct response to her experience of visiting the war-torn country of the former Yugoslavia, director Katie Mitchell uniquely staged *Henry VI Part III* on its own at The Other Place in 1994, retitling it *Henry VI: Battle for the Throne*. Plunging the audience straight into Part III of the trilogy, and therefore straight into the middle of a war, had the desired effect. Mitchell felt:

> she had a moral responsibility to respond to what she'd seen. *Henry VI* does this brilliantly: it isn't telling us anything new about the civil war because there is nothing new to tell. Power and greed, fear and jealousy. Same problems, different century.[28]

In order to belittle the goal for which so many are sacrificed, the emblems of kingship were completely deglamorized:

> The throne the characters spend the evening battling to obtain is a squat, chunky lump, more desirable than the wooden chairs beside it only because it has arms and some rudimen-

tary carving at the top. It goes very well with the crown, which is a flimsy band of metal with a tiny cross pathetically protruding from its front, and the palace carpeting, which consists of dead leaves. Why the rough feel? . . . Mitchell is clearly telling us what she thinks of the Wars of the Roses. Rough theatre suits rough people doing rough things in rough times.[29]

The Christian idealism to which the warring lords pay lip service was shown to be a sham, the remains of some residual memory like indelible learned behavior that has ritual actions but no active meaning:

both Yorkists and Lancastrians swear oaths on a Bible placed at the entrance to the Parliament and, in an extraordinary moment, both join forces in a Latin anthem outside the walls of Coventry before hacking each other to pieces. But there is no cynicism in Mitchell's constant invocation of religion. Instead she turns the play into a moving lamentation over the reduction of Christian amity to the temporary advantages of political power.[30]

Nature, too, played its part in the exposure of the warring factions, bringing extra dimensions to the play: the idea of England's "green and pleasant land" violated but ultimately enduring; and also the thought that the brutal behavior of the warring lords is something inherent, an animalistic instinct for survival perverted into violence and pointless destruction:

Heavy rain, snowstorms, bright, falling autumnal leaves and clear dawn light—the full gamut of the English climate was heard or seen. The production's meteorology was supported by hints of an animal world, bird-song and sheep bleating, sounds that were both reassuring in their normality and disturbing in their transformations into the sounds of horses in pain during the battles. There was a reminder of a natural world in the bark that covered the stage floor : . . . and in a pine-tree on the side of the stage from which Margaret tore a branch to serve as the mocking crown she put on the Duke of York before killing him in [Act]1 [Scene]4 . . . Most strongly it was there most exquisitely, to the accompaniment of bird-song and a babbling brook, in the tuft of feathers Henry plucked from one of the wings that dangled on the belt of a gamekeeper and blew into the air: "Look, as I blow this feather from my face, / And as the air blows it to me again" [*Part III*, 3.1.84–85]. Suggesting continuity in a world beyond the political . . . [31]

In 2000, Michael Boyd also found a vital contemporary relevance in the plays, in the "story of a world cracking apart along divisions of family and belief and value systems flooded out to embrace contemporary global cultures, from Israel and Palestine to Yugoslavia, the former Soviet Union and Rwanda as well as the U.S."[32] In this production England became an abattoir in which men and women constantly preyed upon each other. There was a vivid sense of the absence of God, with Henry VI himself the only advocate of his word on earth. David Oyelowo in his long white robes looked otherworldly, an angel of innocence among the dark costumes and settings, at odds with the corruption that surrounded him: "The first sight is of Henry V's corpse resting on a cross and lowered by a pulley into his grave—a trap-door in the floor springing open. The rule of Christian assurance is over."[33] The impression was one of a warrior hell, where the warring nobles were trapped in an inescapable circle of violence, destined to die and be born again into the same fight, to repeat the cycle:

Boyd treats the trilogy as, above all, an extended essay on time. The young, callow Henry VI is haunted by his grandfather's usurpation of the throne. But the characters also exist in a nightmare present. And death is seen as an entrance as well as an exit: corpses rise up to be guided offstage by a mysterious gatekeeper only to re-appear, like the Duke of York, in the thick of battle. It's a very Eliotesque idea that time present and time past are both present in time future.[34]

The dark set was hung with chains, which actors clung to and swung on during battles, or dangled from when dead:

> Boyd and his designer, Tom Piper . . . re-aligned The Swan so that the stage-floor is an irregular oblong . . . they have realised the virtue of the building lies in its height. Actors are constantly scaling ladders and ropes to remind us of the vertical nature of siege-warfare.[35]

The feeling of suspension, generated by much of the fighting taking place midair, was counterbalanced by the solidity of the large steel doors that dominated the set:

> The action [of all three parts] takes place on a vast, bare stage with the audience seated almost all the way round. At one end are two great metal doors with a balcony above. This becomes a castle in the wars with France, but the doors are also the gates of death through which the trilogy's vast cast of casualties disappear. The play's vision of humanity preying upon itself may be bleak—and is often downright barbaric in Boyd's visceral, gory staging—but there is a strong underlying sense of the possibility of goodness, order and hope.[36]

The 2006 production developed this in the enlarged playing space of the Courtyard Theatre with its thrust stage and galleries—what it lost in intimacy it gained in breadth and the sense of a wider political backdrop to play across.

By cutting and rewriting the plays in 1963, Peter Hall and John Barton:

> narrowed the focus of the plays to centre upon the workings of *history* as a grand narrative force, and John Bury's set was constructed as a giant steel cage, materialising these forces upon the stage as an oppressive trap for its participants. History was both the centre of the production, its "main protagonist," and its surface, its body and its soul, leaving the human subject to the desolate battleground constituted by its mise-en-scène.[37]

1. Michael Boyd's RSC 2000 production of *Henry VI Part III* with David Oyelowo as Henry VI: The dark set was hung with chains, which actors clung to and swung on during battles, or dangled from when dead.

This took the form of "a cruel, harsh world of decorated steel, cold and dangerous."[38] As designer John Bury explained:

> The Wars of the Roses was designed in steel—the steel of the plate armour—the steel of the shield and the steel of the broadsword . . . the central image—the steel of wars—has spread and forged anew the whole medieval landscape. On the flagged floors of sheet steel tables are daggers, staircases are axeheads, and doors the traps on scaffolds. Nothing yields: stone walls have lost their seduction and now loom dangerously—steel-clad—to enclose and to imprison. The countryside offers no escape—the danger is still there in the iron foliage of the cruel trees and, surrounding all, the great steel cage of war.[39]

Bury described how the costumes for 1963 reflected the progressive disintegration of the country during the plays:

> The costumes corroded with the years. The once-proud red rose of Lancaster became as a rusty scale on the soldiers' coats; the milk-white rose of York was no more than a pale blush on the tarnished steel of the Yorkist insurrection. Colour drained and drained from the stage until, among the drying patches of scarlet blood, the black night of England settled on the leather costumes of Richard's thugs.[40]

In Terry Hands' 1977 production each play was given a distinctive feel but with a progression prompted by the different styles of the plays; the closing down of the action and the sense of claustrophobia demonstrated by stage space and color:

> First we see sombrely-dressed nobles round the tomb of Henry V. A black divider foreshortens the stage and gives it a cramped solemnity. But within minutes solemnity is kicked aside and the nobles are squabbling . . . This scene, a dark egg of chaos, is cracked open when the divider lifts to display the full stretch of the battlefield at Orléans. From it crawls the rest of the play:

in embryo we see how the child Henry VI's reign is ruptured by civil dissension and unsuccessful wars in France.[41]

For *Part II* and *Part III* a shaggy green carpet covered the stage floor and a red rope signified divisions within the country:

> It cordons off the commoners from the king in the various official ceremonies. The festive connotation deteriorates in spectacular fashion and the implication of officialdom, order in the sternest sense, and bloody execution moves into the foreground as the rope turns halter for Jack Cade's followers . . . Part III, from King Henry's pastoral speech in [Act] II [Scene] 5 onwards, is characterized by a more and more insistent use of the front of the stage at crucial moments. One feels that Henry and his supporters are about to be pushed over the side.[42]

Costuming in its color and texture also played an important part in emphasizing certain elements in the play:

> The wicked French are dressed in black and blue, an inkling perhaps of the military thrashing that the English are wishing on them. Alexander Iden, Cade's conqueror, looks every inch "the lord of the soil" when he sports in his orchard a furry green jerkin cut in the same material as the floor carpeting. The treatment of the red and white roses is likewise thoughtful. A deliberate progression is observed from the natural flowers originally plucked by the two opposing sides to badges in the shape of red or white neckerchiefs, or, obviously for better wear, as the conflict is drawn out, in the guise of breastplates in which the symbols are coined. Alone Richard Plantagenet affectedly sticks to a natural rose to the end.[43]

Those who survive are revisited in the subsequent plays: Margaret, Henry VI, and York are the center around which the other characters revolve. With limited casts but a large number of characters, the actors playing subsidiary characters who die in battle often return to play someone else. This necessary doubling can be disguised with makeup and costuming or can be used to advantage, promoting a sense of continuity with poignant relevance.

Michael Boyd was inventive in 2000 with his cross-casting of the three plays. Character continuity even extended into the afterlife, with the ghosts of those who had been murdered returning to haunt the subsequent plays in the cycle. In the 2006 revival he took this idea further: "the ghost of Henry V starts events memorably here, and introduces us to one of the staging's motifs: the walking dead."[44] The most striking example of this, appropriately, was the father and son relationship of the Talbots:

> Constellated within Boyd's metaphysical, supernatural world . . . the Talbots remain in a kind of theatrical purgatory from which they repeatedly appear, both as themselves and as others. At Angiers, their bloodied figures appeared on ladders at either side of the catwalk, framing Joan's figure; descending, they walked off the stage, leaving her alone. In *2 Henry VI* . . . [the image of] Young Talbot slung in a harness above the stage, his father looking up at him—recurs, for the spirit summoned in the conjuration scene from a trap beneath the stage was Young Talbot, again suspended, speaking the spirit's prophecy of violent death; his father was there, too, sword in hand, as though still trying to recover his son. Later, Talbot emerged from under the blue sheets that had covered the bed where the raving Winchester dies: now he is the Pirate Captain; Young Talbot, Walter Whitmore. As the father who has killed his son and the son who killed his father, the two apotheosise their own deaths as well as those of others. Haunting the *Henry VIs* like demented spirits, they leave the realm of the undead, coming back in *Richard III* as another father (in-law) and son, Lord Stanley and Richmond.[45]

Boyd also created a character named in the program "The Keeper," who acted as a guide to the dead. As keeper of the gates of hell he would guide the slaughtered through the large metal doors that dominated the set. As the dead reappeared to interfere with the action it reminded the audience of the terrible cost of civil war as well as its cyclical and self-destructive nature. These strong and willful characters refused to lie down and be forgotten, but played an active part in the world of the living and the future of their descendants. Now and again "Red and white feathers [fell] from on high symbolising both fluctuating fortunes, fickleness and human transience."[46]

Blood Will Have Blood

The violence in *Henry VI* is one reason why it was seldom performed prior to the twentieth century. As an expression of the futility and brutality of war the *Henry VI* plays have enjoyed a revival since the 1960s. The relatively fresh memories of the horrors of the Second World War and the emergence of the shocking footage of violence and its effects from newsreels of Vietnam on television made it inappropriate to shirk from the visceral effects of war. Maybe it was hoped that the graphic portrayal of violence in all forms of art, whether theater, film, art, or literature, would be part of the learning process—the fear of physical violence being one thing that might stop humanity from repeating the same atrocities. Peter Hall stated:

> These history plays with their bloody heads, brutal carnage and sense of fate were not appreciated by the nineteenth century. This is not surprising, it was hoped then that such horrors were past. We know now that this optimism was premature.[47]

Of the violence in Hall's 1963 production John Russell Brown wrote:

> The plays became a high class cartoon, a relentless horror comic . . . horror and violence were presented by liberal splashes of blood, and by inventive business that elaborated every opportunity for the exhibition of cruelty and pain that the text suggested . . . Joan of Arc cut her own wrist like a Tamburlaine with a very large sword; Young Clifford's head was cut off on stage and carried around upon a spear . . . In the Paper Crown scene, the cruel humour of the lines was played close to hysteria. When Margaret stabbed York it was with a quick movement, and then she wept. Then the tears stopped with a wild, painful cry. In this scene the violence was emphasised as much

as anywhere, but there was also rhetorical and musical control and a daring, emotional performance revealing depths of unwilled and conflicting desires.[48]

Many critics found the violence in this production excessive but it certainly spoke to a generation of theatergoers who never forgot the experience. The battle scenes themselves were staged in a minimalist way with the effective use of music and movement:

> most of the fighting is relegated to musical representation, so that instead of being presented with the ultimately comic spectacle of hordes of sweaty actors convulsed in a succession of Douglas Fairbanks' sword fights, the thrust and parry is ominously represented by musical sound—complementing a visual impression of a few silhouetted figures in battle.[49]

Similarly, in 1977: "The battle-scenes are somewhat scantly populated, but director Terry Hands' aim is not to create a realistic illusion but to conjure up an effect that will bring the battles into our minds."[50]

In these productions, and those that have followed, it was the more intimate moments of violence that were graphically depicted. This difference in staging between battles and torture emphasized the anonymity of war as opposed to the very personal acts of torture and retribution. In a review of Peter Hall's 1963 production, one critic described how the production:

> has three climaxes, each of them a curdling climax of blood-letting. The first is the capture and torture of Richmond with Margaret exulting in the indignities that precede his death. The second is the reverse of this situation, where the young brothers capture Margaret and her son and carve up the boy before her eyes. The last is where young Richard, the Crookback king-to-be, comes to the Tower with a curiously loving indifference and slashes the silly saintly Henry to pieces. In the part of the young Richard Ian Holm is deadly accurate and vilely terrible.[51]

Adrian Noble, in 1989, wrote: "As one reads the play in the twentieth century, one is forcibly struck by the potential for violence latent in most of the political confrontations."[52] In 1977 this fact was especially evident in the rebellion of Jack Cade, which contained scenes visually reminiscent of recognizable historical atrocities:

> The communion of the rebels in blood after their first killing looks like a popular action out of Brutus' exhortation to the citizens of Rome, whilst the gory Punch and Judy act performed by Dick the Butcher with two severed heads stuck on pikes fetches its inspiration from the worst scenes of the French revolution.[53]

> The rebels' ineptitude is comic; they kill so badly, a group of them straining at ropes, botching each other's work as they labour for several minutes to strangle the clerk of Chatham. But their technique improves. Dick the Butcher wheels on the audience, his face a massive display of demented glee, his hands and face cleaver clotted with blood. Hands clasp his, faces are smeared, the mood grows maniacal. Cade has been played with an undercurrent of frustration. He is a man trying desperately to articulate real grievances, but illiteracy defeats him . . . violence stands for words; the legitimate grievances get swamped in the blood-lust . . . [54]

In 1994, Katie Mitchell used symbolic representations of blood and violence. In the allegory of the son who has killed his father and the father who has killed his son, the two men juxtaposed onstage held a red rose and a white rose: "No blood-dripping corpses or medical materialism, instead each party unwraps a symbolic human fragment while Jonathan Firth's . . . sweet-souled, quietly spoken king invokes heaven's pity."[55] For the staging of the battles, Mitchell took the language used in the plays as her cue:

> The animal imagery with which the battles are described finds its way into the soundtrack that resounds with the cries of wild beasts. The fighting is not staged but thrillingly implied as

troops march on to intimidating drumbeats under swirling
snow and then hurtle out to battle. At one point, in the tense
pause before they make their deadly charge, the lovely drift of
innocent birdsong drops into the moment like an ache of nos-
talgia and a moral judgement on the scene.[56]

She also emphasized the rituals of death inherent in the play with
music and liturgies, but:

Instead of sentimentalising the play, these ritual moments
highlighting the self-serving cynicism of the warmongering
nobles, just as the Bayeux-like representation of St George slay-
ing the dragon emblazoned on the back wall merely empha-
sises how, in a war that has largely degenerated into personal
vendettas, national interests are increasingly overlooked. The
production brings out well the black comedy implicit in much
of this, as in the scene where the Yorkists are reduced to hurling taunts at the corpse of Clifford, who has tactlessly died

2. In 1994, Katie Mitchell used symbolic representations of blood and violence . . . the two men onstage held a red rose and a white rose in her
small-scale touring production of *Henry VI Part III* entitled *The Battle for the
Throne*.

before they could crow over him. Tom Smith's wizened skin-head of a Richard even plants a desecrating kiss on the dead man's lips.[57]

In the RSC's most recent productions by Michael Boyd the violence was far more visceral than symbolic: "nervous theatre-goers are warned to look away when Joan is pinioned to the stake and when Jack Cade's rebels prepare to execute their prisoner":[58]

> Events on the ground . . . make it clear that, as the chorus in *Henry V* said, England is bleeding . . . some people are garrotted or suffocated. The purple-faced ghost of Richard Cordery's Gloucester is one of several men Boyd asks to wander the stage after their deaths. But what these spooks are watching is an abattoir England in which character after character is stabbed or sliced. An innocent victim of the brutish, vivid recreation of the Cade rebellion gets his liver cut out. Aidan McArdle's Crookback cheerfully tosses aside a dying foe's tongue. His murder of Henry VI leaves so much blood on the stage that the cast must virtually wade in it for its curtain-call.[59]

Of the 2006 revival Benedict Nightingale claimed, "Boyd's revival strikes me as less gory than the version he staged in 2000." Despite this, he concludes "yet we end up with Crookback and his brother ripping out a foe's tongue, eye and penis."[60] In 2006 Richard of Gloucester was played by Jonathan Slinger—a "mesmerisingly horrible young Crookback Richard."[61]

"Foule Fiend" and the "She-Wolf" of France

> Shakespeare feels compelled, in this trilogy, to personify that evil in the form of two aggressive warrior women, the French soldier-sorceress Joan la Pucelle (Joan of Arc), and Henry's ferocious and sexually powerful queen, Margaret. This gives the plays a horrifying and yet oddly recognisable gender politics, as teams of men surge across the stage roaring their contempt for "effeminate peace," and yet vent their implacable hatred on women who dare to dabble in war.[62]

Political crisis in Shakespeare's work is deeply imbedded in the break-down of the family. The family was seen as a microcosm of the state in both literature and in reality. Those who stepped outside the social norms would be punished for their deviant behavior—especially women who assumed a dominant role over their husbands. *Henry VI* includes a number of women whose "unnatural" behavior symbol-izes the chaos and unnatural order of the state.

Our perception of Joan la Pucelle/Joan of Arc today is drastically at odds with the portrayal of the witch in Shakespeare's plays. For the modern actor playing the part, ambiguity as to whether Joan's inspiration is either divine or demonic is something which can add an extra dimension to an otherwise two-dimensional character. In 1977, Charlotte Cornwell's performance divided critics, but incorpo-rated the various elements of this legendary character:

> The French declare her "France's saint," the English call her a witch, and her performance underscores these ambiguities. She takes a child's delight in seeing through the Dauphin's attempted deception, but when she begins to laugh, the laugh-ter is a disturbing cackle. We become aware that she is clutch-ing a fetish that hangs from her neck. She is alternately seductress, fishwife, and Amazon, beating first the Dauphin and then Talbot into the ground, enticing Burgundy back to the French, throwing her boots and berating the soldiers for their slackness. But when the French hold out a torch of vic-tory before her, she starts back, terrified. She has disdained to kill Talbot, telling him "Thy hour is not yet come," but when that death finally arrives, she spends a long minute alone on stage, staring at the body, aware that her own usefulness to France is exhausted and that *her* hour has come.[63]

Fiona Bell in 2000 played Joan as a young woman who had found power in the supernatural to escape an abusive father, and to over-come prejudices of class. This, however, was only a veneer of strength that failed her when she was faced with her own inadequacies. The turning point for this Joan was Act 4 Scene 7 when Sir William Lucy pays tribute to the dead Talbot and his son:

3. Terry Hands' 1977 production of *Part I,* with Charlotte Cornwell as Joan la Pucelle: "The French declare her 'France's saint,' the English call her a witch, and her performance underscores these ambiguities."

I ended up laughing at Lucy throughout the whole scene. He refuses to give in to her and continues to venerate the dead soldier, and they end up trying to outdo each other, her laughter becoming more and more deranged . . . [Talbot] has been brave and courageous, unquestioningly performing his duties

to the crown. He is the antithesis of Joan . . . she will never
achieve the status she needs. She is put face to face with pure
nobility, who can see her for what she is, or for what she feels
herself to be. I think it crushes her, and the only way she can
hide her fear is to laugh at Lucy . . . she knows that the end is
in sight . . . [64]

Margaret appears after Joan's death as if her spirit has been resurrected to plague the English throne. She possesses many of Joan's
qualities: as an object of desire, an instrument for ambitious lords, as
the warrior queen, the "she-wolf" of France. The parallels with Joan
and with witchcraft were obvious to the Elizabethan playgoer. In
Michael Boyd's staging the link between Joan and Margaret was
taken further by having the same actor play both parts—Fiona Bell
in 2000, Katy Stephens in 2006:

Fiona Bell begins the trilogy as a vigorous Joan of Arc, a figure
Shakespeare notoriously saw as a Satanic witch and crossdressing fiend, but spends most of it as a Margaret beneath
whose pale, demure looks lie arrogance, fierce ambition and
sadistic delight in her enemies' setbacks. [65]

Katy Stephens was described as "beautiful and formidable as Joan
la Pucelle"[66] and "fiercely Amazonian"[67] as Queen Margaret. The
"dual" casting of Joan and Margaret had a deliberate effect in emphasizing the nature of Margaret's character, as well as providing a
through-line in the three plays. Margaret descended in a picture
frame at the end of *Part I* just after Joan had been burned at the stake.
Bell explained:

In this production Joan informed Margaret throughout. [Boyd]
had transposed two scenes (Part I, Act 5, Scenes 3 and 4),
which resulted in Margaret's first entrance coming directly on
the heels of Joan's burning. I would appear, literally in a puff of
smoke, as though emerging from the embers, a new, more
advanced model of Joan. The metaphysical world is ever present in these plays . . . It was the impression that this idea

gave . . . rather than the actuality, that was important. It added another dimension to Margaret and reinforced the milieu of the plays, the under-carriage of which is a never-ending, nigh-on-apocalyptic struggle between good and evil.[68]

Similarly, in 1988 the first appearance of Margaret was moved to immediately after the execution of Joan. Penny Downie, who played Margaret, explained:

Our intention was to show Margaret in a sense taking over where Joan left off, a new Frenchwoman to be a scourge to the English. With Joan of Arc at the stake and dead bodies on the stage, I came on covered in a brown cloak, hungry, a scavenger on the battlefield, like a sewer rat sniffing for the remnants of the picnic that York and Warwick had been eating while Joan was burning.[69]

In 1963 Peggy Ashcroft's performance as Margaret became central to the tetralogy. Tackling the part aged fifty-six, her skill as an actor and her maturity made her the more dominant partner in the trilogy. Although David Warner received great plaudits for his performance, Ashcroft's development from young French princess to matriarchal harridan dominated and pulled together the plots of the three plays:

The extraordinary thing about Ashcroft's performance is its development. The young bride brushing aside with a girlish gesture the embarrassment of her dowry-less arrival in England; the foreign queen tentatively sitting at a remote corner of her husband's council chamber; the dominating partner fighting his battles; the stricken mother deprived of her own child—all these facets are there and they seem to grow inevitably one from the other.[70]

John Barton also cut the plays to emphasize the strength of her individuality: Reignier, her father, was cut from the meeting with Suffolk and bargaining on the battlefield; she was invited to join the "council board," the council-of-war table around which the lords sat; "in explicit language added by Barton, Margaret takes the initiative in calling for Humphrey's impeachment, and goes on to plot his death, in conspiracy with her lover Suffolk."[71] Importantly the final scene in the first play ended with Margaret entering with the head of Suffolk:

> Bending her wild grief and anger into a protective embrace of her weak husband, and breathing defiance to their enemies, she charges him:

> > Steel thou thy heart to keep thy vexed kingdom,
> > Whereof both you and I have charge and care.

4. In *Part III* of Terry Hands' 1977 production, Helen Mirren's "deviant sexpot" as Margaret taunts Emrys James as York: "Margaret is all the more horrible in that her torturer's body moves as sensuously as ever it did in loving Suffolk. She caresses York's face—but leaves it smeared with his child's blood."

These salient lines, which Shakespeare might have written, had not Sackville and Norton and Barton thought of them first, leave us with no doubt of whose play this has become, as the royal couple exit to confront England's uncertain future at the final fade-out.[72]

In 1977, Terry Hands' casting of the young Helen Mirren as Margaret meant that the emphasis moved to Henry, played by the more experienced Alan Howard. The casting of Mirren also deliberately added an overtly sexual element to the relationships in the play. On meeting Henry she was as entranced by him as by Suffolk: "Helen [Mirren]'s Margaret is less harridan than deviant sexpot, never more intimate and loving than when a murder is rising to its climax."[73] After the murder of Suffolk this sexuality became perverted into sadistic pleasure:

> Margaret is all the more horrible in that her torturer's body moves as sensuously as ever it did in loving Suffolk. She caresses York's face—but leaves it smeared with his child's blood. She watches his agony in twitching, feline fascination. When he collapses in her lap, she rocks him maternally before clasping a sword and thrusting him through, a final erotic release.[74]

The linking of sex with violence in the character of Margaret was also built into Fiona Bell's portrayal in 2000. There were clear indications that Joan la Pucelle was sleeping not only with the dauphin but with any member of the French court who was politically expedient. With instruction from Michael Boyd to "keep the memory of the burning [of Joan] with me when . . . playing Margaret," Fiona Bell recalled how the brutality of York's torture of Joan was repaid by Margaret in *Part III*:

> The burning scene was directed to be very vicious. With the words "And yet, forsooth, she is a virgin pure" [*Part I*, 5.4.83] York would stab me in the genitals and show his hand with the

blood on it, ironically suggesting that he has broken her hymen. Their cruelty helps set these Englishmen apart from the likes of Henry V and the two John Talbots, and shows they are no better than the young girl they are torturing:

> Where York mutilates Joan, Michael [Boyd] had Margaret's henchmen slashing at York with their knives throughout his speech. If Margaret eschewed her sensuality with Suffolk's death, I think it is replaced in Part Three with a visceral delight in the pain of her enemies. I thought she should be practically salivating when she is humiliating York and definitely be sexually aroused.[75]

At the Center of This Maelstrom Sits Henry[76]

Looking back on his role as Henry VI in 1993, Ralph Fiennes remarked:

> My main recollection of the part was of this pathetic figure, lovable but frustrating because, although he was clearly a good man, he was completely unable to control the forces of ambition and dissent around him.[77]

Henry is a man at odds with the world in which he lives, unprepared and unable to compromise his own ideals and morality in order to rule. His failure to match up to his father is an inability to carry on the ethos of war into civilian life. The nobles, who have been fighting foreign wars, now see their chance for power and in their desperate attempt to attain it turn their feudal energies in upon themselves.

Henry's first major difficulty as a ruler is his age. Surrounded by people of greater years and with more experience, in *Part I* he is often painfully out of his depth. In 1977 Terry Hands emphasized Henry's youth in the staging, making him appear almost childlike:

> the new King Henry (played throughout the trilogy by Alan Howard), [is] a vulnerable child, his throne much too large. His feet would dangle as if they didn't rest on a step. When he

5. Ralph Fiennes as Henry VI in Adrian Noble's 1988 RSC production: "My main recollection of the part was of this pathetic figure, lovable but frustrating because, although he was clearly a good man, he was completely unable to control the forces of ambition and dissent around him," with Penny Downie as Margaret.

6. In 1963 in Peter Hall's RSC production: David Warner gave a touching performance as "a novice-like figure in a coarse gown pitiably reliant on Gloucester for advice."

kneels to be crowned he needs help to rise to his feet. His uncles flank his throne—as they did his father's coffin—shouting the ancient abuse at each other over his bowed and bewildered head. He is no match for the stamping, strutting little York who sniffs his rose and plots his plots. Because Henry shrinks from kingship, the kingdom fractures. There is no more eloquent emblem for dissolution than this: Henry's venerable uncles fall to fisticuffs, using their staves of office to beat each other over the head.[78]

In 1963 David Warner gave a touching performance as:

> a novice-like figure in a coarse gown pitiably reliant on Glouces-ter for advice and, at moments of tension, given to sweeping the whole company with a sweet nervous smile in anxiety to win everyone's approval. In the second play his situation is changed and his original appeal gives way to mere pathos . . . [79]

David Oyelowo was the first black actor to play Henry VI for the RSC in 2000. However, it was his youth that set him apart from the other nobles in *Part I*:

> Oyelowo's Henry as a young boy clutches his royal robes for reassurance as he forces himself to be bold. With age he gains authority but, fatefully, puts his reverence for justice above his subjects' need for a leader they can hold in awe.[80]

As Henry ages, his determination in upholding of Christian law again puts him at odds with the real world, a barbaric world which pays lip service to God only. As critic Benedict Nightingale observed:

> Oyelowo's fine, gentle Henry is alone in his love of peace and even lonelier in the quiet wisdom he acquires as the evening progresses. It's as if the Dalai Lama were not just caught in a cannibal orgy but married to the hungriest eater.[81]

For the opening of Act III Scene 1, the King and Queen stood together at one end of the stage, awaiting the entry of the peers through the huge double doors opposite. After a tense pause filled with an ominous drumbeat, the doors opened and four ranks of straight-backed, stern-faced men strode forward. The two parties faced each other. No sign of deference or submission was given by the peers, who looked more like a fighting squadron than obedient subjects. At last, Henry made a slight movement forward and the peers scattered, making brief bows. It was clearly never going to be easy for the gentle Henry to master this group's power and independence.[82]

For the Complete Works' revival in 2006, Henry was played by another black actor, Chuk Iwuji, described as "a Henry VI with the simplicity, charity, kindness and moral outrage that fits a Christ-figure who discovers he is living in Golgotha."[83] Henry takes his role as the anointed Deputy of God on earth seriously, determinedly sticking to the principles of a spiritual rather than a political leader. Ralph Fiennes commented:

> his whole dilemma was that he could not find a way to assert his rule through purely Christian values. The area an actor has to tackle in playing the role of Henry VI is *faith* . . . At times this approach leads Henry into vengeful, "Old Testament" actions; at others he follows an approach of forgiveness, toler-ance, and pacifism.

Alan Howard similarly pointed up Henry's failure but also em-phasized his growing isolation from the world which surrounds him in *Part II* and *Part III* with bouts of madness: "His swoon on hearing the news of Duke Humphrey's death left him in a catatonic trance, from which Margaret strove to rouse him by means of her long, highly rhetorical speech."[84] The division of purpose between kingly duty and his faith created a schism in Howard's Henry; aware of who he ought to be but unable to forget who he really is:

> His childish curls are gone. His voice, once tremulous, making every sentence seem to end in a question, is now firmer. He rises to moments of majesty, but then backs off from them bewildered, as if he did not recognize himself as the man who had just spoken. When he asks Gloucester to resign his Protec-torship, the entire court is stunned. But Henry has no stomach for blood and no joy in power. He becomes a figure of increas-

ing detachment, sitting on the fringes smiling wanly—it is all
so absurd!—a painfully bemused spectator viewing the chaos
he has no power to control. [85]

Henry's nemesis or alter ego takes the form of Richard of
Gloucester:

They are both isolationists. Hunchbacked Richard is "myself,
alone"; Henry longs for shepherd's weeds. But Henry knows
what dying Warwick learned, that pomp is only "earth and
dust," while Richard is willing to "Torment myself, to catch the
English Crown."[86]

Primarily a fighter, Richard is a creature of war: "In the field of battle, if nowhere else, he has transcended his disabilities: here he is the
fastest, moves with the greatest alacrity, is the most lethal, and yet
the effort takes less toll of him than anyone else."[87] The murder of
Henry by Richard can often be the most disturbing and deeply shocking part of the play. On one level, Richard's prominence in the cycle
comes to a head as he disposes of his family's enemy; on another,
Good comes face-to-face with Evil in a metaphysical battle of wills.

Preempting the "make love not war" attitude of the 1960s by
facing violence with loving gestures, David Warner's Henry (1963)
maintained his Christian ethos to the end, planting: "a kiss of forgiveness on murdering Richard's cheek . . . a sublime end. This
Henry is the archetype of every honest CND demonstrator who ever
sat down in Trafalgar Square."[88] Deprived of the pleasure of the kill
by Henry's taunting and his furious and maniacal reaction, the
unsatisfied Richard "further mutilated his body after the murder:
and like some terrible puppy scrabbles at and worries the dead body
with his hacking dagger."[89]

In Terry Hands' 1977 production, religious imagery emphasized
this clash between the two:

When the two finally come face to face, it is for one to kill the
other. A trap in the forestage opens; the king crouches on a
grilled floor through which light streams upward. His hands

are manacled to chains attached from above. His hair is grayed [*sic*]. Richard appears from below like some demon; his black against Henry's white smock is obviously emblematic. Richard grins, but . . . [he] is finally discomfited, and it is fury that makes him silence Henry by lunging forward to stab and stab again. The king sags into a crucifix.[90]

Alan Howard played Henry as if he wanted to die, goading Richard into killing him. Finally able to release the anger which had built up in him throughout, Henry let rip at Richard in shocking form, purging himself of pent-up emotion, cursing Richard with future prophecy, and also ensuring his own death.

Anton Lesser, who essayed Gloucester in this production, played Richard again in 1988 to Ralph Fiennes' Henry. Despite their differences there was an understanding between the two men, which Fiennes described as:

an understanding deriving paradoxically from their utterly opposed set of values. Because of this they can talk to each other quite easily. There is the possibility of an almost conversational start to the scene which builds into Henry's frightening prophecy and condemnation of Richard. It is as if Henry is taken over by a peculiar power: he knows he is going to die and is given the gift of prophecy which allows him to make a terrible judgement on Richard.[91]

Lesser explained how:

Richard decides he has had enough at the prospect of being told the significance of his own presence in the world. This is something that must not be uttered—like having the future read, even having one's fortune told. To know one's future destroys the sanctity of unknown destiny and for Richard (certainly the way I played him) his running condition depends upon experiencing the eternal now: every minute is fresh and full of possibility. Prophecy always panics him . . . He suffers from the fear that someone who has vision, by uttering what that vision is, can make it happen—and, of course, it does. Henry's switch from past to future triggers that reaction. Richard kills him and utters one of his most remarkable statements of self-awareness and of present-tense self-assertion:

> I have no brother, I am like no brother.
> And this word 'love', which greybeards call divine,
> Be resident in men like one another
> And not in me: I am myself alone. [*Part III*, 5.6.80–83][92]

What is left at the end of the three plays is a country in as much peril as it was at the start, but this time peril from within. Moving from wars with France, to wars between families, Richard of Gloucester points forward to a future in which the family will devour itself. Left at the end of the play holding Edward IV's baby, his nephew, the audience are already aware of his murderous intent. As at the end of Boyd's production: "we leave this sly, wry psychotic standing in a puddle of blood, [the blood of Henry VI] clucking over the swaddled nephew he'll be murdering in the final episode in the RSC's Bardathon."[93] In 1988 the final word of the *Henry VI* plays was Richard's "Now!"—ominously pointing forward to the opening words of *Richard III*.

The tragedy of Henry VI's failure to rule was poignantly symbolized in Terry Hands' production. The long wars have so distorted civilian and private life that when Edward calls for music to lead his family in a dance: "they stand there confused. The wars are over, but no one can remember the steps."[94]

In set design, costuming, and casting these directors visually unified the plays so that through-lines were there for the audience to connect to. They also managed to express a level of connection between characters and events, which made these three very different plays, with massive casts, easier to follow. The emphasis of certain contemporary themes also helped to bring a direct level of understanding to a modern audience, and bring these neglected plays back to life. In their notions of absurdity, black humor, cynicism, and in their depiction of violence, the *Henry VI* plays stand up today among the best antiwar fiction. They ask:

7. At the end of *Part III* in Michael Boyd's 2000 production: "we leave this sly, wry psychotic standing in a puddle of blood, clucking over the swaddled nephew he'll be murdering in the final episode in the RSC's Bardathon [*Richard III*]," with Aidan McArdle as Richard Duke of Gloucester.

a series of disturbing questions about the nature of political power, questions that seemed to have been resolved with the advent of democracy, but that have now returned to haunt us with a vengeance; above all, the question of whether the exercise of power is always tainted with evil, murderous violence, coercion, dishonesty, and betrayal . . . But this is finally a story about the endless, incoherent cycle of fratricidal horror that civil war becomes; and it is a measure of the greatest art that it can deal with such terrible subjects and still leave the audience, at the end, feeling exhilarated, uplifted, better able to endure and oppose the cruelties of the world.[95]

THE DIRECTOR'S CUT: INTERVIEWS WITH EDWARD HALL AND MICHAEL BOYD

Edward Hall, son of the RSC's founder Sir Peter Hall, was born in 1967 and trained at Leeds University and the Mountview Theatre School before cutting his teeth at the Watermill Theatre in the 1990s. His first Shakespearean success was a production of *Othello* in 1995, though he used the experience as inspiration to found Propeller, an all-male theater company with whom he directed *The Comedy of Errors* and *Henry V*, which ran together in repertory during the 1997–98 season, and *Twelfth Night* in 1999, all at the Watermill. In 1998 he made his directorial debut with the RSC on a production of *The Two Gentlemen of Verona*, and would go on to work again with the company on *Henry V* in 2000–01, and, in the 2001–02 season, the production of *Julius Caesar*. In between *Henry* and *Caesar* that year, Hall returned to the Watermill to direct *Rose Rage*, his (in)famous and celebrated abattoir-set adaptation of the *Henry VI* trilogy that he discusses here. He left the RSC in 2002 and has continued to work with Propeller on such productions as *A Midsummer Night's Dream* in 2003 and *Twelfth Night* and *The Taming of the Shrew* in 2007. He became artistic director of Hampstead Theatre in 2010.

Michael Boyd was born in Belfast in 1955, educated in London and Edinburgh, and completed his MA in English literature at Edinburgh University. He trained as a director at the Malaya Bronnaya Theatre in Moscow. He then went on to work at the Belgrade Theatre in Coventry, joining the Sheffield Crucible as associate director in 1982. In 1985 Boyd became founding artistic director of the Tron Theatre in Glasgow, becoming equally acclaimed for staging new writing and innovative productions of the classics, including *Macbeth* with Iain Glenn and an award-winning adaptation of Janice Galloway's *The Trick is to Keep Breathing*. He was drama director of the *New Beginnings Festival of Soviet Arts* in Glasgow in 1999. He joined the RSC as an associate director in 1996 and has since directed numerous productions of Shakespeare's plays. He won the Laurence Olivier Award for Best Director for his *Henry VI* trilogy with the RSC's *This England: The Histories* cycle in 2001, which he discusses here. He took over as artistic director of the RSC in 2003. In 2006 he revived the celebrated saga as part of the company's Complete Works Festival, going on to direct them along with the other five history plays that together form Shakespeare's two tetralogies, and presenting the entire sequence in 2008 as *The Histories*. The productions won The Evening Standard Theatre Editor's Award and Olivier Awards for Best Company Performance, Best Revival, and Best Costume Design.

Putting on the *Henry VI* saga means directing at least two shows, possibly three, or working hard to come up with some sort of mammoth adaptation. What inspired you to want to take on that challenge?

Hall: It started through wanting to direct all three plays. The sweep of the story is fantastic and I'd already directed *Henry V,* so I felt drawn to the next chapter. At the Watermill Theatre in Newbury I didn't have the luxury of doing a three-hour-long show, because the last train to London left at about 10:35 p.m. So, quite simply, my co-adaptor Roger Warren and I sat down and worked out that all three plays had to be done within four to four and a half hours because we couldn't come down later than ten past ten. That was how I was constricted: the rail timetable had a lot to do with the creation of it. There is a mistaken view that people cut the plays because they think they are not good enough, but that certainly wasn't the case with us. I would have happily done much more of it if I'd had the time to do it in.

When we set to thinking about how to boil the text down it was much more a case of looking at what was there, rather than looking at what we would cut. With any great piece of work, cutting it is always painful and if you look back at what you have cut you'll never actually go through with it. You have to focus on the story you are telling. Essentially, the first part of *Rose Rage* was *Henry VI Parts I* and *II* squeezed together and the second part was *Part III*. In our first part we had a war abroad going wrong as a metaphor for how bad government at home was. Bad government at home was causing a war to go wrong abroad and the death of Talbot, the great hero, was a direct result of squabbling politicians in Whitehall. Within that you saw the rise of Suffolk, the splitting of York and Lancaster and the Rose Garden scene, the capture of Margaret of Anjou and the affair between Suffolk and Margaret, and the influence of Margaret and Suffolk on the boy king causing all sorts of factions to develop at court. That was broadly the sweep of the first two hours, finishing with Jack Cade's revolt. We began the second part with the Yorkists breaking into Parliament and York being crowned, rolling into the murder of York and Rutland and the arrival of Richard Duke of Gloucester. We did the whole thing with twelve people, so there was an incredible amount of doubling going on: I think one of the actors got killed five times. We weren't able to do Joan of Arc and France which was the part that suffered most. Audiences did one of two things: they either sat down and watched what was in front of them; or, if they wanted to take a belligerent view, they sat down and complained about what had been cut.

Boyd: For us, the *Henry VI* plays were to be the opening salvo of an eight-play cycle. In our 2000 productions the key inspirations were the Corpus Christi mystery cycles, Lincoln and Norwich Cathedrals, and the legacy of civil strife and cultural poverty left by the English Reformation. We worked on the assumption that Shakespeare was writing about his own time through the protective prism of the past.

By 2006, when we revisited the cycle, Britain was engaged in two wars, post 9/11, and I was now in charge of the RSC as artistic director, looking for a project of sufficient ambition and substance to headline our yearlong Complete Works Festival and open our temporary Courtyard Theatre. I was also looking to test the potential of the RSC as an ensemble company on the European model; a community of artists, with a long-term project, and working on the largest canvas the theatrical canon can provide.

All this colored our Complete Histories Cycle.

Do you think perhaps the scale of the undertaking is what makes them such rarely performed plays? Or are they, as very early Shakespeare efforts, inferior in some way?

Hall: In no way are they inferior. I think it's all to do with resources. Because what's the point of only seeing one part? You have to bring three plays together and you need a lot of resources to do that. It is a major event for a company to take on those plays because of their scale. If you squeeze them down to a cast of twelve you are pushing it, but that's still quite large. Even when you are doing a four-hour version of the three plays you need a six-week rehearsal period. So I think it's much more to do with resources and practical issues than it is to do with the quality of the writing.

Boyd: There has been an intellectual laziness and a sort of apolitical shallowness in the way these plays have been addressed which has led to them being misunderstood and underestimated as the naive work of a journeyman.

We respond very easily to the "modernity" of the Henry IV and V plays, and even "the birth of the interior monologue" with *Richard III*. We are so keen to see ourselves in Shakespeare that we always show him looking in our direction: the "First Great Modern" casts his searching but ultimately benign gaze upon his true inheritors. We twist his neck to make sure that he sees things the way we do and we torture Hamlet on Freud's couch to reveal the "First Great Modern Masterpiece."

But Shakespeare is not always looking in our direction. He looks away from us as well, envisioning a lost medieval Catholic England, banished and criminalized as recently as his father's lifetime—an England at one with itself, and able to share a common vocabulary whose meaning was still physically embodied in the coherent and magical symbolism and song of a shared faith. Perhaps Shakespeare is also the "Last Great Medieval," and his first tetralogy the "Last Great Medieval Masterpiece"?

Judged by the criteria of modern psychological realism these plays might look patchy, naive, and odd, but set them in the context of the great medieval cathedrals, the liturgy, and devotional drama and painting of the fifteenth and sixteenth centuries, and they shine with precocious sophistication.

In performance the plays also consistently display the theatrical flair that made them the most popular of their time and secured Shakespeare's early reputation.

Many scholars now view *Part I* as a collaborative "prequel" (Shakespeare is thought to have written about 20 percent) and it's often seen as a bit of a misfit within the trilogy. What's your take on the play? Does it work as a coherent opening chapter, or do you need to work to bolt it on to the other two? Does the Joan of Arc/Talbot struggle inform the other two plays?

Hall: I never thought about it being a collaboration at the time. *Part I* begins the story with a very broad horizon that slowly focuses down and down. The pressure that it keeps up is intense. There might have been more than one person involved, but that never influenced the way we worked on material or chose what to cut. I don't think it makes *Part I* inferior to the other two: there is so much to set up and establish in *Part I* which pays off as you run through *Parts II* and *III*. If there were more than one author in *Part I* then I'd say Shakespeare was certainly clever enough and collaborative enough to bring their work to bear and use it to his advantage. Whichever way you look at it does, I think, put Shakespeare as an author at the forefront of the work.

Boyd: One scene in *Part I* that struck me as tonally alien to Shakespeare was Suffolk's wooing of Margaret. It felt self-conscious and brittle and so I loyally attributed it away from William to Nashe. But even here you are aware of a corrupt version of Harry's later wooing of the French Kate [in *Henry V*], and you have Shakespeare's trademark gag (almost overworked throughout the canon) of "Would he were here." Perhaps Shakespeare later stole it from Nashe.

For us, *Part I* was the theatrical blockbuster of the tetralogy: a grand set piece state funeral is followed by fighting on the streets of London, and then a cannonade at Orléans—great costumes, comedy, and bombast from the overblown French Court, magic and sorcery from the charismatic Joan of Arc, whose swordplay skillfully builds into major battles on the fields of France. We enjoyed the matrix of antagonisms between Gloucester and Winchester, Talbot and Joan, York and Somerset, all around the quiet vulnerable center of Henry and the English Crown.

The Corpus Christi plays provided us with one key to coherence throughout the tetralogy: their potent and efficient recycling of iconic characters, objects, and situations which thereby accumulate a sublime significance proved a valuable model for our aesthetic. Just as the Pharoah shares a rhyme scheme with Herod and Satan, and Isaac prefigures Christ, and the timber from the Tree of Knowledge returns later to provide the hull of Noah's Ark and the Cross of Christ's Passion, our characters and our objects and actions found powerful refrains. We noticed, for instance, that the French Court speaks the language and wears the clothes of Satan's vainglorious minions gathered outside the Hell Mouth and throwing sweeties to the children from their pageant wagon. Richard III later refers to himself as a Vice figure from the Mysteries. The actors playing the French court in our *Part I* became, in turn, the leaders of the Kentish Rebellion and the York brothers in *Part II* as they carried strife across the English Channel from a seemingly defeated France. The Talbots recalled to us Abraham and Isaac and they in turn became powerfully reprised and tested as father and son throughout the entire eight-play cycle. Joan of Arc, in typically Shakespearean fashion, is both magical and fraudulent, and her last trick for us was to re-emerge from her own ashes to take vengeance on York, Warwick, and all the English who had brutally burned her alive, as the next and greatest scourge of England, Margaret of Anjou. The audience gasped, consistently.

Others among the greatest of Shakespeare's characters, who will stride across the later Henry plays, are also forged in the heat of *Henry VI Part I*: Humphrey of Gloucester (Richard Cordery), Richard of York (Clive Wood), Warwick (Geff Francis 2000/01, Patrice Naiambana 2006/08), Suffolk (Richard Dillane 2000/01, Geoffrey Streatfeild 2006/08), and the extraordinary Henry himself.

In the theater, this is a wonderful play.

What about *Parts II* and *III*; what's the essence of each one? *Part II* seems like a very bleak political satire in many respects while *Part III* has the feel of more straightforward tragedy. What were some of your experiences of the particular challenges of working on them?

Boyd: An excessively pessimistic and over-schematic reading of the Henries could go as follows: Talbot and the true values of chivalry are betrayed and killed by the politicking of a divided England in *Part I*, Humphrey and the values of benign pragmatic Humanism are murdered in *Part II*, Henry and England's "Spiritual Soul" are murdered in *Part III*.

Talbot and son played an important role in our *Part II* as the executioners of Suffolk. Not pirates in our show, but now embittered ghosts of the Talbots floating on the Styx in Charon's boat, they challenged and beheaded the selfish duke and sent his head to Margaret, who had earlier bedevilled them as Joan of Arc. Suffolk's headless body was then dragged ashore and abused by two fishermen who turned out to be Alençon and Orléans from *Part I*, who would now drum up the Kentish Rebellion with Jack Cade/the dauphin before reincarnating as Richard and Edward the sons of York.

Driving all three Henry plays is anger and grief about the destructive schism dividing the body politic of England, and an impassioned search for coherence and harmony. The trilogy reaches its nadir with the depth of man's inhumanity in *Part III*: the murder of Rutland, torture and murder of York, mutilation and murder of Clifford, and the greatest ever human slaughter on English soil at Towton. We travel through Shakespeare's hellish vision of an England out of joint with nothing more than Henry's trembling candlelight to guide us. When that, too, is extinguished by the murder of Henry, we are ready to say with Edgar that "This is the worst." And then comes Richard III.

The glimmer of hope toward the end of *Part III* comes not from the son of York cradled in Richard's murdering arms, but from Henry's miraculous prophecy and blessing of the young boy Richmond. In our production Richmond was played by the same actor (Sam Troughton in 2000/01 and Lex Shrapnel 2006/08) who had played John Talbot sacrificed to the devilish French in *Part I*, no longer as Young Talbot's ghost, but still scarred with John Talbot's exact head wounds, inflicted by the French in *Part I*.

There is something remarkable about following these characters over eight or nine hours in performance, especially as the plays are so unfamiliar, the audience not only has more time to suffer alongside the protagonists, but also has largely no idea what the outcomes will be. Did you find the plays a liberating prospect to work on in this respect?

Hall: It has never really bothered me when I've done *A Midsummer Night's Dream* and people know that Bottom is going to wake up with Titania. This knowledge never seems to spoil the experience of the audience so I didn't really notice a lack of foreknowledge watching the history plays. What you do get with these plays is an immediate piece of living English history. You can still see the characters from their pages alive and well today. Just as you still see Falstaff, Pistol, and Bardolph, you still see Jack Cade and his cohorts, the Clerk of Chatham, Clarence, Richard Duke of Gloucester, the father who killed his son: you see all these people, they're all there in front of you. They are quintessentially English. There's something about the way these people speak and behave, the places they talk about and their family history, that a British audience instantly plugs into. It's rooted in our DNA. There's an excitement about a five-hundred-year-old story talking to us today and these people being as recognizable today as they were then. There's something about the national character that Shakespeare captured in the history plays and it's still with us. If you look at relatively recent British history there have been two huge civil conflicts: the English Civil War and the Wars of the Roses. We don't have the great work of art about the English Civil War. The Wars of the Roses lives more strongly in our culture than the English Civil War—as a period, as a story, and as a piece of living history—because of Shakespeare.

Boyd: One potent case of our production benefiting from both these factors was how shocked and horrified audiences always were by the death, halfway through the trilogy, of Richard Cordery's seemingly indestructible Humphrey, and how grateful they were that I brought him back to haunt the ensuing chaos, and then to gloat on England's troubles as the King of France in *Part III*.

I always try to work on a Shakespeare as if it were a new text, but it is rare for most of the audience to be following the narrative innocently. Imagine what *Hamlet* would be like to watch if the shifts of his fate were as surprising as those of Margaret and Henry are to most people over the course of the tetralogy.

The plays depict brutal power struggles on a level surely unmatched elsewhere in Shakespeare, and reminders of death were ever present in the visuals of both your productions. Could you discuss that and give us an insight into the process of arriving at those design choices?

Hall: Our setting was an abattoir. People call each other butchers in the play and England is talked about as a slaughterhouse, which is what first led me to think of that image. The question is how do you do a historical play with an extraordinary amount of violence in it? How do you abstract that into a metaphorical world where people can be violent to each other in a way that doesn't involve restraint? In a stage fight when an actor is pretending to stab someone, what is actually at the forefront of their mind is being careful not to actually kill them. I wanted to work out a way of presenting the violence so that the audience could get a proper sense of it, with no danger to anyone onstage. So the actors could really let themselves go, but where there were dots that the audience had to join up so that their imaginations would be engaged. We used a butcher with a huge meat slab with real offal being chopped to pieces and pulled apart. It

8. Edward Hall's *Rose Rage* (2001) at The Watermill: "Our setting was an abattoir. People call each other butchers in the play and England is talked about as a slaughterhouse, which is what first led me to think of that image . . . In a stage fight when an actor is pretending to stab someone, what is actually at the forefront of their mind is being careful not to actually kill them."

meant that you could get the full visceral experience of the violence. You could smell it. At one point we cooked some of the offal in a sizzling hot pan and it was eaten onstage. It engaged the imagination in a different way than a stage fight would. When Warwick died we had a large bucket being filled with a stream of blood running from a tap. It ran as the wounded Warwick gave his dying speech and then when he died the tap stopped. You saw his blood drain away in front of you.

When we came to Jack Cade and the executions we used big red cabbages to represent people's heads. We put an actor's head at one end of a long chopping block and put the red cabbage on the other end and then smashed the cabbage with a baseball bat. The actor would roll off and disappear into the wings while everyone tore the cabbage to bits and ate bits of it. Not only did it work to watch, it was good for the company because they were doing something quite animal and were able to sort of explore the feelings of violence that might come with that kind of behavior. Imagination is a wonderful thing. We had a man playing a woman, Margaret of Anjou, walking on in tears with the head of her dead lover, as represented by a red cabbage in a sack, and no one laughed. Everyone understood exactly what was going on. To me that's interesting because you're embracing the idea of theater. You're absolutely free from any twentieth-century naturalism and free to explore the plays in a metaphorical way, which is the spirit in which they were written.

Boyd: Our complete 2008 cycle (in the order of writing) began with Henry V's coffin descending from the black heavens and ended with Henry V wooing Katherine of France on a stage made out of the coffins of the French dead.

We connected Joan to the other world with the reassembled sacrificial bones of a dead bird, and later the same actress (Fiona Bell in 2000/01 and Katy Stephens in 2006/08) reassembled the bones of her dead son Edward to empower her curses on the House of York. Memorial stones were assembled by York as he enlisted his dynastic forefathers to his claim to the throne, and his grandson later did the same, in miniature now, and as a game with only half-remembered significance. White feathers fell at Joan's death and later again at

Towton and Tewkesbury where they intermingled with the red of blood and of the House of Lancaster.

Later in the cycle sand fell onto kings and told them their time, too, would pass. We were trying to dramatize two interlocking types of cycle: the blind and solipsistic cycle of revenge, and the Mystery Cycle, where revenge is finally halted by sacrificial love. A third cycle, of repeated history, would have been evident to the Elizabethan audience: the providential conclusion of Shakespeare's first tetralogy, with Henry Tudor finally triumphant over evil (so pleasing to the authorities and their censors), would have been qualified by theatergoers as they wandered home. It was, after all, another Henry Tudor who brought about the great religious and political divisions of their own time, for which the conflicts between York and Lancaster had just served as metaphor.

How do you see the roles of the female characters in the plays? In many ways, Henry is the most traditionally "feminine" character in a world inhabited by powerful, martial women.

Hall: I'm not sure I agree with that about Henry. I think he's a deeply spiritual man who is desperate not to do the wrong thing. The pressure around him is so intense that he gets to a point where he cannot do anything without ostracizing a group of people he doesn't want to ostracize. He falls into a catch-22 situation, which is also a metaphor for how difficult it is to stop a civil conflict like this happening. I think you have to be very careful with that character; he is a man under a lot of pressure and he is very sensitive. Feminine in terms of expressing vulnerability? No. Feminine in terms of sensitivity? Yes.

Boyd: Both Joan and Margaret exploit their femininity in the wooing of the French court and Suffolk respectively, and Elizabeth Grey, later Queen Elizabeth, exhibits femininity and vulnerability throughout her story, finding her tigress's strength only as the mother of two murdered children in *Richard III*. One of Shakespeare's finest and most characteristic achievements in the trilogy is to reverse for one scene our great animosity toward the adulterous, murderous couple of Suffolk and Margaret, and invite us to feel deep compassion for them as they are forced apart in *Part II*. Both here, and in her motherly protection of her son, Margaret is all woman.

The need in Shakespeare's women for self-determination is consistently denied by brutal patriarchy, and the author consistently reveals how this need is then sublimated into sexual, or supernatural, control. Joan of Arc, Margaret, the Countess of Auvergne, and Eleanor, Duchess of Gloucester, are just the first of many.

Shakespeare also gives his disempowered women astonishing insight. There is no more devastating critique of cannibalistic court politics than Eleanor's warning to her husband, Humphrey, on the eve of his arrest.

What was your vision of the character of Henry? He is often disregarded because he seems a weak, ineffectual, and uncharismatic pawn in a deadly game for which he is not suited, and yet it seems Shakespeare gives him opportunities to show tremendous strength and dignity.

Boyd: Henry's journey is both a paradox and a pilgrimage. He begins as an ignored and powerless child, overwhelmed by a factious court and the memory of his father, Henry V. Supported by the loyal and pragmatic counsel of Humphrey Duke of Gloucester, he grows in stature, speaks better than anyone of the dangers of internal dissent on the field of France, and makes the best possible effort to balance and neutralize the opposing dynastic factions within the court. His moment of greatest human folly (and the undoing of the English court) is the moment where he most insists upon his will being done: his marriage to Margaret and crowning her Queen of England.

The mistake most often made in interpreting Henry is the anachronistic, modern assumption (Freud's couch again) that his victimhood must be entirely the result of some internal psychological pathology, which ignores the external geological pressures which form his fate in his four-play journey. Henry is England embodied throughout the first trilogy, and the plays print themselves upon his mind and body as England suffers.

By coincidence, both our Henries were Nigerian and both practicing Christians (David Oyelowo 2000/01, Chuk Iwuji 2006/08).

9. Michael Boyd's 2006 RSC production with Katy Stephens as Margaret and Chuk Iwuji as Henry VI whose "moment of greatest human folly (and the undoing of the English court) is the moment where he most insists upon his will being done: his marriage to Margaret and crowning her Queen of England."

Both were alert to the savagery of civil war and both embraced the opportunity to play a lifetime pilgrimage where Henry grew in strength and authority the further he removed himself from power. Pragmatists who scoff at such a paradox are ultimately aligning themselves with the sterile Machiavellianism of Richard III and most modern power politics. Henry is seemingly omnipotent in death as he leads the armies of the dead and the living against the tyrant at Bosworth Field.

Historically Henry VI became an unsuccessful candidate for beatification and sainthood, and Shakespeare is undoubtedly endowing him with the prophetic and miraculous martyrdom of England's one sainted king, Edward the Confessor. [Stephen] Greenblatt has talked eloquently of Shakespeare's boldness in staging purgatory on a Protestant London stage [*Hamlet in Purgatory*, 2002]. This portrait of Henry, at such a vulnerable point in Shakespeare's career, shows an even greater daring.

I remember reacting with an equal measure of surprise and glee at the appearance onstage of the character we realize is going to become Richard III in the future, who seems "good" at first before finally setting out his stall in a remarkable soliloquy in *Part III*. Do you see the family-centric struggles of *Part II* giving way to a sort of angel/devil binary between Henry and Richard toward the end of the saga, looking forward unavoidably to the one-man show that is *Richard III*?

Hall: The death of Richard's father has a profound effect upon him, and that's the thing that unhinges him completely. One cannot over-emphasize the effect York's death has on his sons. For Richard, the relationship with his father almost allows him to ignore the fact that he's deformed, because his father is such a tower of strength to him and so envelops him with love. When he's gone I think that's the first time he has to look at himself in the mirror on his own. His brother Edward was famous for going into battle with his troops, on foot and with sword drawn. He was a real bruiser and the moment he got the crown he spent the next decade drinking and shagging. By the time he'd drunk himself to his grave and realized he was about to die, he hadn't organized what was going to happen next and it was too late. Mix those things together: you have the elder brother suddenly going bananas—he's got his money, he's got his crown, and he's going to enjoy himself. And you have a disgruntled younger brother who has lost his father and suddenly feels like he doesn't fit. Then you have a middle brother who doesn't know who he is—he's very articulate but is clearly blown whichever way the wind goes, and has already shown himself untrustworthy once. You add that all together and you can see where Shakespeare's going.

Boyd: From out of England's corrupt and wounded womb comes forth a distorted monster. The same forces which bring about the pseudo-judicial murder of Humphrey, the misshapen false rebellion of Jack Cade, and which bring England, Margaret, and Henry to the brink of madness, squeeze Richard and his teeth into the horrified arms of the midwife. That is the perspective as seen from the end of the trilogy and our productions did emphasize the cosmology of good and evil by casting the minor Vice figures of France in *Part I* as those who would later preside over England's descent into chaos in *Part III* and *Richard III*, but Shakespeare's secular humanist side was also evident: Henry's mentor Gloucester gives good counsel which is wholly secular, and Henry only retreats from this world toward the status of angel when he has no other choice. When there is no other place available where human truths can be cherished.

Richard of Gloucester refers to himself in terms of the Vice figure in the medieval morality and mystery plays, but he, too, excites our compassion as he absorbs horrific personal attacks from Margaret, Clifford, and eventually even his own mother. And the audience member who has empathized with Richard of York's arduous and impassioned three-play struggle for the throne can also carry a candle for all of his orphaned sons, including Richard, as they seek dynastic justice where their murdered father failed. Both Aidan McArdle (2000/01) and Jonathan Slinger (2006/08) had been tremendous and very different Pucks for the RSC, and their Richards reflected the same differences: Aidan winning us against our better judgment with great psychotic charm, and Jonathan gradually blackmailing us with the morbid exhibition of his physical and psychic wounds.

It's interesting, however, to view the plays alongside *Richard III* as structurally they work very differently in their democratic distribution of character. What were they like to work on with your respective companies of actors? Could you give us a little insight into the process of working on such a large-scale, ensemble-rich project?

Hall: If you have a smaller cast you absolutely have to decide who is on which side. You have to mark that out quite carefully so people know who is sitting on which side of the fence, and who is in the middle. You can use costume for that as well. You have to go through the family tree and look at where everybody is. When you conflate characters together you have to look at where that places them relative to the family. You have to make sure people are clearly identifiable all the way through, because the big fear audiences have about the history plays is that they won't know who anyone is. You have to help a little bit with that. It's a bit of a detective journey to begin with to work out exactly who is motivated by what. It is in the end like doing a soap opera. Family is the most important thing: it is a massive family squabble played out on a big stage.

What is absolutely crucial to making the plays work is to make sure you get the right political atmosphere. And it's very simple: there is no such thing as the middle way. There is no such thing as liberal compromise. If you are not for something, you are by definition against it. There's no in between. People's lives and lands and titles could be decided and disappear in a moment if they made a slightly wrong call, and even sometimes a small mistake. So it's an incredibly dangerous and difficult atmosphere to operate in. There is no such thing as debate, and you have to create that atmosphere and get people to understand that. It explains why people behave as they do, why they are so guarded and so mistrustful and so careful. Ultimately and famously in *Richard III* it partly explains why Stanley sits on the top of the hill with his army and refuses to join in the battle until he's sure which side is winning. That sort of political atmosphere is a key thing to understand and to communicate in the way you play those big court scenes. It could all fall apart for anybody in a second and no one's quite sure what's going to happen next. If you get that then you have real tension, the potential of a good thriller.

Boyd: It's impossible *not* to view these plays alongside *Richard III*. Few Hollywood movies have so obviously trailed a sequel as *Henry VI Part III* and a good third of *Richard III* is incomprehensible or looks clumsy and dull without the experience of the preceding trilogy.

My favorite moment of enhanced insight might be Katy Stephen's aging Margaret reassembling the skeletal remains of her murdered son as a vessel through which to channel her curses on the Yorks and the Greys, much as she had done with the bones of a bird in *Henry VI Part I*, as Joan of Arc, to channel her cursing of Talbot and the English. She passes her targeted curses around the room until she is interrupted by the young Marquis of Dorset, a small part, but played here by Wela Frazier, who had also played Edward, Margaret's son, in *Henry VI Part III*. Katy stops, is choked, and her aggression collapses into uncontrollable grief as she and the audience both see a vision of her slaughtered boy.

True: more members of the ensemble had a quieter time of it in *Richard III*, but when Stanley and Richmond are played by the Talbots (with Stanley handing Richmond the very sword that Talbot had handed to his son, three plays ago, as he went into battle), and when Richard can be haunted not just by Henry VI, Hastings, and Buckingham, but by his own father, Richard of York, it becomes an easy task to make the "small" parts count, and thereby tell the whole story of the play, avoiding the common error of limiting it to an undramatic monologue.

DESIGNING *HENRY VI*: TOM PIPER

Tom Piper was born in London in 1964 and graduated from Trinity College, Cambridge, before studying theater design at the Slade School of Art. In 1990 he worked with Peter Brook in Paris on his production of *The Tempest* and then worked as a freelance designer. He won the London Fringe Best Design Award for *Cat in the Ghetto* at Tabard Theatre in Chiswick, West London. He first worked with Michael Boyd at the Tron Theatre in Glasgow on his production of *Jack and the Beanstalk*. They have worked together regularly since then and Tom was appointed associate designer with the RSC in 2004. His work there includes designs for *The Broken Heart, Spring Awakening, A Patriot for Me, Much Ado About Nothing, The Spanish Tragedy, Bartholomew Fair, Measure for Measure, Troilus and Cressida, A Month in the Country, A Midsummer Night's Dream, Romeo and Juliet, Henry VI, Richard III, The Tempest, King Lear, Twelfth Night, Hamlet* and *The Histories, As You Like It, The Drunks, The Grain Store,* and *Antony and Cleopatra.* He won the Laurence Olivier Award for Best Costume Design in 2009 for his work on Shakespeare's Histories that he's discussing here.

Could you first explain what is the role of the designer and how your work relates to that of the director?

Piper: The designer works with the director through discussions, sketches, and models to create the world of the play—an environment in which the actors can tell the story dressed in clothes that reflect their nature, wealth, and status within that world. That world may alter over time as characters and their situations change. With a Shakespeare play especially, where so much of the sense of location is given by the language, the design needs only to be suggestive and does not have to slavishly create a real location. As the *Henry VI* plays move swiftly from England to France, street to tower to court to battle, the set design needs to be a springboard for the imagination of the audience, to transport them instantly from place to place. The director then works with the actors through rehearsal to discover the meaning of the text, and how best to tell the story in the created world.

In terms of Shakespeare's vision of the Wars of the Roses and the eventual resolution at Bosworth Field, with Henry Richmond becoming king and inaugurating the Tudor dynasty, the world of the play is very medieval, very fifteenth century. At the same time, the rise and fall of a tyrant is a perennial historical theme, and there have been very successful productions set in, say, 1930s Germany or the Baghdad of Saddam Hussein. What sort of a setting did you and your director choose, and why?

Piper: I tend to believe that there are broadly three periods in which you can set a play: the period it is set in, the time it was written, or now. Any other time-setting risks adding another layer of interpretation; for example, seeing a play set in 1930s Germany has all the layers of our twenty-first-century interpretation of that time and place imposed on a play written in the sixteenth century.

My initial research started with images of medieval battlefields, castles, and the paintings of Hieronymus Bosch, especially his depictions of hell with devils herding the damned through gaping hell mouths. But I also covered contemporary artists such as Francis Bacon and Louise Bourgeois, for their tormented figures and sculptural use of space. As an ex-biologist I am fascinated by the double helix of DNA and its echo in man-made forms such as staircases, and given that so much of the plays revolves around who is descended from whom, a subtle link to genetics seemed appropriate. The design was developed through many models, exploring the shapes of a tower, how the musicians would be integrated into the world, what the textures would be. The metal finish came partly from a response to the outside of the theater clad in rusty metal sheets, but also from the faceted panels of suits of armor. At one point in the design the tower was almost too literally a helmet with a visor slot. I still like to think of the stage as the body of England, the walkways entrances its arms and legs, the central tower its head with doors as the mouth (often the gates to hell), and the trapdoors its guts.

Staging either of Shakespeare's tetralogies is a mammoth undertaking. How did you manage to cover such a broad sweep of history and such different narratives from Joan of Arc to Jack Cade and ghostly visitations? Was the challenge as a designer to try to marry the plays to create a seamless whole or did you try to differentiate them in specific ways?

Piper: The plays of this cycle require too many different locations to describe, let alone design, but somehow the theater space must be capable of suggesting them all. The key is in the text and what we know of Shakespeare's own playhouse with its balconies, tiring-house, traps, and few entrance doors. Shakespeare always tells us where we are and the architecture of his space allows us suggestive possibilities for locations without requiring new scenery for each one. Was it possible in a single environment to create a versatile enough space in which we could imagine every scene required, without having to have endless scene changes? The plays have many different locations: castles, the Tower, numerous French towns which all seemed to need a higher level in which one group can lord it over another. Other scenes need gates or doors that can be broken down, or barred, within which traitors are imprisoned. Grand council chambers, parliaments, and battlefields can be the whole theater space, with the audience as fellow lords, commons, or foot soldiers. Ghosts or entrenched soldiers can burst from beneath the stage. The stage needs to be flexible and neutral enough to allow us to imaginatively leap from location to location.

Within the basic environment we still had to solve the staging requirements of particular scenes. The thrust space forces you to think as a sculptor rather than in a painterly way; every scene is viewed from multiple angles, so elements introduced have to work from all sides and be transparent enough not to create too many sight line problems. Most importantly it's a shared space in which both audience and actors are in continual dialogue. Within this space the clothes are vital to help tell the story. Joan's supernatural nature was enhanced by a chorus of three women in red who echoed her every move; the factions of York and Lancaster were marked by a clear color scheme of black and silver versus rust browns that chimed with the colors of the metal environment. Certain episodes within the plays needed a new visual language. The Cade rebellion was dramatized as a disturbing descent into a Boschian hell in which we mixed periods and the living with the dead. We suspended a cage within the space that became a climbing frame for rebels and an abstract tree for Cade to hide in at the end.

The plays depict brutal power struggles on a level surely unmatched elsewhere in Shakespeare, and reminders of death were ever present in the visuals of your production. Could you discuss that and give us an insight into the process of arriving at those design choices?

Piper: I looked at images from abattoirs and battlefields and we found, through the use of ropes and ladders hung within the space, a way of suspending bodies that could echo the twisted figures on the barbed wire of the trenches or hanging carcasses. The death of John Talbot was inspired in part by Rembrandt's *Descent from the Cross*. He was winched into the air in slings and then brought down to be cradled "pieta"-like by his father. Throughout there was an emphasis on the vertical axis in the space moving from hell below to the heavens above. The nature of the thrust stage makes the audience implicit witnesses to all the power struggles and political fighting, so the whole theater could become the debating chamber at court. I think that really helped the audience follow the shifts in allegiances. It created a sense of immersion in the whole rather than viewing it through a frame, as would have happened if we had been in a proscenium house.

10. In Michael Boyd's 2006 production of *Henry VI* designed by Tom Piper, "[t]he Cade rebellion was dramatized as a disturbing descent into a Boschian hell in which we mixed periods and the living with the dead."

How did you differentiate between France and England/the French and the English, or did you see them as essentially the same?

Piper: In *Part I* the French are very much the light entertainment, seen by Shakespeare almost as caricatures in quite a deliberately jingoistic way. So we emphasized this through costume: the French at the beginning are overblown and overconfident in the face of a famished English force led by Talbot. The French were all blue silk brocades and golden trim, while Talbot was in far more naturalistic filthy gray battledress. When we came to stage *Henry V* (after we had rehearsed the *Henry VI* plays) we took the idea even further: the French were dressed as exotic acrobats, almost birds of paradise with long-tailed coats who lived on trapezes floating above the world. The Countess of Auvergne was also seen through English eyes as a devilish temptress dressed in red. Later, by the time of Lady Bona's rejection by Edward, the French inhabited a more civilized and rational world that seemed very honorable in comparison to the madness of the English court. I kept with the blue color scheme, but made the clothes more muted and real.

And what about the women who often seem central and peripheral at the same time?

Piper: The women's journey through the plays was especially interesting and reflected Michael's strong through-casting. Each new role an actor took on brought with it the history of past characters they had played. So Katy Stephens who played Joan was reborn, so to speak, as Margaret; in fact Joan's attendant fiends were costumed in red velvet in the final preexecution scene, so when Margaret emerged onstage in the same dress, only two minutes after Joan had been lowered into her burning pit, it was clear that the spirit of evil had not been extinguished but was now taking on a new, subtler guise that the English, through Suffolk, were seduced into bringing into the English court. In later battle scenes we gave Margaret Joan's breastplate as a subtle echo.

And for all the blood, the murders, the choreographed onstage fighting: I suppose there's a basic choice between "stylization" (slow-motion battles, red silk for blood) and "realism" (the clash of metal, lashings of mud, and Kensington Gore): where did you aim to find yourselves on that spectrum?

Piper: We used many approaches within the plays, from naturalistic hand-to-hand fighting with broadswords through to large choric moments when the whole company acted as a stylized image of the flow of battle, for example lifting the defeated Talbots into the air. The choice depended on the dramaturgical needs of the moment. So it was important to see Joan of Arc actually fight and overpower Talbot, and the bloody brutality of the murders of York, Rutland, and Edward needed to be seen in their full horror to understand the vicious cycle of revenge within the plays. These were often moments of close-up action focusing on individual stories; to get the sense of the reality of the whole battlefield is far harder in theater, so we explored a more stylized language for these moments, sometimes in slow motion, or with nonnaturalistic swordfights, or through the use of ropes and aerialists. The fight director, Terry King, and movement director, Liz Ranken, worked very closely together on this fusion. Other moments became even more deliberately stylized, as for example in the battle of Towton, for which we decided to focus on Henry VI, alone in the tower hundreds of miles from the battlefield but feeling the battle fought in his name. So the only elements of actual warfare we used were the sounds of arrows, while a column of white feathers fell, through which Henry walked. The feathers turned red, as had the snow which fell in Towton.

SHAKESPEARE'S CAREER
IN THE THEATER

BEGINNINGS

William Shakespeare was an extraordinarily intelligent man who was born and died in an ordinary market town in the English Midlands. He lived an uneventful life in an eventful age. Born in April 1564, he was the eldest son of John Shakespeare, a glove maker who was prominent on the town council until he fell into financial difficulties. Young William was educated at the local grammar in Stratford-upon-Avon, Warwickshire, where he gained a thorough grounding in the Latin language, the art of rhetoric, and classical poetry. He married Ann Hathaway and had three children (Susanna, then the twins Hamnet and Judith) before his twenty-first birthday: an exceptionally young age for the period. We do not know how he supported his family in the mid-1580s.

Like many clever country boys, he moved to the city in order to make his way in the world. Like many creative people, he found a career in the entertainment business. Public playhouses and professional full-time acting companies reliant on the market for their income were born in Shakespeare's childhood. When he arrived in London as a man, sometime in the late 1580s, a new phenomenon was in the making: the actor who is so successful that he becomes a "star." The word did not exist in its modern sense, but the pattern is recognizable: audiences went to the theater not so much to see a particular show as to witness the comedian Richard Tarlton or the dramatic actor Edward Alleyn.

Shakespeare was an actor before he was a writer. It appears not to have been long before he realized that he was never going to grow into a great comedian like Tarlton or a great tragedian like Alleyn. Instead, he found a role within his company as the man who patched up old plays, breathing new life, new dramatic twists, into tired repertory pieces. He paid close attention to the work of the university-educated dramatists who were writing history plays and tragedies for the public stage in a style more ambitious, sweeping, and poetically grand than anything that had been seen before. But he may also have noted that what his friend and rival Ben Jonson would call "Marlowe's mighty line" sometimes faltered in the mode of comedy. Going to university, as Christopher Marlowe did, was all well and good for honing the arts of rhetorical elaboration and classical allusion, but it could lead to a loss of the common touch. To stay close to a large segment of the potential audience for public theater, it was necessary to write for clowns as well as kings and to intersperse the flights of poetry with the humor of the tavern, the privy, and the brothel: Shakespeare was the first to establish himself early in his career as an equal master of tragedy, comedy, and history. He realized that theater could be the medium to make the national past available to a wider audience than the elite who could afford to read large history books: his signature early works include not only the classical tragedy *Titus Andronicus* but also the sequence of English historical plays on the Wars of the Roses.

He also invented a new role for himself, that of in-house company dramatist. Where his peers and predecessors had to sell their plays to the theater managers on a poorly paid piecework basis, Shakespeare took a percentage of the box-office income. The Lord Chamberlain's Men constituted themselves in 1594 as a joint stock company, with the profits being distributed among the core actors who had invested as sharers. Shakespeare acted himself—he appears in the cast lists of some of Ben Jonson's plays as well as the list of actors' names at the beginning of his own collected works—but his principal duty was to write two or three plays a year for the company. By holding shares, he was effectively earning himself a royalty on his work, something no author had ever done before in England. When the Lord Chamberlain's Men collected their fee for performance at court in the Christmas season of 1594, three of them went along to the Treasurer of the Chamber: not just Richard Burbage the tragedian and Will Kempe the clown, but also Shakespeare the scriptwriter. That was something new.

The next four years were the golden period in Shakespeare's

career, though overshadowed by the death of his only son, Hamnet, aged eleven, in 1596. In his early thirties and in full command of both his poetic and his theatrical medium, he perfected his art of comedy, while also developing his tragic and historical writing in new ways. In 1598, Francis Meres, a Cambridge University graduate with his finger on the pulse of the London literary world, praised Shakespeare for his excellence across the genres:

> As Plautus and Seneca are accounted the best for comedy and tragedy among the Latins, so Shakespeare among the English is the most excellent in both kinds for the stage; for comedy, witness his *Gentlemen of Verona*, his *Errors*, his *Love Labours Lost*, his *Love Labours Won*, his *Midsummer Night Dream* and his *Merchant of Venice*: for tragedy his *Richard the 2*, *Richard the 3*, *Henry the 4*, *King John*, *Titus Andronicus* and his *Romeo and Juliet*.

For Meres, as for the many writers who praised the "honey-flowing vein" of *Venus and Adonis* and *Lucrece*, narrative poems written when the theaters were closed due to plague in 1593–94, Shakespeare was marked above all by his linguistic skill, by the gift of turning elegant poetic phrases.

PLAYHOUSES

Elizabethan playhouses were "thrust" or "one-room" theaters. To understand Shakespeare's original theatrical life, we have to forget about the indoor theater of later times, with its proscenium arch and curtain that would be opened at the beginning and closed at the end of each act. In the proscenium arch theater, stage and auditorium are effectively two separate rooms: the audience looks from one world into another as if through the imaginary "fourth wall" framed by the proscenium. The picture-frame stage, together with the elaborate scenic effects and backdrops beyond it, created the illusion of a self-contained world—especially once nineteenth-century developments in the control of artificial lighting meant that the auditorium could be darkened and the spectators made to focus on the lighted stage. Shakespeare, by contrast, wrote for a bare platform stage with a standing audience gathered around it in a courtyard in full daylight. The audience were always conscious of themselves and their fellow spectators, and they shared the same "room" as the actors. A sense of immediate presence and the creation of rapport with the audience were all-important. The actor could not afford to imagine he was in a closed world, with silent witnesses dutifully observing him from the darkness.

Shakespeare's theatrical career began at the Rose Theatre in Southwark. The stage was wide and shallow, trapezoid in shape, like a lozenge. This design had a great deal of potential for the theatrical equivalent of cinematic split-screen effects, whereby one group of characters would enter at the door at one end of the tiring-house wall at the back of the stage and another group through the door at the other end, thus creating two rival tableaux. Many of the battle-heavy and faction-filled plays that premiered at the Rose have scenes of just this sort.

At the rear of the Rose stage, there were three capacious exits, each over ten feet wide. Unfortunately, the very limited excavation of a fragmentary portion of the original Globe site, in 1989, revealed nothing about the stage. The first Globe was built in 1599 with similar proportions to those of another theater, the Fortune, albeit that the former was polygonal and looked circular, whereas the latter was rectangular. The building contract for the Fortune survives and allows us to infer that the stage of the Globe was probably substantially wider than it was deep (perhaps forty-three feet wide and twenty-seven feet deep). It may well have been tapered at the front, like that of the Rose.

The capacity of the Globe was said to have been enormous, perhaps in excess of three thousand. It has been conjectured that about eight hundred people may have stood in the yard, with two thousand or more in the three layers of covered galleries. The other "public" playhouses were also of large capacity, whereas the indoor Blackfriars theater that Shakespeare's company began using in 1608—the former refectory of a monastery—had overall internal dimensions of a mere forty-six by sixty feet. It would have made for a much more intimate theatrical experience and had a much smaller capacity, probably of about six hundred people. Since they paid at least six-pence a head, the Blackfriars attracted a more select or "private" audience. The atmosphere would have been closer to that of an indoor performance before the court in the Whitehall Palace or at Richmond. That Shakespeare always wrote for indoor production at court as well as outdoor performance in the public theater should make us cautious about inferring, as some scholars have, that the opportunity provided by the intimacy of the Blackfriars led to a sig-nificant change toward a "chamber" style in his last plays—which, besides, were performed at both the Globe and the Blackfriars. After the occupation of the Blackfriars a five-act structure seems to have become more important to Shakespeare. That was because of artifi-cial lighting: there were musical interludes between the acts, while the candles were trimmed and replaced. Again, though, something similar must have been necessary for indoor court performances throughout his career.

Front of house there were the "gatherers" who collected the money from audience members: a penny to stand in the open-air yard, another penny for a place in the covered galleries, sixpence for the prominent "lord's rooms" to the side of the stage. In the indoor "private" theaters, gallants from the audience who fancied making themselves part of the spectacle sat on stools on the edge of the stage itself. Scholars debate as to how widespread this practice was in the public theaters such as the Globe. Once the audience were in place and the money counted, the gatherers were available to be extras on-stage. That is one reason why battles and crowd scenes often come later rather than early in Shakespeare's plays. There was no formal prohibition upon performance by women, and there certainly were women among the gatherers, so it is not beyond the bounds of possi-bility that female crowd members were played by females.

The play began at two o'clock in the afternoon and the theater had to be cleared by five. After the main show, there would be a jig—which consisted not only of dancing but also of knockabout comedy (it is the origin of the farcical "afterpiece" in the eighteenth-century theater). So the time available for a Shakespeare play was about two and a half hours, somewhere between the "two hours' traffic" men-tioned in the prologue to *Romeo and Juliet* and the "three hours' spectacle" referred to in the preface to the 1647 Folio of Beaumont and Fletcher's plays. The prologue to a play by Thomas Middleton refers to a thousand lines as "one hour's words," so the likelihood is that about two and a half thousand, or a maximum of three thousand lines, made up the performed text. This is indeed the length of most of Shakespeare's comedies, whereas many of his tragedies and histories are much longer, raising the possibility that he wrote full scripts, possibly with eventual publication in mind, in the full knowledge that the stage version would be heavily cut. The short Quarto texts published in his lifetime—they used to be called "Bad" Quartos—provide fascinating evidence as to the kind of cutting that probably took place. So, for instance, the First Quarto of *Hamlet* neatly merges two occasions when Hamlet is overheard, the "Fishmonger" and the "nunnery" scenes.

The social composition of the audience was mixed. The poet Sir John Davies wrote of "A thousand townsmen, gentlemen and whores, / Porters and servingmen" who would "together throng" at the public playhouses. Though moralists associated female playgoing with adultery and the sex trade, many perfectly respectable citizens' wives were regular attendees. Some, no doubt, resembled the modern groupie: a story attested in two different sources has one citizen's wife making a post-show assignation with Richard Burbage and ending up in bed with Shakespeare—supposedly eliciting from the latter the quip that William the Conqueror was before Richard III. Defenders of theater liked to say that by witnessing the comeuppance of villains on the stage, audience members would repent of their own wrongdoings, but the reality is that most people went to the theater then, as they do now, for entertainment more than moral edification. Besides, it would be foolish to suppose that audiences behaved in a homogeneous way: a pamphlet of the 1630s tells of how two men went to see *Pericles* and one of them laughed while the other wept. Bishop John Hall complained that people went to church for the same reasons that they went to the theater: "for company, for custom, for recreation . . . to feed his eyes or his ears . . . or perhaps for sleep."

Men-about-town and clever young lawyers went to be seen as much as to see. In the modern popular imagination, shaped not least by *Shakespeare in Love* and the opening sequence of Laurence Olivier's *Henry V* film, the penny-paying groundlings stand in the yard hurling abuse or encouragement and hazelnuts or orange peel at the actors, while the sophisticates in the covered galleries appreciate Shakespeare's soaring poetry. The reality was probably the other way around. A "groundling" was a kind of fish, so the nickname suggests the penny audience standing below the level of the stage and gazing in silent openmouthed wonder at the spectacle unfolding above them. The more difficult audience members, who kept up a running commentary of clever remarks on the performance and who occasionally got into quarrels with players, were the gallants. Like Hollywood movies in modern times, Elizabethan and Jacobean plays exercised a powerful influence on the fashion and behavior of the young. John Marston mocks the lawyers who would open their lips, perhaps to court a girl, and out would "flow / Naught but pure Juliet and Romeo."

THE ENSEMBLE AT WORK

In the absence of typewriters and photocopying machines, reading aloud would have been the means by which the company got to know a new play. The tradition of the playwright reading his complete script to the assembled company endured for generations. A copy would then have been taken to the Master of the Revels for licensing. The theater book-holder or prompter would then have copied the parts for distribution to the actors. A partbook consisted of the character's lines, with each speech preceded by the last three or four words of the speech before, the so-called "cue." These would have been taken away and studied or "conned." During this period of learning the parts, an actor might have had some one-to-one instruction, perhaps from the dramatist, perhaps from a senior actor who had played the same part before, and, in the case of an apprentice, from his master. A high percentage of Desdemona's lines occur in dialogue with Othello, of Lady Macbeth's with Macbeth, Cleopatra's with Antony, and Volumnia's with Coriolanus. The roles would almost certainly have been taken by the apprentice of the lead actor, usually Burbage, who delivers the majority of the cues. Given that

11. Hypothetical reconstruction of the interior of an Elizabethan playhouse during a performance.

apprentices lodged with their masters, there would have been ample opportunity for personal instruction, which may be what made it possible for young men to play such demanding parts.

After the parts were learned, there may have been no more than a single rehearsal before the first performance. With six different plays to be put on every week, there was no time for more. Actors, then, would go into a show with a very limited sense of the whole. The notion of a collective rehearsal process that is itself a process of discovery for the actors is wholly modern and would have been incomprehensible to Shakespeare and his original ensemble. Given the number of parts an actor had to hold in his memory, the forgetting of lines was probably more frequent than in the modern theater. The book-holder was on hand to prompt.

Backstage personnel included the property man, the tire-man who oversaw the costumes, call boys, attendants, and the musicians, who might play at various times from the main stage, the rooms above, and within the tiring-house. Scriptwriters sometimes made a nuisance of themselves backstage. There was often tension between the acting companies and the freelance playwrights from whom they purchased scripts: it was a smart move on the part of Shakespeare and the Lord Chamberlain's Men to bring the writing process in-house.

Scenery was limited, though sometimes set pieces were brought on (a bank of flowers, a bed, the mouth of hell). The trapdoor from below, the gallery stage above, and the curtained discovery-space at the back allowed for an array of special effects: the rising of ghosts and apparitions, the descent of gods, dialogue between a character at a window and another at ground level, the revelation of a statue or a pair of lovers playing at chess. Ingenious use could be made of props, as with the ass's head in *A Midsummer Night's Dream*. In a theater that does not clutter the stage with the material paraphernalia of everyday life, those objects that are deployed may take on powerful symbolic weight, as when Shylock bears his weighing scales in one hand and knife in the other, thus becoming a parody of the figure of Justice who traditionally bears a sword and a balance. Among the more significant items in the property cupboard of Shakespeare's company, there would have been a throne (the "chair of state"), joint stools, books, bottles, coins, purses, letters (which are brought onstage, read, or referred to on about eighty occasions in the complete works), maps, gloves, a set of stocks (in which Kent is put in *King Lear*), rings, rapiers, daggers, broadswords, staves, pistols, masks and vizards, heads and skulls, torches and tapers and lanterns which served to signal night scenes on the daylit stage, a buck's head, an ass's head, animal costumes. Live animals also put in appearances, most notably the dog Crab in *The Two Gentlemen of Verona* and possibly a young polar bear in *The Winter's Tale*.

The costumes were the most important visual dimension of the play. Playwrights were paid between £2 and £6 per script, whereas Alleyn was not averse to paying £20 for "a black velvet cloak with sleeves embroidered all with silver and gold." No matter the period of the play, actors always wore contemporary costume. The excitement for the audience came not from any impression of historical accuracy, but from the richness of the attire and perhaps the transgressive thrill of the knowledge that here were commoners like themselves strutting in the costumes of courtiers in effective defiance of the strict sumptuary laws whereby in real life people had to wear the clothes that befitted their social station.

To an even greater degree than props, costumes could carry symbolic importance. Racial characteristics could be suggested: a breastplate and helmet for a Roman soldier, a turban for a Turk, long robes for exotic characters such as Moors, a gabardine for a Jew. The figure of Time, as in *The Winter's Tale*, would be equipped with hourglass, scythe, and wings; Rumour, who speaks the prologue of *2 Henry IV*, wore a costume adorned with a thousand tongues. The wardrobe in the tiring-house of the Globe would have contained much of the same stock as that of rival manager Philip Henslowe at the Rose: green gowns for outlaws and foresters, black for melancholy men such as Jaques and people in mourning such as the Countess in *All's Well That Ends Well* (at the beginning of *Hamlet*, the prince is still in mourning black when everyone else is in festive garb for the wedding of the new king), a gown and hood for a friar (or a feigned friar like the duke in *Measure for Measure*), blue coats and tawny to distinguish the followers of rival factions, a leather apron and ruler for a carpenter (as in the opening scene of *Julius Caesar*—and in *A Midsummer Night's Dream*, where this is the only sign that Peter Quince is a carpenter), a cockle hat with staff and a pair of sandals for a pilgrim or palmer (the disguise assumed by Helen in *All's Well*), bodices and kirtles with farthingales beneath for the boys who are to be dressed as girls. A gender switch such as that of Rosalind or Jessica seems to have taken between fifty and eighty lines of dialogue—Viola does not resume her "maiden weeds," but remains in her boy's costume to the end of *Twelfth Night* because a change would have slowed down the action at just the moment it was speeding to a climax. Henslowe's inventory also included "a robe for to go invisible": Oberon, Puck, and Ariel must have had something similar.

As the costumes appealed to the eyes, so there was music for the ears. Comedies included many songs. Desdemona's willow song, perhaps a late addition to the text, is a rare and thus exceptionally poignant example from tragedy. Trumpets and tuckets sounded for ceremonial entrances, drums denoted an army on the march. Background music could create atmosphere, as at the beginning of *Twelfth Night*, during the lovers' dialogue near the end of *The Mer-*

chant of Venice, when the statue seemingly comes to life in *The Winter's Tale*, and for the revival of Pericles and of Lear (in the Quarto text, but not the Folio). The haunting sound of the hautboy suggested a realm beyond the human, as when the god Hercules is imagined deserting Mark Antony. Dances symbolized the harmony of the end of a comedy—though in Shakespeare's world of mingled joy and sorrow, someone is usually left out of the circle.

The most important resource was, of course, the actors themselves. They needed many skills: in the words of one contemporary commentator, "dancing, activity, music, song, elocution, ability of body, memory, skill of weapon, pregnancy of wit." Their bodies were as significant as their voices. Hamlet tells the player to "suit the action to the word, the word to the action": moments of strong emotion, known as "passions," relied on a repertoire of dramatic gestures as well as a modulation of the voice. When Titus Andronicus has had his hand chopped off, he asks, "How can I grace my talk, / Wanting a hand to give it action?" A pen portrait of "The Character of an Excellent Actor" by the dramatist John Webster is almost certainly based on his impression of Shakespeare's leading man, Richard Burbage: "By a full and significant action of body, he charms our attention: sit in a full theatre, and you will think you see so many lines drawn from the circumference of so many ears, whiles the actor is the centre. . . ."

Though Burbage was admired above all others, praise was also heaped upon the apprentice players whose alto voices fitted them for the parts of women. A spectator at Oxford in 1610 records how the audience were reduced to tears by the pathos of Desdemona's death. The puritans who fumed about the biblical prohibition upon crossdressing and the encouragement to sodomy constituted by the sight of an adult male kissing a teenage boy onstage were a small minority. Little is known, however, about the characteristics of the leading apprentices in Shakespeare's company. It may perhaps be inferred that one was a lot taller than the other, since Shakespeare often wrote for a pair of female friends, one tall and fair, the other short and dark (Helena and Hermia, Rosalind and Celia, Beatrice and Hero).

We know little about Shakespeare's own acting roles—an early allusion indicates that he often took royal parts, and a venerable tradition gives him old Adam in *As You Like It* and the ghost of old King Hamlet. Save for Burbage's lead roles and the generic part of the clown, all such castings are mere speculation. We do not even know for sure whether the original Falstaff was Will Kempe or another actor who specialized in comic roles, Thomas Pope.

Kempe left the company in early 1599. Tradition has it that he fell out with Shakespeare over the matter of excessive improvisation. He was replaced by Robert Armin, who was less of a clown and more of a cerebral wit: this explains the difference between such parts as Lancelet Gobbo and Dogberry, which were written for Kempe, and the more verbally sophisticated Feste and Lear's Fool, which were written for Armin.

One thing that is clear from surviving "plots" or storyboards of plays from the period is that a degree of doubling was necessary. *2 Henry VI* has over sixty speaking parts, but more than half of the characters appear only in a single scene and most scenes have only six to eight speakers. At a stretch, the play could be performed by thirteen actors. When Thomas Platter saw *Julius Caesar* at the Globe in 1599, he noted that there were about fifteen. Why doesn't Paris go to the Capulet ball in *Romeo and Juliet*? Perhaps because he was doubled with Mercutio, who does. In *The Winter's Tale*, Mamillius might have come back as Perdita and Antigonus been doubled by Camillo, making the partnership with Paulina at the end a very neat touch. Titania and Oberon are often played by the same pair as Hippolyta and Theseus, suggesting a symbolic matching of the rulers of the worlds of night and day, but it is questionable whether there would have been time for the necessary costume changes. As so often, one is left in a realm of tantalizing speculation.

THE KING'S MAN

On Queen Elizabeth's death in 1603, the new king, James I, who had held the Scottish throne as James VI since he had been an infant, immediately took the Lord Chamberlain's Men under his direct patronage. Henceforth they would be the King's Men, and for the rest of Shakespeare's career they were favored with far more court performances than any of their rivals. There even seem to have been rumors early in the reign that Shakespeare and Burbage were being considered for knighthoods, an unprecedented honor for mere actors—and one that in the event was not accorded to a member of the profession for nearly three hundred years, when the title was bestowed upon Henry Irving, the leading Shakespearean actor of Queen Victoria's reign.

Shakespeare's productivity rate slowed in the Jacobean years, not because of age or some personal trauma, but because there were frequent outbreaks of plague, causing the theaters to be closed for long periods. The King's Men were forced to spend many months on the road. Between November 1603 and 1608, they were to be found at various towns in the south and Midlands, though Shakespeare probably did not tour with them by this time. He had bought a large house back home in Stratford and was accumulating other property. He may indeed have stopped acting soon after the new king took the throne. With the London theaters closed so much of the time and a large repertoire on the stocks, Shakespeare seems to have focused his energies on writing a few long and complex tragedies that could have been played on demand at court: *Othello, King Lear, Antony and Cleopatra, Coriolanus,* and *Cymbeline* are among his longest and poetically grandest plays. *Macbeth* survives only in a shorter text, which shows signs of adaptation after Shakespeare's death. The bitterly satirical *Timon of Athens,* apparently a collaboration with Thomas Middleton that may have failed on the stage, also belongs to this period. In comedy, too, he wrote longer and morally darker works than in the Elizabethan period, pushing at the very bounds of the form in *Measure for Measure* and *All's Well That Ends Well.*

From 1608 onward, when the King's Men began occupying the indoor Blackfriars playhouse (as a winter house, meaning that they only used the outdoor Globe in summer?), Shakespeare turned to a more romantic style. His company had a great success with a revived and altered version of an old pastoral play called *Mucedorus.* It even featured a bear. The younger dramatist John Fletcher, meanwhile, sometimes working in collaboration with Francis Beaumont, was pioneering a new style of tragicomedy, a mix of romance and royalism laced with intrigue and pastoral excursions. Shakespeare experimented with this idiom in *Cymbeline,* and it was presumably with his blessing that Fletcher eventually took over as the King's Men's company dramatist. The two writers apparently collaborated on three plays in the years 1612–14: a lost romance called *Cardenio* (based on the love-madness of a character in Cervantes' *Don Quixote*), *Henry VIII* (originally staged with the title "All Is True"), and *The Two Noble Kinsmen*, a dramatization of Chaucer's "Knight's Tale." These were written after Shakespeare's two final solo-authored plays, *The Winter's Tale*, a self-consciously old-fashioned work dramatizing the pastoral romance of his old enemy Robert Greene, and *The Tempest*, which at one and the same time drew together multiple theatrical traditions, diverse reading, and contemporary interest in the fate of a ship that had been wrecked on the way to the New World.

The collaborations with Fletcher suggest that Shakespeare's career ended with a slow fade rather than the sudden retirement supposed by the nineteenth-century Romantic critics who read Prospero's epilogue to *The Tempest* as Shakespeare's personal farewell to his art. In the last few years of his life Shakespeare certainly spent more of his time in Stratford-upon-Avon, where he became further involved in property dealing and litigation. But his London life also continued. In 1613 he made his first major London property purchase: a freehold house in the Blackfriars district, close to his company's indoor theater. *The Two Noble Kinsmen* may have been written as late as 1614, and Shakespeare was in London on business a little over a year before he died of an unknown cause at home in Stratford-upon-Avon in 1616, probably on his fifty-second birthday.

About half the sum of his works were published in his lifetime, in texts of variable quality. A few years after his death, his fellow actors began putting together an authorized edition of his complete *Comedies, Histories and Tragedies*. It appeared in 1623, in large "Folio" format. This collection of thirty-six plays gave Shakespeare his immortality. In the words of his fellow dramatist Ben Jonson, who contributed two poems of praise at the start of the Folio, the body of his work made him "a monument without a tomb":

And art alive still while thy book doth live
And we have wits to read and praise to give . . .
He was not of an age, but for all time!

SHAKESPEARE'S WORKS: A CHRONOLOGY

1589–91	*? Arden of Faversham* (possible part authorship)
1589–92	*The Taming of the Shrew*
1589–92	*? Edward the Third* (possible part authorship)
1591	*The Second Part of Henry the Sixth*, originally called *The First Part of the Contention betwixt the Two Famous Houses of York and Lancaster* (element of coauthorship possible)
1591	*The Third Part of Henry the Sixth*, originally called *The True Tragedy of Richard Duke of York* (element of co-authorship probable)
1591–92	*The Two Gentlemen of Verona*
1591–92; perhaps revised 1594	*The Lamentable Tragedy of Titus Andronicus* (probably cowritten with, or revising an earlier version by, George Peele)
1592	*The First Part of Henry the Sixth*, probably with Thomas Nashe and others
1592/94	*King Richard the Third*
1593	*Venus and Adonis* (poem)
1593–94	*The Rape of Lucrece* (poem)
1593–1608	*Sonnets* (154 poems, published 1609 with *A Lover's Complaint*, a poem of disputed authorship)
1592–94/ 1600–03	*Sir Thomas More* (a single scene for a play originally by Anthony Munday, with other revisions by Henry Chettle, Thomas Dekker, and Thomas Heywood)
1594	*The Comedy of Errors*
1595	*Love's Labour's Lost*

1595–97	*Love's Labour's Won* (a lost play, unless the original title for another comedy)
1595–96	*A Midsummer Night's Dream*
1595–96	*The Tragedy of Romeo and Juliet*
1595–96	*King Richard the Second*
1595–97	*The Life and Death of King John* (possibly earlier)
1596–97	*The Merchant of Venice*
1596–97	*The First Part of Henry the Fourth*
1597–98	*The Second Part of Henry the Fourth*
1598	*Much Ado About Nothing*
1598–99	*The Passionate Pilgrim* (20 poems, some not by Shakespeare)
1599	*The Life of Henry the Fifth*
1599	"To the Queen" (epilogue for a court performance)
1599	*As You Like It*
1599	*The Tragedy of Julius Caesar*
1600–01	*The Tragedy of Hamlet, Prince of Denmark* (perhaps revising an earlier version)
1600–01	*The Merry Wives of Windsor* (perhaps revising version of 1597–99)
1601	"Let the Bird of Loudest Lay" (poem, known since 1807 as "The Phoenix and Turtle" [turtledove])
1601	*Twelfth Night, or What You Will*
1601–02	*The Tragedy of Troilus and Cressida*
1604	*The Tragedy of Othello, the Moor of Venice*
1604	*Measure for Measure*
1605	*All's Well That Ends Well*
1605	*The Life of Timon of Athens*, with Thomas Middleton
1605–06	*The Tragedy of King Lear*
1605–08	? contribution to *The Four Plays in One* (lost, except for *A Yorkshire Tragedy*, mostly by Thomas Middleton)

1606	*The Tragedy of Macbeth* (surviving text has additional scenes by Thomas Middleton)
1606–07	*The Tragedy of Antony and Cleopatra*
1608	*The Tragedy of Coriolanus*
1608	*Pericles, Prince of Tyre,* with George Wilkins
1610	*The Tragedy of Cymbeline*
1611	*The Winter's Tale*
1611	*The Tempest*
1612–13	*Cardenio,* with John Fletcher (survives only in later adaptation called *Double Falsehood* by Lewis Theobald)
1613	*Henry VIII (All Is True),* with John Fletcher
1613–14	*The Two Noble Kinsmen,* with John Fletcher

KINGS AND QUEENS OF ENGLAND: FROM THE HISTORY PLAYS TO SHAKESPEARE'S LIFETIME

	Life Span	*Reign*
Angevins:		
Henry II	1133–1189	1154–1189
Richard I	1157–1199	1189–1199
John	1166–1216	1199–1216
Henry III	1207–1272	1216–1272
Edward I	1239–1307	1272–1307
Edward II	1284–1327	1307–1327 deposed
Edward III	1312–1377	1327–1377
Richard II	1367–1400	1377–1399 deposed
Lancastrians:		
Henry IV	1367–1413	1399–1413
Henry V	1387–1422	1413–1422
Henry VI	1421–1471	1422–1461 and 1470–1471
Yorkists:		
Edward IV	1442–1483	1461–1470 and 1471–1483
Edward V	1470–1483	1483 not crowned: deposed and assassinated
Richard III	1452–1485	1483–1485
Tudors:		
Henry VII	1457–1509	1485–1509
Henry VIII	1491–1547	1509–1547
Edward VI	1537–1553	1547–1553

	Life Span	*Reign*
Jane	1537–1554	1553 not crowned: deposed and executed
Mary I	1516–1558	1553–1558
Philip of Spain	1527–1598	1554–1558 co-regent with Mary
Elizabeth I	1533–1603	1558–1603
Stuart:		
James I	1566–1625	1603–1625 James VI of Scotland (1567–1625)

THE HISTORY BEHIND THE HISTORIES: A CHRONOLOGY

Square brackets indicate events that happen just outside a play's timescale but are mentioned in the play.

Date	Event	Location	Play
22 May 1200	Truce between King John and Philip Augustus	Le Goulet, Normandy	*King John*
Apr 1203	Death of Arthur	Rouen	*King John*
1209	Pope Innocent III excommunicates King John		*King John*
18/19 Oct 1216	Death of King John	Swineshead, Lincolnshire	*King John*
Apr–Sep 1398	Quarrel, duel, and exile of Bullingbrook and Mowbray	Coventry	*Richard II*
3 Feb 1399	Death of John of Gaunt	Leicester	*Richard II*
Jul 1399	Bullingbrook lands in England	Ravenspur, Yorkshire	*Richard II*
Aug 1399	Richard II captured by Bullingbrook	Wales	*Richard II*
30 Sep 1399	Richard II abdicates	London	*Richard II*
13 Oct 1399	Coronation of Henry IV	London	*Richard II*
Jan–Feb 1400	Death of Richard II	Pontefract Castle	*Richard II*
22 Jun 1402	Owen Glendower captures Edmund Mortimer	Bryn Glas, Wales	*1 Henry IV*
14 Sep 1402	Henry Percy defeats Scottish army	Homildon Hill, Yorkshire	*1 Henry IV*

Date	Event	Location	Play
21 Jul 1403	Battle of Shrewsbury; death of Henry Percy (Hotspur)	Battlefield, near Shrewsbury, Shropshire	*1 & 2 Henry IV*
Feb 1405	Tripartite Indenture between Owen Glendower, Edmund Mortimer, and Northumberland (Henry Percy)	Bangor	*1 Henry IV*
May–Jun 1405	Rebellion of Archbishop of York (Richard Scroop), Earl of Norfolk (Thomas Mowbray), and Lord Bardolph	Yorkshire	*2 Henry IV*
8 Jun 1405	Trial and execution of Archbishop of York and Earl of Norfolk	York	*2 Henry IV*
20 Mar 1413	Death of Henry IV	Westminster Abbey	*2 Henry IV*
9 Apr 1413	Coronation of Henry V	Westminster Abbey	*2 Henry IV*
c. 1415–16?	Death of Owen Glendower	Wales?	*2 Henry IV*
Early Aug 1415	Execution of Earl of Cambridge, Lord Scroop, and Sir Thomas Grey	Southampton	*Henry V*
14 Aug–22 Sep 1415	Siege of Harfleur	Harfleur, Normandy	*Henry V*
25 Oct 1415	Battle of Agincourt	Agincourt, Pas de Calais	*Henry V*
31 Aug 1422	Death of Henry V	Bois de Vincennes, near Paris	*1 Henry VI*
18 Jan 1425	Death of Edmund Mortimer	Ireland	*1 Henry VI*
Oct 1428–May 1429	Siege of Orléans	Orléans	*1 Henry VI*
17 Oct 1428	Death of Lord Salisbury	Orléans	*1 Henry VI*

Date	Event	Location	Play
18 Jun 1429	Capture of Lord Talbot at battle of Patay	Patay, near Orléans	*1 Henry VI*
18 Jul 1429	Coronation of Charles VII	Rheims Cathedral	*1 Henry VI*
6 Nov 1429	Coronation of Henry VI as King of England	Westminster Abbey	[*1 Henry VI*]
23 May 1430	Capture of Joan of Arc	Compiègne, near Soissons	*1 Henry VI*
30 May 1431	Execution of Joan of Arc	Saint-Ouen, near Paris	*1 Henry VI*
16 Dec 1431	Coronation of Henry VI as King of France	Notre Dame Cathedral, Paris	*1 Henry VI*
14 Sep 1435	Death of Duke of Bedford	Rouen	*1 Henry VI*
Summer– Autumn 1441	Arrest and trial of Eleanor Cobham and accomplices	London	*2 Henry VI*
20 May 1442	Lord Talbot created Earl of Shrewsbury	Paris	*1 Henry VI*
23 Apr 1445	Marriage of Henry VI and Margaret of Anjou	Titchfield, Hampshire	*2 Henry VI*
23 Feb 1447	Death of Humphrey, Duke of Gloucester	Bury St. Edmunds	*2 Henry VI*
11 Apr 1447	Death of Cardinal Beaufort	Winchester	*2 Henry VI*
2 May 1450	Death of Earl of Suffolk	English Channel	*2 Henry VI*
Jun–Jul 1450	Rebellion of Jack Cade	Kent and London	*2 Henry VI*
Spring 1452	Richard, Duke of York, marches on London	London	*2 Henry VI*
17 Jul 1453	Death of Lord Talbot at battle of Cantillon	Cantillon, Gascony	*1 Henry VI*
22 May 1455	First battle of St. Albans	St. Albans, Hertfordshire	*2 Henry VI*

Date	Event	Location	Play
10 Jul 1460	Battle of Northampton	Northampton	[*3 Henry VI*]
Oct 1460	Richard, Duke of York, holds Parliament	London	*3 Henry VI*
30 Dec 1460	Battle of Wakefield	Wakefield, Yorkshire	*3 Henry VI*
2 Feb 1461	Battle of Mortimer's Cross	Near Wigmore, Herefordshire	*3 Henry VI*
29 Mar 1461	Battle of Towton	Near Tadcaster, Yorkshire	*3 Henry VI*
28 Jun 1461	Coronation of Edward IV	Westminster Abbey	*3 Henry VI*
1 May 1464	Marriage of Edward IV and Elizabeth Woodville	Northamptonshire	*3 Henry VI*
Jul 1465	Henry VI captured	Lancashire	*3 Henry VI*
26 Jul 1469	Battle of Edgecote Moor	Near Banbury, Oxfordshire	*3 Henry VI*
Oct 1470–Apr/ May 1471	Readeption (restoration) of Henry VI	London	*3 Henry VI*
14 Apr 1471	Battle of Barnet; death of Warwick	Barnet, near London	*3 Henry VI*
4 May 1471	Battle of Tewkesbury; death of Edward, Prince of Wales	Tewkesbury, Gloucestershire	*3 Henry VI*
21 May 1471	Death of Henry VI	Tower of London	*3 Henry VI*
12 Jul 1472	Marriage of Richard, Duke of Gloucester, to Anne	Westminster Abbey	*Richard III*
18 Feb 1478	Death of Duke of Clarence	Tower of London	*Richard III*
9 Apr 1483	Death of Edward IV	Westminster	*Richard III*
Jun 1483	Death of Lord Hastings	Tower of London	*Richard III*

Date	Event	Location	Play
6 Jul 1483	Coronation of Richard III	Westminster Abbey	*Richard III*
2 Nov 1483	Death of Duke of Buckingham	Salisbury	*Richard III*
16 Mar 1485	Death of Queen Anne	Westminster	*Richard III*
22 Aug 1485	Battle of Bosworth Field	Leicestershire	*Richard III*
30 Oct 1485	Coronation of Henry VII	Westminster Abbey	[*Richard III*]
18 Jan 1486	Marriage of Henry VII and Elizabeth of York	Westminster Abbey	[*Richard III*]
Jun 1520	Meeting of Henry VIII and Francis I	"Field of the Cloth of Gold," near Calais, France	[*Henry VIII*]
17 May 1521	Death of Duke of Buckingham	Tower Hill, London	*Henry VIII*
29 Nov 1530	Death of Wolsey	Leicester	*Henry VIII*
25 Jan 1533	Marriage of Henry VIII and Anne Bullen (Boleyn)	Whitehall	*Henry VIII*
1 Jun 1533	Coronation of Anne Bullen (Boleyn)	Westminster Abbey	*Henry VIII*
7 Sep 1533	Birth of Princess Elizabeth	Greenwich Palace	*Henry VIII*
10 Sep 1533	Christening of Princess Elizabeth	Greenwich Palace	*Henry VIII*

FURTHER READING AND VIEWING

CRITICAL APPROACHES

Bevington, David, "1 Henry VI," in A Companion to Shakespeare's Works Volume II: The Histories, ed. Richard Dutton and Jean E. Howard (2003). Excellent introductory essay that marries consideration of the authorship of the play with engaging critical analysis of it as a piece of drama.

Cartelli, Thomas, "Suffolk and the Pirates: Disordered Relations in Shakespeare's 2 Henry VI," in A Companion to Shakespeare's Works Volume II: The Histories, ed. Richard Dutton and Jean E. Howard (2003). In-depth analysis of one of the play's major characteristics, riot and disorder.

Goy-Blanquet, Dominique, Shakespeare's Early History Plays: From Chronicle to Stage (2003). Excellent study of the plays as representations of chronicle history that takes analysis of Shakespeare's pragmatic need to structure stageworthy narratives as its starting point.

Grene, Nicholas, Shakespeare's Serial History Plays (2002). Argues that all of Shakespeare's histories were meant to be staged as a serial sequence and pursues critical links between them all accordingly: chapters 3–5 deal with the Henry VI trilogy and Richard III.

Hodgdon, Barbara, The End Crowns All: Closure and Contradiction in Shakespeare's History (1991). Magisterial study of the idea of "endings" in Shakespeare's histories: chapter 3 deals with the Henry VI trilogy.

Holderness, Graham, Shakespeare: The Histories (2000). Influential reevaluation of the historical contexts through which we might better understand Shakespeare's writing of his history plays: chapter 5 deals with Henry VI Part I.

Lull, Janis, "Plantagenets, Lancastrians, Yorkists, and Tudors: *1–3 Henry VI, Richard III, Edward III*," in *The Cambridge Companion to Shakespeare's History Plays*, ed. Michael Hattaway (2002). Excellent overview of Shakespeare's early history plays.

Pendleton, Thomas A., ed., *Henry VI: Critical Essays* (2001). Excellent and diverse collection of essays on a range of themes spanning all three plays.

Riggs, David S., *Shakespeare's Heroical Histories: Henry VI and Its Literary Tradition* (1971). Excellent study contextualizing the production of the plays within early 1590s literary and dramatic culture.

Schwarz, Kathryn, "Vexed Relations: Family, State, and the Uses of Women in *3 Henry VI*," in *A Companion to Shakespeare's Works Volume II: The Histories*, ed. Richard Dutton and Jean E. Howard (2003). Interrogates the relationships between family and state in the play, particularly the ways in which women are used in transactions of marriage to this end.

Taylor, Gary, "Shakespeare and Others: The Authorship of *Henry VI Part One*," in *Medieval and Renaissance Drama in England*, Vol. 7 (1995). Excellent and persuasive model of the coauthorship of *Part I*.

THE PLAY IN PERFORMANCE

Hampton-Reeves, Stuart, and Carol Chillington Rutter, *Shakespeare in Performance: The Henry VI Plays* (2006). Excellent study of all the major stage and screen realizations of the trilogy since the turn of the twentieth century.

Holland, Peter, *English Shakespeares: Shakespeare on the English Stage in the 1990s* (1997). Features analysis of the RSC's 1994 rendering of *Henry VI Part III*, entitled *The Battle for the Throne*.

Jackson, Russell, and Robert Smallwood, eds., *Players of Shakespeare 3* (1993). A treasure house for those interested in the acting of these plays, featuring Ralph Fiennes on playing the role of Henry, Penny Downie on Queen Margaret, and Anton Lesser on Richard of Gloucester.

Oyelowo, David, *Actors on Shakespeare: Henry VI Part 1* (2003). Intriguing rehearsal diary by Oyelowo, whose performance as Henry won widespread critical acclaim in Michael Boyd's 2000–01 productions for the RSC.

Pearson, Richard, *A Band of Arrogant and United Heroes, The Story of the Royal Shakespeare Company Production of The Wars of the Roses* (1990). Full account of the epic 1963 Peter Hall/John Barton saga that helped to establish the RSC as we know it today.

Smallwood, Robert, ed., *Players of Shakespeare* 6 (2004). A volume devoted entirely to history plays, featuring Fiona Bell and Richard Cordery on their respective roles as Queen Margaret and Humphrey Duke of Gloucester in Michael Boyd's 2000–01 productions for the RSC.

AVAILABLE ON DVD

Henry VI Parts One, Two and Three, directed by Jane Howell for the BBC Shakespeare series (1983, DVD 2005). Howell's epic trilogy is widely acclaimed as perhaps the crowning glory of the entire BBC Shakespeare canon, with the cast across the three films boasting such talent as Peter Benson (Henry), Brenda Blethyn (Joan la Pucelle), Trevor Peacock (Talbot/Jack Cade), Julia Foster (Margaret), Ron Cook (Richard of Gloucester), Bernard Hill (York), Paul Jesson (Clarence), and Brian Protheroe (Edward IV).

REFERENCES

1. In his pamphlet *Greene's Groats-worth of Wit bought with a million of Repentance,* Robert Greene makes the first published reference to William Shakespeare: "for there is an upstart Crow, beautified with our feathers, that with his Tygers hart wrapt in a Players hyde, supposes he is as well able to bombast out a blanke verse as the best of you: and being an absolute Johannes fac totum, is in his owne conceit the onely Shake-scene in a countrey"; the line "his tygers hart wrapt in a Players hyde" is an allusion, it's argued, to the description of Queen Margaret in *Henry VI Part III,* "O, tiger's heart wrapt in a woman's hide" (1.4.137).
2. *Stratford Herald,* 26 April 1889.
3. Carol Chillington Rutter and Stuart Hampton-Reeves, *The Henry VI Plays* (2006), p. 27.
4. Rutter and Hampton-Reeves, *The Henry VI Plays,* p. 30.
5. Stanley Wells, *Shakespeare in the Theatre: An Anthology of Criticism* (1997), p. 52.
6. Rutter and Hampton-Reeves, *The Henry VI Plays,* p. 36.
7. Reynolds, quoted in Wells, *Shakespeare in the Theatre,* pp. 52–3.
8. *Birmingham Daily Mail,* 24 April 1889.
9. *Stratford-upon-Avon Herald,* 26 April 1889.
10. *Birmingham Gazette,* 22 April 1899.
11. *Stratford-upon-Avon Herald,* 11 May 1906.
12. Rutter and Hampton-Reeves, *The Henry VI Plays,* p. 39.
13. Rutter and Hampton-Reeves, *The Henry VI Plays,* p. 53.
14. Foster Hirsch, *Shakespeare Quarterly* 21 (1970), pp. 477–79.
15. *New York Times,* 2 July 1970.
16. Alan C. Dessen, *Shakespeare Quarterly* 28 (1977), pp. 245–46.
17. Dessen, *Shakespeare Quarterly* 28, pp. 245–46.
18. Alan C. Dessen, *Shakespeare Quarterly* 29 (1978), pp. 283–85.
19. *Guardian,* 13 February 1989.
20. *Guardian,* 10 February 2001.
21. Stuart Hampton-Reeves, "Theatrical Afterlives," *The Cambridge Companion to Shakespeare's History Plays,* ed. Michael Hattaway (2002).
22. J. C. Trewin, *The Illustrated London News,* 3 August 1963.
23. Michael Billington, *Guardian,* 16 December 2000.

24. Peter Roberts, *Plays and Players*, 12 September 1963.

25. Michael Boyd in an interview with Maddy Costa, *Guardian*, 19 July 2006.

26. Hampton-Reeves, "Theatrical Afterlives."

27. Peter Hall, Introduction to *The Wars of the Roses Adapted for the Royal Shakespeare Company from William Shakespeare's Henry VI, Parts I, II, III and Richard III* by John Barton in collaboration with Peter Hall (1970).

28. Nicola Barker, *Observer*, 14 August 1994.

29. Benedict Nightingale, *The Times* (London), 12 August 1994.

30. Michael Billington, *Guardian*, 11 August 1994.

31. Peter Holland, *English Shakespeares: Shakespeare on the English Stage in the 1990s* (1997).

32. Barbara Hodgdon, "The RSC's 'Long Sonata of the Dead,'" in *Re-Visions of Shakespeare*, ed. Evelyn Gajowski (2004).

33. Nicholas de Jongh, *Evening Standard*, 14 December 2000.

34. Billington, *Guardian*, 16 December 2000.

35. Billington, *Guardian*, 16 December 2000.

36. Charles Spencer, *Daily Telegraph*, 15 December 2000.

37. Hampton-Reeves, "Theatrical Afterlives."

38. Hall, Introduction to *The Wars of the Roses*.

39. Barton and Hall, *The Wars of the Roses*.

40. *A Band of Arrogant and United Heroes, The Story of the Royal Shakespeare Company Production of The Wars of the Roses* (1990).

41. Sally Emerson, *Plays and Players*, September 1977.

42. J. M. Maguin, *Cahiers Élisabéthains*, No. 12, October 1977.

43. Maguin, *Cahiers Élisabéthains*.

44. Dominic Cavendish, *Daily Telegraph*, 11 August 2006.

45. Hodgdon, "The RSC's 'Long Sonata of the Dead.'"

46. Billington, *Guardian*, 16 December 2000.

47. Hall, Introduction to *The Wars of the Roses*, 1970.

48. John Russell Brown, *Shakespeare's Plays in Performance* (1966), pp. 196, 215–16.

49. Peter Roberts, *Plays and Players*, 12 September 1963.

50. B. A. Young, *Financial Times*, 13 July 1977.

51. T. C. Worsley, *Financial Times*, 18 July 1963.

52. Adrian Noble, Introduction from *The Plantagenets*, 1989.

53. Maguin, *Cahiers Élisabéthains* 7.

54. Carol A. Chillington, *Educational Theatre Journal*, 4 December 1977.

55. Michael Billington, *Guardian*, 11 August 1994.

56. Paul Taylor, *Independent*, 12 August 1994.

57. Taylor, *Independent*, 12 August 1994.
58. Rhoda Koenig, *Independent*, 14 December 2000.
59. Benedict Nightingale, *The Times* (London), 15 December 2000.
60. Benedict Nightingale, *The Times* (London), 11 August 2006.
61. Dominic Cavendish, *Daily Telegraph*, 11 August 2006.
62. Joyce McMillan, *Scotsman*, 20 December 2000.
63. Carol A. Chillington, *Educational Theatre Journal*, 4 December 1977.
64. Fiona Bell, "Joan of Arc and Margaret of Anjou," in *Players of Shakespeare 6*, ed. Robert Smallwood (2004).
65. Nightingale, *The Times*, 15 December 2000.
66. Cavendish, *Daily Telegraph*, 11 August 2006.
67. Nightingale, *The Times*, 11 August 2006.
68. Bell, "Joan of Arc and Margaret of Anjou."
69. Penny Downie, "Queen Margaret," in *Players of Shakespeare 3*, ed. Russell Jackson and Robert Smallwood (1993).
70. Peter Roberts, *Plays and Players*, 12 September 1963.
71. Robert Potter, "The Rediscovery of Queen Margaret: The Wars of the Roses," 1963, *New Theatre Quarterly*, Vol. 4, No. 14, May 1988.
72. Potter, "The Rediscovery of Queen Margaret: The Wars of the Roses" (1988).
73. Benedict Nightingale, *New Statesman*, Vol. 94, No. 2418, 22 July 1977.
74. Carol A. Chillington, *Educational Theatre Journal*, 4 December 1977.
75. Bell, "Joan of Arc and Margaret of Anjou."
76. Rebecca Brown, "The Play in Performance," *Henry VI Part 2* (2005).
77. Ralph Fiennes, "Henry VI," in *Players of Shakespeare 3*, ed. Russell Jackson and Robert Smallwood (1993).
78. Chillington, *Educational Theatre Journal*, 4 December 1977.
79. *The Times* (London), 18 July 1963.
80. Rhoda Koenig, *Independent*, 15 December 2000.
81. Nightingale, *The Times*, 15 December 2000.
82. Brown, "The Play in Performance."
83. Nightingale, *The Times*, 11 August 2006.
84. Brown, "The Play in Performance."
85. Chillington, *Educational Theatre Journal*, 4 December 1977.
86. Chillington, *Educational Theatre Journal*, 4 December 1977.
87. Anton Lesser, "Richard of Gloucester," in *Players of Shakespeare 3*, ed. Russell Jackson and Robert Smallwood (1993).
88. B. A. Young, *Punch*, Vol. CCXLV, No. 6411, 24 July 1963.
89. Frank Cox, *Plays and Players*, Vol. 11, No. 6, 1964.
90. Chillington, *Educational Theatre Journal*, 4 December 1977.

91. Fiennes, "Henry VI."
92. Lesser, "Richard of Gloucester."
93. Nightingale, *The Times*, 15 December 2000.
94. Chillington, *Educational Theatre Journal*, 4 December 1977.
95. McMillan, *Scotsman*, 20 December 2000.

ACKNOWLEDGMENTS AND PICTURE CREDITS

Preparation of *"Henry VI* in Performance" was assisted by a generous grant from the CAPITAL Centre (Creativity and Performance in Teaching and Learning) of the University of Warwick for research in the RSC archive at the Shakespeare Birthplace Trust.

Thanks as always to our indefatigable and eagle-eyed copy editor Tracey Dando and to Ray Addicott for overseeing the production process with rigor and calmness.

Picture research by Michelle Morton. Grateful acknowledgment is made to the Shakespeare Birthplace Trust for assistance with picture research (special thanks to Helen Hargest) and reproduction fees.

Images of RSC productions are supplied by the Shakespeare Centre Library and Archive, Stratford-upon-Avon. This library, maintained by the Shakespeare Birthplace Trust, holds the most important collection of Shakespeare material in the UK, including the Royal Shakespeare Company's official archive. It is open to the public free of charge.

For more information see www.shakespeare.org.uk.

MODERN LIBRARY IS ONLINE AT
WWW.MODERNLIBRARY.COM

MODERN LIBRARY ONLINE IS YOUR GUIDE TO CLASSIC LITERATURE ON THE WEB

THE MODERN LIBRARY E-NEWSLETTER

Our free e-mail newsletter is sent to subscribers, and features sample chapters, interviews with and essays by our authors, upcoming books, special promotions, announcements, and news. To subscribe to the Modern Library e-newsletter, visit **www.modernlibrary.com**

THE MODERN LIBRARY WEBSITE

Check out the Modern Library website at
www.modernlibrary.com for:

- The Modern Library e-newsletter
- A list of our current and upcoming titles and series
- Reading Group Guides and exclusive author spotlights
- Special features with information on the classics and other paperback series
- Excerpts from new releases and other titles
- A list of our e-books and information on where to buy them
- The Modern Library Editorial Board's 100 Best Novels and 100 Best Nonfiction Books of the Twentieth Century written in the English language
- News and announcements

Questions? E-mail us at **modernlibrary@randomhouse.com**.
For questions about examination or desk copies, please visit
the Random House Academic Resources site at
www.randomhouse.com/academic